CONFERENCE ON BRITISH STUDIES
BIOGRAPHICAL SERIES
Editor: PETER STANSKY
Consultant Editor: G. R. ELTON

RADICAL JOURNALIST:
H. W. MASSINGHAM (1860–1924)

OTHER BOOKS IN THIS SERIES

RADICAL JOURNALIST: H. W. MASSINGHAM

(1860–1924)

ALFRED F. HAVIGHURST

AMHERST COLLEGE

CAMBRIDGE UNIVERSITY PRESS

Published by the Syndics of the Cambridge University Press
Bentley House, 200 Euston Road, London NW1 2DB
American Branch: 32 East 57th Street, New York, N.Y.10022

Library of Congress Catalogue Card Number: 73-83106

ISBN: 0 521 20355 4

First published 1974

Printed in Great Britain by
Alden & Mowbray Ltd
at the Alden Press, Oxford

FOR MILDRED

CONTENTS

CONTENTS

Preface

This book is hardly a biography. It is rather a study of the professional career of a brilliant journalist who, as reporter, leader-writer, literary critic and editor, was in the main stream of English life at a time when the press was the leading medium for informing the public and influencing its opinions.

Concerning H. W. Massingham virtually nothing has been written since 1925 (the year after his death) when Harold J. Massingham published a memorial volume with selections from his father's writings introduced by essays written by distinguished journalists who had been members of his staffs. I have deliberately refrained from making extensive use of these essays. For one thing, they are readily accessible. More importantly, they are hardly historical statements. Informed and perceptive these essays certainly are and they stand up well some fifty years later, but inevitably they are eulogistic in tone and represent subjective judgment. Indeed, though historians have invariably regarded Massingham with respect and have treated his papers as significant forces in English life, the man himself has remained a shadowy figure.

The reasons are not far to seek. It has been difficult to study Massingham apart from the papers associated with him. His own articles for the *Star*, the *Daily Chronicle* and the *Nation* (the *Speaker* and the *Daily News* are exceptions) were generally unsigned. Thus these journals have usually been cited and excerpted anonymously – as in 'Massingham's *Nation* said . . . ', or, less cautiously, the editor is made responsible for all statements. In Massingham's case the difficulties are compounded for he preserved little of the record of his life. He kept no journal, maintained no diary of appointments; he preserved almost no correspondence before 1914 and very little thereafter. His own letters are generally brief with little in them but the actual business in hand. No family papers have survived and it has been possible to reconstruct only the barest outline of his personal life. His children left home early for school with but slender family ties thereafter. In later years their interest in family matters was slight and their memories dim. Apart from what this suggests of Massingham's own personality, it matters little – his entire life was devoted to journalism.

In my endeavour to reconstruct Massingham's professional life I have examined nearly all his prolific writing – in one manner or another close examination usually establishes authorship of unsigned material, or, failing that, distinguishes between his responsibility as leader-writer and that as editor. And while he did not preserve his letter files, many of his correspondents did theirs. And so through the papers of W. E. Gladstone, Bernard Shaw, John Burns, H. W. Nevinson, J. L. Hammond, Arnold Bennett, Lord Northcliffe, Ramsay MacDonald and many others I have been able to construct detail and chronology and to comprehend the stress and strain which was the essence of his life and work.

In so doing I have incurred indebtedness quite beyond adequate acknowledgment and have made many warm friends. Above all others is Miss Gertrude M. Cross, Massingham's secretary from 1918 to 1924. Without her keen interest, wide knowledge, wise counsel and constant assistance truly this book could not have been written. She has read the entire manuscript as has Professor Peter Stansky, the series editor. Their close scrutiny detected many errors in statement and raised many questions of judgment which make this a better book than it would otherwise have been. Also I have been fortunate in coming to know, on informal terms, members of the Massingham family, particularly Mr Hugh Massingham, himself a fine journalist, and Mr Godfrey Massingham, also a man of perception, who provided an insight into their father's talents and personality I could not have found elsewhere. Mrs Penelope Massingham, widow of Harold, turned over to me a packet of important correspondence and Mrs Betty Massingham, widow of another son, Richard, loaned me correspondence between Massingham and his daughter, Dorothy. In Norwich I received generous assistance from Mr Philip Hepworth and Mr Frank Sayer of the Central Library, Mr Rex L. Beaumont and Mr Eric Fowler of the *Eastern Daily Press*, Mr Andrew Stephenson of the Norwich School, Mr Basil Cozens-Hardy and Miss Lilian E. Parish. In due course I propose to give to the Norwich Central Library my collection of Massingham material.

It has been my pleasure and privilege to converse with many who knew Massingham well, among them: Mr Edmund Blunden, Professor G. P. Gooch, Mrs Frida Laski, Mrs Lucy Masterman, Mr Frank Swinnerton and Mr Leonard Woolf. And I have corresponded with others: Padraic Colum, Lady Constance Malleson, R. H. Mottram, Bertrand Russell, Siegfried Sassoon, Sir Osbert Sitwell and Sir Oswald Mosley.

In common with all who labour in the materials of British history I owe much to libraries and archives and their staffs. Some are cited elsewhere but I wish also to make mention of the Amherst College Library, Amherst, Massachusetts (Mr Floyd Merritt); the Smith College Library, Northampton, Massachusetts (which provided a complete file of the *Nation*); the Beaverbrook Library (Mr A. J. P. Taylor, Mrs Sheila Elton and Miss Rosemary Brooks); the British Library of Political and Economic Science (Mr Geoffrey Allen); the Bodleian Library, Oxford (Mr D. S. Porter); and the staffs of the British Museum and of the British Museum Newspaper Library at Colindale. Lord Ponsonby kindly sent me a selection from the papers of his father, Arthur Ponsonby, and Sir Geoffrey Harmsworth from the Northcliffe Papers. Miss Joan Sharp made available in London the diary of Henry W. Nevinson. Mr David Ayerst and Mr Trevor Wilson put in my hands relevant materials from the C. P. Scott Papers in the *Guardian* archives; Professor Joseph C. Baylen made available correspondence in the W. T. Stead Papers, Professor Everett W. Ferrill from the Norman Angell Papers and Professor Stephen E. Koss from the Sir John Brunner Papers. It was my pleasure and privilege to examine the papers of Baron Fisher, Admiral of the Fleet, at Lennoxlove. Mr and Mrs Patrick Gardiner gave me a free hand at the A. G. Gardiner Papers in their attic at Wytham.

Quotations from unpublished journals and correspondence of Arnold Bennett and from correspondence of H. W. Massingham are included with the permission of the Henry W. and Albert A. Berg Collection, The New York Public Library, Astor, Lenox and Tilden Foundations. By courtesy of the Humanities Center, the University of Texas at Austin, I am using correspondence from the Edward Garnett Papers, the H. M. Tomlinson Papers and the Bernard Shaw Papers in their possession. The J. L. Garvin Papers were consulted in

London by courtesy of Miss Viola Garvin and Mr Tristan Jones. By permission of the Harvard College Library I have used extracts from the Oswald Garrison Villard Papers and the William Rothenstein Papers in the Houghton Library.

Archivists, scholars and friends who have assisted me along the way are almost legion. I should like to give special thanks to: Mr G. Awdry, Miss Eva Faye Benton, Mr Kenneth Blackwell, Mr Victor Bonham-Carter, Miss Lela Cryz, Professor H. N. Fieldhouse, Mr A. R. Ford, Mr David Garnett, Mr Martin Gilbert, Professor Alfred Gollin, Dr R. Hale White, Miss Josephine L. Harper, Mr Cameron Hazlehurst, Mr James C. Hepburn, Mrs Mary M. Hirth, Mr Michael Holroyd, Miss Carolyn Jakeman, The Rt Hon. Roy Jenkins, Professor Dan H. Laurence, Mr P. J. Law, Mr John Lehmann, Professor Arthur Marder, Mr John L. Nevinson, Sir Mark Norman Bt, Miss F. Ranger, Miss Margaret Ratcliffe, Mr E. F. D. Roberts, Professor Blair Rouse, Mr B. Philip Rowntree, Mr Stanley Rypins, Mr Charles Seaton, Mr Wilfred Stone, Mrs Lola L. Szladits, Mr H. A. Taylor, Miss D. Tindall, Miss Dorothy Tomlinson and Mr Peter Weiler.

I gratefully acknowledge permission from copyright-holders to publish certain correspondence and other documentary material: the British Library of Political and Economic Science (Passfield, Courtney, Harrison, Wallas and Morel Papers); Mr Brian Jones (the *Guardian*); His Grace the Duke of Hamilton (Baron Fisher Papers); the Hogarth Press; Sir Geoffrey Harmsworth Bt (the Northcliffe Papers); William Heinemann Ltd and Houghton Mifflin Co. for quotations from Randolph S. Churchill and Martin Gilbert, *Winston S. Churchill*; Mr Malcolm MacDonald; Mr Godfrey Massingham; Mr Hugh Massingham; the National Library of Scotland (Rosebery Papers); Baron Ponsonby; Mr Arthur Leonard Ross; Mr Pratap C. Chitnis (Rowntree Trust Papers); Viscount Runciman and the Hon. Sir Steven Runciman; the Strachey Executors (the John St Loe Strachey Papers); the University of Illinois and Mr G. P. Wells (the H. G. Wells Papers); the Yale University Library (Wm H. Buckler and E. M. House Papers); the State Historical Society of Wisconsin (Henry Demarest Lloyd Papers). Shaw texts © 1974 by the Trustees of the British Museum, The Governors and Guardians of the National Gallery of Ireland, and Royal Academy of Dramatic Art. Extracts from texts by Bernard

Shaw have been used with the permission of the Society of Authors, on behalf of the Bernard Shaw estate. My sincere apologies to other copyright-holders whom I have tried in vain to locate or to reach.

A. F. H.

Amherst, Massachusetts
July 1973

Abbreviations

Berg	Berg Collection, New York Public Library
B.L.P.E.S.	British Library of Political and Economic Science, London School of Economics
B.M.	British Museum, London
Bodleian	Bodleian Library, Oxford
B.P.	John Burns Papers
D.C.	*Daily Chronicle*
D.P.	Sir Charles Dilke Papers
G.B.S.P.	George Bernard Shaw Papers, British Museum
G.P.	William E. Gladstone Papers
H.G.P.	Viscount Gladstone Papers
Houghton	Houghton Library, Harvard University, Cambridge, Massachusetts
H.P.	Viscount Haldane Papers
H.W.M.	H. J. Massingham (ed.), *H.W.M.: A Selection from the Writings of H. W. Massingham* (London, 1925)
J.L.H.P.	J. L. Hammond Papers
Laurence	Dan H. Laurence (ed.), *Bernard Shaw: Collected Letters*, vol. 1, *1874–1897* (New York, 1965)
L.G.P.	David Lloyd George Papers
M.P.	H. W. Massingham Papers
N.D.	Diary of Henry W. Nevinson
P.P.	Passfield Papers
P.R.O.	Public Record Office, London
R.P.	Earl of Rosebery Papers
Shaw Diary	Diary of George Bernard Shaw

Introduction

H. W. Massingham, editor of the *Star* (1890–1), editor of the *Daily Chronicle* (1895–9) and editor of the *Nation* (1907–23) is indelibly associated with two significant aspects of English journalism in his time – first, that of the impact of the 'Radical' press on society and politics, and second, that of the 'New Journalism' which transformed the press into an organ of information and opinion for the middle classes and the working man. Massingham constantly articulated that opinion and very often determined its substance. He 'knew everyone', it is frequently observed, and his life story is a very considerable part of the biographies of political leaders and of prominent men of letters of his day.

Consider the end of his story. Massingham died on 27 August 1924, at Tintagel, Cornwall, at the age of sixty-four, and was buried on 2 September in Old Brompton Cemetery in London. In the half hour before the service old friends and associates gathered, representing, as the *Manchester Guardian* suggested, in a striking manner those areas of journalism, politics and letters in which Massingham had been prominent. Liberalism, reaching back to the 1880s, was represented by John Burns, and later associations by Lady Courtney and Augustine Birrell. Of men of letters there were John Galsworthy and R. B. Cunninghame Graham, and a veteran publisher, T. Fisher Unwin. Fellow editors included A. G. Gardiner formerly of the *Daily News*, Clement Shorter of the *Sphere*, J. C. Squire of the *New Statesman* and the *London Mercury*, H. D. Henderson of the *Nation and Athenaeum*, J. S. Braithwaite of the *Christian Science Monitor*. Michael MacDonagh, chairman of the Parliamentary Press Gallery was there, as was A. Cozens-Hardy of the Norwich *Eastern Daily Press* where Massingham learned his trade. From Massingham's own staff on the *Daily Chronicle* came Vaughan Nash and W. D. Morrison, and from the *Nation*, J. A. Hobson, H. N. Brailsford, H. W. Nevinson, S. K. Ratcliffe, and F. W. Hirst. There was a veteran Socialist, E. Belfort Bax, and restless eager younger men – Harold Laski and Oswald Mosley. The Prime Minister, James Ramsay MacDonald, from his home in Scotland, sent a telegram of condolence to Mrs Massingham. Dr Morrison, rector of St Marylebone, conducted the service.[1]

Over a span of thirty-five years Massingham's contact with prominent political figures was recurrent and significant – W. E. Gladstone, Rosebery, Dilke, Asquith, John Burns, Campbell-Bannerman, Churchill, Lloyd George, and MacDonald. As a journalist he is sometimes credited with revolutionising press reporting from the House of Commons and is invariably listed among the outstanding parliamentary reporters of his day. Looking back in 1918, George Bernard Shaw wrote:

> Mr. Massingham, in the teeth of his proprietors and of all the vested interests, political and commercial, which controlled the daily papers he edited, succeeded in changing the politics and outlook of the *Star* and the *Chronicle* from the Whig-ridden Socialist Radicalism of the 'eighties to the Collectivist Progressivism of the 'nineties.[2]

And he created the *Nation*, one of the significant weeklies of the twentieth century. Testimony to his quality as writer and editor is abundant. G. P. Gooch referred to him as 'perhaps the most brilliant journalist of his time', and, more recently, Randolph Churchill spoke of him as 'perhaps the most powerful of the political journalists of that decade [1900–10]'. In another vein, Lloyd George, long after his complete break with Massingham, remarking on the intolerably 'dull' character of controversy in the *Nation* after Massingham, referred to him as 'a man of genius' who 'could make even bickering attractive'.[3]

It is commonplace to speak of 'a golden age of editors' during the first quarter of the twentieth century. Along with Massingham were others, including C. P. Scott of the *Manchester Guardian*, J. L. Garvin of the *Observer*, J. A. Spender of the *Westminster Gazette*, A. G. Gardiner of the *Daily News*, and A. R. Orage of the *New Age*. With

---

[1] *The Times, Manchester Guardian,* and *Eastern Daily Press* for 3 Sept. 1924; personal knowledge of Miss Gertrude M. Cross.

[2] *Nation,* 9 Feb. 1918, quoted in G. B. Shaw, *Pen Portraits and Reviews* (London, 1932), 42–3.

[3] F. J. C. Hearnshaw (ed.), *Edwardian England, A.D. 1901–1910* (London, 1933), 22; Randolph S. Churchill, *Winston S. Churchill*: volume 2, *Young Statesman, 1901–1914* (Boston, 1967), 11; L.G.P., Lloyd George to E. D. Simon (draft), 23 Feb. 1926.

his paper each editor identified his own personality and philosophy. And it is often observed that such editors, whose associations and knowledge were wide and whose productivity almost incredible, were equal in political stature to the chief ministers of state.[1] How they rank comparatively is a matter of opinion. Shaw's judgment about it all was this: 'A first rate editor is a very rare bird indeed: two or three in a generation, in contrast to swarms of authors, is as much as we get; and Massingham was in the first of that very select flight.'[2]

But there was still another side to him, 'this master of nervous, vivid English', who hardly wrote what can be called a book, yet 'was a joy to the craftsmen of letters'.[3] A. G. Gardiner declared that there was none like him 'in the impetus of his attack, his sense of an occasion, and in the swift magical phrases that leapt from his pen in the feverish hurry of the spirit'. This impression endured. On the centennial of his birth, and thirty-six years after his death, a writer for the *Guardian* quoted a remark made soon after Massingham's death that he 'could stamp a whole paper, as he stamped a sentence, with the impression of his passion and thrust'.[4] And so it was that this man, whose formal education ended when he was not yet seventeen, made the *Star*, the *Daily Chronicle* and the *Nation* organs of great literary influence, and was as much at home among men of arts and letters as with men of public affairs. Shaw was a close friend for more than thirty-five years. When the *Nation* moved its office in 1912 to the quiet backwaters of Adelphi Terrace overlooking the Embankment and the Thames, the Shaws were neighbours in a flat above. Across the street were J. M. Barrie and Joseph Pennell. Other neighbours were John Galsworthy and the publisher, T. Fisher Unwin.

Massingham's literary associations were astonishingly wide and varied. He and Meredith were mutual admirers; nearly all the writing of 'Mark Rutherford' in his last years appeared in the *Nation*. There Galsworthy was frequently published, and Sir Rabindranath Tagore as well. H. G. Wells' *Tono-Bungay* was considered by Massingham for serialisation and *Mr. Britling Sees it Through* did first appear in the

---

[1] Alfred M. Gollin, *The Observer and J. L. Garvin, 1908–1914* (London, 1960), 27.
[2] *H.W.M.*, 216.
[3] Composite of A. G. Gardiner in *Nation*, 6 Sept. 1924, p. 686 and J. A. Spender, *Life, Journalism and Politics*, 1 (New York, n.d.), 138–9.
[4] *Nation*, 6 Sept. 1924, p. 686; the *Guardian*, 25 May 1960.

pages of the *Nation*. When Arnold Bennett was first invited to contribute to the *Nation*, his reaction was, 'No editorial invitation has ever flattered me as much as this.'[1] Over the years, a small host of younger writers – among them Padraic Colum, R. H. Mottram, Siegfried Sassoon, Osbert Sitwell, Aldous Huxley and Edmund Blunden – first found a public in the *Nation*'s columns and were everlastingly grateful for the encouragement of its editor.

As a person Massingham was an enigma, with conflicting forces constantly bearing down upon him. The result was turbulence of mind, even from his youth. The precepts of his home and of his school nurtured an evangelicalism which persisted in a puritanical outlook bordering on self-righteousness. His childhood days left unpleasant memories of a sombre world with limited values and of a home where his mother was always partial to an older son. His home life as an adult, and increasingly so, was apart from his professional career; at his funeral a close associate remarked that he had not been aware that Massingham was married. To his first wife, a woman of rare gifts of mind and spirit, Massingham was devoted. But she died in 1905 leaving him with six children, including one just born. Before long Massingham married his first wife's sister who, while conscientious was unimaginative and insensitive, failing to win the affection of the children and doing little for her husband. But, in fact, Massingham had already deserted his home for Fleet Street. He was not, testify two of his sons, 'a good father'.[2] He captured 'citadel after citadel of the Paynim of Fleet Street and never removed his armour at home until long after we were abed. We stood in palpitant awe of him; living for ideas, he had little fondness or time for children'. Thus writes the eldest son, Harold J. Massingham. On the other hand, surviving letters from Massingham to Dorothy, his only daughter, reflect warmth and fatherly affection.[3] And his close friend, Vaughan Nash, with whom he spent holidays in Ireland and on the Continent, writes at length of his love for children and their adoration of him. His youth apart, he had no definable religious faith and yet remained deeply interested in the

---

[1] Arnold Bennett, *Journal of Arnold Bennett*, I (New York, 1932), 347, 26 Nov. 1909.
[2] Author's interviews with Godfrey Massingham, Hugh Massingham and Miss G. M. Cross.
[3] H. J. Massingham, *Remembrance: An Autobiography* (London [1941]), 5–6; Massingham letters to Dorothy Massingham in possession of Mrs Betty Massingham.

public manifestations of religion and was, in later years, frequently at services in the King's Weigh House Church, London. Religion – he declared in some initial pages of an intended autobiography – as he was introduced to it as a child, was both 'terrifying' and 'ridiculous'. And so, in his own words, he became 'a heathen, with religious intervals'.[1]

To different people he was different things, almost invariably expressed in positive terms and usually in contradiction. Indeed, many observers, to their own surprise, found their judgments inconsistent. He was, writes his son, 'a melancholy and lively man all at once'.[2] He had few close friends. On the other hand, the *Outlook*, whose political attitudes were quite different from Massingham's, upon his departure from the *Daily Chronicle* in 1899, referred to his 'electric personality', and as one 'capable of prejudice and impulse, but incapable of unkindness'. Padraic Colum, who knew Massingham in the early *Nation* years, recalls that 'he was a very thoughtful, very considerate man; when he smiled a friendliness radiated from him'.[3] But characteristic of the impression he made in later years is a reference to 'the singular contrast between his soft voice and scholar's face and, the extraordinary ferocity of his invective at its height'. To Leonard Woolf who saw him regularly and frequently over many months Massingham was a famous editor, 'yet a strange, rather disquieting person'. After Massingham's death, J. A. Spender remarked: 'The thing that puzzled . . . was that with [a] . . . very delicate literary gift – gift of the artist and detached observer of men and things – he had the vehement dogmatic temperament which is usually that of the rhetorician'. And to Lloyd George he became 'that anemic tapeworm'. When H. G. Wells created Mr Peeve in *Men Like Gods* (1923) he very likely had Massingham in mind; on the other hand, an attractive character, Mr Markington in Siegfried Sassoon's *Memoirs of an Infantry Officer*, was certainly Massingham. Frank Swinnerton found him a 'Jeremiah' and yet the one person he ever knew 'who really doubled up with laughter'.[4] H. W. Nevinson once described him as a 'delightful combination of

[1] *H.W.M.*, 270, 294.
[2] *Ibid.*, 234.
[3] *Outlook*, 2 Jan. 1899, p. 564; Colum to the author, 23 June 1966.
[4] Leonard Woolf, *Downhill All the Way* (London, 1967), 92; J. A. Spender, *Westminster Gazette*, 2 Sept. 1924, p. 4; author's interview with Frank Swinnerton, 16 Nov. 1964.

St. Francis and Rabelais'.[1] To Stephen McKenna he was 'a thin bitter-tongued, sea-green incorruptible'. The historian of the *New Statesman* suggests that Massingham's attitude toward his readers implied the toast, 'Here's to us; there's none like us.' But that writer never knew Massingham. F. W. Hirst, editor of *The Economist* and a member of the *Nation* staff over a period of years respected Massingham but remarks that he 'was not always a trustworthy guide in politics'. And Hirst recalls L. T. Hobhouse, another writer for the *Nation*, as saying of Massingham, 'his ship is moored, though it swings with the tide'.[2]

Thus Massingham's personality, his talents and his career invite comment, often disparate comment. In search of a statement detached, yet informed and comprehensive, we come across a judgment made long after his death by a popular historian – a reference to Massingham as 'the most gifted, most influential, most acrimonious and erratic' of all the Liberal journalists.[3] Here, perhaps, is a preliminary text for our examination of Massingham's career.

1 Henry W. Nevinson, *Changes and Chances* (New York, 1923), 187; N.D., 8 Sept. 1902, 9 Jan. 1904, etc. H. N. Brailsford once asked Nevinson if they would be 'as bawdy minded as H.W.M.' if they 'lived his shut-up kind of life' (N.D., 12 Apr. 1910).
2 McKenna to the author, 1 Dec. 1964; Edward Hyams, *The New Statesman* (London, 1963), 97; Francis W. Hirst, *In the Golden Days* (London, 1957), 205.
3 Peter de Mendelssohn, *The Age of Churchill*, I (London, 1961), 320.

CHAPTER I

From Norwich to London (1860–1888)

Henry William Massingham was born on 25 May 1860, in Old Catton, on the northern fringe of the ancient East Anglian city of Norwich. He was the second of three sons. His father, Joseph Massingham, was secretary to a Norwich banker, Joseph Gurney, but it is more to the point to say that he was an active Radical in politics and a lay preacher in the Methodist Church. For the strongest influence in Henry Massingham's youth was not his father who died when Henry was but six, nor his mother, with whom there developed no strong bonds of affection,[1] but rather that of evangelical Wesleyanism and political nonconformity – convictions and associations which reach back in the Massingham family to the late eighteenth century, when one Joseph Massingham (Henry's grandfather, a schoolmaster at Coltishall, just north of Norwich) was 'converted' and became the leader of a Wesleyan society. In 'Norwich as I Remember It', a piece written in 1924, Massingham dwelt at length upon the distinctions, in his boyhood, of Church and Chapel – Anglicanism and Nonconformity. 'Each section lived apart and regarded the other with no favourable eyes.'

The glimpses we have of Massingham's youth are, for the most part, associated with Chapel and School. He is closely identified with the New Catton Sunday School, often referred to as the Sun Lane School. The brownish red brick building stands today, an incongruity in the midst of urban renewal. There he received, in the day school, his elementary instruction; and when fourteen he received first prize for excellence in a Norwich Sunday School Union scripture examination. One of his boyhood friends, in old age, recalled lads of the district throwing snowballs at young Massingham's 'top hat' as he came down

[1] A psychologist would no doubt dwell upon this hostility between the boy Henry Massingham and his mother. Shaw returns repeatedly to this subject. See *H.W.M.*, 214, Shaw's letter to Dorothy Massingham, 13 Jan. 1925 (University of Texas) and his preface to Stephen Winsten, *Salt and His Circle* (London, 1951), 10. This chapter is largely based on Massingham's reminiscences in *H.W.M.* and information from Miss G. M. Cross and Mr Frank Sayer.

Sun Lane to the school. At the Calvert Street Methodist Chapel the Massingham pew was directly behind that of the Cozens-Hardy family, prominent in Norwich.[1]

Upon the death of his father, Henry Massingham came under the guardianship of a relative, Jacob Henry Tillett (1818–92), whose outlook and interests were similar to those of Joseph Massingham. Both lay preachers and also trustees of the New Catton Sunday School, in 1845 they were among the founders of the *Norfolk News* from which developed the *Eastern Daily Press* in 1870. But Tillett, himself, was a person of further accomplishment. He was twice mayor of Norwich and was a member of the House of Commons, 1880–5. As the political leader of Norwich Liberalism and Nonconformity he had come to know Richard Cobden, John Bright and John Morley. Methodist lay preacher, orator, Radical journalist, Liberal politician, in time Tillett became young Massingham's model and inspiration.

But in his youth, more immediate was the influence of Norwich School (at this time known as the Norwich Grammar School or King Edward VI's School) with its extraordinary headmaster, Augustus Jessopp. From the age of ten to seventeen Massingham attended and, of all his early memories of Norwich, he loved most to recall his school. 'In the noble old school room under the shadow of the still nobler cathedral . . . my happiest days were spent. . . I read voraciously, and at sixteen I was a better scholar than I have ever been since.' He remembered Jessopp

of a stature and mien to impress school boys as Arnold had impressed Rugby, and for beauty and sonority his voice equalled, I think, Gladstone's. I shall never forget his reading of the collect 'Lighten our Darkness' with which he used to close the afternoon school, so that to an imaginative boy the growing gloom of a winter's day seemed shot with spiritual light.

Only one letter, but that one quite remarkable, survives from these years, written when young Massingham was thirteen. It is dated 10 February 1874, just after the General Election, addressed to his older brother then at Oxford, and written from Hewitt's Villas, St Augustine's Road, in the parish of St Clement where Mrs Massingham and the children were living. It warrants extensive quotation. Christmas

[1] J. W. Robertson-Scott, *'We' and Me* (London, 1956), 160; Report of the Sun Lane School, Norwich, 1874, M.P.; Lilian E. Parish of Norwich to author, 31 Jan. 1965.

recess at an end, he writes that in his brief speech reconvening the school, Dr Jessopp referred to

Briscoe, who is a master now, as the 'strong, sturdy, stalwart, stedfast standby' of the school and advised the upper boys in the school to take measures against the habit of swearing that had arisen in the school. Lohr and Harry Brightwell have been moved into the Upper 6th; but neither of them have at *present* evinced signs of genius. The Dr. makes their lives intensely miserable, by the ways in which he abuses them. 'A *feeble* lot, unfortunate boy'; 'is there nothing you know? Nothing? . . .'

Now as to our work. We began with the 1st book of Horace's Epistles, but we have now left it off and begun some Homer. . . I have a great deal of work to do. . . I should think I have done a *score* copies of Elijiac verses and only *one* piece of Prose!!! . . .

Now I suppose you would like to know something about the Election. It has been very exciting, and a little stormy, and has roused sleepy old Norwich up thoroughly. Both parties have done their utmost, by squibs, torchlight processions, meetings etc, to gain the election. There has been some fighting, (two or three men were sent to the Hospital) and a little window-breaking by the Liberal roughs, and I imagine some bribery by the Tories. One incident is too good to pass over. Twenty-six voters had been shut up by the Tories till nearly four o'clock (when the poll closed) in a public-house, but when the Tories came for them with cabs, they found the Liberal roughs had blockaded the entrance, and in short they couldn't vote. . . .[1]

Young Massingham's interest in politics was not unassociated with his studies. Thirty years later he wrote: 'When I was a boy, my interest in politics was formed by the reading of long columns of speeches, records of Homeric encounters, where heroes fought with heroes.'[2]

At the Norwich Grammar School he had, as he says, the 'habit of hard and regular study'. From year to year he won prizes, and so eventually considered seeking a university scholarship. His mother urged Cambridge; he much preferred Oxford. Mr Tillett, now a prominent member of the staff of the *Norfolk News*, intervened with the proposal of an immediate start in journalism. 'I jumped at the chance', he tells us.[3]

He left the Grammar School in April 1877, shortly before his seven-

[1] M.P.
[2] *Contemporary Review*, 85 (June 1904), 842.
[3] Records of the Norwich Grammar School; *H.W.M.*, 322.

teenth birthday. Already his mother had written to the *Norfolk News* about a post on the reporting staff for her son and it was soon arranged that he was to be 'articled' to J. H. Tillett for four years. From Joseph Massingham the family had inherited substantial shares in the *Norfolk News* and young Henry's relationship in time became that of a proprietor as well as a reporter. In March 1886, to his considerable satisfaction he became a member of the General Committee representing the stockholders. He attended meetings of the Committee occasionally until 1896 but did not resign until 1904.[1]

And so in the editorial rooms of the *Eastern Daily Press*, which had been established by the *Norfolk News*, Massingham's journalistic career was launched. In reminiscing, years later, he recalls that he was

a great hand at Latin hexameters and Greek iambics, and with about as much knowledge of nineteenth century England and Norwich as if I had been brought up in Babylon. . .

Was I happy? I was utterly miserable. . . I could not, at once, reconcile myself to the various and shallow interests of journalism. And after a year or so I fell into a melancholy of soul, which I think only my kind old editor suspected. . . Taught to do everything exactly and nicely, remembering my Horace and Virgil, I could not, for the life of me, apply myself to the work of the police-court, the descriptive 'par', the 'leaderette', the thousand and one tasks of the provincial newspaper, in which one kind of function melts into another. It seemed to me everything was at an end. . . I hung over the bridge on my way home, and wondered what so useless a creature was made for. At length a strong and gentle hand [his editor] drew me out of the depths.

He tells us that at first he

suffered from fastidiousness of style. It became so acute that I lost the power of writing altogether, and for fear of using the wrong word would sit in miserable vacancy before the virgin page, while the clock raced its way to the fatal hour of going to press. This over-delicacy soon passed away and I got to write as carelessly as the rest of the world.

One of his first duties was a weekly pilgrimage to Carrow Abbey, home of Mr Tillett, to take a 'leader' by dictation. 'I transferred its wisdom to the compositors in a script which for thirty years has earned me their undying hatred', he remarked later. And a colleague recalled,

---

[1] Records of *Eastern Daily Press*, Norwich, including Massingham to Managing Committee of *Norfolk News*, 12 Dec. 1885; 9 Jan. 1886 and 2 Mar. 1904.

'Oh, the language that fizzed and exploded because of his squiggly writing, his copious interlineations, his crossings out and his "stettings" in.'[1] Tillett was somewhat Olympian in manner and young Massingham moved much closer to his editor, James Spilling, to whom religion was more important than politics. 'Mr. Spilling . . . tried to make me a Swedenborgian, and did in fact convince me that it was possible to be both an editor and saint. . . It was his sweetness of character and the gentle determination of his mind to goodness and charity, which drew me even more than his intellectual gifts.'

The bright spot each week was holding the 'copy' for the proof-reader of the 'London Letter' by William Hale White. 'The young reader loved those interludes in his weekly task of checking the items in the auctioneer's lists and rehearsing the simple ritual of tea-meetings in country chapels.'[2] He did not then know that Hale White also wrote as 'Mark Rutherford'. And it was at the Easter season, 1880, on the eve of a tumultuous General Election, that he came to know Clement Shorter, another young journalist – their association continued until Massingham's death. Shorter retained a 'vivid memory of this youthful enthusiast [Henry Massingham] . . . His keenness for books and reading, his genuine love for scholarship, positively dazzled me'.[3]

As an apprentice, young Massingham of course learned his trade; but fully as important was the new world into which he entered. The transition was intellectual and spiritual – the words are chosen deliberately – and was dramatic in the extreme, as indicated by his own remarks forty years on, no less revealing because somewhat blurred, in detail, by time. He had been nurtured in Wesleyan theology and Puritan morality, builders of strong character both of them, but not always inspiration for talent. Norwich was then a city of some 70,000 but nineteenth-century technology had yet to make its transformation. Massingham never forgot its 'rows of old houses of soft brown colouring, and many little crooked streets, whose outline was broken up with little old churches, and with openings into covered pathways,

[1] *Eastern Daily Press*, 9 Sept. 1924.
[2] Reuben Shapcott (ed.), *The Autobiography of Mark Rutherford* (London, 1936), 'Memorial Introduction' by H. W. Massingham (p. 1). This Memorial Edition was first published in 1924.
[3] J. M. Bullock (ed.), *C.K.S., An Autobiography: A Fragment of Himself* (London, 1927), 50.

which in turn led to "yards", set around with tiny houses'. Churches dominated, some thirty-three of them within an area of a square mile, and many chapels and meeting houses besides.

At the Grammar School Massingham's schooling had been traditional. 'The intellectual atmosphere of the Norwich of those days was not specially bracing', he tells us. The Cathedral was served by a fine organist but there was no 'vital connection between the Cathedral and the musical taste of the citizens'. A theatre of sorts, there was, but its fare was thin, and in puritanical Norwich regarded by most 'as the way to the pit'. 'What spiritual home was here for an imaginative youth, beginning to read Shelley and Byron, Voltaire and Strauss, Arnold and *Supernatural Religion*?' To Massingham as his boyhood years passed, Norwich was no sanctuary of piety. The Church of England was for the aristocrats; in any case for him sacramentalism had no appeal. And in those who dutifully went to service in the Chapel he found more hypocrisy than faith – the shop, he decided, was both their present world and their other world.

These remarks indicate something of young Massingham's state of mind during the early years of his apprenticeship. Suddenly, in November 1878, came the tragic death of his older brother, Joseph John; the coroner's inquest in Devon recorded death as resulting 'from injuries received from accidentally falling into fire'. Joseph was twenty-three. The *Norfolk News* set forth at length his brilliant record as a student at the Norwich Grammar School and then at Oxford where he attained 'first class' honours and won a fellowship in Merton College.[1] His death had an impact on Henry Massingham beyond any previous experience. 'The only being whom I loved, and who had any power of God over me, was dead.' Uncertain as he was of his own future and haunted with doubts about the meaning of life and death, he was deprived of the support of a sensitive and powerful intelligence which he sorely needed. Fortunately he was able to turn even more to his editor, Mr Spilling, who reinterpreted Christianity for him – as a creed of divine love and not of eternal vengeance. And in the small but select circle of Unitarians, he also found intellectual stimulus and religious direction.

[1] The Register of Deaths, Somerset House; *Norfolk News*, 17 Nov. 1878, p. 7.

In more worldly matters his maturity, he suggests, came through the theatre, limited as it was in Norwich, and in the newspaper office. In his sixties he lived again the thrill at sixteen of the curtain rising on his first play. The theatre at once became one of his great loves. The newspaper office opened up to him a pagan world of pains and pleasures, of transitory experience, of success and failure, of man's humanity and inhumanity to man. But if Massingham drifted away from institutional religion, he never forsook the Puritan ethic with its strong call of duty, its sensitivity to conscience, its self-righteousness. For his journalistic career, Massingham's Norwich background was fully as important for what it was as for his leaving it.

In the minutes of meetings of shareholders of the *Eastern Daily Press* in March 1882 appears a notice that Henry Massingham had been added to the staff at a salary of £100. His apprenticeship was over. A note of self-satisfaction is evident in a letter of 31 January 1883, in his hand, addressed to the editor and directors, stating that members of the staff were 'desirous of signalizing the pleasure we find in your employment and the general harmony of our relations with you and each other, by a trip together to London, a dinner there, and a visit to some place of amusement' and suggesting that the annual gift of the directors for a social occasion be used in this manner.[1]

Beginnings in London

Early in 1883, Massingham, now twenty-two, armed with introductions, went off to London. There he decided to remain, rejecting Edmund Yates' offer of a post in Norwich as correspondent for the *World*. Soon he looked up Shorter, now a clerk in Somerset House, and announced that he (Massingham) was to write the 'London Letter' for the *Norfolk News* in succession to Hale White who had written the letter since 1872. The Letters are unsigned but according to Hale White's biographer, his last piece appeared on 17 March 1883. Presumably, 'London Letter' is thereafter Massingham's column, though we know that others substituted occasionally. It is likely that Shorter wrote the Letter for several weeks in 1883 while Massingham, under

---

[1] Records of *Eastern Daily Press*, Norwich. In 1920 Massingham attended the Jubilee celebration of the *Eastern Daily Press*. Glasses were raised to one 'who now rules the *Nation*'. *Eastern Daily Press*, 11 Oct. 1920.

doctor's orders, had a complete rest. Massingham wrote at length to Mr Spilling about his health, a recurrent problem throughout his life. On 9 June 1883 he married Emma Jane Snowdon, daughter of a Norwich draper, Henry Snowdon. Massingham's schoolmaster, the Rev. Augustus Jessopp, now rector of Scarning, Norfolk, performed the ceremony in St Matthew's Church in the hamlet of Thorpe on the edge of Norwich. The newly-married couple settled down in Gresley Road, Highgate, not far from their friend, Shorter.[1]

In addition to his 'London Letter' Massingham soon found employment with the National Press Agency which supplied news to provincial papers. His training was under its well-known chief, Dawson Rogers. Massingham was with Rogers on a celebrated occasion in December 1885 when Herbert Gladstone, in an effort to bolster up the Liberal Party, went down to the Agency office and in effect reported his father's conversion to Irish Home Rule. The sensational news was a scoop, Massingham himself sending the report to Norwich and relating the circumstances in a letter to J. H. Tillett.[2] By then Massingham was one of the Agency's chief reporters. For a few weeks in the summer of 1886, J. A. Spender worked alongside him. Years later Spender wrote: 'He terrified me by the speed with which he turned out his work . . . I remember being struck by the remarkable quality of his lightning performance and the peculiar blend of intricacy and lucidity which he achieved.'[3]

Through Tillett, an M.P., Massingham had secured entrée to the Press Gallery of the Commons and though at first he 'stood unknown, gauche, timid', he was soon launched, in occasional pieces for the Press Agency and in his articles for the Norwich papers, on parliamentary reporting, the area of his greatest claim to fame as a reporter. Through his Westminster associations he was soon admitted to a little gathering of journalists at the National Liberal Club which he had joined in 1883.

---

1 Two undated letters, Massingham to Spilling [1883] in Records of *Eastern Daily Press* Norwich. Register of Marriages, 9 June 1883, Somerset House.
2 Sir Charles Mallet, *Herbert Gladstone: A Memoir* (London, 1932), 119. Massingham to Tillett (n.d.), Records of *Eastern Daily Press*, Norwich. See also H. W. Massingham, *The Life and Political Career of the Right Hon. W. E. Gladstone* (London [1898]), 28–30.
3 *Westminster Gazette*, 2 Sept. 1924, p. 4.

Of his day-to-day life, we have fairly frequent and revealing glimpses, thanks to his 'London Letter' for the *Norfolk News*. As one reads it week after week, one at first doubts whether it was indeed written by a young reporter of twenty-three or twenty-four, just come to London from provincial Norwich. The youthful exuberance is convincing enough but there is knowledge and sophistication which is startling. Yet the articles, with a few exceptions, are clearly those of young Massingham with references to Norwich scenes and friends, special reference to his schoolmaster, Augustus Jessopp, his clear understanding of the issue of Methodist reunion with, in fact, allusion to his own father, mention of his own presence at the Socialist and Radical meeting in Trafalgar Square on 'Bloody Sunday' in November 1887, and mention of his holidays in France in August 1883, June 1885, and May 1887.

The 'London Letter' reveals Massingham's great zest for politics in general, and his devotion at an early stage to Liberalism and Gladstone in particular. On 2 May 1885, he praises Gladstone's speech (27 April) on a Vote for Credit to meet a Russian threat in Afghanistan, as his 'greatest', and a little later, on 27 June 1885, he contributes a remarkable description of the parliamentary session when Gladstone turns over power to Salisbury. The entire Letter for 26 December 1885 is devoted to Gladstone and Irish Home Rule, recognising and asserting the professional responsibility which accompanied the *coup* of the National Press Agency in announcing Gladstone's support.

Massingham also refers frequently to literary matters, as, for example, his attendance in 1883 at the Shelley Society to hear readings by Henry Irving, and at the Wordsworth Society to hear James Russell Lowell. He makes special mention of seeing Sarah Bernhardt and by 1886 his 'London Letter' incorporates his own critical comment on drama and the theatre. He describes art exhibitions which he visits, such as the Millais Collection in the Grosvenor Gallery. He attends lectures by Bernard Shaw, Frederic Harrison, Michael Davitt. When he heard Charles Bradlaugh and H. M. Hyndman discuss the question of whether Socialism would benefit the English people, he commented that both speakers needed advice and guidance. He followed closely Henry George's activities in England, getting acquainted with him in April 1884 and attending the farewell dinner in his honour.

His interest in religion continued. In 1883 we find him at the Temple Church to hear the Archbishop of Canterbury, and at the Nonconformist City Temple to hear its famous preacher, Joseph Parker, and later the American, Henry Ward Beecher. In December 1885 he wrote his mentor in Norwich, J. H. Tillett, a letter which reveals the distance Massingham had travelled from East Anglia:

Are you not . . . rather glad to note the Reform movement in the Church of England, and are you quite sure that we shall have disestablishment after all as the end of all the talk and agitation. It seems to me that if we can get a free, self-governed, universal church – not State trammelled but perhaps State-recognized – we shall get all that friends of liberty want, and be rid of the cramping narrowness, and often plutocratic exclusiveness, of the sects.

Creeds and sects – these bothered him. He found more congenial the Bedford Chapel in Bloomsbury of the Rev. Stopford Brooke, Unitarian preacher, Fabian Socialist, and scholar. Any humanist atmosphere where politico-religious ideas flourished attracted Massingham. Thus one evening, with Shaw, he attended in Bethnal Green a meeting of the Guild of St Mathew – Christian Socialists – sponsored by Stewart Headlam. It was through Headlam that he met Henry George.[1]

For London life there is manifest at once a special concern. In the 'London Letter' 18 December 1886, he tells of conversations with forgotten souls spending their lives in the recesses of the Thames Embankment. We are told that he spent a night there and wrote up his experiences for the *Eastern Daily Press*.[2] And the 'London Letter' reports with excitement the legislation which created the London County Council in 1888.

In such ways, and sundry others, young Massingham's activities and associations grew. Friendship developed with two other East Anglians, Herbert Burrows (ardent member of the Social Democratic Federation – S.D.F.) and William Clarke (Fabian journalist who would in time be a leader-writer for the *Daily Chronicle*). Along with Shorter they forgathered frequently, 'little dreaming what the future had in

---

[1] Massingham to J. H. Tillett [Dec. 1885], Records of *Eastern Daily Press*, Norwich; F. G. Bettany, *Stewart Headlam: A Biography* (London, 1926), 87.

[2] Robertson-Scott, *'We' and Me*, 138, mentions the article on the Embankment but I have been unable to locate it.

store for any of us', wrote Burrows. And there was Henry Norman, roving journalist of the *Pall Mall Gazette*, later to be assistant editor of the *Daily Chronicle*. In 1887 Norman set out on a round-the-world assignment and his fortunes in the United States were passed on by Massingham to Norman's chief, W. T. Stead.[1]

All this time Massingham read regularly under the great dome in the Reading Room of the British Museum. There he renewed his student days and developed 'the first sense of what the underside of journalism meant'. There he met William Archer, whose career as dramatic critic was already well under way, and through him, Bernard Shaw. In later life Shaw could not recall their first meeting. 'I was certainly not introduced to him; he arises in memory as a person known to me quite intimately and often called The Boy.'[2]

And so it was, wrote Massingham in 1898, that

slowly the door of journalism opened out to me. What delight to see and talk to a great man made visible flesh at last, or even to some working journalist who wrote for the great papers I had read all my life, [and who] walked in and out of the sacred temples where Truth lit her nightly lamp, and did not seem even overpowered by the honour!

[1] [Herbert Burrows and John A. Hobson (eds.)], *William Clarke; A Collection of his Writings, with a Biographical Sketch* (London, 1908), xxiii; Bullock (ed.), *C.K.S., An Autobiography*, 42; Massingham to Stead, 18 Nov. 1887 (courtesy of J. O. Baylen).
[2] *H.W.M.*, 209.

CHAPTER 2

The 'Star' Years (1888–1891)

The 'New Journalism'

Massingham did not linger long in the shadows of routine journalism. In 1890, at the age of thirty, he found himself editor of the *Star*, a half-penny evening daily launched in London two years before by T. P. O'Connor. The *Star* had promptly established itself as embodying those changes in the newspaper world known as the 'New Journalism' (a phrase attributed to Matthew Arnold): meeting the interests and needs of all classes after the coming of household suffrage; extension of news coverage from that chiefly political to various aspects of English life; transformation of the colourless report to the human-interest story, including the 'interview'; a typographical revolution in which the paragraph superseded the column and the headline overshadowed the paragraph, and with 'cross-heads' to break up solid masses of print and facilitate rapid reading. Massingham himself in writing in 1892 about the transformation of the press emphasised news reporting as now presenting 'a picture of men and women' instead of 'a dry clatter of words, words, words'; the headline, he said, constituted 'a short hand description' of the event.[1]

Stanley Morison, a discerning historian of journalism, has remarked: 'The "New Journalism" made its way into the English newspaper world by way of the evening papers, to be precise, in the later *Pall Mall Gazette* under Stead; and it made itself at home in *The Star*, from its beginning under T. P. O'Connor in 1888.'[2] For the morning dailies, the half-penny paper in the new style awaited the appearance of the *Daily Mail* in 1896.

In the initial issue of the *Star*, 17 January 1888, T. P. O'Connor in 'Our Confession of Faith' promised

---

[1] H. W. Massingham, *The London Daily Press* (London, 1892), 183–5.
[2] Stanley Morison, *The English Newspaper, 1622–1932* (Cambridge, 1932), 279. Cf. *History of The Times*, III (London, 1947), 97, 'the change became explicit with evening journalism in the *Star*'.

plenty of entirely unpolitical literature – sometimes humorous, sometimes pathetic; anecdotal, statistical, the craze of fashions, and the arts of house-keeping – now and then a short, dramatic and picturesque tale. In our reporting columns we shall do away with the hackneyed style of obsolete journalism; and the men and women that figure in the forum or the pulpit or the law court shall be presented as they are – living, breathing, in blushes or in tears – and not merely by the dead words that they utter.

Gathering and writing up the news for an evening paper involved techniques different from those for a morning paper. A few years later Massingham wrote of his own experience on the *Star*:

Haste . . . is the moral and material rule of the evening newspaper. A leader written after the writer has raced through the morning paper in the dimly-lit morning train, may have to be dashed off in three quarters of an hour. . . The descriptive report . . . must be written up within a few minutes of the spoken word. [Of the Parnell Commission which began hearings in September, 1888] I remember that Mr. T. P. O'Connor, who is the fastest descriptive writer I ever knew, and myself had to finish our three or four, or possibly five columns of description within a minute or so of the rising of the court. The copy in cases of this kind is always carried in batches to the office by a constant service of messenger boys.[1]

'Our Confession of Faith' also established the *Star*'s political tone:

The *Star* will be a Radical journal. It will judge all policy – domestic, foreign, social – from the Radical standpoint. This, in other words, means that a policy will be esteemed by us good or bad as it influences, for good or evil, the lot of the masses of the people.

By chance, the advent of the *Star* coincided exactly with the trials in the Old Bailey of Socialists and Radicals charged with riotous assembly in Trafalgar Square the previous 13 November ('Bloody Sunday'). 'Very well I remember the first issue of "The Star" . . . as at that moment I was standing my trial with Mr. John Burns', R. B. Cunninghame Graham tells us years later. We encounter personalities who were to be prominent in Massingham's life henceforth. R. B. Haldane stood bail for Cunninghame Graham, and Stewart Headlam for Burns. Defence counsel included H. H. Asquith. Massingham himself was a witness, for he had observed the assembly from a window in Northumberland Avenue. He testified that he saw nothing

---

[1] *The London Daily Press*, 181.

of the matter at issue and that he believed the 'London roughs' were not present. The prisoners, found guilty, were sentenced to six weeks in jail.[1]

The *Star* also came to life at the time of the 'new unionism', which may be described, in uncontroversial terms, as the expansion of trade-union organisation and activity in 1888–9 and after. No doubt the sharp differences between the organisation and principles of trade unionism, 'old' and 'new', were played up at the time, but that there was a conflict is no 'myth', nor is the part of Socialists and Radicals in this conflict. Massingham's role is that of the journalist, with convictions, but not that of the labour agitator.

In the Match Girls' Strike of July 1888, one of the organisers was Massingham's friend, Herbert Burrows. Massingham himself helped to collect strike money. With *Star* support the National Union of Gas-workers and General Labourers was organised in 1889 and the Beckton Gas Works in the East Ham section of London granted an eight-hour day without a strike. In August 1889 came the London Dock Strike. Vaughan Nash, a chronicler of the Strike, tells us that he first encountered Massingham 'as a pale, tired looking, detached and rather stern figure' on a Sunday morning at Strike headquarters at Wade's Arms in Poplar. On 8 September Massingham along with Shaw and Belfort Bax attended a strikers' meeting in Hyde Park.[2] From 24 August to 16 September the *Star*'s leading article, one day excepted, supported the Strike. Without much question, Massingham wrote most if not all of these articles. Complete lists of subscribers to the Strike Fund were published. The *Star* for 24 August admonished: 'STAND FIRM, STRIKERS'; on 14 September it declared: 'Today the curtain rings down on the Great Strike. Soon it will rise again on the drama of the final emancipation of Labour.' Massingham had become a Radical journalist.

T. P. O'Connor, Irish journalist, Member of Parliament from 1880 to 1929, and ardent Parnellite, founded the *Star* to strengthen the

[1] *Star*, 17, 18, 19 Jan. 1888 and 6 May 1920; *The Times*, 18 Jan. 1888. Massingham contributed £1 to the Law and Liberty League of W. T. Stead, on behalf of the demonstrators. Massingham to Stead, 18 Nov. 1887 (courtesy of J. O. Baylen).
[2] Shaw Diary, 21 July 1888 and 8 Sept. 1889; *H.W.M.*, 292.

cause of Irish Home Rule in London. He had the blessing and financial support (£40,000 in his own telling) of such Liberal Radicals in the Commons as John Morley, Henry Labouchere, John Brunner and Professor James Stuart. The latter, Professor of Mechanical Science at Cambridge, became chairman of the Board of Directors.

O'Connor employed Henry Massingham as assistant editor and chief leader-writer. 'I engaged him a bit on trust . . . and largely at the recommendation of an old associate . . . I soon found that I had made the discovery of a journalist of genius.' So O'Connor wrote in obituary notices in 1924. It was one Devenish, business manager for the *Star* and formerly foreman printer at the National Press Agency, who had suggested Massingham.[1] As for Massingham's own interest, as early as 30 July 1887 he was reporting in his 'London Letter' to the *Norfolk News* the plans for the new paper.

The remainder of the staff was assembled with the aid, sometimes on the initiative, of Massingham. Of Bernard Shaw he spoke to O'Connor 'with rapture'. In December 1887 Massingham wrote Shaw 'You have heard of the intention to start a new Radical paper called the "Star" . . . We have thought of you as a possible contributor and we should be glad to secure your services for occasional "notes".'[2] Shaw became a leader-writer at two guineas a week.

All in all, in retrospect, it was an extraordinary staff; as often remarked, it included a small host of individuals who subsequently achieved considerable reputations as editors: Massingham himself; Ernest Parke, the sub-editor, later editor of the *Star* whom O'Connor referred to as 'almost the first choice on my staff'; Robert Donald, founder of *London* (later *Municipal Journal*) and editor of the *Daily Chronicle*; Clement Shorter of the *Sketch* and later the *Sphere*; Thomas Marlowe (*Daily Mail*); Lincoln Springfield (*London Opinion*); W. J. Evans (*Evening News*); R. A. Bennett (*Truth*); James Douglas (*Sunday Express*). The book reviewer was Richard Le Gallienne, and the drama critic was A. B. Walkley (later on *The Times*) who wrote as 'Spectator'. Joseph Pennell tells us that it was through Shaw that he

---

[1] *Daily Telegraph*, 29 Aug. 1924; *Sunday Times*, 7 Sept. 1924; [Wilson Pope and others], *The Story of 'The Star', 1888–1938* (London [1938]), 16; T. P. O'Connor, *Memoirs of an Old Parliamentarian*, II (New York, 1929), ch. XIV.

[2] O'Connor, *Memoirs*, II, 256; G.B.S.P., Add. MS. 50511/95, Massingham to Shaw, 12 Dec. 1887.

became the *Star*'s art critic. 'I drew all the London art world to the paper and dragged it into endless controversies', he modestly added. The music critic was Belfort Bax. When the *Star* was launched, Clement Shorter said to Massingham, 'Give me the opportunity of a weekly column of gossip about books. I will write it for nothing.' He was promptly employed at a guinea a week and in the third issue (19 January 1888) began his column, 'Books and Bookmen', concerning literary personalities and fortunes, signed 'Tattler' (later 'Tatler'). Soon it appeared twice a week and opened up larger opportunities to Shorter.[1]

Many other features developed, including Ernest Parke's sensational stories about 'Jack the Ripper', and 'Captain Coe' (really E. C. Mitchell) on sports. The often gossipy column 'Mainly About People' dates from the first issue of the *Star* and by 1892, according to Massingham, had published 'some thousands of biographies, in brief, of famous and infamous folk'. The anonymous but celebrated reporter, 'The *Star* man', seemed always on hand. Thus he turned up at the offices of the *Pall Mall Gazette* on 27 April 1888 just in time to catch the editor, W. T. Stead, leaving for St Petersburg to cover the Russian crisis. Result – a 'scoop' for the *Star*. The sections on books, music and the arts, as well as on politics, invited reader comment, a device deliberately employed. Walkley wrote to Shaw:

One of Archer's suggestions . . . is that I should aim at starting topics from time to time likely to provoke correspondence: a capital way of getting one's copy done *gratis*. Your name occurs to me as that of the great Impolite Letter Writer of the Day. . . Is there any topic you would like to write about? If so I would insert the necessary paragraph next week.

The idea may well have come from Massingham, for he used it to advantage in all of his editorial chairs, having been introduced to the stunt by James Spilling, his old chief in Norwich.[2]

Journalistically and, at least for a time, commercially, the *Star* was a sensational success. O'Connor had said that perhaps 30,000 or 40,000

---

[1] Joseph Pennell, *The Adventures of an Illustrator* (Boston, 1925), 160; Bullock (ed.), *C.K.S., An Autobiography*, 52–3.

[2] O'Connor, *Memoirs*, II, 256–7; Massingham, *The London Daily Press*, 183; G.B.S.P., Add. MS. 50512, Walkley to Shaw, 7 Oct. 1888.

readers the first year would make him happy.[1] OUR FIRST DAY /
AN EPOCH IN JOURNALISM / THE WORLD'S RECORD
BEATEN / 142,600 COPIES SOLD – thus the cross-heads in a
single half-column in the second day's issue, 18 January. At the end of
the first week it proclaimed, 'Already we have laid our hands on the
pulsating heart of the greatest city in the world.' It was clearly reaching
the working class with circulation averaging 125,000. In June, O'Connor celebrated his success with a reception at the office in Stonecutter
Street. In the *Norfolk News* (30 June 1888), Massingham reports it as
'one of the most successful parties of the season . . . a kind of christen-
ing of the paper which in five months has attained unprecedented
circulation in evening journalism'. We are told that the circulation
reached 279,000 by the summer of 1889,[2] a pace which nearly finished
its rival, the *Daily News*, 'a prosy Victorian paper', orthodox Liberal
in persuasion, whose circulation sharply declined after 1890.[3] Kennedy
Jones who, along with Alfred Harmsworth, revived the *News* in 1895,
later wrote that the *Star* established the reputation as 'being the most
advanced and best written evening paper in London'.[4]

We can now follow Massingham's life more closely, thanks to the
entries in the diary of 'the ubiquitous Mr. Shaw' (probably Massingham's phrase). They came together as friends, as well as associates on
the *Star*. On 24 May 1888 Massingham went with Stewart Headlam
and Graham Wallas to the Bedford Debating Society to hear Shaw and
then proceeded to Headlam's house to argue 'about religion until
1 a.m.' At the Shelley Society, one evening, both Massingham and
Shaw spoke. Luncheon and dinner meetings, often at the National
Liberal Club, were frequent, sometimes with Sidney Webb, Walkley,
Shorter, or Belfort Bax. There were chess games at the Club. They
met at the British Museum and chatted 'over chocolate'. Shaw was a
frequent visitor and guest in the Massingham home. On Sundays there
were long walks, four miles or more, in Highgate and Hampstead.
Says Shaw: 'We thus became *bona fide* travellers in the legal sense,
entitled to obtain drinks as such, and second, to buy a copy of the

[1] [Wilson Pope], *The Story of 'The Star'*, 17.
[2] Paul Thompson, *Socialists, Liberals and Labour: The Struggle for London, 1885–1914*
(London, 1967), 97.
[3] Oron James Hale, *Publicity and Diplomacy . . . 1890–1914* (New York, 1940), 22–3.
[4] Kennedy Jones, *Fleet Street & Downing Street* (London [1920]), 130.

Observer.' The *Observer* was still trading on the fame of its reports of week-end battles during the Franco-Prussian war. 'Massingham would solemnly waste fourpence every Sunday morning – when any of the penny weeklies would have served him better.' After considerable deliberation Shaw (February 1890) bought Massingham's 'Bar-lock' typewriter for £13, 'on credit of course', and used it with some difficulty for years.[1]

One evening in February 1889 was recounted by Shaw at length:

Went to Croydon by the 7:17 train to meet Massingham at Bax's. After some singing, we began spirit rapping and table turning, and in the excitement of it I forgot the last train. I cheated from the first, and as soon as Massingham detected me, he became my accomplice and we caused the spirits to rap out long stories, lift the table into the air, and finally drink tumblers of whisky and water, to the complete bewilderment of Bax. . . I have not laughed so much in years.

Massingham was fond of this story, too, but in later years he made the victim not Belfort Bax but Edward Clodd. In 1925 Shaw wrote to Dorothy Massingham: 'Your father could not have exaggerated the seance; the truth has to be toned down to make it credible.' It was such episodes which Shaw had in mind when he spoke of Massingham's 'big high shoulders into which his cheeks sank readily when his unsleeping sense of humor set him chuckling'.[2]

The politics of the 'Star'

In analysing the role of the *Star* in politics, the salient fact is Liberal Party recovery after the disaster of 1886. Our focus is on London where the working-class vote was recaptured, and the climax was the General Election of 1892 in which the Liberals won 17 of the 22 constituencies in which over 80 per cent of the voters were working class. Before that came notable success in local elections, especially the victory of a majority of seats by the Progressive Party in the first London County Council. How to explain these results? The best historical scholarship concludes that 'the real motive forces in the Liberal recovery were the *Star* newspaper and the trade union boom

---

[1] Shaw Diary, 1888–90, *passim*; *H.W.M.*, 214–15.
[2] Shaw Diary, 16 Feb. 1889, as found in St John Ervine, *Bernard Shaw: His Life, Work and Friends* (London, 1956), 150; Shaw to Dorothy Massingham, 13 Jan. 1925 (U. of Texas); *H.W.M.*, 209.

of 1889–92'. This interpretation rejects the statements of Fabian historians, until recently generally accepted, that Liberal revival in London resulted from Fabian 'permeation' of the Liberal Party, transforming its policies and influencing its selection of candidates.[1]

As to the *Star*, the Fabians have insisted that they transformed it into their own organ, appropriating its columns for their own purposes. The classic statement is in Fabian Tract No. 41, *The Fabian Society: Its Early History* written by Shaw and published in 1892. Concerning the year 1888, he wrote:

We collared the *Star* by a stage army stratagem, and before the year was out had the assistant editor, Mr. H. W. Massingham, writing as extreme articles as Hyndman had ever written in *Justice*. . . [It became] far more advanced than the wildest Socialist . . . ever hoped to see a capitalist paper.

Shaw elaborated this theme, in and out of season, then and thereafter. 'The stage army stratagem', he explained, came when O'Connor would not publish Shaw's articles. The Fabian Society ordered all its members to write to the *Star* expressing indignant surprise. 'In 1888 it cost only twenty-eight post cards written by twenty-eight members to convince the newly born *Star* newspaper that London was aflame with Fabian Socialism.' In a much later account, Shaw added: 'and though Massingham assured his chief that all the letters were written by me (which was near enough to the truth . . .) T. P. was none the less impressed'.[2]

In February and March 1890, when it seemed that the *Star* might lose the services of both Massingham and Shaw, Shaw wrote Massingham of the 'Fabianism which made it [the *Star*] famous' and warned O'Connor of 'the *Star* drooping without its magic Fabian atmosphere on the first page and its Bassetto enchantments inside'.[3]

But the *Star* hardly mentions the Fabians before July 1888.[4] Shaw's own political leaders last less than a month, from January to February 1888. Thereafter his political writings were limited to occasional notes and these ended early in 1889 when he succeeded Belfort Bax as music

---

[1] On Fabian claims and the role of the *Star*, see Thompson, *Socialists, Liberals and Labour*, 97 and chs. 5 and 7; A. M. McBriar, *Fabian Socialism and English Politics, 1884–1918* (Cambridge, 1962), ch. 9.
[2] Fabian Tract No. 41, pp. 18, 26; two other accounts by Shaw: 'In the Days of Our Youth', *Star*, 19 Feb. 1906, and 'When We Were Very Young', *Star*, 7 Jan. 1938.
[3] Laurence, 244–5.
[4] Thompson, *Socialists, Liberals and Labour*, 98.

critic. On the other hand the *Star* espoused Radicalism closely associated with Liberalism. It enthusiastically supported the objectives worked out at the Liberal Party Conference of 1888, eventually incorporated in the Newcastle Programme of 1891. These included certain Radical proposals: Home Rule for Ireland and disestablishment of the Church in Scotland and Wales, an end to plural voting, institution of parish and district councils, legislation fixing the employer's liability for accidents in industry. In broader terms Liberalism advocated land reform, housing legislation, progressive taxation. By 1889 and 1890 it was favouring a statutory eight-hour day as well as free education, poor law reform and prison reform. This programme emphasised both progressive legislation and revival of the Liberal Party. Socialists were welcomed if they supported the second as well as the first of these objectives.

It was in London that the *Star* made a difference. 'We regard the organization of London Radicalism as the first great work of the *Star*', declared the first issue. Agencies were at hand which the *Star* vitalised. To attract the newly-enfranchised voters, democratic Liberal caucuses had been organised and federated in the London Liberal and Radical Union (L.R.U.). Professor Stuart, chairman of the Board of Directors of the *Star*, was one of its chief sponsors. In addition there were some 300 Radical Clubs associated together in the Metropolitan Radical Federation, in effect an organisation rivalling the L.R.U. Both organisations were politically apathetic before 1888. Now, as the new political voice of the London working classes, the *Star*, with its extraordinary circulation, brought together Liberals, Radicals and Socialists into a new Progressivism. To the *Star* may be attributed in considerable part the Progressive victories in the Vestries (May 1888) and in the School Boards (November 1888) but it was positively spectacular in the election of the first London County Council in January 1889. In August 1888 the London L.R.U. drafted a programme on housing and public services which was the basis for the *Star*'s 'Questions to Candidates'. Just before polling the *Star* issued a list of endorsed candidates. Out of 119 members the Progressives elected 68. O'Connor later remarked that the first London County Council was largely nominated in the offices of the *Star*.[1] When the County Council set

[1] O'Connor, *Memoirs*, II, 267.

to work, its steady support in the London press came from the *Star* and the *Daily Chronicle*.

Looking back in 1920, Massingham's own version was: 'The *Star* accomplished nearly everything it set out to do. It destroyed the Salisbury Government, created the London Progressive Party, knocked the old journalism into fits, and made even the Liberal Party think.'[1] Of Massingham's role we can be fairly sure even to the point of identifying with some confidence many of his own (unsigned) leaders. Take the Irish problem. There was the case of John Mandeville, famous in the annals of the *Star*. Mandeville, a tenant farmer in Mitchelstown in County Cork, was convicted in 1887 of inflammatory speech-making and imprisoned for two months under the Crimes Act. His death in July 1888, according to the verdict of the inquest jury, resulted from his 'brutal and unjustifiable' treatment in prison. The *Star* pronounced his death 'murder' and Balfour proposed criminal proceedings against the paper.[2]

Massingham's feelings on the Irish question were so strong that it is likely that most of the *Star*'s comment on the McFadden Case came from his pen. Father McFadden, a priest in the 'straggling parish of Gweedore [Co. Donegal] with its 44,000 acres of black bog, brown heather, and grey granite' (Massingham's words) had served a jail sentence on conviction of conspiracy under the Crimes Act. Now he was charged with murder in the death of Inspector Martin, who died in a riot when he sought to arrest McFadden on a second charge of conspiracy. A party of English journalists, including Massingham as the 'Special Commissioner of the *Star*', went to Maryborough in Ireland in October 1889, to cover the trial. His substitute on the 'London Letter' for the *Norfolk News* refers to his 'slashing editorials on Ireland' in the *Star*. In one of his own 'London Letters', Massingham tells us that he went to Ireland 'representing a London daily paper, the name of which horses will not drag from me but which, I flatter, represents the opinion of a number of average Englishmen'. His extended account

[1] *Star*, 6 May 1920.
[2] L. P. Curtis, Jr, *Coercion and Conciliation in Ireland, 1880–1892* (Princeton, 1963), 223–5.

appeared in the *Star*, and in certain other papers, including the *Scottish Leader*, *Western Daily Mercury*, and *Bristol Mercury*.[1]

Massingham's reporting in the McFadden Case is indicative. By 1889, the second year of the *Star*, he was generally credited with a strong role in determining its policy. Comment after he left the paper in 1891 attributed to him most of the Radicalism of the paper, and *Pearson's Monthly* says he originated the term 'Progressive' as applied to Radicals in the London County Council. Shaw emphasised Massingham's initiative. In 1906 Shaw wrote that by 1889 Massingham's articles on London politics had 'become more and more Progressive, then ultra-Progressive, then positively Jacobin'. In December 1889, Shaw advised the editor of *La Revue Socialiste* (Paris) that a copy of his paper sent to O'Connor would be 'simply wasted; but one to H. W. Massingham, as the Social Democratic editor of the *Star*, would secure a notice. He is nominally the assistant editor, but it is he who really forces the socialist programme into the *Star* in spite of T.P.' And soon after Shaw was writing to the editor of the new weekly, the *Speaker*, about the 'irreconcileable hostility between the New Radicalism & the Old ... Read the *Star* & watch the struggle between *our* Social Democratic editor [Massingham] & *your* Home Rule editor [O'Connor]'. And as Massingham's relations with O'Connor reached breaking point, the strength of Massingham's hand and voice is clear, at least to Shaw.[2]

But Massingham's Radicalism and his Progressivism did not in the *Star* period lead him to organised Socialism. In these years he saw very little of Sidney Webb and Graham Wallas who together with Shaw were the most active Fabians. Massingham's own interest in Fabian principles and tactics was then that of an interested but detached observer. For his 'London Letter' he wrote (18 February 1888) 'I had thought the *Star* was Radical enough, but I find that Socialists are profoundly disgusted with it as not going far enough'. In November 1888, after a talk with Stuart, he suggested to Shaw that he or some other Fabian (perhaps Clarke) be a candidate in the approaching

---

1 'London Letter', *Norfolk News*, 19, 26 Oct. and 2 Nov. 1899. Massingham published in *The Gweedore Hunt: A Story of English Justice in Ireland* (London, 1889) an account based on his articles for the *Star*.
2 *Pearson's Monthly* (June 1892), p. 269; Shaw in the *Star*, 19 Feb. 1906; Laurence, 233–5, 245.

London County Council elections.[1] 'Local Government is a way that would be certain to do your cause good ... It seems to me a very important period in the development of your party.' Then in a discussion of Socialism in his 'London Letter' for 15 December 1888 Massingham remarked that 'The Fabians have the only promising approach to the problem'. In broader terms his political outlook is evident in his lecture, 18 September 1889, on 'Liberalism and Labour Politics' before the Central Democratic Club (probably a Radical Club) in Gray's Inn Road. Massingham was not favourable to the idea of an independent labour party; he thought the interests of labour could better be served through the new Radical programme. 'There was no use', the summary in the *Star* continues, 'in attaching a party label to a social force that belonged exclusively to neither party ... socialism as an organization had not been growing, but as a force was becoming constantly more manifest.'[2]

Massingham's key role on the *Star* emerges most clearly in the conflicting views which divided the staff and led to his elevation to the editorship in July 1890 and six months later to his resignation. The first breach back in 1888, as we have seen, was between O'Connor, an Irish Home Rule Radical, and Shaw, a confirmed Socialist, a fact which O'Connor discovered somewhat to his surprise. The issue was John Morley and the crisis was immediate. In recounting the episode years later, O'Connor tells us 'You may judge of my confusion when John Morley brought up to me in the Division Lobby of the House of Commons a paragraph, written by Shaw, I am sure, in which he is dealt with more faithfully than fairly'.[3]

Shaw wrote O'Connor a letter of resignation (9 February) as leader-writer:

You will be more at your ease without having constantly to suppress my articles... Tell John Morley ... that the latest principles from Voltaire & Bentham will not do for Stonecutter St, and that your Star must cross his sooner or later if he persists in his 18th century Rip-van-Winkleism.

And to Massingham, Shaw wrote: 'T.P.'s attachment to John Morley

[1] G.B.S.P., Add. MS. 50543/96, 98–9, Massingham to Shaw, 30 Nov. and 3 Dec. 1888.
[2] Shaw Diary, 18 Sept. 1889; *Star*, 19 Sept. 1889.
[3] O'Connor, *Memoirs*, II, 266 (Shaw's paragraph on Morley in the *Star* cannot be identified).

is the final blow. It is impossible to attain even high mud marks in politics without taking that solemn literary obsolescence and shaking the starch out of him twice a week regularly.'

References to Massingham in Shaw's diary become scant and it may be that their relations for a time were strained. Some ten days after his resignation Shaw wrote Massingham a long letter about *Star* policy but it has not survived. Several months later in a letter to Mrs T. P. O'Connor Shaw referred to 'mossy-headed Massingham. How I should like to get hold of that paper just for a fortnight'.[1]

But Massingham had his own differences with O'Connor. Let us begin with an account of what was presented to the reading public – this is found in W. T. Stead's *Review of Reviews*. We are told (March 1890) that almost from the start the control of *Star* policy fell more and more into the hands of the assistant editor, Massingham, 'an ardent Social Radical'. But O'Connor and Massingham differed over a significant legislative proposal, the Eight Hours Bill for miners – a difference compounded by the fact that O'Connor had at first embraced it and then, apparently on the remonstrances of Morley and some of the *Star* shareholders, repudiated it. When the miners' demand for an eight-hour day was rejected by O'Connor, Massingham appealed over his head to directors and shareholders. In June 1890 the *Review of Reviews* reported that T.P., as O'Connor was invariably known, had bought out the shareholders supporting Massingham, but this statement was corrected in the July issue – it was T.P. who was being bought out, for £15,000. Stuart and Massingham took charge, with Massingham undertaking the normal duties of editor.

In later years both Massingham and O'Connor, good friends, played down these differences. Massingham took pleasure in relating how T.P. got him off the *Star* and how he in turn succeeded in ousting T.P. and returning as editor himself. In an obituary notice, generally complimentary, after Massingham's death, T.P. admitted that Massingham 'was not altogether a comfortable colleague', and that he was often surprised to find in the *Star*

very nasty little flicks at the Liberal Party and its leaders. The result was that after a night in the House of Commons . . . I had to drag myself out of

---

[1] Shaw in the *Star*, 19 Feb. 1906; Laurence, 183–5, 189; Shaw Diary, 17 and 20 Feb. 1888.

bed, not merely to write my own article . . . but also to scrutinize severely the articles of my assistants.[1]

But we can get closer to what it was all about originally. The *Star* had moved a considerable distance from the policy which the directors had envisaged. In Norwich the more conventional Liberals thought the *Star* 'rather sensational and cheap' and 'below Stuart's standard'. Stuart's father-in-law, Jeremiah Colman, wrote from Norwich that the paper had a vulgar tone. When T.P. said that 'London electors had to be stirred up to vote Progressive', Colman responded: 'I cannot conceal from myself nor can I conceal from you the strong dissatisfaction which is felt by a section of the Liberal Party as to the line which the paper has taken.' O'Connor did face opposition from his directors but the role of individuals, such as John Brunner, is clouded.[2]

The most revealing account of the final break between Massingham and O'Connor is in T.P.'s *Memoirs* where references to Massingham are veiled but none the less recognisable. The problem of watching over 'the indiscretions of Mr. Massingham and Mr. Shaw had got on my nerves', O'Connor wrote. But 'the blow which thoroughly paralysed me' was a printed indictment 'full of misrepresentation and deadly in its venom' sent out to the shareholders by 'a man on the staff whom I regarded as my greatest and most faithful friend'. This person is not identified further, but it was clearly Massingham. The Massingham version, as his *Nation* associates later represented it, was that the issue was a clear matter of principle – the policy of the *Star*. A somewhat different comment came from Robert Donald, in 1890 a member of the *Star* staff. 'I think that "T.P." was badly treated and that Mr. Massingham failed in loyalty when he prepared a return showing that Mr. O'Connor was spending little time at the office and was not keeping up his contributions.' O'Connor and Donald had the same document in mind.[3]

Here and there we catch glimpses of the controversy as it developed. In the midst of arguments over the *Star*'s finances Massingham dropped

[1] Miss G. M. Cross to Oswald Garrison Villard, 22 Nov. 1929, Houghton; *Daily Telegraph*, 29 Aug. 1924.
[2] Basil Cozens-Hardy to the author, 11 Aug. 1969; [Henry] Hamilton Fyfe, *T. P. O'Connor* (London, 1934), 152–4. Stephen E. Koss, *Sir John Brunner: Radical Plutocrat, 1842–1919* (Cambridge, 1970), 158.
[3] O'Connor, *Memoirs*, II, 269–70; Fyfe, *T. P. O'Connor*, 153.

a note to T.P.: 'Of course after your expressions to me this morning, it would be quite inconsistent with my self-respect to continue a member of the staff of the *Star*.' Early in April 1890, in accepting a dinner invitation from Sir Charles Dilke, O'Connor wrote 'I sincerely trust that Massingham will not be in the company; he has treated me so badly that I could not feel comfortable at the same table. . . I am in the midst of a struggle here but I am going to beat up my enemies.'[1]

Shaw knew what was up, for he was seeing Massingham frequently at this time. In February he tells us that Massingham was 'very full of his quarrel with T.P.' Shaw was involved because he felt underpaid and had complained to Massingham. On 4 March Shaw received a letter from T.P. suggesting that the *Star* could do without him. He sat up until 3 a.m. drafting a reply:

If Massingham goes, my going with him will (1) double the *éclat* of his martyrdom, and (2) be an additional proof of your alleged bad editing. . . There is a difference between M's line of battle with you and mine. [Our differences over Morley] are the commonplaces of political warfare. Massingham has gone beyond this, and is fighting with both hands by attacking not only your policy, but your diligence in fulfilling your Stonecutter St. official functions. With that I have nothing to do. . . I propose, then . . . to hold on until your difference with M. is settled. He is now in high spirits, riding for a fall.[2]

The clash with O'Connor shows Massingham's adherence to principle, yes, but also his impulsiveness and impatience. And some would add, daring. The strange admixture of the intellectual and the emotional, of principle and pride, of the conscious and the unconscious, of self-control and of hasty action are qualities in Massingham which close associates all remark on later and which emerge clearly for the first time in his differences with O'Connor over the *Star*. To all outward appearance he won this battle, but Shaw's shrewd comment was that he was 'riding for a fall'. He at once found himself even more at odds with Stuart. Their relation was, in fact, somewhat ambiguous – each in effect regarding himself as the editor – and Massingham's tenure lasted but six months. He resigned in January 1891. As the story came to be told among newspapermen, the paper was no more successful,

---

[1] Fyfe, *T. P. O'Connor*, 151–2; D.P., Add. MS. 43914/229.
[2] Shaw Diary, 20 Feb. and 4 Mar. 1890; Shaw to Massingham, 28 Feb. 1890, and Shaw to O'Connor, 4 Mar. 1890 in Laurence, 243–6.

financially, under Massingham than it had been under O'Connor. This along with Massingham's 'Socialism' forced his resignation. According to Brailsford, the final break came with a leader written by Stuart in Massingham's absence, in criticism of John Burns for his support of a protracted railway strike in Scotland.[1] The comment of the *Review of Reviews* (January and February 1891) is perceptive. It reported that when Massingham became editor the directors called on him 'to moderate his zeal for social reform'. Massingham 'is young and impetuous, exceedingly sensitive. He was not tough enough to stand the strain of a false position and he resigned'.

Of course we do not know the story in any detail. But the sudden advent of the O'Shea Divorce Case, involving the Irish leader, Parnell, in November 1890, was a complicating factor. English Radicals tended to support Parnell's fight to remain leader of the Irish Party while other influential elements of the press, notably, Hugh Price Hughes of the *Methodist Times*, W. T. Stead of the *Review of Reviews* and E. T. Cook of the *Pall Mall Gazette* opposed. Hughes had not been favourably inclined towards Massingham. Now, in December the *Methodist Times* was assailing the *Star* for joining up with Labouchere in support of Parnell. The 'disgusting' *Star* was accused of publishing 'scandalous falsehoods about Price Hughes' and was charged with 'alienating the only people that can save the Liberal Party from ruin'. Massingham was apparently caught between Stuart and Hughes and he unburdened himself to Stead:

I have rarely had more troubled times than during this last fortnight or so – troubles which I [fear] ... will end my connection with the *Star*. Price Hughes does his best to incite Stuart to interference, & he has succeeded. I am in the grips of Whig wire pulling, & I shall never be quit of them, either till they have sucked all the lifeblood out of me, or I assert my independence. And I propose to do the latter.

Massingham apologised for failure of courtesy and patience in commenting on Stead's attitude towards the Parnell Case.[2] And so in a confusion of reason and emotion he asserted his independence, as he was to do again and again, under similar circumstances.

---

[1] *History of The Times*, III, 99; *H.W.M.*, 95.
[2] *Methodist Times*, 10 July 1890, p. 693, and 4 Dec. 1890, pp. 1236–7; Massingham to Stead, 9 Dec. 1890 (courtesy of J. O. Baylen). See Shaw's comment, Laurence, 277.

After Massingham's resignation the *Star* became more orthodox as a Liberal journal; as Shaw put it, the paper proceeded to 'Gladstonize' its politics. Massingham's own comment not long after was

The *Star* presents a curious instance of transition from fiery and impatient Radicalism, with a certain socialistic bias, to a faithful representation of the ordinary party creed. It owes this change to Mr. James Stuart, M.P., who has successfully resisted the effort to maintain the paper in its earlier lines.[1]

'A certain socialistic bias', says Massingham. But his formal 'Socialist' phase, if there was one, was limited to 1891–3 when he was actively associated with the Fabian Society. As a prelude to that episode it is interesting to examine his relations, during his *Star* period, with Socialist groups more militant than the Fabians.

That he had good friends and acquaintances in these groups is evident. There was Herbert Burrows, already mentioned as a leading member of the S.D.F. and a contributor to its organ, *Justice*. But Massingham seems to have seen more of Belfort Bax, a cultivated man, social philosopher of some Marxist persuasion, close friend of both Shaw and Engels, and co-founder with William Morris of the Socialist League. Massingham was now well acquainted with Hyndman and, very likely as early as this, with Morris as well. Eduard Bernstein, in exile, and publishing the *Sozialdemokrat* in London since 1888, tells us that at this time the only important London journalist he came to know was Massingham.[2]

But Massingham kept his distance from the S.D.F. Likewise, *Justice* was wary of the *Star* from the beginning, declaring that 'Mr. T. P. O'Connor will have to go beyond mere Radicalism if he carries out his confession of faith in its entirety'. As the London County Council elections approached Massingham wrote to Shaw that he did not think Hyndman himself was valuable as a candidate, while Hyndman in turn told Shaw that he did not favour negotiations with a Liberalism which merely had in mind absorbing the S.D.F. To be

---

1 Shaw, Fabian Tract No. 41, p. 18; *The London Daily Press*, 190. Despite Stuart's return to orthodox Liberalism, the view of the Cozens-Hardy family in Norwich, closely associated with Stuart, was that his connection with the *Star* barred him from Cabinet office under Gladstone. (B. Cozens-Hardy to the author, 11 Aug. 1969.)
2 Eduard Bernstein, *My Years of Exile: Reminiscences of a Socialist*, trans. Bernard Miall (London, 1921), 252–3.

sure, *Justice* and the *Star* had much in common in London politics with the *Star* supporting three S.D.F. candidates for the County Council and *Justice* applauding the Progressive victory. After the internal crisis in the S.D.F. with the expulsion of Henry Champion in November 1888 and the resignation of John Burns in 1889, *Justice* turned to emphasising social change through the parliamentary process and welcomed the *Star*'s programme of New Radicalism.[1] But all this was a matter of politics not of principle.

Massingham's aloofness from doctrinaire Socialism is illustrated in his attitude towards the controversy among Socialist groups for control of a workers' congress scheduled for July 1889 in Paris and over plans for a new Socialist International. Two opposing groups emerged. One, orthodox Marxist, led by Paul Lafargue (Marx's son-in-law), developed in France under the name of the Blanquists and was supported in England by Friedrich Engels, Edward Aveling and his common-law wife, Eleanor Marx, and Eduard Bernstein. It also had the support in England, strangely enough, of moderate elements, but elements hostile to the S.D.F., and as such hoped to win over the columns of the *Star* to offset the influence of *Justice*. On the other hand, Hyndman and his Marxist S.D.F. favoured the other French group, the unorthodox and more moderate Possibilists, who likewise sought support from English Radicals and Socialists, and thus the *Star*. Eventually, in July, two rival congresses met in Paris.

In the clash between the groups, prior to the congresses, the *Star* took the position (3 May) that the two factions really had nothing to quarrel about and that 'it was more than ever necessary that the workmen ... should show a united front'. The whole episode would have been insignificant in *Star* annals had not Massingham himself gone to Paris in early May to cover the Exhibition celebrating the centenary of the French Revolution. Even so, our knowledge of efforts to gain *Star* support is limited to the correspondence of Engels in London and Paul Lafargue and Laura Marx Lafargue in Paris.[2]

When further comment by the *Star* (3 and 7 May) on the Socialist

[1] *Justice*, 20 Jan. 1888; 20 April 1889. Massingham to Shaw, 30 Nov. 1888 and Hyndman to Shaw, 6 Dec. 1888 in G.B.S.P., Add. MSS. 50543/96 and 50538/113–14. *Star*, 12 Apr. 1889.
[2] Friedrich Engels, Paul and Laura Lafargue, *Correspondence*, trans. Yvonne Kapp, II (Moscow, 1960); Chüshichi Tsuzuki, *Life of Eleanor Marx, 1855–1898* (Oxford, 1967).

controversy in France was somewhat favourable to the Possibilists and suggested a connection between the Blanquists and the supporters of General Boulanger, a deputation in London (Eleanor Marx, Edward Aveling and Belfort Bax) protested at the *Star* office, and Engels wrote Paul Lafargue at length (11 May):

What we need are letters from Paris, sent direct to the STAR, bearing Paris postmarks, *refuting the Possibilist slanders*. . . The STAR is the daily paper which is most read by the workers and the only one that is open to us, however little. [Massingham was captured by the Possibilists who] would not let go of him, made him tipsy with absinthe and vermouth and thus succeeded in winning over the STAR for their congress and in making him swallow their lies. If you want us to be useful to you here, help us to recover some influence with the STAR by showing him that they have set his feet on a dangerous path. . . And to that end there is no other way than letters of protest against these articles, *reaching him direct from Paris*.

But the Lafargues in Paris considered this 'impracticable'. There was some hope that the *Star* would publish the official convocation of the Blanquist Congress with signatures. Engels wrote again (14 May): 'If only we can be supported by a few blows from Paris' which urge Massingham '*to insert the proclamations when they come*'. But Paul Lafargue responded from Paris: 'The only way to answer the reports from Paris in the *Star* would be to show . . . that the Possibilists treated Massingham as an imbecile who could be made to believe that black is white. . . You must admit that this would be an unlikely way of winning over the director of the *Star*.'

The *Star* did publish (14–15 May) some letters received from the Blanquist element, but the circular about their Congress was not printed despite Bernstein's efforts to persuade Massingham, and Engels abandoned hope of any support from the *Star*. Henceforth the Engels–Lafargue correspondence, while much concerned with events in England, makes no further reference to the *Star*. Massingham was a newspaper man, not a politician nor a revolutionary. So we are not surprised that when the last English issue of Bernstein's *Sozialdemokrat* was published in London on 27 September 1890, the *Star* (29 September) carried an interview with Bernstein, by Massingham: 'Socialist Smugglers: Germany Flooded with Papers from Kentish Town: a Talk with the Editor.' Bernstein explained how the paper had been produced and distributed in London.

From 'Star' to 'Daily Chronicle'

Uncomfortable as were the circumstances of his leaving the *Star*, in so doing Massingham did not seem to lose stature. In Radical circles, particularly, his years with the *Star* left him admired as well as respected. *Pearson's Monthly* said he had emerged from his clash with the *Star*'s proprietors, 'with all the honours of war', and may now be said 'to be the most prominent and brilliant member of the younger group of journalists' in London. The *Review of Reviews* in reporting T. P. O'Connor's plans for a new Sunday paper, remarked: 'The question of whether he succeeds or not will depend upon the question whether or not he has found another assistant like Mr. Massingham.'[1]

Massingham left the editorship of the *Star* in January 1891; little more than four years later he became editor of the *Daily Chronicle*. In the interval he had varied opportunity to test and develop his powers as a writing journalist – for dailies, for weekly newspapers, and for periodicals. His interests widened and his knowledge increased and he displayed that capacity for versatility and output which throughout his life astonished associates and readers alike.

His first formal assignment, that with the *Sunday World* was, to be sure, short-lived. Massingham's concern for Irish tenant farmers and his enthusiasm for Gladstone and Home Rule had brought him in close touch with Michael Davitt, Irish land reformer and labour leader. In September 1890 Davitt launched a weekly newspaper, the *Labour World*, described as 'a journal of progress for the masses', and directed at the concerns of labour throughout the British Isles. For a Sunday edition, called the *Sunday World*, Massingham wrote from 29 March to 26 April 1891, a series of articles entitled 'Peter's Net' and signed 'The Fisherman'.

In his first article Massingham wrote that he proposed to deal

week by week with matters that interest the democracy of London and Great Britain. . . I shall mainly though not exclusively, treat of political matters . . . not . . . the barren tract of party polemics, but the field . . . of the peoples' politics. . . Don't be afraid of what is called the State. The State is the people organized as a Government. It can do for you many things which singly you cannot do for yourselves.

[1] *Pearson's Monthly* (June 1892), p. 269; *Review of Reviews*, III (May 1891), 479.

In the next issue (5 April) he emphasised a series of lectures on the Co-operative Movement by Miss Beatrice Potter. And (12 April) while applauding the nomination of Tom Mann to the Royal Commission on Labour, created in 1891 ('barring that of John Burns, it is the best that could be made') he directed serious charges at the Commission:

A hollower fraud it would be impossible to imagine... Just a sufficient number of labour representatives to enable the Government to pretend that it is playing fair to the workers, when, in reality, it is selling them... Of the new elements of social progress – such as the new unionism and the new economy – there is either no representation at all or a ludicrously inadequate one. Where's land nationalisation? Where's Fabian Socialism? Where's even latter day Radicalism? Where's the live impulse that serves nine-tenths of the working class fighters today? Not on the Commission – and for a very good reason.

Massingham seemed to be making the most of this opportunity. But Davitt was not a success as an editor. His opposition to Parnell after the Divorce Case weakened his appeal. He had difficulties with staff and finances and had to abandon the project. In May the editorship passed briefly from him to Massingham, who, said the *Review of Reviews* (May 1891), 'may be relied upon to do his level best to make the paper the leader of the politico-Socialists of Great Britain'. But Massingham had much the same financial problem as Davitt and the *Labour World* soon ceased publication, on 30 May.[1]

During the remainder of 1891, until Massingham became associated with the *Daily Chronicle*, his writing was varied. He had in progress the series of articles on the newspapers of London, published in the *Leisure Hour* between February and September 1892. He wrote a piece for the *Contemporary Review* for September 1891 on 'The Nationalization of Cathedrals', inspired very likely by Jessopp. Massingham lamented the collapse in the administration of Church endowments and proposed that the Deans and Chapters be 'divested of any control over their landed estates... The time is surely coming when the effective nationalization of cathedrals will be seen to be necessary to the organ-ization of democracy and a valuable aid to the enrichment of its provincial life'. And in November he organised a 'London Letter', to

[1] On Davitt, see T. W. Moody, 'Michael Davitt and the British Labour Movement, 1882-1906', in *Transactions of the Royal Historical Society*, 3 (1953), 53-76. Massing-ham's tribute to Davitt, on his death, is in the *Speaker*, 2 June 1906.

which Shaw and Webb contributed, which appeared briefly in the *Bradford Observer*.[1]

Late in 1891 Massingham joined the staff of the *Daily Chronicle* as a leader-writer – the first leader which can be identified as his appeared in the issue for 28 November. We know nothing of the circumstances of his initial association but of his immediate success there is abundant testimony. Within a year or so he became the assistant editor. By June 1892 the admiring *Pearson's Monthly* was saying that 'some of the best political and literary writing in the *Daily Chronicle*' was coming from his pen. He returned to the House of Commons, his 'Parliamentary Notes' beginning in August 1892. His more significant 'House and Lobby' dates from 2 February 1893; its distinctive feature was that Massingham mixed straight news with commentary. Though it was unsigned, we may be sure that week in and week out it is his except for an occasional issue in which the column was prepared by 'our special correspondent'. 'Our Gallery Man', in the issue of 1 February 1893, describing the opening of a parliamentary session, is almost certainly Massingham. In its issue for 13 December 1893, the *Sketch* featured an interview with E. A. Fletcher, the *Daily Chronicle* editor, which singled out Massingham and his 'House and Lobby' for special praise. He continued writing the column after he became editor in March 1895, but only until September.

Massingham's reputation was enhanced when his articles for the *Leisure Hour* were published in book form late in 1892. Here are two comments: '*The London Daily Press* treats the press as a great organ of education, a great leader of thought; it suggests its responsibilities and sketches its powers'. And again, it is 'obliging but perilous – lifting the *yashmak* from the blushing and bowing physiognomies of the London journalists and revealing them in all their nakedness. One can but thank him, however. . . His seven chapters are mines of information, popularly and accurately given'.[2]

There is an urbanity about these essays which came out of Massingham's widening experience. His enthusiasm for change in orthodox journalism was now tempered. The 'New Journalism', he said, has sharper limits to its sphere than was at first predicted for it. . . The belief

---

[1] Shaw Diary, 14, 25, 26 Nov. 1891; *Bradford Observer*, 16 Nov. 1891.
[2] *Westminster Review*, 39 (Feb. 1893), 198; *Critic*, 22 (11 Mar. 1893), 141.

so conspicuously shared by the early promoters of the *Star*, that a newspaper could shape the whispers of democracy, and mould the vague desires for a new social synthesis, has not been developed. Journalism, new and old, is after all, too dependent on the party machine. . . The average journalist is still too slight, too unbelieving, too conventional a citizen to rule his country.

Two years later, in articles on 'How a Morning Newspaper is Produced', he spoke more boldly, perhaps reflecting his growing reputation with the *Daily Chronicle*. The morning papers in London, he said, suffer from want of single-minded direction which can be secured only by 'constant cooperation between the head of a newspaper and every member of his staff. There should, indeed, be the same transmission of orders and intelligence as goes to the planning of a great battle'. The reader should be aided 'in his search for what is truly significant in life', this by 'vivifying' the material. Thus foreign intelligence with its 'diplomatic nothings, vague and worthless echoes of uninteresting opinion' should be replaced with 'brief paragraphs of literary, social, dramatic and personal intelligence'. He urged 'more knowledge and sympathy' in treatment of Indian and colonial affairs. Of special urgency was the need to humanise the news reporting of London. Mechanical aids such as the headlines should tell a story, and type should be discreetly used 'to point a moral and adorn a tale'. The individual journalist should be emancipated from his anonymity; articles of criticism, in particular, should be signed. 'Look at the admirable results of giving Mr. Archer, Mr. Pennell, Mr. Bernard Shaw and Mr. Walkley their head in dramatic, artistic, and musical criticism, or of allowing Mr. T. P. O'Connor to sign his daily impressions of Parliament and politics.' He all but mentioned the *Star* by name. 'All these changes', he concluded, 'have been initiated in the evening, not in the morning press, though the *Daily Chronicle* is fast following a good example.'[1] Massingham was of course now the assistant editor of the *Daily Chronicle*.

1 *The London Daily Press*, 191–2; *The Young Man*, July 1894, and Aug. 1894.

CHAPTER 3

Fabian Socialist (1891–1893)

Soon after Massingham's resignation from the Fabian Society, Beatrice Webb noted: 'One feels that to be safe with him one ought to keep him very much in tow.' And not long after she referred to 'the mercurial H. W. Massingham'.[1] These remarks may serve as introduction to Massingham's dramatic rise to prominence with the Fabians and the early end of his interest and membership.

In March 1891, shortly after he left the *Star*, Massingham, on the recommendation of Graham Wallas and Sidney Webb, was elected to membership in the London Fabian Society. He was promptly (10 April) elected to the Executive Committee of 15, with 82 out of a possible 117 votes. Later in the year he joined Shaw and Wallas on the Executive's 'General Committee', empowered to reach decisions on routine matters. He at once took on countless duties. He assisted with publication of the *Fabian News* and preparation of Fabian Tracts. He revised the circular list of contributors to the *News* and arranged with the *Daily Chronicle* for publicity for the Society in reporting lectures by its members. He and the secretary, Edward R. Pease, drafted a report on Fabian Societies for the Fabian Conference early in 1892. He was exceedingly active in preparations for the General Election of 1892. He and Webb were asked to draw up a census of parliamentary candidates and Massingham himself organised the Fabian campaign fund for Ben Tillett at Bradford, now a Fabian and running as an independent Socialist, and drafted his election manifesto. He attended 35 out of 51 meetings of the Executive – a record exceeded only by the secretary – and he frequently presided. In April 1892 he was re-elected to the Executive, with 127 out of a possible 152 votes; only Wallas, Shaw and Webb received more votes.[2] He was a promi-

---

[1] Beatrice Webb, Diary, 12 March 1894 and March 1895, in *Our Partnership*, ed. Barbara Drake and Margaret I. Cole (London, 1948), 71, 116.

[2] Fabian Society, Executive Committee Minutes: for 1891 (20 Mar., 10 April, 10 June, 6 Oct., 13 Oct., 20 Oct., 1 Dec., 8 Dec.); for 1892 (5 Jan., 18 Jan., 19 Jan., Feb. *passim*, 1 Mar., 15 Mar., 29 Mar., 1 April, 2 May). *Fabian News*, Apr. and May 1891 and Apr. and May 1892.

nent Fabian, and his months of freedom from daily responsibilities with the *Star* provided the opportunity to become an energetic Fabian as well. He even, briefly, tried out Socialist language.

In June 1892, *Pearson's Monthly* was able to say of Massingham. 'He has become the specialist in all Labour Questions, and probably no man in London knows as well as he does the real truth about the . . . worker's problems that are now puzzling the rulers of Great Britain'. Perhaps the writer had read Massingham's article 'Wanted, A New Charter', which appeared in the *New Review* in March 1891, in which he spelled out a programme of social reform to be achieved through the Liberal Party. Undismayed by the period of 'capitalist rally' of 1890 following 'the great proletariat revival of 1889' he speaks out. The remedy for the working man's discontent will be found in the 'New Unionism' which provides another Chartist movement, 'social as to its end and political as to its means'. The working man, armed with the vote, can bring force to bear upon Parliament. To the working man's query: Who will open the way? the answer is the Radical Party; in every recent by-election campaign the Liberal candidate combined with the Irish Home Rule issue a social programme designed to attract the new voters. Massingham proposes a seven-point charter: land for the people, an eight-hour day, the educational ladder, a people's Parliament, the free commune (open district and parish councils with power), taxation of the idlers, and pensions for the aged. With the articulation of the Newcastle Programme, of October 1891, says Massingham, the Liberal Party is moving in the right direction. But, at the same time he warns in the *Labour Leader* (10 October) that 'these principles have got to be seen and felt in the Budgets they produce on the floor of the House of Commons, or from the benches of the County Councils'.

Massingham's Liberal Radicalism and his Fabianism were for a time compatible. The Fabian Executive asked him to issue as a leaflet his *Daily Chronicle* article (1 December 1891) on the Duke of Westminster, attacking the unearned increment in the value of his lands. His statement, designed as a Fabian Tract, was put aside but he and Pease were appointed to confer with societies interested in land reform. Though his name is not listed in the file of Fabian lecturers, he did deliver at least one Fabian lecture – at Essex Hall on 5 February 1892.

In 'The Method of Fabianism' he analysed the fortunes of Socialism in British politics – Conservative and Liberal Parties, London County Council, Radical organisations. We have a summary. 'Amidst perplexities of parties we must remember that Socialism is a principle of action to be applied at once and decisively to the whole field of current politics.' The time for forming an effective Labour Party had not arrived. 'We cannot be certain that this policy of permeating Radicalism with Socialism will prove successful' but a choice must be made between getting perhaps four or five Socialists in Parliament or attempting 'to get in some 200 imperfectly and unwillingly socialized Radicals'. He concludes on a doctrinaire note: 'Whatever happens, at the fit moment the logical development must bring us a true workers' Parliament.'[1]

Massingham was active in the episode of the proposed monster demonstration in the interests of free speech scheduled for the World's End Passage in Chelsea, for 31 January 1892. The police had interfered with open-air meetings at the World's End and late in 1891 the S.D.F. sponsored 'A Defence Committee for Free Speech' composed of representatives from various London Radical and Socialist groups. As the Fabian representatives, Massingham, Shaw, Webb and Wallas urged upon Sir Charles Russell (he had been Attorney General in the previous Gladstone Government) the necessity of rousing Liberal leaders to the defence of free speech. Russell sent the deputation on to the Home Office where they were given satisfactory assurance. All this was reported to the full meeting of the Defence Committee on 17 January but accounts of just what happened vary. According to the *Daily Chronicle*, Shaw said he was taking the place of Massingham (ill with the 'flu), in offering to go down to World's End and speak and be arrested on condition that the mass demonstration be abandoned. There must, under no circumstances, be a clash with the police. This proposal was voted down by 29 votes to 27 and the Fabian Society withdrew its representatives. The *Daily Chronicle* deplored the decision to hold the mass meeting in defiance of the police. Eventually the demonstration was rescheduled for 28 February but on that day,

---

[1] Fabian Society, Executive Committee Minutes, 1 Dec. 1891; 18, 19 Jan. 1892. *Fabian News*, Mar. 1892. Shaw Diary, engagement section, 5 Feb. 1892 (courtesy of Stanley Rypins).

though a much larger crowd than usual gathered at World's End, there was no formal demonstration and the crowd soon dispersed.[1] As Massingham entered his second year on the Executive Committee his participation in Fabian affairs sharply declined. From April 1892 to April 1893 he attended only 11 out of the 50 meetings of the Executive, and his formal activity, as recorded in the Minutes, almost ceased.[2] In the Progressive victory in London County Council elections of March 1892 and in the Liberal victory in the General Election in July, Massingham's energy and devotion is not with the Fabian Society but with the *Daily Chronicle*. Massingham reveals himself as a Radical journalist, not as a politician. And Massingham's close association is now not with Shaw or Webb but rather with John Burns who was re-elected to the London County Council as a Socialist but also as a Progressive with Radical support, and who was returned to Parliament in July, running as an Independent Labour candidate supported by the Liberal Association. This was the kind of connection which Massingham liked. Burns had left the S.D.F. in 1889 and both his temperament and ambitions led him towards Liberalism and away from doctrinaire Socialism and trade unionism alike. He and Massingham met frequently for tennis or to watch cricket on the Kennington Oval, but more often to discuss London politics.[3]

Prior to the London elections in March 1892, the *Daily Chronicle* carried a series of articles (23 January through to 20 February) on the general theme 'What the County Council has Done for London'. Subtitles were: 'As its Working Conscience'; 'For Administration'; 'For Economy'; 'For its Health and Safety'; 'For its Poor and Suffering'; 'For its Pleasure'; 'For its Labour'. Behind these articles were lengthy conferences between Massingham and Burns as they pored over reports of the County Council. On 30 January they went down the Thames to Barking and Crossness to inspect the new Sewage Works. Burns comments: 'Home to London at 8; Massingham dead beat; without food for nine hours, a frequent occurrence for members of the Committee on London Works.'[4] The *Daily Chronicle* had now

[1] *Fabian News*, Feb. 1892; Shaw Diary (Rypins' transcription), 11 and 13 Jan. 1892; Laurence, 341; on the Chelsea demonstration see *D.C.*, 18–19 Jan., 29 Feb. 1892, and *Justice*, 23 and 30 Jan. and 5 Mar. 1892.
[2] *Fabian News*, Apr. 1893.   [3] B.P., Add. MS. 46312, Burns Diary, 1892, *passim*.
[4] B.P., Add. MS. 46312, Burns Diary, 1, 3, 24, 27, 30 Jan. 1892.

replaced the *Star* as the most influential friend of the Progressives in the London press.[1]

When the new Parliament met in August, Burns, accompanied by Massingham, went to the Commons and received, Burns tells us, 'a good reception inside and out'. The leader in the *Daily Chronicle* (5 August) almost certainly written by Massingham, commented on the seating of Burns and also of Keir Hardie in the Commons, the latter in his cloth cap, but Burns in a new suit. During August, Shaw and Burns as well as Champion and other Socialists wrote a series of letters, published in the *Daily Chronicle*, dealing with the political situation and in particular with John Morley's campaign in the Newcastle by-election.[2] Shaw wrote to Burns at length about the questions raised by Morley's refusal to support the Eight Hours Bill. Shaw said that lacking a working-class candidate, the workers of Newcastle should be instructed by Burns to vote for Morley. He concludes: 'Whatever policy you adopt, make Massingham back it up.' The next day Massingham and Burns discussed the problem. Soon after (21 August) the three met on a Sunday afternoon at Massingham's home.[3] And so though Shaw still wrote for the *Daily Chronicle*, the closer association was that of Massingham and Burns. In October, on a Sunday walk to Barking, they discussed unemployment and Burns' article on the subject appeared in the *Nineteenth Century* for December.[4]

Despite Massingham's declining role in the Fabian Executive, he remained loyal to the Fabian cause in 1892. He accepted Party policy towards parliamentary candidates and approved Shaw's election manifesto of 1892 (Fabian Tract No. 40). The Fabians, including Massingham, supported John Morley in the by-election at Newcastle in August. On the other hand, Independent Labour, particularly Keir Hardie and Cunninghame Graham, opposed Morley because of his opposition to the eight-hour day, a principle accepted in the course of the campaign by the Conservatives.[5]

[1] A. G. Gardiner, *Sir John Benn and the Progressive Movement* (London, 1925), *passim*.
[2] Shaw's letters concerning Morley's campaign are in *D.C.*, 20 and 24 Aug.; his third letter (25 Aug.) was a reply to Champion and other Socialists.
[3] Shaw to Burns, 12 Aug. and Shaw to Webb, 22 Aug. in Laurence, 355–8, 361–2; Shaw Diary (Rypins' transcription), 21 Aug.; B.P., Add. MS. 46312, Burns Diary, 13 and 21 Aug.
[4] B.P., Add. MS. 46312, Burns Diary, 23 Oct. 1892.
[5] *Fabian News*, Mar. 1892; D. A. Hamer, *John Morley* (Oxford, 1968), 277–9. Many

Massingham took part in the formation on 26 October 1892 of the London Reform Union, a propaganda agency for the support of the Progressive Party, but dominated by Fabian members and policies. Its purpose was 'to assist in finding a remedy for the social and municipal wants of the metropolis'. The next day a *Daily Chronicle* leader declared: 'The formation of the London Reform Union ... is, we hope, destined to mark a new epoch in metropolitan politics. It denotes at all events a definite stage in the awakening of London.' It was written by one who attended the meeting, and Massingham was there. He assisted in the establishment of the official organ, *London* ('devoted to the interests of local government and the Progressive cause'), was one of its directors and gave the early issues his counsel and enthusiastic support. The editor was Robert Donald, formerly with Massingham on the *Star*.[1]

Also, the Webbs and Massingham seemed harmonious in their attitude towards the Royal Commission on Labour. Sidney Webb gave evidence at length on 17 and 18 November 1892. Beatrice Webb called the entire undertaking a 'gigantic fraud' and capable of doing great harm if their report was taken seriously. They were supported in this view by an article by Massingham in the *Daily Chronicle*, a re-expression of his scepticism when the Commission was formed.[2]

Massingham's writing in 1892 reveals no sign of defection from Fabianism. In an article in the *Fortnightly* (October 1892) celebrating the permeating of the old unionism by the new, he declared that they had come together in the Trades Union Congress (T.U.C.) of 1892, with agreement on the eight-hours question. In time a Radical Parliament would produce legislation satisfactory to the Parliament of labour. As to the political activity of the T.U.C. he seemed a little guarded. In another article, in the *New Review* (October 1892), he asserted that while not Radical enough, the new Gladstone Govern-

years later, in assessing Morley's career, Massingham, in a much-quoted passage, declared that Morley's opposition to an Eight Hours Bill for miners cost him the Liberal leadership – *H.W.M.*, 25–6.

[1] *London*, Prospectus, and other Robert Donald Papers (courtesy of H. A. Taylor); *London*, vol. 1; McBriar, *Fabian Socialism and English Politics*, 197, 201.

[2] Royal Commission on Labour, C-7063-I, 1893–4, pp. 245–327 for Webb's evidence; B.L.P.E.S., Diary of Beatrice Webb, 24 Dec. 1892 (erroneously given as 24 Dec. 1893 in *Our Partnership*, ed. Drake and Cole, 40).

ment was democratic 'in a sense which represents a more hopeful approach to the social problem than any Liberal Government . . . ever made before'. Gladstone's hand, he said, 'is still on the lever of the instrument of progress'. Some such theme was developed in his talk, 'The New Purpose in Politics' which he gave in November to the Russell Club at Oxford. The *Fabian News* (December) reported a 'large attendance' but provides no text of the talk. By the end of 1892, the *Daily Chronicle*, which had previously not committed itself on Irish Home Rule, came out in its support, O'Connor Power, M.P. and member of the *Daily Chronicle* staff, bringing the paper around, according to Herbert Gladstone.[1] The following year, 1893, Massingham called on E. R. Pease, secretary of the Fabian Society, to supply Sir Charles Dilke, who was striving to enact the Miners' Eight Hours Bill, with names of M.P.s on the Fabian list of those who had pledged their support. Massingham had himself favoured the eight-hour day, in principle at least, since 1890.[2]

In October 1893 Massingham resigned from the Fabian Society. The occasion was the sudden reversal of Fabian policy towards the Liberal Party and towards Independent Labour politics. To be sure the Fabians had participated in the inaugural conference of the national Independent Labour Party (I.L.P.) at Bradford in January 1893 but Fabian leadership (particularly Webb and Shaw) had been hostile towards efforts of 'Socialist Unity' with the S.D.F. and the Hammersmith Socialist Society, and had dropped out of these negotiations. In particular they opposed efforts to merge the Fabian Society in the I.L.P.

Then suddenly, or so it appeared to Massingham, on the matter of labour politics there was an about-face, dramatically enunciated in a manifesto, 'To Your Tents, Oh Israel!' published in the *Fortnightly* for November 1893. The explanation of this new direction in Fabian policy was in part the early good fortune of the I.L.P. but more especi-

---

[1] H. Gladstone to Lord Ripon, 3 Dec. 1892, B.M., Add. MS. 43543/157.

[2] Massingham to Pease, n.d., Fabian Society Papers. While with the *Star* Massingham responded (12 Dec. 1890) to a request for information as to the operation of the eight-hour day: 'The Eight Hours System has been carried out in our office with little friction. . . . The relations between employer and employees on the STAR have always been excellent, and have been in a measure improved by the introduction of the Eight Hours System. . . . I need not add that the system does not apply to the editor.' (Sidney Webb and Harold Cox, *The Eight Hours Day* (London [1891]), 261–2.)

ally the creation by the T.U.C. in 1893 of a political fund for supporting Labour and Socialist candidacies in local and General Elections. Webb, in particular, was now convinced of the importance of capitalising on this identification of trade unionism with Independent Labour politics.[1]

Once we look back, we find differences in attitude in the contributions of Massingham, Shaw and Webb in a symposium, 'What Mr. Gladstone Ought to Do' in the *Fortnightly* for February 1893. Massingham speaks of the election results of 1892 as very stimulating; he stresses the potentialities in the new Liberal Government and he points out that the programme of the new I.L.P. is but an elaboration of the Newcastle Programme of the Liberal Party. On the other hand Shaw speaks of Liberalism as 'a spent projectile' and asserts that 'the substitution of Progressivism for Liberalism was the key to the political history of the last two and the next six years'. Webb, for his part, asserts 'that Gladstone and his Cabinet do not share the aspirations of the great mass of wage earners. . . If the present Liberal leaders are not in earnest about social reforms on collectivist principles, it is high time that the working man took the matter into his own hands'.[2]

Pease tells us that Massingham was on the Continent when 'To Your Tents, Oh Israel!' was drafted and that otherwise he might have accepted it. But Massingham was absent only briefly and he insisted that he had no advance word whatsoever. In that case Massingham must have become completely out of touch for the manifesto was authorised in June and during September and October Shaw was working on it almost daily and discussing it frequently with Webb; the latter wrote to Wallas that he 'wanted a strong tract showing up the Liberal party'.[3]

On 13 October at a private meeting of the London Fabian Society Shaw read the document: it was unanimously adopted and publication authorised – it appeared in the *Fortnightly* for 1 November 1893. From 1886 to 1892, the manifesto declared, the Liberal Party had made 'desperate efforts' to take on

[1] McBriar, *Fabian Socialism and English Politics*, 247–50.
[2] *Fortnightly*, Feb. 1893, pp. 271–2, 280, 286.
[3] Edward R. Pease, *History of the Fabian Society* (London, 1916), 116. Massingham to Webb, 18 Oct. 1892, P.P. Shaw Diary, 20, 23, 30 Sept. and 5 Oct. 1893. Webb to Wallas, 12 Sept. 1893, quoted in Thompson, *Socialists, Liberals and Labour*, 147, n.

some semblance of democratic condition. . . . A new daily paper was started in London and run on the assumption – pure bluff at the moment – that Liberal politics were Collectivist Radical politics. This paper, *The Star*, was a huge success. . . . At the election of the first London County Council Liberalism was openly superseded by Collectivist Radicalism under the new name of Progressivism.

The Liberals worried little about fine distinctions in Progressivism.

Municipal Socialism, Collectivist Radicalism, Trade Unionism, Fabianism, everything was swallowed with more or less wry faces. . . The *Daily Chronicle* followed the *Star* as if to the manner born. . . Finally, the New-castle Program was reached in 1891 bristling with . . . Collectivist measures.

Victory came to the Liberals in 1892, but now sixteen months had elapsed with little result and the opportunity was past. So the manifesto swept through the period 1886–93, in some ways a biography of Henry W. Massingham. The conclusion: working-class allegiance must be transferred from the Liberals to Labour candidates backed by the trade unions. Fabian permeation had done all it could and had done it well – a Collectivist Parliamentary Committee now represented the T.U.C. The trade unions should provide a parliamentary fund of 'at least £30,000' and should place fifty Independent Labour candidates in the field at the next General Election.[1]

Massingham's reaction is found in a series of letters which he wrote to Shaw, Webb, Wallas and Pease. (Since Massingham did not pre-serve correspondence, we do not have the letters in reply.) When he first read the manifesto he wrote to Webb, 18 October: 'I disagree with everything in this unhappy and ridiculous document.' It ignored, he said, a respectable record already made by the Liberal Government. The appeal to the trade unions was

in contradiction to everything you and others have taught inside the Fabian Society and out. . . Fancy the trade unions in the trough of the depression setting aside £30,000 for a labour fund. Talk about fifty labour members. You know very well there are not five who would be worth putting into parliament. . . I must absolutely disassociate myself from [this document].

And he did so, the same day, in a letter of resignation to Pease: 'I will not and cannot remain a member of a society which has publicly gone

[1] *Fabian News*, Nov. 1893; *Fortnightly*, Nov. 1893, pp. 569–89.

back on its wisest teaching & has made a spectacle of itself to the world.'[1]

At Fabian headquarters a day or so later Shaw read this letter, and went home to find a letter from Massingham addressed to himself, probably in reply to a letter he had written urging Massingham to withdraw his resignation. 'I have given you righteous anger,' Massingham wrote; 'now I will give you solid argument.' That is, he adds, if one can take seriously a manifesto 'full of levity, of unreal and insincere argument, of unverified statements, and of purposeful exaggeration', representing Mrs Webb's desire to try Chamberlainism as a 'speculation', Sidney Webb's 'smallness of view' and Shaw's 'flippancy'. Massingham puts his own position thus 'I have been a permeator all my days, a Collectivist Radical. . . And that I remain. It is Fabianism which has changed and I who remain Fabian, declining . . . to turn a somersault as you have done to wreck our influence with the Radicals.' The Fabian Executive urged Massingham to reconsider (Wallas in particular was conciliatory) but Massingham found no occasion;[2] his action, indeed encouraged other resignations from the Society soon after.

Massingham disclaimed responsibility for an article in the *Daily Chronicle* suggesting that the authors of the manifesto secured from it personal gain.[3] But on 30 October undoubtedly in Massingham's words, the *Daily Chronicle* did say: 'What we call the dilettante spirit in Labour Politics will be agreeably stimulated by an amusing contribution to the November number of the *Fortnightly Review*.'

Fabians, the *Daily Chronicle* continued, may be Socialistic, but there is no Socialism in the manifesto. And it concluded: 'We do not feel bound to interest ourselves greatly in an intrigue, pursued in a school boy humour, of which we are quite sure its authors will have reason to be ashamed.'

In direct answer to 'To Your Tents, Oh Israel!' Massingham wrote an article, 'Government and Labour' for the *Contemporary Review* (December 1893). He declared that a trade union parliamentary fund

---

[1] Massingham's letters to Webb and Shaw are in P.P., and the letter to Pease is in Fabian Society Papers.
[2] Fabian Society, Executive Committee Minutes, 20 Oct. 1893; Shaw Diary, 18, 27 Oct. and 1 Dec. 1893.
[3] Massingham to Wallas, 30 Oct. [18]93, Wallas Papers, B.L.P.E.S.

of £30,000 was unlikely and that Independent Labour candidates in any considerable number would weaken the Liberals and ensure Tory rule. He set forth the legislative accomplishments of the Gladstone Government and declared that 'the Government had, by an intervention unique in the history of English politics, settled the Coal Strike'. He concluded that in the session just at an end the Liberals stood for 'Socialism' while the Tories stood for 'individualism'. Massingham's rejection of the manifesto was supported by Michael Davitt in the December issue of the *Nineteenth Century*.

Labour papers generally welcomed the manifesto, though the important *Workman's Times*, Joseph Burgess' mouthpiece for the new I.L.P., spoke of 'the unprincipled character of Fabian tactics' and emphasised the resignation of Massingham, 'one of the men who invented the Newcastle Programme'. Commenting on Massingham's reply to the manifesto, the *Workman's Times* was respectful, up to a point. Reference is made to

the principal leader writer of the *Daily Chronicle*, sometime editor of the *Star*. . . No man has given more signal proof of fidelity to WHAT HE BELIEVES, to be the best interests of Labour. . . No man has striven more earnestly to use the Liberal Party for Labour ends. No man is more utterly blind to the extreme urgency of the political situation.[1]

The *Speaker*, the most important weekly organ of the Radicals, refused to take the manifesto seriously and spoke of it as the work of 'some unknown and obviously ignorant rhetorician. . . The appearance of the present effusion has had only one result – a division in the ranks of the society itself, and the withdrawal of perhaps its most influential member. . .' Massingham was moved to write to Webb: 'You see the article in the "Speaker." Now perhaps you can realize the extent of the mischief the manifesto has done. It is the opening of an unhappy era of mutual distrust and of a final collapse of the labour movement'.[2]

A breach developed at once between the Fabians and the London Radical and Liberal Association, an organisation close to Massingham's heart. It was a not unexpected development to Shaw. At the Council

[1] *Workman's Times*, 11, 16, 23 Nov. 1893.
[2] *Speaker*, 4 Nov. 1893; Massingham to Webb, 3 Nov. 1893, P.P. The *Speaker* for 4 Nov. was undoubtedly in Massingham's hands on 3 Nov.

meeting of the Association on 6 November, Sir Charles Russell, the Attorney General, made light of the manifesto as well as of Shaw and Webb and lauded the Government's record. Shaw was present and tells us: 'I spoke recklessly without tact or temper, and probably did more harm than good.'[1]

But tensions relaxed somewhat. Early in November Massingham was writing to Shaw:

What rot you talk about my going over to Chamberlainism. The thought never entered my head. And your Manifesto is a ridiculous failure. *The Times* are of course patting you on the back and telling you to go ahead. By all means, go, and share the fate of Champion. Of course I'll talk it over with you. Come dine on Sunday.

Somewhat to Massingham's surprise, Shaw did turn up. He wrote to Beatrice Webb:

He [Massingham] had not yet received my card. . . He was so amazed at my appearance that he yelled with laughter. . . [But] as he cannot very well assume that his old invitation remains unaffected by his Chronicle sallies, I suggest that you write him a reassuringly goodhumored note to the effect that you hope that his feelings as expressed in print will not cut him off from our Saturdays.

Mrs Webb extended Massingham an invitation for the coming Saturday and he responded amiably 'I'm afraid I've rampaged around in fine style over the Manifesto but I think I'm cool enough now.'[2]

The *Fabian News* for January 1894, declared that Massingham's article in the *Contemporary Review*, 'while purporting to be a reply, is in the main an able restatement of the Fabian case and is worth careful study'. With some modifications and extensions, in part suggested by the Massingham and Davitt replies, the manifesto was published in January 1894 as Fabian Tract No. 49, *A Plan of Campaign for Labour*.

In Massingham's first letter to Webb about the manifesto, on 18 October 1893 he had exclaimed: 'What, think you, will Burns say to this kind of thing?' We can be sure that Burns and Massingham discussed the manifesto – they saw each other frequently at this time. Burns had joined the Fabians in June 1893 and his article on un-

---

1 *Speaker*, 11 Nov. 1893. Shaw Diary quoted in Laurence, 407.
2 P.P., Massingham to Shaw [5 Nov?] and Massingham to Webb, 10 Nov. Shaw to B. Webb, 6 Nov., in Laurence, 407.

employment was republished as Fabian Tract No. 47. By February 1894 Webb and Shaw were working through Burns to win Massingham back to the cause. A dinner meeting was arranged. Shaw wrote to Burns

We want to show you the sort of calculation on which we ventured the Fabian Manifesto & to get your opinion as to whether anything can be done with the Parliamentary Committee [of the Trades Union Congress]... Make Massingham come, anyhow, alive or dead, if you can't come yourself.[1]

It is doubtful that Massingham turned up. He had lost interest in Fabianism and had moved back to Liberalism. It is no mere coincidence that Massingham's active service in the Fabian Society came during the interval between his association with the *Star* and that with the *Daily Chronicle*. For one thing he had time. Also, his fortunes with the *Star* left him temporarily soured on Liberal politics and it was natural for him to turn to Fabianism in March 1891. But a year later the situation had changed. The Liberals had won at the polls and Massingham himself was established in Salisbury Square with the *Daily Chronicle*. When Shaw was occupied with the manifesto in 1893 Massingham's mind was on the Second Home Rule Bill and as the author of 'House and Lobby' he was building a reputation as a parliamentary reporter. By early 1894 when Fabians were concerned with electoral tactics towards labour Massingham was agitating for prison reform and, politically, could think of little save Gladstone and the question of the Liberal Party leadership.

Incidentally, it may also have been no coincidence that the short period of his preoccupation with 'practical politics' came at the time of close association with political clubs. From June 1889 until January 1893 he served on the 'Political Sub-Committee' of the National Liberal Club – a Committee which solicited support for Liberal electoral candidates. He also joined the Eighty Club in 1892 and served on its Executive Committee in 1894.[2]

[1] Webb to Burns, 21 Feb. 1894, B.P., Add. MS. 46287/269; Shaw to Burns, 22 Feb. 1894, Laurence, 420; Shaw Diary, 24 Feb. 1894.
[2] Minutes of Political Sub-Committee, National Liberal Club Records; '*Eighty*' *Club Reports*, 1891–9 (London, 1892–1900); *Eighty Club: Objects, Rules, Reports, List of Members* (1892–1903).

CHAPTER 4

'The Daily Chronicle' (1891–1899)

'The most influential paper in this country' – with this remark by 'a shrewd politician' Massingham begins his description and analysis of the *Daily Chronicle*, written in 1892. In his language is both pride and aspiration as he tells us that the *Daily Chronicle* is 'an independent paper' but at the same time 'probably nearer the inner mind of the left wing of the Radical Party' than any other Liberal paper, enjoying to a conspicuous degree 'the confidence of trade unionism and of the London working-men'. And he continues: 'Its circulation increases daily [in 1892 it claimed the largest circulation of any daily paper in London]. Its liveliness, variety, serious tone, and intellectual thoroughness afford a welcome relief to the slovenly and unthinking opportunism which is the curse of the modern newspaper. In a word, it has gone far and it ought to go farther.' Against this judgment we might set a more objective comment from *Sell's Press Guide, 1892*. Of the *Daily Chronicle*:

Its leaders are sometimes a little woolly and lacking in snap and grit – there is, in short, not sufficient evidence of the audacity and the dash of real leadership – but the *Daily Chronicle* has a future. Alone among its penny contemporaries it shows evidence of growth.

In Massingham's telling, the *Daily Chronicle*'s importance as a journal of opinion dates from the appointment in 1890 of A. E. Fletcher as editor – a man who joined with the gifts of a great journalist 'a real love of literature, a special knowledge of educational questions, and a sympathetic temper which readily grasped the significance of the labour movement which began with the Dock Strike of 1889'. In 1890 the *Star* 'represented the most complete embodiment of the London democracy'. Now, in 1891, this place is occupied by the *Daily Chronicle* which 'curiously enough, does not stand in complete accord with the main body of the Liberal Party'. And so Massingham concludes:

The *Daily Chronicle* has perhaps a more interesting, and at the same time a more indeterminate, future than that of any other English paper. It has practically ceased to represent any militant form of Unionism and its free and intelligent expression of the later movements of advanced social opinion will probably bring it more or less in touch with the New Radical Party. Or . . . it may remain a paper with a message and a mission, but without a client.[1]

Massingham seems to be anticipating the future.

Fletcher was more catholic in his interests, particularly in his concern for 'causes', even than Massingham. Fletcher's *Daily Chronicle* stimulated London's pride in elected School Boards and County Councils. It publicised the lot of the poor. During the Great Lockout in the coal industry in 1893, the *Chronicle* was perhaps the most active of the journals in relief work – with subscription lists, news stories of hard times, and facilities for passing on gifts of clothing to distressed families. Fletcher joined the I.L.P. and was one of its candidates for Parliament in 1895.[2] His contribution, somewhat overshadowed by Massingham's brilliance, has never been sufficiently recognised. When Fletcher left the *Daily Chronicle* in 1895, the *Review of Reviews* remarked that he had raised the paper from a position of comparative unimportance to the first rank of metropolitan journalism. On Fletcher's death in 1915, Massingham referred to him 'as something of a Quixote in Fleet Street; he loved journalism, but he loved causes more'.[3]

In March 1895, less than four years after he joined the staff of the *Daily Chronicle*, Massingham became, at the age of thirty-four, the editor – when W. T. Stead was editor of the *Review of Reviews* and Edmund Yates was with the *World*, when J. A. Spender was about to become the editor of the *Westminster Gazette* and E. T. Cook editor of the *Daily News*, and when Alfred Harmsworth was ready to launch the *Daily Mail*. Some friends were at hand to welcome and praise an advancing career. The *Sketch* (with Clement Shorter as editor)

[1] Massingham, *The London Daily Press*, 121–2, 132 ,143–4. R. D. Altick, in *The English Common Reader: A Social History of the Mass Reading Public, 1800–1900* (London, 1957), makes no reference either to the *Star* or the *Daily Chronicle*. This would appear to be an oversight. *Sell's Press Guide* is quoted in *Review of Reviews* (Oct. 1891), p. 414.
[2] Sir James Marchant, *Dr. John Clifford, C. H., Life, Letters and Reminiscences* (London, 1924), 109; R. Page Arnot, *The Miners: A History of the Miners' Federation of Great Britain, 1889–1910* (London, 1949), 241.
[3] *Review of Reviews*, XII (Apr. 1895), 313; *Nation*, 20 Nov. 1915, p. 284.

remarked that his new position 'is one which gives splendid opportunities for an individuality so striking and a temperament so hopeful of the future of social progress'. After Massingham had been in the editorial chair less than a year, the *Review of Reviews* declared:

He has risen by virtue of sheer ability from a subordinate position in the ranks of London newspaper men to a place of commanding influence. He is a leader among the municipal reformers of London, has shown himself unequalled as a Parliamentary reporter, is a champion of the labour movement, and is master of an editorial style that is at once trenchant and of pure literary quality.

By this time, E. T. Cook's biographer tells us, the *Daily Chronicle* had outdistanced the *Daily News* as a Liberal paper – this by spending money on its development, enlarging its size and scope, as well as by its literary excellence.[1]

Massingham remarks that under Fletcher, the *Daily Chronicle* reached a new standard of literary excellence through a specialisation in its editorial staff more complete than in any other paper, except *The Times*. In the Fletcher period, the political leader-writers were Robert Wilson, whom Massingham singles out as distinctly 'brilliant', O'Connor Power, M.P., William Clarke (a specialist on economic problems and on American affairs, generally), and then, in 1891, Massingham himself. Shaw takes credit for recommending Clarke in 1890 to write on labour politics in London, and soon these leaders had commanding influence. As early as 1891 Charles Williams was the paper's war correspondent, making the *Daily Chronicle* 'the soldiers' paper' – so established was Williams' reputation as a military expert. Naylor wrote on labour questions, W. D. Morrison on prisons and penal reform.[2]

Under Massingham's editorship this specialization became expertise. His assistant editor and literary editor was Henry Norman, whom Massingham had known as early as 1887 and who had been with the *Chronicle* since 1893. The news editor was Robert Donald, whose venture with *London* had proved a disappointment. Harold Spender took over 'House and Lobby', the form of which he testifies came from

[1] *Review of Reviews*, XIII (Feb. 1896), 131–3; *Sketch*, 27 Mar. 1895; *History of The Times*, III, 830.
[2] Massingham, *The London Daily Press*, 134–5; Shaw Diary, 2 Sept. 1890; C. H. Norman in *Cosmopolis*, XI (Jan. 1898), 91.

the genius of Massingham, and Vaughan Nash became the *Daily Chronicle*'s labour expert. In 1897, in connection with the Jubilee, the *Chronicle* ran a series, 'Sixty Years of Empire', from 7 June to 26 June, with Nash's famous article, 'Factory and Mine Legislation' (24 June), Sir Charles Dilke's 'The Growth of Greater Britain' (8 June) and an article by Walkley on the Victorian stage. Perhaps it was the vogue of this series which led Shaw to insist that Massingham be invited to the 'Women's Jubilee Dinner and Soirée' in the Grafton Galleries on 14 July, given by a hundred distinguished women to a hundred distinguished men.[1] Joseph Pennell remarked that the *Daily Chronicle* became 'violently literary and artistic'. He and his wife wrote art criticism and he enlisted some of the great illustrators of the day – Whistler, Burne-Jones, William Morris, Aubrey Beardsley – in developing, in the *Chronicle*, the large drawing as a feature of daily journalism. William Rothenstein's drawings were published serially.[2]

With Henry W. Nevinson we must pause longer, for he was to succeed Norman as literary editor in May 1899 and later to be one of the mainstays of the *Nation* staff. Many have marvelled at his versatility. Felix Frankfurter who came to know him during the *Nation* days remarked that he had no counterpart in American journalism and that soaked in classical and modern literature, master of many languages, he would have made a better head of a Romance Language Department, a Classics Department or a German Department than is often found in many American universities.[3] Nevinson's association with the *Daily Chronicle* and later the *Nation* takes two forms: as a war correspondent, and as an essayist. William Rothenstein, on assignment, encountered Nevinson in Cologne after the First World War. He refers to Nevinson as 'a noted pacifist, who looked like a Confederate General, had missed no war during the last thirty years, and really loved military life'.[4]

Nevinson had fallen in love with Greece after a brief trip in 1894 and when the war for Cretan independence broke out in 1896, he importuned his friend, Vaughan Nash, for aid in gaining a post as

[1] Shaw to Ellen Terry, 14 July 1897, Laurence, 781–3.
[2] Pennell, *Adventures of an Illustrator*, 247, 250; Robert Speaight, *William Rothenstein* (London, 1962), 61.
[3] Harlan B. Phillips (ed.), *Felix Frankfurter Reminisces* (New York, 1960), 93.
[4] William Rothenstein, *Men and Memories, 1900–1922*, II (New York, 1932), 358.

correspondent with the *Daily Chronicle*. On 14 March 1897 he was Nash's guest at the National Liberal Club. There, Nevinson tells us in his dramatic way,

he introduced me to H. W. Massingham, editor of the 'Daily Chronicle' which in the previous year or two he had raised to a height of perturbing power, and it was he and his paper that inspired the more Quixotic or enthusiastic of the pro-Greek partisans. Within half a minute he asked me to write him letters from the front, if war should be declared. I instantly accepted, and in less than sixty seconds the whole course of my life was changed. On St. Patrick's Day, 1897, I sailed again for Greece.

In Greece Nevinson became the paper's regular correspondent for the 'Thirty Days' War'. He passed Greek sentries, if we may believe his own account, by shouting the Greek for '*Daily Chronicle*', so well known was the paper as a supporter of the Greek cause. On 26 May, Massingham wrote Nevinson's wife 'I have wired to Mr. Nevinson to return; I have nothing but praise for his work which under circumstances of great difficulty has been unequalled for dispatch, finish and critical faculty.'[1] This was the beginning of a life-long association between Massingham and Nevinson, chronicled in detail in Nevinson's diary, which runs with almost daily entries, from 2 June 1893 until 20 October 1941.

Upon his return from Greece Nevinson became a regular member of the *Chronicle* staff. In 1898 he thought he was down for the Sudan and Khartoum when Williams suddenly decided to go. Likewise he was frustrated in his desire to report from America the war between the United States and Spain. He was overpowered by jealousy when J. A. Hobson went out to the Transvaal for the *Manchester Guardian* in July 1899, though very soon, in September, he too was on his way to South Africa. His nature was so highly strung, his vanity so consuming, his sensitiveness to criticism so acute, and his attachment to causes so fanatic that one often hesitates to accept his account of just what happened. His impatience became irrational when despairing over the 'poor D. C., the champion of lost causes' (17 January 1898), ridiculing A. E. Fletcher 'now a doddering old piece of insignificance' (21 June 1899), and patronising Shaw who 'is regarded as dead and finished now,

---

1 Nevinson, *Changes and Chances*, 145; Henry W. Nevinson, *Fire of Life* (London, 1935), 74; Massingham to Mrs Nevinson, 26 May 1897, Nevinson Papers.

through his marriage and money' (26 January 1899). His life was 'full of doubts and fears' while he waited for Norman and Williams to resign, months after he had been told he was to succeed them both.

Finally in May 1899 he replaced Norman and now he viewed *his* staff (his literary staff) with pride – with Lionel Johnson and William Archer as literary and dramatic critics, with the Pennells for art books, Hubert Bland for novels, Edward Clodd for folklore, Arthur Waugh for poetry, and occasionally Massingham himself for almost anything.[1] Shaw was also occasionally available. With him there was at once a spirited exchange over terms for a long review of musical subjects. Nevinson wrote: 'The editor instructs me to inform you that he will see you damned rather than give you more than £5-5-0.' Shaw responded that only personal regard for the editor restrained him from reporting this instance of 'literary sweating' to the Authors' Society. 'I will see the paper and its proprietors boiled in hell before I will work on such terms.' But apparently he did, for Nevinson recorded in his diary, 26 May, 'Shaw capitulated'.[2]

Towards Massingham, also, Nevinson's impatience sometimes turned to anger. He writhed when his unsigned material was cut for reasons of space or because of a conflict of opinion. Pressure of time annoyed him. But Nevinson is usually enthusiastic, even ecstatic, about Massingham and his diary is a labour of love when he records his admiration. Highly sensitive himself he was quick to perceive this quality in Massingham. He obviously was beside himself with excitement on one occasion when he hurried to the office to make a verbal change in an article only to find that Massingham had already himself inserted just the sentence he had in mind (14 December 1898). In retrospect, in a book published in 1923, Nevinson referred to 'the happy years while the "Chronicle" was still a paper of light and we were all serving the editor with the enthusiasm that raises journalism to the level of a Church or Sacred Order'.[3]

---

[1] Nevinson, *Changes and Chances*, 192–3.
[2] G.B.S.P., Add. MS. 50503, Nevinson to Shaw, 18 May 1899; Shaw to Nevinson, 19 May 1899, Sotheby Cat., 1964, Lot 585, 1 Dec. (The story is also told in *Changes and Chances*, 191–2.) In 1896, Shaw's terms for newspaper work were £3 per thousand words, with a minimum of £5, which, he says, the *Chronicle* pays him 'with melancholy resignation' and intimates with every cheque an end to their connection and 'complains bitterly when I cheerfully act on that understanding' – Laurence, 596–7.
[3] *Changes and Chances*, 197–8.

On 21 December 1891, the *Daily Chronicle* announced an increase, for most issues, from eight pages to ten, in recognition of the success of the literary section which had brought an 'unprecedented' increase in circulation. The literary supplement which previously had appeared only with the Wednesday issue, became a daily feature of one or two pages. The *Review of Reviews* remarked on this 'bold breaking with the old tradition of the eight-page paper', an important step in journalism, soon followed by other papers.[1] On 16 May 1896, the *Chronicle* announced that the Saturday issue was to be enlarged to twelve pages, the extra pages 'dealing specially with matters interesting the social and literary world'. The issues for 2, 3, and 4 November 1896 were increased from ten to twelve pages to carry Fridtjof Nansen's account, with drawings, of his recent polar expedition.

In retrospect, the literary pages of the *Daily Chronicle* seem more enduring than the political, however important the latter were at the time. Along with the *Daily News*, after its return to life in 1895, the *Daily Chronicle* established a reputation for influencing the taste and ideas of the middle and lower classes. Sir Henry Newbolt, whose verse was reviewed by Archer in 1897, spoke of the paper as 'the most literary of the dailies and constantly in my hands'. H. N. Brailsford, in his obituary sketch of Massingham, remarked: 'For me and most of my fellow students, the *Chronicle* was the only paper we cared to read.' Page three was that 'wonderful literary page' which Massingham made 'a criticism not merely of letters but of life, a vehicle for every group of thinkers and artists which was struggling to escape from the prison house of Victorian conventions'.[2]

The contacts of the *Daily Chronicle* were wide and varied. And for Henry Massingham himself, there were interests outside Fleet Street. In September 1891 he proposed for himself a two-week excursion of the Art Workers' Guild, to Italy – the Art Workers' Guild sought to stimulate home arts and crafts; for some reason he did not go.[3] He became a member of J. M. Barrie's 'Allahakbarries' Cricket team, along with A. Conan Doyle, Bernard Partridge and John Davidson. And

[1] *Review of Reviews*, VII (Feb. 1893), 129.
[2] Henry Newbolt, *My World as in My Time: Memoirs* (London, 1932), I, 196; H. N. Brailsford in *New Leader*, 5 Sept. 1924.
[3] Shaw to Emery Walker, 11 Aug. 1891, Laurence, 305.

Sir Charles Dilke's article, 'Athletics for Politicians' in the *North American Review* for August 1899 fascinated him.[1] Another interest took Massingham with Shaw to Bayreuth in July 1896 for the Wagner Festival. From Victoria Station to Nuremberg, in Shaw's telling, Massingham whistled 'I dreamt that I dwelt in marble halls'.[2]

In 1898 Massingham became very much exercised over one 'de Rougemont', a Swiss, who claimed to have spent several years as a modern Robinson Crusoe on an island in the Pacific after being marooned in the course of a pearl-fishing expedition. The Geographical Section of the British Association accepted his story as genuine – it appeared at length in the *Wide World Magazine*. But references to 'turtle-riding', and the like, aroused suspicion. To test its authenticity Massingham produced Louis Becke who had been born in New South Wales and had lived on various Pacific islands. De Rougemont's statements were examined in two interviews, with Edward Clodd present as 'the honest broker'. The story and the controversy together with considerable correspondence appeared in the *Daily Chronicle*, under the heading 'Rougemont Day by Day', with the conclusion on 10 October, that the story was a fraud.[3]

If Massingham ever indulged himself, it was in his passion for drama and the theatre. For him the stage as well as the press replaced the church and the lecture platform as a forum for ideas and ideals. We have frequent references to Massingham the critic. In March 1891 he replaced William Archer as the *Manchester Guardian* reviewer of the first performance of Ibsen's *Ghosts* at the Royalty Theatre. Archer had translated the play. After the production Massingham, along with Archer, Shaw and Florence Farr (the actress), spent the remainder of the evening at the home of Henry Norman.[4] When *Arms and the Man* opened in April 1894, Shaw requested seats for 'three powerful journalistic allies of mine' – Massingham, Henry Norman and Ernest Parke. In January 1895 Massingham invited R. B. Haldane, along with

[1] Denis Mackail, *The Story of J. M. B.* (London, 1941), 261; Massingham to Dilke, 26 July 1900, D.P., Add. MS. 43916/238–9.
[2] Bernard Shaw, *How to Become a Musical Critic*, ed. Dan H. Laurence (London, 1961), 233, 237.
[3] *D.C.*, Sept. and Oct. 1898; Edward Clodd, *Memories* (London, 1916), 123. Dan H. Laurence (ed.), *Bernard Shaw: Collected Letters*, vol. 2, *1898–1910* (London, 1972), 68.
[4] Shaw to Archer, 14 Mar. 1891, Laurence, 285; Shaw Diary, 13 Mar. 1891.

'one or two critics', to his home in Nightingale Lane, to hear Shaw read 'his new play'. This was *Candida* which Shaw read on the evening of 19 January in the presence of Massingham, the Joseph Pennells, A. B. Walkley, and one or two others – Haldane apparently was not there.[1]

The arts, literature and politics often come together in the pages of the *Daily Chronicle*, as in the career of William Morris. We find there his controversy with H. M. Hyndman over the S.D.F. During the Miners' Lockout in 1893 Morris' ideas concerning the future of the arts were discussed in the *Daily Chronicle*, Morris himself writing a letter (published 10 November 1893) in which he declared that the arts could not be kept alive by small groups set apart from the mass of the people incapable of understanding and enjoying their work.

All worthy schools of art must be . . . the outcome of the aspirations of the people towards the beauty and true pleasure of life. . . These aspirations . . . can only be born from a condition of practical equality of economical conditions amongst the whole population.

In 1894 Morris protested, in the *Chronicle*, against a new mortuary chapel, proposed as an addition to Westminster Abbey, and in 1895 he pleaded for the preservation of native trees, the hornbeams, in Epping Forest. He also attacked imitation and falsification in the restoration of Rouen Cathedral; he lamented mistakes in renovation at Peterborough; he applauded the work of the Trinity Almshouses in the Mile End Road.[2]

When Morris died in 1896, Arnold Bennett noticed that most daily papers made but brief reference to his career. Extensive coverage was found only in the *Daily Chronicle* which spoke of 'a delightful poet, a matchless artist, a noble and potent personality, the most picturesque and forceful figure that socialism has produced. . . Morris was in truth of the race of Giants' and included a tribute by Shaw. Massingham wrote to Morris' daughter, Mrs Sparling, that though he had talked

---

1 Laurence, 424. H.P., Massingham to Haldane, 14 Jan. [?], 1895; Pennell, *Adventures of an Illustrator*, 160. Information from Shaw's diary, courtesy of Professor Dan H. Laurence in letter to author, 31 July 1973.

2 Paul Thompson, *The Work of William Morris* (New York, 1967), 202, 206, citing *Daily Chronicle*, 9 Oct. 1893. Other communications to *D.C.* are reprinted in Philip Henderson (ed.), *The Letters of William Morris . . .* (London, 1950), 363, 365, 377–9.

with her father only a few times, he 'loved and admired him more than any other person in England. . . He will never, I am sure, be forgotten by London, or England or the world'.[1]

Henry Norman encountered George Moore shortly after his book of essays, *Modern Painting*, appeared in 1893. 'I have', said Norman, 'a review of your book in type by the greatest writer in the world.' Walter Pater's review appeared in the *Daily Chronicle*, and an interview with the author as well.[2] While on the *Star* Massingham had become acquainted with T. Fisher Unwin, the London publisher who published *The Gweedore Hunt* in 1889. Now, in 1893, Massingham inquired of Unwin: 'Who is the author of the Mark Rutherford series? I have been reading *The Revolution in Tanner's Lane* and have been much struck with it.' Massingham soon read in the *Autobiography* of Rutherford's engagement years before to write the 'London Letter' for the *Norfolk News*, and identified him as William Hale White.[3]

Massingham was a frequent attendant at the annual country dinners of the Omar Khayyam Club, an informal society of literary journalists organised in 1892. In July 1895 some thirty or forty people, including Massingham, Henry Norman, Edmund Gosse, E. T. Cook, George Gissing, Clement Shorter and Robertson Nicoll gathered at the Burford Bridge Hotel in Surrey to do honour to George Meredith who lived nearby. Massingham had come to know Meredith through Clement Shorter as early as 1891, and visited Meredith at Boxhill occasionally thereafter.[4]

Normally the Omar Khayyam Club met at Aldeburgh in Suffolk. Massingham's name was carved on the Arthurian table in the meeting hall. A regular feature of the gathering was a poem written and read by one of the company. Edward Clodd, a Massingham admirer, tells us that at the meeting of Whitsuntide 1897, the poem was read by

[1] *Journal of Arnold Bennett*, I, 19; *D.C.*, 5 Oct. 1896; Massingham to Mrs Sparling, 5 Oct. 1896, Morris Papers, B.M., Add. MS. 45346.
[2] Joseph Hone, *Life of George Moore* (New York, 1936), 183–4.
[3] Massingham to Unwin, 23 Jan. 1893, Berg. Shapcott (ed.), *Autobiography of Mark Rutherford*, Memorial Edition Intro. by H.W.M., 1–2.
[4] Siegfried L. Sassoon, *Meredith* (London, 1948), 227–8; W. Robertson Nicoll, *A Bookman's Letters* (New York, 1913), 'Memories of Meredith', p. 5. C. L. Cline (ed.), *Letters of George Meredith* (3 vols., Oxford, 1970), II, 1,021–2, 1,023, 1,114, 1,126; George Meredith, *Various Readings and Bibliography* (New York, 1911) lists references in the *D.C.*

Massingham, with a reference to 'best son of Earth, warm-hearted Clodd'. H. G. Wells attended the 1896 meeting of the Club and it may be that on this occasion he and Massingham met initially. In the columns of the *Daily Chronicle* Wells received some of his first recognition.[1]

R. B. Cunninghame Graham, in custody of the Caid in the Atlas Mountains, addressed a letter, dated 22 October 1897, to the *Daily Chronicle*, telling of his plight in the hope that when printed it would come to the attention of the Foreign Office. He had sought first, in the disguise of a Turkish doctor and then posing as a Moorish shereef, 'Mahmmed el Fasi', to journey some 150 miles beyond the Atlas Mountains to the southern province of Sus and the 'forbidden city' of Tarudant. He had been forced to abandon the adventure as almost certain to cost his life. His letter was published in the *Daily Chronicle* on 15 November, a few days before the announcement in the press of his release by the Sultan's orders.[2]

Some of William Archer's best pieces appeared in the *Daily Chronicle* (these are collected in *Study and Stage*, 1899), and his controversy with Shaw over the years is there well documented. A celebrated subject of contention was Ibsen whom Archer regarded as poet and dramatist and Shaw as philosopher and social thinker. In December 1894, Archer read his translation of *Little Eyolf* a week before publication to a group of friends including Massingham and Shaw. Massingham reviewed the Archer translation in the *Daily Chronicle*, on 12 December and it was first produced two years later, Shaw encountering Massingham at the opening performance.[3] For Ibsen's seventieth birthday on 20 March 1898, Archer and Gosse organised a 'Recognition' in England. On behalf of the *Chronicle* Massingham signed the appeal for funds to provide a gift. To the whole affair there was a variety of reactions, all reflected in the pages of the *Chronicle*, including a somewhat injured Massingham because of the omission, by error, of his name from the letter accompanying the presentation to Ibsen. Along with Archer,

---

1 Massingham's poem is in *H.W.M.*, 354; presentation copy to Clodd, Whitsuntide 1897, signed by Massingham and others, is in Berg. Ingvald Raknem, *H. G. Wells and his Critics* (Oslo, 1962), 446–7.

2 A. F. Tschiffely, *Don Roberto, Being the Account of the Life and Works of R. B. Cunninghame Graham, 1852–1936* (London, 1937), ch. XIV.

3 Archibald Henderson, *George Bernard Shaw: Man of the Century* (London, 1956), 410. Shaw to Archer, 6 Dec. 1894, in Laurence, 467–9; Shaw Diary, 3 Nov. [*sic*], 1894; Shaw to Charlotte Payne-Townshend, 23 Nov. 1896, in Laurence, 704.

Elizabeth Robins and others, Massingham was a member of the initial committee behind the London Stage Society, started in 1899 though not incorporated until 1904, which grew out of Elizabeth Robins' efforts to produce Ibsen experimentally.[1]

Massingham was an admirer of the poetry of Francis Thompson, whose contributions to the *Daily Chronicle* included his 'Ode for the Diamond Jubilee of Queen Victoria', written at three weeks' notice in June 1897, and his 'Ode on the Nineteenth Century'. In January 1899 the *Daily Chronicle* carried a lively controversy between Archer and George Moore over Archer's review of Edward Martyn's play, *The Heather Field*; there was a comment by W. B. Yeats, and a caricature by Max Beerbohm.[2]

These accounts of the role of the *Daily Chronicle* in the literary history of the period could be multiplied; for the lives and fortunes of less successful writers, the *Chronicle* was an important as for the great.

Massingham's interest in writers is not always literary. Oscar Wilde's writing, for example, was little noticed in the *Daily Chronicle*. Nor was there any particular interest or concern in his trials. But the Wilde Case brought to public attention the issue of prison reform, and the medium was the press, in large part the *Chronicle*. The Home Secretary between 1892 and 1895 was Herbert Asquith, then on friendly terms with Massingham, and the Departmental Committee on Prisons, established in 1894, was the responsibility of the Under Secretary, Herbert Gladstone. Both he and R. B. Haldane, another member of the Committee, were within easy reach of Massingham.

From Massingham's correspondence we learn that in the autumn of 1893 he visited prisons in and out of London.[3] On the staff of the *Daily Chronicle* was the Rev. W. D. Morrison, who had been a chaplain at Wandsworth Prison since 1887. Presumably Morrison consulted with Massingham, for in January 1894 the *Daily Chronicle* ran a series of

1 Sir Edmund Gosse, *Correspondence with Scandinavian Writers* (Gyldendal, 1960), 48, 182; Archer's account in *D.C.*, 26 Mar. 1898. For London Stage Society, see Janet Dunbar, *Mrs. G. B. S.* (New York, 1963), 120–1.
2 Everard Meynell, *The Life of Francis Thompson* (New York, 1913), 332; Allan Wade (ed.), *Letters of W. B. Yeats* (New York, 1955), 308–11; Rupert Hart-Davis (ed.), *The Letters of Oscar Wilde* (London, 1962), 778.
3 H.G.P., Add. MS. 46042/54–5, Massingham to H. Gladstone, 16 Oct. 1893; P.P., Massingham to B. Webb, 10 Nov. 1893.

three articles by Morrison on 'Our Dark Places: The Prison System'. A leader, almost certainly by Massingham, introduced the series, observing that there was a minimum of parliamentary or ministerial supervision over funds available to the prison commissioners. A concluding leader declared that 'the articles have not been conceived in a spirit of exaggeration or even of loose humanitarianism, nor designed to reflect on public officials . . . [but] we are convinced that a case has been made out for inquiry'. 'Letters to the Editor' were generally sympathetic. Morrison also published in the *Fortnightly* (April 1894) an article 'Are Our Prisons a Failure?', emphasising the growth of 'recidivism' and advocating an inquiry as 'to what extent it is produced by our present principles of prison discipline'.[1]

The Home Secretary read the articles in the *Daily Chronicle* and to their influence is generally attributed the appointment, soon after, of the Departmental Committee on Prisons. But, as often happened in Massingham's advocacy of causes, he annoyed as well as stimulated. To James Granville Legge, Herbert Gladstone's Private Secretary, was assigned responsibility for following the discussion on prison reform in the *Daily Chronicle*. In passing along the first two articles, Legge commented (27 January): 'It is a pity that if he [Massingham] thought it necessary to deliver himself of these portentous articles he did not really study prisons abroad, *e.g.*, America, where 'experiments' have so far ended only in failure. . .' Two days later, he sent along the last of the articles:

On Saturday night I spent three hours talking with him [Massingham] on the subject. I pointed out what damage he was doing to his case by making it so much of a personal attack and by reckless and gross exaggeration. He admitted nearly all my points after some argument but he pleaded that to get what he and his friends do want they must ask for a good deal more. . . I told him it was absurd to suppose [there was] a case for anything like a Royal Commission, and that he had better rest content with the knowledge of the fact that the Chief is the kind to do the right thing at the right time of his own initiative. Still I was not expecting that he would climb down as much as he has in the appendix he has added to his article today.[2]

---

[1] Morrison's articles in *D.C.*, 23 25, 29 Jan. are by 'Our Special Correspondent'. Comment is in *D.C.*, 25, 29, 31 Jan., and 1, 2, 3, 5 Feb.

[2] Sir Charles Mallet, *Herbert Gladstone: A Memoir* (London, 1932), 146; George Ives, *A History of Penal Methods* (New York, n.d.), 217. Legge to Gladstone, 27, 29 Jan. in H.G.P., Add. MS. 45990/197–9. For the Committee hearing, see parliamentary

In 1895 the new chairman of the Prison Commission, Evelyn Ruggles-Brise, was instructed to carry into effect as many of the Committee's recommendations as possible. These recommendations were the basis for the Prison Act of 1898.[1] But it was long before then, in 1895, that Wilde's trials and imprisonment took place. The *Daily Chronicle* had previously stood aside from the Wilde Case. Before Massingham's time the *Daily Chronicle* had reviewed unfavourably *The Picture of Dorian Gray* and in Wilde's two trials in 1895 for homosexuality took no side, though it was credited along with *Reynold's Newspaper* with the most impartial reporting of the proceedings. Bail for Wilde in 1895 was in part provided by Stewart Headlam; this action, he tells us, cost him some of his friends, including Massingham (temporarily) and Henry Norman.[2]

But the sponsorship of prison reform by the *Daily Chronicle* in 1894 had attracted Wilde's attention and in its columns Wilde's own story got to the public. On 25 May 1895 he was found guilty of homosexual acts, was sentenced to two years' hard labour, and taken first to Pentonville Prison, in North London. Soon Asquith read in the *Daily Chronicle* (5 June) of Wilde's reported insanity and ordered an investigation; Wilde was pronounced 'perfectly sane'. In July Wilde was transferred to Wandsworth. Through Haldane, who visited Wilde in both Pentonville and Wandsworth, and through Morrison, the chaplain at Wandsworth, Massingham was following the case. On 25 September he wrote to Stead:

don't forget the horror of the [prison] system, which continually presses on my imagination since I went the round of the prisons. The whole thing is torture & nothing but torture. Oscar Wilde is being slowly starved to death, & is now little better than an hysterical imbecile. I hope you will watch this case which is typical, & distasteful as it is to bring him up again, I think we have a duty [about?] him which we must discharge.[3]

papers, *Report of the Departmental Committee on Prisons* (April 1895), in C. 7702, vol. 56. Morrison gave evidence on 31 July and 3 August 1894. The *D.C.* on 24 April 1894 comments on the *Report*.

[1] Sir Evelyn Ruggles-Brise, *The English Prison System* (London, 1921), 75–8.

[2] The *D.C.* review of *Dorian Gray* is abstracted in Stuart Mason, *Bibliography of Oscar Wilde* (London [1914]), 48. Bettany, *Stewart Headlam*, 131–2. According to a statement made in 1968 by C. H. Norman, a member of the *New Age* staff, Massingham sought signatures for a petition to expel Headlam from the National Liberal Club but failed (Norman to the author, 20 July 1968).

[3] Letter to Stead, courtesy J. O. Baylen. For much of the Wilde story I have followed

The *Daily Chronicle* reported, on 28 September, that Wilde was suffering from 'want of nourishment' – this led to a medical inquiry which recommended transfer to a prison outside London where open-air activities might improve his health. In November 1895 Wilde was transferred to Reading Prison where he served out his term. Tom Martin, a kindly warden, smuggled into him copies of the *Daily Chronicle*. On his release in May 1897 Wilde went directly to France where shortly thereafter he read in the *Daily Chronicle* of Warder Martin's dismissal from Reading. This prompted the first of Wilde's extensive letters to the *Daily Chronicle*. It was published on 28 May 1897, under the heading: 'THE CASE OF WARDER MARTIN: SOME CRUELTIES OF PRISON LIFE'. Wilde begins: 'I learn with great regret, through the columns of your paper, that the Warder Martin of Reading Prison has been dismissed by the Prison Commissioners for having given some sweet biscuits to a little hungry child.'[1] The *Daily Chronicle* for 28 May commented sympathetically on the Wilde statement and printed another letter from Martin discussing the statement of the Home Secretary (now Sir Matthew Ridley, in the Salisbury Government): 'I am fully satisfied that the dismissal was fully justified.'[2]

Upon learning by telegram that his letter had actually appeared in the *Daily Chronicle* Wilde wrote at once to his friend, Robert Ross: 'I now think I shall write my prison article for the *Chronicle*. It is interested in prison reform and the thing would not look an advertisement. Let me know your opinion. I intend to write to Massingham.' A day or so later he again wrote to Ross: 'Don't you see how right I was to write to the *Chronicle*?' and added that he had written Massingham to inquire whether he would be interested in publishing his prison experience in three articles, as part of a syndicate. When no encouragement came from Massingham he was disappointed. He wrote Ross, on 3 June: 'I think the *Chronicle* are nervous. They have not answered yet,

---

the detailed and well-documented account in H. Montgomery Hyde, *Oscar Wilde: The Aftermath* (New York, 1963). For Haldane, see Horace G. Hutchinson (ed.), *Private Diaries of the Right Hon. Sir Algernon West, G.C.B.* (London, 1922), 312 and R. B. Haldane, *An Autobiography* (New York, 1929), 166–7.

[1] Hyde, *Oscar Wilde* 26–35, 39, 151. The letter in this *D.C.* for 28 May 1897 was republished in Feb. 1898 as 'Children in Prison and Other Cruelties of Prison Life'; reprinted in Hart-Davis, *Letters of Oscar Wilde*.

[2] Mason, *Bibliography of Oscar Wilde*, 51.

or anything.' A few days later he remarked in another letter to Ross that the *Daily Chronicle* might like to publish his journal, 'Berneval Day by Day'. But nothing further appeared in the *Chronicle* at that time. Massingham's interest was only that of prison reform. In the issue for 15 February 1898 Nevinson reviewed *The Ballad of Reading Gaol*, a long notice on the leader page; the tone was favourable but the emphasis was on the horrors of prison life. Wilde commented: 'The *Chronicle* meant well, but there is more in the poem than a pamphlet on prison-reform.'[1]

In March 1898 the Commons debate on the Prison Bill inspired Wilde's second letter to the *Daily Chronicle*. Dated 23 March, it was published 24 March, under the heading, 'DON'T READ THIS IF YOU WANT TO BE HAPPY TODAY', provided by the editor, and is signed 'The Author of the *Ballad of Reading Gaol*'. It begins:

Sir: I understand that the Home Secretary's Prison Reform Bill is to be read this week for the first or second time, and as your journal has been the one paper in England that has taken a real and vital interest in this important question, I hope you will allow me to point out what reforms in our present stupid and barbarous system are urgently necessary.

His indictment of the existing system followed. The Prison Reform Bill became law in August and some of the changes paralleled proposals made by Wilde.[2]

[1] Hart-Davis, *Letters of Oscar Wilde*, 578, 581–2, 593, 604, 704, 770, 781n.
[2] Stuart Mason, a very reputable bibliographer, includes in his *Bibliography of Oscar Wilde* (p. 445) a reference to a review of *De Profundis* (1905), entitled 'Out of the Depths', in the *Eastern Daily News*, 24 Feb. 1906, and signed 'H.W.M.'. No such review was found in any of the Norwich papers or elsewhere.

CHAPTER 5

Liberalism and the 'Daily Chronicle' (1894–1899)

From Gladstone to Rosebery, Fletcher to Massingham

The Earl of Rosebery succeeded Gladstone as Prime Minister and Party leader in March 1894. In the vicissitudes of the Party – Rosebery's elevation in 1894, the collapse of his Government in 1895 and his resignation from Party leadership in October 1896 – the *Daily Chronicle* and Henry W. Massingham are essential to the story. And there is also the internal history of the paper – divergent views, personal differences, the reputations of the staff, that is of Fletcher, the editor, of Massingham who succeeded him in March 1895, of Henry Norman, a member of the staff since 1893 who became assistant editor in 1895, and of William Clarke, leader-writer.

Political leaders in the *Daily Chronicle* were unsigned – authorship cannot usually be assigned with any certainty. But Massingham's own position until the autumn of 1895, we know to be mirrored in his column, 'House and Lobby'. His confidence in Gladstone, by the end of 1893, had somewhat tempered. Thus, Gladstone's speech in the Commons, on 19 December, in effect hostile to the proposed increase in naval Estimates supported by most of his Cabinet, is termed 'a little too clever, too ingenious'. But Massingham's admiration and loyalty for Gladstone still dominated. He knew that Gladstone read the *Daily Chronicle* regularly and before long a letter was despatched, on 2 March 1894, to Herbert Gladstone – the resignation of his father was then certain. Massingham wrote:

I want to say how much I personally regret that any words I may have used some time ago in criticising Mr. Gladstone's speech should have seemed in the light of later events (of which I then knew nothing whatever) to read unkindly. Believe me, that was far from my intention. Words slip too easily from the journalist's pen. I shall always regret them...

And it may have been Massingham who despatched a telegram to

Gladstone late in January 1894, signed 'The Editor, *Daily Chronicle,* London'. 'Pall Mall Gazette announces on authority your immediately impending resignation. We propose ridiculing it as dishonouring rumour and beg word of confirmation.' Gladstone's answer was ambiguous.[1]

But it was soon generally accepted that his resignation was indeed close at hand. A careful reading of the *Daily Chronicle* discloses a startling variation in tone between 'House and Lobby' and other, unsigned, articles. Massingham praises Gladstone's 'great speech' on local government, 19 February, and is preoccupied on the occasion of Gladstone's final speech (1 March) with recording 'the tumultuous and conflicting waves of emotion [which] flowed over the House of Commons'. But a leader, 21 February, treats Gladstone's speech, the day before, abandoning the Employer's Liability Bill after amendment by the Lords, as part of 'a ghastly failure'. As to the challenge from the Lords:

The Liberal Party has, we think, a right to know where it stands in this matter... Are we to have a country ringing with denunciation of the Lords, and to have a few words of whispering humbleness from the Prime Minister? If Mr. Gladstone feels that age and infirmities press too heavily upon him for the leadership of an uncompromising crusade, it is for him to say so... Let us hear his mind.[2]

Another leader, on 28 February, said bluntly that Gladstone's eyesight 'is no longer equal to the task'. Certainly not the work of Massingham, these leaders may have well have been written by Clarke.

On the issue of Rosebery's leadership contradictory views are not for some time apparent in the *Chronicle*'s columns. Massingham wrote (27 February): 'I find everywhere great hope of him as a man of character, of personal force, even of a certain magnetism.' An unsigned leader (28 February) declared that Rosebery would be adequate to the demands of the party 'and we do not know that we can make the same prediction with confidence of any possible rival'. For some time Radical Liberals had marked out Rosebery for the future. This derived mainly from his role in the London County Council, where, elected as an Independent in 1889, he at once associated himself with the

[1] *D.C.*, 'House and Lobby', 20, 22, 23 Dec. 1893; *Private Diaries of Algernon West,* 276, 263-4, 284; H.G.P., Add. MS. 46042/56-7.
[2] As summarised in *Annual Register, 1894* (London, 1895) [58].

Progressives and served as the first chairman of the Council. 'In many respects', his latest biographer affirms, 'this was the most important single factor in his advance to the Premiership.'[1] Massingham himself, in an article in the *Contemporary Review* (April 1894), declared that Rosebery's main source of strength 'lies in the social movement which made it inevitable that when Mr. Gladstone went he would be succeeded by a municipal statesman'. It became habit, not without basis, for the *Daily Chronicle* to take credit for Rosebery's elevation, in that it was the first paper to press his claims. Also, attention was called to Rosebery's reference 'to some influential letter in some influential paper' (the *Chronicle*), in his remarks at St James's Hall, 21 March 1894 in response to a congratulatory address tendered him by the London County Council.[2]

On Rosebery the *Daily Chronicle* would seem to speak with a single voice. But in view of developments before the end of the year we must listen to a story told by Beatrice Webb, if not told very precisely. She relates that soon after the shift from Gladstone to Rosebery, Massingham sought Sidney's advice concerning *Chronicle* policy 'and his ultimatum to the nominal editor that he would stand no interference in the political editorship'. The impetus had come from Haldane who had supported Rosebery but in the shuffle was left without office and considered some of the appointments 'dreadful'. He was anxious that the *Chronicle* be more critical of the new Government. Massingham, Haldane and Webb 'more or less determined on a plan of campaign', with Haldane inciting Massingham 'to keep the *Chronicle* an independent force'.[3]

---

[1] Robert Rhodes James, *Rosebery: A Biography of Archibald Philip Primrose, Fifth Earl of Rosebery* (London, 1963), 199. In 1901 Massingham remarked ('The Next Government', *Anglo-Saxon Review* (June 1901), 5–14) that only as chairman of the L.C.C. had Rosebery succeeded. In 1923 Massingham recalled that most Liberals favoured Rosebery in 1894 because of his attitude on social questions and the inadequacy of the Gladstonian tradition. *H.W.M.*, 28–9. Lord Eversley (George Shaw-Lefevre) wrote Massingham of the opposition in Gladstone's Cabinet to Harcourt's succession. Eversley to Massingham, 6 Sept. 1923 (Copy), M.P.

[2] *D.C.*, 5 and 22 Mar. 1894. In his St James's Hall speech Rosebery was referring to a 'Letter to the Editor' (*D.C.*, 8 March) objecting to such a meeting during Holy Week. Of his remarks on that occasion, the *D.C.* commented (22 Mar.): No other statesman 'has ever delivered such an exposition of the new politics that one hopes, are one day going "to build Jerusalem in England's green and pleasant land" '.

[3] Webb, *Our Partnership*, ed. Drake and Cole, 114–16, which agrees with the MS. Diary, B.L.P.E.S., with slight verbal change.

Massingham's change in stance, as revealed in 'House and Lobby', comes slowly. The new Prime Minister's blunder, in admitting on his first appearance in the Lords that Home Rule could not come without an English majority behind it, was hardly noticed – instead Massingham chose to praise Rosebery's Edinburgh speech (17 March) in which he endeavoured without great success to explain away that indiscretion. A few days later Massingham referred to Rosebery's 'ample exposition of the new spirit in politics'.[1] In an article in the *Contemporary Review* (April 1894) Massingham labelled the shift from Gladstone to Rosebery 'the landslip from the old to the new radicalism'. In May, in 'House and Lobby' he was impressed by the great hold which Rosebery had on the rank and file of the Party. All this was no doubt read by Harcourt (who had been Rosebery's rival for Party leadership) with mixed feelings. When the Harcourt Budget with its graduated death duty and other innovations was greeted by the Prime Minister with 'apprehensions', Harcourt's son wrote in his journal: 'W.V.H. much amused at the high Tory line by R! I wonder what the *Daily Chronicle* would think if they could see this.'[2]

The Rosebery Government demonstrated its weaknesses soon enough. It is a historian of the 1960s who has said that those who succeeded Gladstone 'neither concerned themselves with continuing the Gladstonian tradition, nor with an attempt to evolve a new sort of Liberalism. Both in foreign and domestic affairs, their policies lacked coherence, consistency, and a clearly defined aim'.[3] It is much the view Massingham came to in time. For a year he groped for alternatives. As early as May 1894 he was dwelling on the lack of leadership in the Commons, and he was suggesting a dissolution and a General Election, a proposal which he developed at length in the *Contemporary Review* for June. In 'House and Lobby' he urged closer rapport between the Government and the National Liberal Federation.

But Massingham did not join Fletcher and Clarke in outright attack on Rosebery. As the parliamentary session ends unsigned leaders score the Government for its failure to establish a position on the issue of the House of Lords, while 'House and Lobby' takes a milder tone,

[1] *D.C.*, 'House and Lobby', 14, 20, 22 Mar.
[2] A. G. Gardiner, *The Life of Sir William Harcourt* (London, 1923), II, 283.
[3] Peter Stansky, *Ambitions and Strategies* (Oxford, 1964), 173.

emphasising the achievements of the Government and regarding Rosebery as still on trial. Massingham's tone registers more disappointment than anger. Parliament was prorogued on 25 August 1894 not to meet again that year. As one reads through the *Daily Chronicle* in the succeeding months, one wonders whether it was in fact a Liberal paper. Margot Asquith tells the story of a conversation with John Morley and Sir William Harcourt in late May 1895. Morley said that like Joseph Chamberlain he would rather have newspapers 'for than against me'. Said Harcourt: 'My dear chap, you would surely not rather have the *Daily Chronicle* on your side... Our party has had more harm done to it through the *Daily Chronicle* than anything else.' At this Margot demurred, saying, 'its screams, though pitched a little high, are effective'. To which Morley said, 'Oh, you like Massingham of course, because your husband is one of his heroes.' And then Harcourt, 'Well... he always abuses me and I am glad of it.' And Morley responded, 'He abuses me too, though not, perhaps, quite so often as you.'[1]

As to Rosebery, the essential fact is that a conflict of views had now developed within the *Chronicle* staff. On 8 October 1894, Fletcher, the editor, wrote to Henry Demarest Lloyd, the American social reformer (in 1894 he published his influential *Wealth and Commonwealth*, an attack on monopolies) that because of disagreement with his proprietors over publication of betting news he had decided to resign. Fletcher, however, was omitting the real problem. This was explained to Lloyd by William Clarke. He singles out 'that scoundrel', Henry Norman, as the chief cause. According to Clarke, Norman, from the start of his association with the *Daily Chronicle*, had endeavoured 'to oust Fletcher by intrigue'. Of late, Clarke continues, 'Norman has succeeded in hypnotising (I can use no other word) the proprietors; & he & Massingham were responsible for the idiotic way in which the paper went into raptures over Rosebery. They are in short, Rosebery's newspaper tools.' Clarke quickly adds that John Burns was also involved, 'a regular intrigue'.[2]

1 Margot Asquith, *An Autobiography*, II (New York, 1920), 257–8.
2 Fletcher to Lloyd, 8 Oct. 1894; Clarke to Lloyd, 12 and 22 Oct., and 21 Nov. 1894. Lloyd Papers.

Even allowing for emotion bordering on hysteria from Clarke, the mystery of the flat and unaggressive character of the *Daily Chronicle* in the closing months of 1894 and the early months of 1895 clears up. Perhaps, as Clarke suggests, the paper *was* 'at the end of its tether'. However, Massingham's 'House and Lobby', which resumes with the new session of Parliament in February 1895, shows some of its customary lustre. He finds that as a spokesman for the Government in the Lords Rosebery has improved.[1]

But Massingham was really in something of a quandary. In January 1895 we find him unburdening himself again to Haldane, as he had the year before. He urges Haldane to get acquainted with Shaw, 'the best talker & the keenest analytical mind in England'. And with the Webbs interested as well there would be a new party.

As to the future I shall pursue a quietly critical & merciless campaign. There is no great man at the head of affairs from whom we can expect initiative. Therefore we must 'fend' for ourselves. One doesn't want to do needless mischief, but even the fighting spirit is wanting and no great intellectual or moral influence is available.

And he continues: 'I am afraid *you* will have to be prime minister.' Massingham's intent is serious. 'Everything in the last resort depends on *you*. You have position, knowledge, industry, & insight – & those qualities are not combined in any other man.' Then he refers to his own problems at the *Daily Chronicle*: 'Newspapers must be backed from within, & as you know I've a hard row to hoe. But I have little fear that in the future things will come right.'

Massingham's immediate concern was the London County Council election in March. He consulted Webb on the role of the *Chronicle*. Haldane had remarked to the Webbs: 'If only you Progressives can hold your own at the L.C.C. elections, you would be a plank saved from the wreck upon which we could build a new combination.'[2] The result, in Vaughan Nash's words, was that Massingham 'turned the *Chronicle* into an electioneering broadsheet'. To Joseph Pennell we go for an account of the drawings of London life which appeared in successive weeks in February and March:

---

[1] *D.C.*, 'House and Lobby', 6 and 22 Feb. 1895.
[2] H.P., 5904/24–5, Massingham to Haldane, 14 Jan. [?] 1895; Webb, Diary, 20 Jan. 1895, in *Our Partnership*, ed. Drake and Cole, 121.

I got Whistler, Walter Crane, Burne-Jones, William Morris, Phil May, Bernard Partridge, Alfred Parsons, Raven-Hill, Maurice Greiffenhagen, E. J. Sullivan, A. S. Hartrick and Aubrey Beardsley to make drawings. . . All were large . . . some half a page. No such illustrations had ever been printed in a daily paper before.[1]

But the poll – collapse of the Progressives – left the Council evenly divided between Progressives and Moderates. Burns had difficulty holding his own in Battersea, as his correspondence with Massingham illustrates. And the breach reopened between Massingham and the Webbs, with Massingham writing Sidney that the Progressive failure, particularly Burns' reduced majority in Battersea, was partly due to Sidney's association with the I.L.P. 'Anyway I am puzzled, doubtful, and also in a sense sore. . . I hope . . . that we shall continue in the main on the same side. But Fabianism is done with & so is the I.L.P. & I don't think you see things as I do.' It must have been this letter which inspired Beatrice Webb's often quoted reference to 'the mercurial' Massingham,[2] a remark which repeatedly returns to mind.

In mid-March 1895 Massingham replaced Fletcher as editor of the *Daily Chronicle*, with Norman as assistant editor. The only comment from Massingham himself is in letters to W. T. Stead. On 27 March Massingham wrote that the actual change in editorship had come suddenly and unexpectedly. 'I have refused all requests for interviews, portraits &c.; in fact I would rather have entered on a difficult experiment without a word being said about it.'

In consequence, the *Review of Reviews* merely carried a brief announcement of the change. In the *Sketch* (27 March), there is a reference to Massingham's 'very swift ascent to one of the highest positions English journalism can offer'. The *Review of Reviews* planned a full length 'character sketch', but Massingham protested. He wrote Stead (3 October): 'I loathe publicity with all the shrinking of a thoroughly nervous man.' There was no sketch. Just at this time, in late 1895, Massingham and Stead were in close converse over prison

---

[1] *H.W.M.*, 291. Pennell, *Adventures of an Illustrator*, 250, 252.
[2] B.P., Massingham to Burns, 23 and 25 Oct. 1894, Add. MS. 46294/211, 213; P.P., Massingham to Webb, 10 Mar. 1895; Webb, *Our Partnership*, ed. Drake and Cole, 71–2.

reform, over articles by Stead for the *Chronicle* and over Stead's 'Penny Poets and other Penny Steadfuls', in *Punch*'s phrase.[1]

But another view of the shift in editorship comes from Clarke. He wrote Henry Demarest Lloyd in March 1895 of the change, 'so disastrous in every way. Fletcher has gone: Massingham a neurotic, hysterical, bad-tempered impressionist is in his place'. Massingham, he admitted, was perhaps well-intentioned

but he is absolutely under the influence of that damned ruffian Henry Norman, who hates me, whom I hate, & who is bent upon the dismissal of myself and two or three others in the office who are not friendly to the new arrangements... I may add that it is in contemplation by these fellows to turn the Chronicle into a jingo-imperialist organ & gradually change its whole character, in which case not one solitary representative of the *right* will be left in the whole London press. A section of the Rosebery gang are really, on the quiet, all in the conspiracy, the silly feather-headed proprietor [Frank Lloyd] all the while utterly unconscious of the game going on all around him.[2]

Clarke before long turned to a venture of his own; the *Progressive Review* began publication in October 1896. The *Daily Chronicle* greeted its appearance: 'It is for the Progressive thinkers of the country to aid in bringing the newer world into birth.'[3] But Massingham never contributed. The *Progressive Review* proved another disappointment to Clarke, for it, too, had staff and financial problems from the start and lasted but two years.[4]

The Liberal débâcle in the summer of 1895 provided Clarke with ammunition for his parting shot. 'The Liberal Party', he wrote Lloyd 'is smashed into atoms... An organized hypocrisy has come to an end.' As to the *Daily Chronicle*, it 'goes steadily on the down grade'.

---

[1] Massingham to Stead, 27 Mar., 19, 21, 25 Sept., 3 Oct., 8 Nov. 1895 (courtesy J. O. Baylen).

[2] Clarke to Lloyd, 23 Mar. 1895. Lloyd Papers.

[3] Quoted in Peter Weiler, 'Liberal Social Theory in Great Britain, 1896–1914' (unpublished Ph.D. Thesis, Harvard U., 1968), 118.

[4] The Lloyd Papers provide additional information on Clarke's relations with Norman and on the *Progressive Review*. According to [Burrows and Hobson (eds.)] in *William Clarke, A Collection of his Writings*, xxi–xxiii, Clarke renewed connections with the *Daily Chronicle*. He wrote the leader, 20 May 1898 on the death of Gladstone and also the article on the International Congress of Women in London, June 1899.

Anyone but an utter fool wd have found out Norman & Massingham by this time, but apparently the deluded proprietors have not. They must, however, be a little staggered by the utter collapse of Massingham's idiotic political predictions.[1]

Massingham, on succeeding Fletcher, had written Stead: 'I confess the idea of the journalist writing always behind the scenes & in the dark appeals to me.'[2] And so from him we have no comment on Clarke.

Liberal débâcle, 1895

The faltering Rosebery Government came to an end on 22 June, choosing to resign rather than to go to the country. The new Conservative Government under Salisbury dissolved at once, and was confirmed overwhelmingly in the General Election in July with the Liberals suffering a crushing defeat. Their majority of 42 established in 1892 was replaced with a Tory-Unionist majority of 152. It was in particular a defeat for Radicalism and Progressivism. In London, in 1892, the Radicals had won 25 seats; in 1895, they won but 8; they lost 11 seats in London districts where the working-class vote was overwhelming. Of the working-class Members of Parliament only John Burns survived; the Liberals seemed once more a middle-class party. That they had polled nearly half the popular vote was little consolation.[3]

With Fletcher and Clarke out of the picture, what of the response of the *Daily Chronicle*? Its general comment on the Liberal disaster was dignified enough. On Rosebery's resignation, an unsigned leader, 24 June, declared: 'The present administration, whatever its shortcomings may be, has died fighting as it lived fighting. . . The men who go out of office have now, on the whole, opened a better chapter in the nation's history.' In the Election campaign there was considerable praise for Asquith, but emphasis was upon the Progressives in London politics, and beginning on 8 July, a column called '*Chronicle Leaflets*', dealing with municipal problems of London, ran for half-a-dozen issues. When the first returns clearly indicated a Liberal disaster, a comment in the *Daily Chronicle*, 16 July, which sounds like Massingham, declared: 'Social Radicalism has not been defeated; it is upon the

[1] Clarke to Lloyd, 18 July 1895. Lloyd Papers.
[2] Massingham to Stead, 27 Mar. 1895 (courtesy J. O. Baylen).
[3] Thompson, *Socialists, Liberals and Labour*, 107–11.

older, stagnant, hopeless form of the Liberal creed that the heaviest blows have fallen. "Manchesterism" has been finally destroyed, and a good thing too.' When Massingham is writing in the *Contemporary Review*, over his name, he says: 'The Liberal forces are now scattered; the party in its old form and strength which, with one exception, it has maintained throughout the century, has virtually ceased to exist.'

His explanation is first of all 'the want of a single great personality'. Also, the social policy of Liberalism while philosophically sound was politically opportunist and had failed. Advocacy of social legislation had not held the working-class vote; indeed the working class had been repelled by the suggestion of a reduction in hours which might reduce their earnings as well. A year or so later he remarked that 'the party which cannot hold London, Birmingham, Manchester, Newcastle, Bradford, and whose most stable following among the workmen are the miners, can hardly claim to speak even for industrial England'.[1] Soon after the Election he had an exchange with Shaw who declared that the results merely emphasised the need for Independent Labour politics. He prepared an article, 'The Political Situation: a Fabian View', which he hoped to get into the *Chronicle* 'if I can persuade Massingham to do it'.[2] It did appear, on 5 October 1895, and was answered the same day in a leader undoubtedly written by Massingham. The leader declared that Shaw was guilty of a fatal contradiction in arguing (1) that the Liberal defeat came from its failure to accept and act upon collectivist ideas; and (2) in also declaring that the tremendous conservatism within the working class was one of the barriers to social progress. If the latter were true, according to the leader, the working class did not desert the Liberals because of their neglect of Socialist legislation.

---

[1] Massingham, 'The Débâcle and After', *Contemporary Review*, LXVIII (Aug. 1895). 299–304. This article was singled out by the *Review of Reviews* (Amer. edit., XII, Sept, 1895, 337–8) as the most interesting of the comments on the Election. Another view is from a pro-Rosebery Liberal, James Annand, who declared that the Election was lost chiefly to the extent that the *Daily Chronicle* and the Fabian Society had raised suspicion in the popular mind as to the labour policy of the Liberal Party. 'Demoralization of Liberalism', *New Review* (Aug. 1895), pp. 248–50. Massingham's statement in 1897 is in Frederick Whelen (ed.), *Politics in 1896: An Annual* (London, 1897), 76.
[2] Shaw to Pease, 17 Sept. 1895, Laurence, 560–1. Shaw's statement was also delivered in a speech at Essex Hall, 4 Oct.

In commenting upon the Election Massingham barely mentions Rosebery by name and then in no complimentary fashion. It is therefore with some surprise that we encounter this statement in a leader in the issue of 1 July:

> We were wholly skeptical of the alleged Russo-French loan to China until official assertions ... compel belief. We did Lord Rosebery ... an injustice ... It seems undoubted that he [Rosebery] achieved during the period of his last Government, perhaps the most striking of his several great diplomatic successes.

This leader was written by Norman. He so reports to Rosebery the very same day:

> In case you did not see this morning's *Daily Chronicle*, may I beg you to spare a moment to read the enclosed. I believe that at only one point did I fail to do justice to your late administration. I have tried to repair any mistake here.
> The political situation seems to a good many of us well-calculated to promote the birth by and by, of that Party, 'unnamed as yet,' at whose head we want to see you.[1]

Pretty clearly Massingham and Norman no longer agreed on Rosebery. But Norman was soon sent abroad, as a special correspondent of the *Daily Chronicle*, first to Montenegro in October, to Constantinople in November and to the United States in December. In this role Massingham found him indispensable.

In the *Daily Chronicle* for 19 October 1895 appeared an interview between Norman and Nicholas I of Montenegro. Massingham sent W. E. Gladstone an advanced proof, for the interview included this request from Nicholas: 'Say for me ... that where the glance of Gladstone has fallen, freedom has sprung up from the ground. And add that I hold his name in my heart of hearts.' Gladstone responded with a 'Letter to the Editor', published on 21 October. 'You have sent me a paper even more interesting than I expected.' And Gladstone's closing words, 'The traditions of Montenegro now committed to His Highness as a sacred trust exceed in glory those of Marathon and Thermopylae', were telegraphed to Nicholas. In turn Nicholas'

---

[1] R.P., Norman to Rosebery, 1 July 1895; Rosebery to Norman, 22 Mar. 1895 (Letter Book) for an exchange earlier in the year.

telegram of acknowledgment was relayed to Gladstone by Massingham.[1]

Soon after, a 'special commissioner' for the *Daily Chronicle*, certainly Norman, was in Constantinople to report on Armenia. Massingham kept Gladstone informed, and the *Daily Chronicle* for 2 November, 1895 carried a dispatch from Constantinople under the heading, 'The Last Days of Sultan Abdul Hamid II.'[2]

Venezuela – Armenia

Two months later, in December, Norman was in Washington, D.C., to report on the Venezuelan question – a boundary dispute of long standing between British Guiana and Venezuela. It had become a critical issue in Anglo-American relations. In July 1895, Olney, the American Secretary of State, had appealed to the Monroe Doctrine as justifying American intervention. In November Salisbury replied that the principle 'that American questions are for American decision ... cannot be sustained by any reasoning drawn from the law of nations'. Then President Cleveland, in a message to Congress, on 17 December, reaffirmed the Olney position and declared that the United States would insist upon investigation by a Commission and would enforce its recommendations. This message, wrote the British ambassador in Washington, sounded 'a note of war'.[3]

There are several versions of the crisis and its solution. One is that of diplomatic historians constructed from official correspondence and telegrams. Another is that of William T. Stead who staged a campaign for arbitration and, autobiographically, took credit for his National Social Union 'producing such an expression of public opinion in favour of arbitration that Lord Salisbury gave way'.[4] And there is the *Daily Chronicle* version.

Henry Norman begins the story:

On the afternoon of the day after President Cleveland's message had thrown

---

[1] G.P., Massingham to W. E. Gladstone, 16, 21, 22 Oct. 1895, in Add. MS. 44521/76–7, 90–3 and Add. MS. 44524/141–3 where the letter is misdated 22 Oct. 1896. Norman's visit was commended to Gladstone in advance by Malcolm MacColl. G.P., 7 Sept. 1895, Add. MS. 44245/190.

[2] G.P., Massingham to W. E. Gladstone, 21 Oct. and 2 Nov. 1895, Add. MS. 44521/90–3, 107–8.

[3] R. A. Humphreys, *Tradition and Revolt in Latin America* (London, 1969) carefully analyses the dispute as an episode in diplomatic history. He does not refer to the press.

[4] Frederic Whyte, *The Life of W. T. Stead* (2 vols., London, n.d.), I, 78–87.

this country into amazement, I was, as usual, discussing the matters of the day with the editor of the *Daily Chronicle*. . . Two hours later as I was sitting at dinner, a telegram was put into my hands. It was an inquiry from Massingham whether I would hold myself in readiness to leave by the next steamer for New York as the special commissioner of the *Chronicle* on a mission of investigation and peace.

Norman continues the story at some length in *Cosmopolis* for March 1896. Arriving in Washington shortly before New Year's Day he was able through a friendly interceder 'to declare with authority the mind and views of the American Government'. He found evidence, he said, that Lord Aberdeen had many years before disavowed the Schomburgk Line between British Guiana and Venezuela which many in England now insisted upon.

Norman's despatches in the *Daily Chronicle*, beginning on 2 January, declared that the American position was entitled to respect, that the people of the United States and their Government would insist upon arbitration, but that everyone worth considering earnestly desired an amicable settlement. On Friday, 3 January, the *Daily Chronicle* published Norman's despatch with documents which questioned the validity of the Schomburgk Line. On the same day came word of the Kaiser's telegram to President Kruger of the Transvaal congratulating him on the defeat of the Jameson Raid. On 7 January the *Daily Chronicle* reported from its Washington representative that 'the tide of opinion regarding England is distinctly turning, owing both to the *Daily Chronicle* utterance and to England's anxious foreign crisis'.

Apparently Massingham asked the venerable Gladstone for support; on 12 January he wired the *Daily Chronicle*: 'My opinion about arbitration unchanged but . . . cannot usefully appear in public at this moment.'[1] From America, Henry Demarest Lloyd, increasingly important as a link with British Radicals, sent a letter to the *Daily Chronicle*, printed in its issue of 28 January, in which he spoke out vigorously for arbitration as the solution which American opinion genuinely sought. Lloyd also wrote personally to Stead in similar vein. Lloyd's biographer concludes that these communications greatly

[1] G.P., Memo 12 Jan. [1896], Add. MS. 44522/12, 29.

strengthened Massingham's efforts in the *Daily Chronicle* to persuade Salisbury to accept arbitration.[1]

When Parliament reconvened on 11 February, Salisbury's statement in the Lords that, while he did not think it necessary for the United States to 'intrude' the Monroe Doctrine, he was in favour of negotiation, was greeted with 'Cheers'. For this statement, 'House and Lobby' had great praise and the *Daily Chronicle* claimed considerable credit for the decision.

> We shall perhaps [be pardoned] . . . if we point back to the fact that little more than a month ago this journal was fighting single handed among the journals of London – first, to convince the British people that the Schomburghk Line was indefensible; secondly, that the American people were profoundly in earnest; and the moment should be seized to render impossible such fateful misunderstandings.

At the outset, declared the *Chronicle*, the London press insisted that England 'could not with honour retreat an inch'. Today, all this has been changed by the 'simple force of publicity'.[2]

The *New York Times* (8 January) concluded that the attitude of the British press was changing. 'What has happened is the enlightenment of the British public on the merits of the Venezuelan debate by the despatches of Norman.' If so, the British press, did not, with a few exceptions, acknowledge it. The only significant recognition of Norman's role came in Stead's *Review of Reviews* (March 1896). Norman is referred to as occupying 'a pedestal of renown at present without rival in the British press'. His famous telegram in which he professed to have evidence that Aberdeen had disavowed the Schomburgk Line was

> a marvellously artful move. . . Here was an English journalist bold enough, brave enough and honest enough to tell old John Bull that he had not a leg to stand upon if he based his case upon the action of Lord Aberdeen. The fact that the old party in question never based his case on anything Lord

---

[1] Lloyd Papers, Lloyd to *Daily Chronicle*, 15 Jan. 1896, and Lloyd to Stead, 24 Dec. 1895. Chester McArthur Destler, *Henry Demarest Lloyd and the Empire of Reform* (Philadelphia, 1963), 448.

[2] *Parliamentary Debates, Lords*, 4th series, vol. 37, cols. 51–4. *D.C.*, 12 Feb., 6–7. After Massingham's death, the *Catholic Times* (6 Sept. 1924) recounted a story that on the eve of the reconvening of Parliament, Massingham had in readiness a whole page on behalf of arbitration. But when he learned that the Government had accepted the principle of arbitration he withheld the page. The story cannot be corroborated.

Aberdeen did or did not do was everywhere ignored. The whole American press fell upon Mr. Norman's neck and called him blessed.

But Stead was amused as well as impressed. He recalled that praise for Norman often got out of hand. And Stead hoped that Norman's success would not contribute to the disease called 'Swelled Head'. Norman was, indeed, a very brash fellow.

As historians have told the story there has been little reference to the press. Occasionally there is mention of amateur diplomats trying 'to smooth the path of settlement'. At the time the professional diplomats were less than tolerant towards Norman. On 3 January, Lord Pauncefote, British Ambassador in Washington, reported to Salisbury that 'a wave of reason' was passing over America after a period of dementia. And he added

I may mention that a Mr. Henry Norman, sub-editor of the *Daily Chronicle*, has recently arrived here and is making himself very busy about the Venezuela Question & Behring Sea. I believe he cabled something foolish to London yesterday which has been published here under the heading of 'England Backs Down' . . . I am rather suspicious he is 'anguis in herba.'

But Salisbury accepted, reluctantly, the view that the United States had justifiably intervened and that arbitration was in order. Official negotiations began 4 February and proceeded until the final settlement was announced by Salisbury the following November.[1]

In his essay on Liberalism in 1896 Massingham remarked that 'Salisbury is entitled to the credit of a statesman who puts his pride in his pocket'. This is fair enough. Massingham added that, in demonstrating that both nations desired arbitration, 'the press cleared the ground which the statesmen had cumbered'.[2] Closer at hand we have the comment of the *Review of Reviews*. In February, the American edition, now quite separate from the English, summarised the affair:

The inestimable service which the *Chronicle* . . . [has] rendered in these past weeks, has been that of setting before the English people some of those plain facts in the Venezuela case which almost all other English newspapers have succeeded so remarkably in avoiding.

[1] J. A. S. Grenville, *Lord Salisbury and Foreign Policy: The Close of the Nineteenth Century* (London, 1964), 69; Pauncefote to Salisbury, 3 Jan. 1896, Salisbury Papers, Christ Church, Oxford.
[2] Whelen (ed.), *Politics in 1896*, 53–4.

Stead in the English edition, in March:

The really important work which he [Norman] did was in convincing the ordinary newspaper reader here that the citizens of the United States had worked themselves up to an almost incredible state of excitement . . . and that the only way out was by the adoption of some system of arbitration.

As contemporary comment this is reasonable, and it remains convincing. One can hardly say that Salisbury was persuaded by the *Daily Chronicle* (his brief reference to Norman is unapproving),[1] but he and the Cabinet were influenced by public opinion, and Pulitzer's *New York World* in the United States and Massingham's *Daily Chronicle* in England calmed rising voices and established an atmosphere conducive to peaceful arbitration.

When Massingham resigned from the *Daily Chronicle* in 1899, the *Outlook* remarked that the *Chronicle* was the only newspaper 'which called Lord Rosebery to assume the cloak of Mr. Gladstone and presently tore that garment from Lord Rosebery's back'.[2] The resignation of Rosebery as Liberal leader, in October 1896, is one of the more dramatic episodes in the political history of the *Chronicle*. The wider context is the Armenian atrocities which made the Eastern Question a Massingham crusade.

The first reports – wholesale slaughter in certain Armenian villages – came to England in the summer of 1894. An early protagonist for intervention, Canon Malcolm MacColl, vainly bombarded Rosebery with appeals for action.[3] While atrocities were checked in Constantinople, they continued in Asia Minor. By June 1895, when Salisbury returned to office, public opinion for British intervention, led by the Liberal press, began to build up.

But Salisbury was hopeless on Armenia, said 'House and Lobby' on 12 February 1896. Massingham looked for results through Gladstone and in June 1896 sent him a copy of MacColl's review (*Daily Chronicle*, 18 June) of the Duke of Argyll's *Our Responsibilities for Turkey* (1896). The very next day Gladstone responded:

[1] Salisbury to Lord Pauncefote, 7 Feb. 1895, as cited in Grenville, *Lord Salisbury and Foreign Policy*, 69.
[2] *Outlook*, 2 Dec. 1899, p. 564.
[3] R.P.

Neither the Duke nor anyone else that I have read uses language half strong enough against the Sultan and his agents. To describe guilt beyond all bounds language ought to go beyond all bounds.

My choice is between out Heroding everybody, and absolute silence. For my language might be plausibly set down to temper whereas it would be perfectly cold-blooded. I remain silent only for fear of doing harm.

Massingham sought permission to publish this letter; it is likely that Gladstone's reply is found in an undated memo in his cramped hand: 'My personal participation in a movement of a political nature would be injurious and I must avoid it. But would heartily agree with your [efforts] . . . to assist the Armenian cause.'[1]

If Rosebery's position on Armenia was constantly shifting, the position of the *Daily Chronicle* on Rosebery was also sometimes cloudy. To be sure, there was not much question when certain leaders appeared, as on 30 January 1896: 'The Liberal Party is not only not in power – it is incoherent, apathetic, disorganized and dumb. Its leaders do not lead, and its followers have no idea to which point of the political compass they should march.'[2] But then, there was an occasional leader, quite partial to Rosebery, very likely the work of Norman, such as flattering comment (4 March) on Rosebery's Eighty Club address. Norman apart, Rosebery himself quite naturally had more confidence in the *Westminster Gazette* with its 'preeminent usefulness to the Liberal Party. It is moderate and therefore strong; it gives the tone that is wanted, and inspires the provinces'. Thus he wrote to Sir George Newnes. But all this is of only incidental interest; more central to the issue is that while crowds at the City Temple in London heard Dr Joseph Parker denounce 'Abdul the Damned on his Accursed Throne', much of the newspaper-reading public followed the *Daily Chronicle* as it steadily espoused the cause of the Christian subjects of the Porte.[3]

[1] G.P., MacColl to Gladstone, 17 June [1896], Add. MS. 44245/311. G.P., Massingham to Gladstone, 18 June 1896; Gladstone to Massingham, 19 June 1896 (Copy): Massingham to Gladstone, 24 June 1895 and undated memo in Gladstone's hand. Add. MS. 44523/14–15, 62–4, 178.
[2] Weiler, 'Liberal Social Theory in Great Britain', 105; Stansky, *Ambitions and Strategies*, 208.
[3] R.P., Rosebery to Sir George Newnes, 7 Jan. 1896; Newnes to Rosebery, 9 and 14 Jan. 1896. I am reminded of Dr Parker by J. Cruickshank, *The Roaring Century, 1846–1946* (London, 1946), 243.

On 26–7 August 1896, the *Daily Chronicle* and the *Daily News* carried ghastly tales, replete with pseudo-illustrations, of the massacre of Armenians at Constantinople. At the same time, *The Times* was referring to disorders 'provoked by Armenians'. The *Chronicle* soon became a forum for stimulating and clarifying Liberal Party statement. The weight of its leaders bore down on Rosebery. On 5 September: 'so far, Lord Rosebery cannot be said to have shown a burning interest in the matter... Now we are entitled to know what, in Lord Rosebery's opinion, ought to be done'. And seemed to have more confidence (8 September) in Salisbury who 'should realise that now is the time for action with which, we believe, he strongly sympathizes'.

But again it was chiefly to Gladstone that Massingham turned. On 10 September he wrote in swift, urgent language that judging from the flood of letters to his office and innumerable conversations with men of classes and all opinions, at last there was 'a strong popular movement... without reference to party consideration'. But the public mind lacked leadership. He wrote, said Massingham, to emphasise the 'exceeding weight' attached to Gladstone's 'action and opinion'. The *Daily Chronicle* 'would be most honored to be allowed to give the widest publicity to your view, in whatever form you might be disposed to express it'.

The tone of Gladstone's response, on 13 September, was quite different from the previous June. He had no confidence in 'the powers' but thought they would not interfere if Britain acted alone. Salisbury should be encouraged to protest and to act. In several letters and telegrams Massingham emphasised 'the responsibilities of England' and urged Gladstone to make a public statement. 'I need not say how eagerly we look forward for any word of counsel from you – more especially in the unhappy circumstances in which the Liberal Party is placed.'[1]

Gladstone now told the press that nothing but force would avail against the 'Great Assassin' and that mere remonstrance by the Powers had been a mockery. And Asquith in a message to the *Daily Chronicle*, published on 12 September, and quoted in *The Times* on 14 September declared 'I am in entire accord with the conviction that the time has

[1] G.P., Correspondence 10 to 17 Sept. is in Add. MS. 44523/253–6, 264–5, 279–84, 289–92.

come when Great Britain should refuse to hold further terms with a Government which has become a mere instrument for executing the purposes of a will either criminal or insane.'[1]

The same day, the *Chronicle* editorially acclaimed Asquith for breaking the silence of the official Opposition. Rosebery responded to these statements, in *The Times* (for 14 September), that though he shared 'the indignation almost past the power of expression at these last atrocities', it was a 'national question' and that any 'impulse' to action from the leaders of the Liberal Party would be a mistake. While it was a statement not sufficiently moderate for *The Times*, it exhausted Massingham's impatience and he came out the same day with his famous 'Veiled Prophet' leader. He agreed that British action should be non-partisan, and that if the Powers refused to act 'a United England should press upon Lord Salisbury the duty of intervening by force'. And he continued

There is nothing in this statement to offend any adherent to the Prime Minister and even any adherent to the mysterious scruples of Lord Rosebery which have at last found mysterious utterance. On the very day when Gladstone urges coercion and Asquith, still one of Rosebery's colleagues, declares the time has come for breaking the power of the Sultan, the Veiled Prophet of the Liberal leadership tells us that any 'impulse' from him would be 'a mistake.' Anybody might suppose from this that Rosebery stands outside the nation.

Massingham seldom did anything by halves. Rosebery's moribund interest in reform and now his failure to reaffirm British moral leadership in the Armenian question led Massingham to abandon him completely. The *Daily Chronicle* became the strongest voice of protest in the Liberal press. In Robert Rhodes James' phrase, Massingham 'savaged' Rosebery at every opportunity. Even Salisbury won more favour. On 17 September the *Chronicle* declared:

if it were proposed in any quarter to substitute Rosebery for Lord Salisbury as Premier and Foreign Minister, we should offer the most strenuous opposition to any such movement. [Lord Rosebery] has done nothing to merit such a choice; he has done much to make it impossible. And, indeed it is to Lord Salisbury that we turn with much sympathy.

MacColl now tried to establish rapport between Salisbury and

[1] As quoted in *Annual Register, 1896* (London, 1897) [183–4].

Massingham. On 13 September MacColl wrote Salisbury: 'The most powerful organ of the Liberal Party is now the *Daily Chronicle*. I know the editor, a strong Radical, but a thoroughly honest and manly fellow who has but a small opinion of the leaders of his own party.' And on the day of the 'Veiled Prophet' leader MacColl wrote that he had written to Massingham 'to suggest that he should trounce Lord Rosebery, and he had done it, as you will see in his first leader today'. Undoubtedly Massingham listened to MacColl and from 17 September to 14 October, the *Chronicle* ran his series of articles on the Armenian question. The purpose, in part, MacColl mentioned to Salisbury, was 'to vindicate your Lordship's whole position'.[1]

On 24 September, at Liverpool, Gladstone made his major effort. He scored 'the Great Assassin' and called for positive British action in line with treaty obligations. He did not, however, suggest just what action that should be. It was a moderate speech, but the *Daily Chronicle* (25 Sptember) made the most of it, devoting an entire page to the occasion. The Paris correspondent reported that 'Mr. Gladstone's solemn appeal has electrified Europe.'

Thus far, only Asquith among leading Liberals had sided with Gladstone in advocating British unilateral action. Henry Campbell-Bannerman, on the Continent, wrote on 2 October assuring Rosebery of his support. John Morley was equivocal, though according to MacColl, in early October he told Massingham he would stand with Gladstone against Rosebery.[2] And Morley added that he thought Harcourt would do the same. But thus far Harcourt had kept his counsel. The 'Veiled Prophet' leader on Rosebery in the *Daily Chronicle*, had merely amused him.[3] As early as 12 September Massingham besought him to speak. On receipt of Massingham's telegram Harcourt told his son, Loulou, he would make no public statement, but was uncertain what to reply to Massingham. On 16 September Massingham renewed his appeal to Harcourt, even suggesting what he should say. Harcourt now answered, without committing himself: 'There are many things I should like to say to you on the situation

---

[1] George W. E. Russell (ed.), *Malcolm MacColl: Memoirs and Correspondence* (London, 1914), 157ff.
[2] R.P., Campbell-Bannerman to Rosebery, 2 Oct. 1896. G.P., MacColl to Gladstone, n.d., Add. MS. 44245/265; the date suggested, 11 October, is clearly wrong.
[3] Harcourt to Lewis Harcourt, n.d., quoted Gardiner, *Harcourt*, II, 414.

which I cannot well write.' In fact his position was much closer to Rosebery than to Gladstone. He felt that Britain, alone, could do nothing for Armenia, but that Britain should denounce the Cyprus Convention which protected Turkey from intervention. This was the essence of his address to his constituents of Ebbw Vale on 5 October and so his remarks were generally interpreted.[1] But not by the *Daily Chronicle* (6 October) which represented the speech as strongly anti-Turk, and a sharp divergence from Rosebery's view – this the *Chronicle* made out by emphasising Harcourt's plea for a complete understanding with Russia on the Eastern Question. Massingham – for without question he wrote the leader – used Harcourt's speech as the basis for an attack on Rosebery. Harcourt had spoken 'with authority, with weight, with wisdom'; it was 'the most impressive speech since the controversy arose'. Massingham then turned on Rosebery, to whom the *Daily Chronicle* has 'an exceptional right to speak with franknese . . . for that statesman owes more to it than to any journal in ths United Kingdom'.

We cannot turn to a speech or a letter of Lord Rosebery without finding some new indiscretion. The one point that sticks out in his utterances is a fear for an Austrian–Russian war against the U.K. Nothing of England's Duty – nothing of England's Honour.[2]

The authorities on this episode have concluded that Massingham deliberately misrepresented Harcourt's speech in order to divide him from Rosebery and provide opportunity for further attack on the Liberal Party leader.[3] This judgment is circumstantial enough, but it fails to take into account Massingham's general reputation for honesty of intention. On the other hand he was by nature impetuous and volatile. In the heat of an issue he was seldom coldly deliberate.

But the 'savaging' by Massingham, especially the leader of 6 October, was an important factor (perhaps 'the decisive factor') in Rosebery's decision to resign the Party leadership. This he did on 6 October, the very day of the *Chronicle* leader. He had little confidence in Harcourt. This was emphasised by Munro Ferguson, Rosebery's

[1] Stansky, *Ambitions and Strategies*, 209–11.
[2] *D.C.*, 6 Oct. 1896, p. 5.
[3] Stansky, *Ambitions and Strategies*, 212, and James, *Rosebery*, 391; James concludes that the *D.C.* article was the decisive factor.

Parliamentary Secretary, in a letter to Campbell-Bannerman on 12 October. Ferguson added, 'The *Chronicle* has irritated R. but he did not give any importance to its action alone. Our press, however, what there is of it, was v. lukewarm.'[1] A letter from Lady Betty Balfour, Arthur Balfour's sister-in-law, whose information came from Margot Asquith, said that 'apparently resentment of Harcourt's behaviour, & the attitude of the *Daily Chronicle* were the two things which decided Lord R'.[2] Rosebery himself made no reference, in correspondence, to the *Chronicle*. But there was Gladstone. Rosebery wrote Asquith: 'I consider that Mr Gladstone's return to public life is the last straw on my back, for it gives . . . all the disloyal intriguers in the party a shelter and a rallying point.' And he wrote in much the same vein to Gladstone himself.[3] D. A. Hamer in his recent study of Liberal politics emphasises Gladstone's role, but also points out that Massingham capitalised on that role. Rosebery's decision to resign came shortly after he had read the *Daily Chronicle* on Harcourt. This perhaps was the precipitating cause.[4]

Surprisingly, the *Daily Chronicle* leader (8 October) on Rosebery's resignation was mild, remarking that Rosebery's work for his country was not yet finished and suggesting that he had stressed perils which might attend any British action in support of treaty obligations. But a strong leader on 9 October declared that the attempt to lead the Progressive forces of the nation from the House of Lords had failed. Presumably Massingham wrote those leaders. There is no question that the *Daily Chronicle* comment on Rosebery's Edinburgh Speech of 9 October was from Massingham's pen. That speech was Rosebery's valedictory. Some have said he held his vast audience in thrall as he said that perhaps Gladstone had been 'the latest indirect cause' for his resignation. And then he proceeded to laud Gladstone. He declared that intervention by Britain alone in the Armenian Question was impossible. And that he had resigned for the sake of party unity.

The *Daily Chronicle* on 10 October carried a news story under the

---

[1] Campbell-Bannerman papers, Munro-Ferguson to Campbell-Bannerman, 12 Oct. 1896, Add. MS. 41,222/264–5.
[2] Lady Betty Balfour to Mrs Barbara Webb, as quoted in James, *Rosebery*, 393–4.
[3] Stansky, *Ambitions and Strategies*, 212–13.
[4] D. A. Hamer, *Liberal Politics in the Age of Gladstone and Rosebery* (Oxford, 1972), p. 256.

heading: 'ATTACK ON MR. GLADSTONE', and put side by side a statement made by Rosebery in July 1895 advocating a strong policy against the Sultan with his statement at Edinburgh that Britain cannot let a matter like the Armenian slaughter control British foreign policy, when in importance it is in the proportion of 1 to 999.[1] The leader must be quoted.

Lord Rosebery has cleared the air. For purposes of Liberal statesmanship he has cleared it of Lord Rosebery. It is the first genuine revelation of his personality and character... The Edinburgh speech was an attack on Gladstone. The *Daily Chronicle* can only regret that Liberalism has been associated with a personality so out of sympathy with its spirit.

And a day or so later the *Chronicle* returned to the attack saying that Rosebery's utterance was a powerful speech 'against the whole body of humanitarian doctrine'. 'His swan song as a Liberal leader is an assertion of the impotence of his country to take an effectual share in the solution of the greatest problem of European statesmanship.'[2]

All this seems straightforward enough. But the fact is that Henry Norman, the assistant editor, had quite different opinions on Armenia and on Rosebery and stated his views in the periodical *Cosmopolis* in a manner he could not well do in the *Chronicle*. Back in the January 1896 issue of *Cosmopolis* he declared bluntly 'that all the Armenians in existence are not worth the risk to the freedom of mankind of England being reduced to the level of a second rate power' should she intervene alone and confront a coalition of other powers. And now in the November *Cosmopolis*, writing under the date of 22 October, Norman declared that Rosebery's Edinburgh speech 'which, to be appreciated, had to be heard as well as read – was in my mind the ablest and most statesmanlike British utterance on foreign affairs since I began to take an interest in such matters'.

Now Norman *had* heard the speech – from a seat on the platform. He had already attracted Rosebery's attention by his pronouncement in the October *Cosmopolis* on the current situation:

---

[1] This was not quite what Rosebery said. The relevant remark was 'The policy of this country consists, if you like, of a thousand portions or a thousand interests, and we cannot allow nine hundred and ninety-nine of those portions or interests to be sacrificed, to the remaining one, however important that one may be.' *Lord Rosebery's Speeches* (*1874–1896*) (London, 1896), 426.

[2] *D.C.*, 10 Oct., p. 12.

What can England do? So far as my limited judgment goes, she must for the present hold her war dogs in leash. I should regard an understanding with Russia as the best of all possible solutions, and if Lord Rosebury had not been turned out by a chance vote upon an absolutely insincere issue I believe we should have had this before now.

Quite understandably this brought a note to Norman from Rosebery, dated 2 October: 'I have read with great pleasure your brave and able article.' And quite as understandably Norman was provided with a chair on the platform in Edinburgh for Rosebery's 9 October speech. West adds a nice touch, which must have intrigued him. He records that 'we heard that Massingham was with Harcourt at Malwood'. This is quite unconfirmed.[1]

Norman did send a news report of that speech to his chief, and this appeared alongside Massingham's leader. Stead's *Review of Reviews*, hitherto consistently friendly toward Massingham, must have received some inside information, perhaps from Norman. Its comment expressed outrage. Lord Rosebery's speech

was described in the *Daily Chronicle* with a licentiousness of misrepresentation, happily rare in the English press, as an attack upon Mr. Gladstone. The description was so monstrous, that in order to give it any colour, the report of the *Chronicle*'s own representative at Edinburgh was mutilated so as to make his description accord with the editorial calumny.[2]

Norman was driven to further action. He wrote to Rosebery on 13 October:

I think it right to tell you what action I have taken with regard to the *Chronicle*.
I have written to Massingham telling him that it is impossible for me to change my opinion upon the present matter of policy and personality at issue, or to modify my public expression of them, and that if he considers the fact . . . to prejudice him or the *Chronicle*, he must accept my resignation.

A few days later Norman wrote again:

The *Chronicle* will not let me go. I stay with my own view and my own freedom of independent utterance. This incident is therefore closed, and I beg of you to dismiss it from your mind. I would not for the world cause Massingham the embarrassment of letting it be known.

[1] R.P. (Letter Book); *Private Diaries of Algernon West*, 331.
[2] *Review of Reviews* (English edition), XIV (16 Nov. 1896), 390. Similar account, with some alteration, is in American edition, Dec. 1896.

There is no evidence that it did become generally known. Probably, so far as the columns of the *Daily Chronicle* were concerned, the issue was soon blurred. In his letter of 16 October to Rosebery, Norman was able to say:

If you have read the *Chronicle* lately you will have noticed a very distinct – and to me most welcome – change of tone. I think I may say now that these later utterances represent Massingham's views upon reflection and consideration. I do not think he would be disposed now to defend his first comments upon your speech.

Rosebery responded (25 October):

I ought long ago to have thanked you for your two letters. The first indeed made me uneasy, for I feared that you might be called on to make a sacrifice, of which I should have been the indirect and innocent cause. I am however greatly relieved to find that you will be able to continue your connection on the *Chronicle*. . .[1]

We are able to carry the Massingham–Norman encounter no further. Canon MacColl, however, remained much in evidence. In January he was still contributing articles to the *Chronicle* on the Eastern Question, 'putting as much meaning into Lord Salisbury's despatches as they can possibly bear', trying to make out that Salisbury was on the Gladstonian side of the issue.[2] But by this time Salisbury had dismissed the Armenian Question and attention had shifted to Crete.

In the Armenian Crisis the *Daily Chronicle* played a strong, important, even a sensational role. But in the matter of Crete, 1896–7, the *Chronicle* never had the story quite right. And its policy to encourage Greek support of Cretan independence won little favour. The Cretan Rising in the spring of 1896 ended when the warships of the Powers arrived to cut off aid from the Greek mainland. On 5 August the *Daily Chronicle* published an ill-founded rumour that the status of Crete was being discussed by the Sultan and Salisbury, who would depend on France for support and wanted nothing to do with the concert of Europe. In truth, at this time Salisbury had in mind working out a common policy with Russia through the concert of Europe, and his design was reinforced by the exigencies of the Armenian Question.

[1] R.P., for Norman–Rosebery correspondence.
[2] Russell (ed.), *MacColl: Memoirs and Correspondence*, 176, 183–4.

His circular of 20 October outlined a proposal for intervention by the Powers to enforce reforms in the Ottoman Empire. Ambassadorial conferences on reform ended abruptly with the Cretan Rising in the spring of 1897 and the ensuing war between Greece and Turkey. The Greek cause was at once hopelessly lost and only peace terms forced upon the Sultan by the Powers prevented a catastrophe.[1] An agitated *Chronicle* was no boon to the Greek cause. As the Cretan Crisis developed in February, Henry Norman was in Athens, interviewing King George, and in his despatches reiterating day after day the Greek determination to support Crete's dreams of total independence.[2] His assessment of Greek and Turkish policy was often incorrect. *Daily Chronicle* leaders steadily pleaded for support of Greek intervention and Massingham turned repeatedly to Gladstone who first calmly replied that Britain should not encourage Greek military action when it was impossible to aid her and then apparently made no answer whatsoever.[3] Other elements of the Liberal press, notably the *Daily News* and the *Westminster Gazette*, supported the Government. Stead's *Review of Reviews* admitted loss of confidence in the *Daily Chronicle*.[4] Altogether, a combination of inaccuracy (some said irresponsibility) and unpopularity for a time injured its reputation.

'Gladstonian Liberal'

In searching for Massingham's political attitudes from 1897 to 1899, we are often at a loss. 'House and Lobby' is not now his column and his leaders are unsigned. Except for his summary of Liberal politics of 1896, written in 1897, he has nothing to say, outside the columns of the *Chronicle*, until November 1899. We have infrequent glimpses of his activity, only an occasional letter of significance, and the general tone of the *Daily Chronicle*.

How, then, to define his political outlook? During the *Star* years he was an ardent Liberal, an ardent Progressive and an ardent Radical. But his one venture into organised Socialism – Fabianism – ended

---

[1] Grenville, *Lord Salisbury and Foreign Policy*, 74–84. Cf. C. J. Lowe, *Salisbury and the Mediterranean, 1886–1896* (London, 1965), 99ff.

[2] D.P., Norman to Dilke, 23 Feb., 1897, Add. MS. 43916/6–7.

[3] G.P., Add. MS. 44525/97, 102, 155–6.

[4] Ernest Gale in *Cosmopolis*, VI (Apr. 1897), 86–7. *Review of Reviews* (English edition), XV (Mar. 1897), 208.

when a matter of tactics came forward. He could not abide strategy of any kind. And Liberalism, in spite of Gladstone's personal victory in 1892, became steadily less articulate, less unified, and less effective. Now at the end of 1896 with the Tories supported by Liberal Unionists solidly in power and with no General Election in sight, with Gladstone out of the picture and Rosebery a bitter disappointment, what did the future hold?

Massingham's own answer is neither optimistic nor aggressive. Liberalism, he says, survives only 'as a critical force'.

What, therefore, seems to be required of Liberalism is a service of more efficient, more adroit, and more commanding talent than its opponents possess, the assertion of the principles that underlie the wise, humane, free government of the modern State, and the realisation of the old Liberal watchword Liberty, for the workers and the non-possessing classes.

Liberals have failed, he recognises, in their search for solutions to problems. He ticks them off – workmen's accidents, taxation, land, old-age pensions, payment of members, suffrage, Lords' veto, education.[1] Later, in 1897, the *Chronicle* declared that a progressive Liberal Party should be the result and not the cause of intellectual change. 'There is nothing so important now as that the party of progress should find out what it means, what it believes, what it wants.'[2]

From 1895 to 1899 the *Daily Chronicle* rings the changes on the idea of a revivified Liberal Party. It must be a 'new party' with 'a new programme'. The Party must address itself 'to the great common life of all the people, the attainment of a certain level of moral strength, mental activity and physical well being'. Such shallow thoughts (one can hardly call them ideas) are a journalistic response to a political situation. Ideas about society germinate elsewhere, in the atmosphere of such groups as the Rainbow Circle and the London Ethical Society, and to such as these Massingham was never attracted.

Where to turn for a hero after Gladstone and Rosebery? Of course there was John Morley; but for him Massingham's respect was often matched by a difference of opinion. The *Chronicle*'s unreserved admiration was for Leonard Courtney, M.P., but now a Liberal Unionist.

---

[1] Whelen (ed.), *Politics in 1896*, 77–9.
[2] Weiler, 'Liberal Social Theory in Great Britain', 129. I have relied heavily on Weiler's digest of editorial comment in the *D.C.* during the years 1896–9.

Massingham would certainly have liked to see him back in the Liberal fold. For more immediate results he seems to have turned to the young Welsh Radical, David Lloyd George, who had entered the Commons in 1890. There must be a story behind and beyond a letter he wrote to his wife, on 9 September 1897: 'Saw Massingham (*Daily Chronicle*) last night. He is anxious I should take in hand the resurrecting of the Liberal Party & do what Lord Randolph Churchill did for the Tory Party. He says I am the man to do it & he'll back me through thick and thin. I told him I would do it provided we could agree on a definite line of policy.' We know that Massingham had been championing the cause of the Welsh quarrymen, in their contest over unionism with Lord Penrhyn, owner of the Bethesda slate quarries. In January 1897 Massingham had conferred with officials of the union along with Lloyd George and other Welsh Liberal M.P.s, and Massingham's efforts on behalf of the quarrymen were long remembered.[1] The Massingham–Lloyd George association had begun.

Of course it was easier to find fault than to find new ideas and new leadership. Liberal Party organisation, particularly the National Liberal Federation (N.L.F.), was under constant attack from the *Chronicle*. The N.L.F. should be more representative of the rank and file of the party. To bourgeois freedom the Party must add working-class freedom. And the N.L.F. should encourage working-class candidates for Parliament within the Liberal Party. But such admonition from the *Chronicle* implied no support for a Labour Party. 'There is no future for the Independent Labour Party if the Liberal Party can transform itself into a genuinely democratic and effective party.'[2]

It may be recalled that in 1892 Massingham had written that the *Daily Chronicle* 'may remain a paper with a mission, but without a client'. Ties with the Liberal Party were growing slender. Of course it was Shaw who said it quite simply and directly when he noted that the *Chronicle* was 'pegging away fairly hard just now at the incompetence of both sides'.[3]

---

[1] Kenneth O. Morgan (ed.), *Lloyd George Family Letters 1885–1936* (London, 1973), 112, 109; *Welsh Gazette*, 12 Sept. 1924.

[2] Weiler, 'Liberal Social Theory in Great Britain', 106–7.

[3] G.B.S.P., Add. MS. 50557, personal memo endorsed: 'August 1898: Shaw report on Manifesto'. R. Spence Watson, *The National Liberal Federation 1877–1906* (London, 1907) makes no reference to the *Star*, the *Daily Chronicle* or Massingham.

In London politics, to be sure, Massingham continued to throw his energies into the Progressive cause. But it must be quickly added that, in order to win back the working-class vote lost in the previous County Council election, Progressivism had emancipated itself from the Liberal Party. Well before the polling in March 1898 Massingham had discussed the problem with John Burns and Robert Blatchford. He was again on friendly terms with the Webbs. The *Chronicle* electioneered for the Progressives and advised voting a straight ticket.[1] In the result the Progressives recouped their previous losses, gaining some 18 seats, emerging with 80 seats out of 118.

Massingham found no occasion for similar satisfaction at Westminster. There was no 'Liberal cause'. This is apparent as we examine some matters of national concern. One is the changing character of the T.U.C. In 1895 its Parliamentary Committee proposed new standing orders by which delegates would cast a vote in proportion to the affiliated membership of their society; trades-councils delegates would be ineligible since their membership was incorporated in unions, and to qualify as a delegate one must be either working at a trade or be a union official. These proposals were in the interests of the large unions and the Congress would thus be more representative of the total membership though less representative of the varied interests and points of view in the Labour Movement.

At first the *Daily Chronicle* supported the proposals – they were favoured by John Burns and represented a victory for the Liberal Party.[2] But we find detachment and independence in comment after formal adoption of the new regulations by the Congress on 3 September. The next day, the *Chronicle* said

We are afraid that yesterday's doings at Cardiff are a setback, and that they may spell trouble for the understanding between workers of all grades that has given hope and life to the Labour Movement and the politics of the last six years.

The *Daily Chronicle* was closely associated with the Workmen's Compensation Bill of 1897, brought forward by the Salisbury Government as an alternative to the Employers' Liability measure which the

[1] Blatchford to Burns, 28 Feb. 1897, B.P., Add. MS. 46287/202; Webb, *Our Partnership*, ed. Drake and Cole, 145; *D.C.*, 3 and 4 Mar. 1898.
[2] B. C. Roberts, *The Trades Union Congress, 1868–1921* (London, 1958), 153.

Liberals had failed to pass in 1893–4. While the measure was largely uncontested in Parliament, it did encounter opposition from the trade unions. Joseph Chamberlain, sponsoring the measure, reported to the Cabinet in February 1897 that the advocacy of the measure by the *Daily Chronicle* 'has made some impression on Trades Union leaders'. When the measure was before the Commons, Massingham gave solid support and referred to Chamberlain's leadership as 'arbitrating, conciliating, reconciling warring interests and stamping the whole proceedings in the House with that spirit of clear and precise bargaining which has always been Mr. Chamberlain's note in politics'. After the measure had passed its second reading, Massingham wrote to Sir Charles Dilke: 'Great triumph for J. C. this Bill. He's a queer dog.' The measure became law on 6 August.[1]

A historian has described the dispute in the engineering industry, from 1897 to 1899, as 'the greatest head-on clash which had ever occurred in British industry on the prerogative of management within the workshop'. Contrary to the press generally, the *Chronicle* was favourable to the union position. Massingham was kept well informed by Burns who was closely associated with George Barnes, the new secretary of the Amalgamated Society of Engineers.[2]

Such matters, significant as they are in themselves, assist us little in attempting to categorise the policy of the *Chronicle* and the outlook of Massingham. It is perhaps of more consequence to reflect that on Gladstone's death in 1898 Massingham wrote a summary of his life and career,[3] published by the *Illustrated London News*, then edited by Clement Shorter. Massingham's attachment to his political heroes was usually short-lived, but for Gladstone there is a loyalty which is steadfast. Certainly Massingham quoted Gladstone more often than any other politician[4] and so it is not surprising that Massingham's Liberalism in the 1890s is often described as 'Gladstonian'.[5] For one

---

[1] J. L. Garvin, *The Life of Joseph Chamberlain*, III (London, 1934), 156–8. D.P., Massingham to Dilke, 27 May 1897, Add. MS. 43916/31. See also Harold Spender, *Fire of Life* (London, 1926), 89.

[2] R. D. Clarke, 'The Dispute in the British Engineering Industry 1897–98', *Economica* (May 1957), pp. 128, 134; B.P., Burns Diary, 1, 6, 14 Jan. 1898, Add. MS. 46316.

[3] *Life and Political Career of Gladstone*.

[4] E.g., 'Parliamentary Sketch', *Manchester Guardian*, 14 Apr. 1900.

[5] G. P. Gooch, *Under Six Reigns* (London, 1958), 79; Jeffrey Butler, *The Liberal Party and the Jameson Raid* (Oxford, 1968), 224; Lucy Masterman, 'A Pilgrim of Eternity', *Weekly Westminster* (13 June 1925).

thing they were much alike in spirit – evangelicalism was as strong in Massingham's 'religious intervals' as in Gladstone's orthodoxy. Neither was intellectual in his attitude toward politics – neither owed any debt to the philosophical radicals. In theoretical terms, Liberalism meant Liberty – freedom of the individual and not much more need be said. In principle they were alike in favouring complete freedom of worship, freedom of trade, freedom for the worker and the employer alike. Conscience was one's guide and opportunity was a call to action. Massingham, like Gladstone, was a moralist and not a politician. Each had a distaste for dogma and Party organisation and thus for class divisions in society. So they distrusted Labour politics. They opposed intervention abroad except when conscience was aroused. They were generally hostile to Imperialism but sympathetic when it was 'responsible'. All told, it is worthy of note that when the Liberal Party faltered in the late 1890s Massingham, instead of moving to the left in the direction of Labour politics, retreated into a shadowland without borders and a guiding light.

Liberal Imperialism – exit from the 'Daily Chronicle'

In 1896, in the three controversial areas of foreign policy, the Liberals 'practically represented the policy of England' – wrote Massingham. While the statement holds up for Venezuela, for Armenia it is nonsense. As for the third area, South Africa, we note first, with something of a start, in a popular account of the Edwardian years, that the idea of Liberal Imperialism was launched in the columns of the *Daily Chronicle*.[1] Now this statement is not without substance. When the *Chronicle* helped propel Rosebery into high office his association with the idea of Imperialism was no barrier. Furthermore in the 1890s Massingham had great respect for and considerable association with two other future 'Limps' – Haldane and Asquith. Haldane was something of a confidant during the dark days after the Election of 1895 and Asquith was regarded by Massingham as one of the ablest of the younger members of the last Cabinet. For Sir Charles Dilke Massingham had even higher admiration. Had he preserved his correspondence we might well have the details of an interesting story.

[1] Whelen (ed.), *Politics in 1896*, 48; W. Macqueen Pope, *Twenty Shillings in the Pound* (London, 1949), 349.

In connection with the Jubilee of 1897 the *Daily Chronicle* ran a series of articles under the general heading 'Sixty Years of Empire'. The second article, 'The Growth of Greater Britain', by Dilke was received by Massingham with great enthusiasm and satisfaction.[1] And again, Dilke's 'responsible imperialism' and his support from the *Chronicle* is apparent in his clash with Curzon in April 1897 in the Commons over slavery and cannibalism in the native army of the Congo Free State.

In the middle nineties W. T. Stead's enthusiasm for Rhodes and a 'responsible' Imperialism – Stead's language was similar to Dilke's – in no way interfered with his friendly relation with Massingham. When Chamberlain went to the Colonial Office in 1895 Massingham interviewed him and subsequently wrote in the *Chronicle*, 'Perhaps the most interesting experiment in administration which has ever been tried in this country will be Mr. Chamberlain's management of our Colonial Empire.'[2]

And it is interesting to follow the *Chronicle*'s statements on the South African Crisis as it developed. While denouncing the Jameson Raid as 'a lawless expedition', the *Chronicle* declared that Chamberlain acted like a statesman in promptly dissociating the Government completely and in calling on the British South African Company to repudiate the raid.[3] While the parliamentary inquiry was in progress Massingham wrote Stead that he still, as always, maintained that neither Chamberlain nor Robinson (High Commissioner in South Africa) had been 'privy' to the Raid. And when Chamberlain, on 26 July 1897 virtually repudiated the censure of Rhodes in the Committee Report which he had signed, Massingham displayed little concern. The *Chronicle* comment was almost certainly written by Massingham, for its tone and language were similar to that of his remarks to the Webbs. The *Chronicle* referred to 'the marvelously clever and adroit speech' of Chamberlain 'which ends the matter'. To the Webbs Massingham spoke of Chamberlain's 'superb rope walking'. His career 'is extraordinarily interesting – every day brings its own trick'. He was not a statesman, but merely 'a great political artist'.[4] It may well be that

[1] *D.C.*, 7–30 June 1897; D.P., 27 May 1897, Add. MS. 43916/31.
[2] *D.C.*, 27 Nov. 1895; Garvin, *Chamberlain*, III, 28.
[3] *D.C.*, 2 and 3 Jan., and 7 Feb. 1896.
[4] Massingham to Stead, 31 Mar. 1897 (courtesy J. O. Baylen). *D.C.*, 27 July 1897, p. 6. Webb, Diary, 30 July 1897 in *Our Partnership*, ed. Drake and Cole, 143. When the inquiry was renewed in January 1900, the *Chronicle*, now out of Massingham's hands, was more critical of Chamberlain. See Garvin, *Chamberlain*, III, 554.

Massingham was somewhat influenced by his enthusiasm for the Workmen's Compensation Bill, sponsored by Chamberlain, in its final legislative stages at this time.

In other respects the *Chronicle* at this time does not bear the marks of a strong foreign policy in opposition. Imperialist diplomacy seemed to be accepted, as, for example, in the possibility, in March 1898, of a tripartite agreement among Britain, Germany and the United States to check France in Africa, Russia in China, and Spain in Cuba.[1] A few months later, as the Fashoda Crisis was shaping up, and many Liberals were looking to their leaders for guidance, the *Chronicle* treated the matter conventionally. The issue for 17 September 1898, ran a large map, two-thirds of a page in size, with an accompanying article, 'Where Two Nations Meet: the Position at Fashoda'. It was just at this time that Henry Fowler spoke of the 'cant' of the *Chronicle* in its complaints about Liberal leadership.[2] Massingham's conception of anti-Imperialism, like Gladstone's, was 'flexible'.[3]

On 8 December 1898 Harcourt resigned Liberal Party leadership and on 17 January following, Morley resigned from the Liberal Front Bench. Both acted in opposition to the prevailing sentiment in the Party supporting Imperialist policies. A leader in the *Daily Chronicle* for 6 December, critical of Party leadership, was apparently the precipitating factor in Harcourt's action.[4]

A *Chronicle* leader for Tuesday, 20 December, cautiously discussed party differences over Imperialism: 'We do believe it is the business of the Liberal Party to concern itself with the Empire, and that there is a right kind of imperialism which is essential to a just conception of the duty of an English Government.' This prompted a letter from Harcourt to Morley, 21 December, that 'friend Massingham has discovered . . . that the opinion of the Provinces is not for, but against, imperialism'. Both Harcourt and Morley regarded their position 'as a stand against a Jingo invasion of the Liberal Party'.[5] The *Daily Chronicle* was somewhat suspicious of Harcourt's intentions and remarked on 18 January

---

[1] *D.C.*, 8 and 14 Mar. 1898 as cited by Simon Maccoby, *English Radicalism, 1886–1914* (London, 1953), 257.
[2] Butler, *The Liberal Party and the Jameson Raid*, 223.
[3] Stansky, *Ambitions and Strategies*, 298.
[4] *Ibid.*, 262, 265–75.
[5] Gardiner, *Harcourt*, I, 477.

that it was unfortunate that Harcourt and Morley were 'standing aloof from the party'.

On 6 February 1899 Sir Henry Campbell-Bannerman was elected Party leader in a meeting of Liberal M.P.s at the Reform Club. On Imperialism he had been considerably closer to Rosebery's position than Harcourt. But Massingham was finding a new hero. On 17 January he wrote Campbell-Bannerman that there was 'a quite unanimous feeling of approval' for him as the new Party leader. And Massingham asked for a statement he might print. Accordingly, on 21 January the *Daily Chronicle* reported that Campbell-Bannerman would accept. Soon, on 24 February, circumstances forced the new Liberal leader to declare himself in the Commons on Imperialism – the issue which divided the Party. On Morley's motion attacking the Government position in the Sudan C.B.'s remarks were cautiously and adroitly middle-of-the-road but he voted for the Morley motion. The *Daily Chronicle* expressed satisfaction.[1] If C.B.'s attitude was indecisive, so at this point was the position of Massingham, as we shall now see as we turn in some detail to the crisis in 1899 in South Africa.

On 21 November 1899 the *Daily Chronicle* carried a leader critical of Government policy in the South African War. The day following, a leader wholeheartedly supported the Government. Between these issues, on 21 November Massingham, along with Harold Spender, the parliamentary reporter, and Vaughan Nash, the labour expert, resigned – a landmark in Massingham's career.

It invited comment. Rosebery could not refrain from writing J. A. Spender: 'The *Chronicle* sheds its chiefs almost as often as the Liberal Party.' J. L. Hammond, new editor of the *Speaker*, remarked, sympathetically, that it would 'be the death of the D.C.' And L. T. Hobhouse commented: 'The men who have constituted the character of the paper have left it.' Beatrice Webb, probably not so sympathetically, noted that 'Liberals of all types are depressed and uncertain of

---

[1] Massingham to Campbell-Bannerman, 17 Jan. 1899, Campbell-Bannerman Papers, Add. MS. 41234/67b. J. A. Spender, *The Life of the Right Hon. Sir Henry Campbell-Bannerman* (2 vols., Boston, 1924), I, 224–5. Late in January Massingham and Morley were invited to dinner by Frederic Harrison. Harrison to Morley [Jan. 1899], Harrison Papers, B.L.P.E.S. Unfortunately the record stops there.

themselves.'[1] Hobson in the *Speaker* (9 December) summarised its effect on journalism. The London daily press

is now virtually unanimous on the side of Mr. Rhodes... Any debate remains represented in London by the *Morning Leader*, the *Westminster Gazette* and the *Star* ... ridiculously outnumbered by the solid phalanx of the entire morning penny press.

Massingham resigned from the editorship of the *Daily Chronicle* rather than support the Boer War – no incident in his career is better known than this. In November–December 1899 his position seemed unequivocal – a ringing dissent from British policy in South Africa. What was little emphasised then and largely forgotten thereafter is that with the outbreak of war in October 1899 his views changed – prior to that he had not been hostile to official policy toward the Boers. Harold Spender later tells us that 'Mr. Massingham was not always a determined supporter of the Boers.' On 26 November 1899 Hobhouse wrote to C. P. Scott, who opposed the war, that 'it was [Harold] Spender who converted Massingham to the right view & Massingham went into it at last with the zeal of a convert'. Just the day before Hobhouse had the story from Spender.[2]

And so we retrace our steps in an effort to follow Massingham's change of heart and mind. Once again we encounter the anonymity of the columns of the *Daily Chronicle*. We do know that as the South African Crisis developed Massingham had been charitable, even friendly towards Chamberlain, that he had little enthusiasm for the political stance of Harcourt and Morley who had led the anti-Imperialist sentiment in the Liberal Front Bench and that he welcomed to Liberal leadership Campbell-Bannerman who had generally supported Tory colonial policy. Another factor, easily disregarded, is that the period between the Jameson Raid and the outbreak of war was not, with some exceptions, one of strong views on South Africa passionately held.

[1] Rosebery to Spender, 25 Nov. 1899, as in Wilson Harris, *J. A. Spender* (London, 1946), 105. Hammond to Hobhouse, 5 Dec. 1899, J.L.H.P. Hobhouse to C. P. Scott, 26 Nov. 1899, Scott Papers, Manchester (courtesy Trevor Lloyd). Webb, *Our Partnership*, ed. Drake and Cole, 190.

[2] Spender, *Fire of Life*, 97. Vaughan Nash, in his account of the episode in *H.W.M.* says nothing of Massingham's change of heart. For Hobhouse letter, Scott Papers, Manchester (courtesy Trevor Lloyd). For characteristic reference by historians to Massingham's role, see John Wilson, *CB: A Life of Sir Henry Campbell-Bannerman* (London, 1973), 301–2, 309.

Among politicians, and journalists as well, there was much shifting of position. The attitude of much of the press, including that called 'Liberal', was ill-defined. Horace Seymour, who had been Private Secretary to W. E. Gladstone, wrote Herbert Gladstone in April 1899 a word of congratulation on being made Liberal Party Chief Whip. He added 'There is not a single Liberal daily now worth the name. The *Daily News* is beneath contempt and the *Chronicle* only a shade better'.[1]

However, careful examination of the *Daily Chronicle* during the months immediately preceding the war, reinforced by Nevinson's diary, reveals sharp differences within the staff. From June 1899 Nevinson is increasingly critical of the developing crisis in the Transvaal. On 11 July he notes that he and Spender were both forbidden to write further on that issue. During August their editor was ill, and in and out of the office. Frederic Harrison wrote Morley (1 August) that 'the *Daily Chronicle* is forming a committee to protest against war'. The columns of the *Chronicle* reveal no such committee but we do find Spender urging Nevinson to write 'a brochure for the Boers'.[2]

As we read through the *Chronicle* we often find a difference in content and tone between leaders presumably written by Massingham, and Spender's 'House and Lobby'. On 11 July an unsigned article declares:

The danger for the moment lies with the Outlanders' Committee who think that Mr. Chamberlain and Sir Alfred Milner are utterly committed to their personal objects. They think that by raising an outcry they can squeeze what they like from two such leaders.

On the other hand 'House and Lobby' (12 July), declares that Chamberlain's listing of grievances of the Uitlanders is designed to embitter feeling against the Transvaal; that of 18 July emphasises Chamberlain's condemnation of the new proposal in the Transvaal Franchise Bill; while that of 28 July declares that the second Transvaal Bluebook indicates that the Government is on the war path. But unsigned leaders continue to find moderation in British policy. 'Mr. Chamberlain has always had justice done to him in this journal for the qualities he really possesses' (10 August).[3]

---

[1] 16 April 1899, H.G.P., Add. MS. 46057/149.
[2] Harrison to Morley, 1 Aug. [1899], Harrison Papers, B.L.P.E.S. N.D., 18 Aug. 1899.
[3] See also leaders, *D.C.*, 12, 18, 28 July.

But we have a more direct confrontation, on 29 July, after a significant debate in the Commons. 'House and Lobby' speaks of the 'warlike speeches of Salisbury and Chamberlain' while a leader merely says that Government statements are ambiguous. The Government had proposed a Joint Commission representing both Britain and the Transvaal to consider a proposal for franchise reform. A leader has this to say (29 July):

Our parliamentary correspondent may well be right that it is another instance of the Government's referring every difficult question to a Commission, as an excuse for doing nothing for the moment. But we prefer to think that it is . . . a concession . . . to the great principle of arbitration which Mr. Kruger pressed so eagerly on Sir Alfred Milner and which the latter accepted as in many ways responsible and expedient.

Massingham's illness, the ban on Nevinson and Spender and Nevinson's trip to Paris from 22 to 26 August probably account for the absence of strong statements in August. But on 4 September, Nevinson notes that Massingham 'at last takes my position on the whole war'. On 6 September there appeared a leader, which we know was by Massingham, declaring that no cause for war exists between Britain and the Transvaal. To this leader Nevinson succeeded in tacking a eulogy of Morley's address (5 September) at Arbroath as 'an eloquent protest against irresponsible elements in this country goading us into war'. In response to the Boer proposals, Nevinson's leader (7 September) said they were more conciliatory than one would venture to expect. Massingham did not entirely approve of this leader.[1] But he was giving way and on 9 September there was a strong leader, almost certainly written by Massingham, deploring the situation – that Britain was about to go to war over one word, 'sovereignty'. 'We shall go to war on an issue which has been deliberately changed during the course of negotiations and we shall earn for ourselves in South Africa a heritage of hatred.' The same day (9 September) he saw Nevinson off for Southampton and a boat to South Africa.[2]

Thereafter the *Daily Chronicle* is consistently critical of the policy of the Salisbury Government. Full publicity was given to the anti-war

[1] N.D., 22–6 Aug., 4–7 Sept.
[2] N.D., 9 Sept. In 1911 Nevinson and Brailsford in discussing the issue of Women's Suffrage spoke of the 'resemblance to Pro-Boer times, [and] the chance of winning the best of *Nation* staff over'. N.D., 6 Mar. 1911.

demonstration in Trafalgar Square on 24 September, Hyndman, one of the speakers, crediting the *Chronicle* with organising the rally.[1] Campbell-Bannerman's speech on 6 October at Maidstone, declaring that war could and should be averted, was praised in a *Chronicle* leader, and even warmer words were accorded Courtney's efforts to organise anti-war feeling. Harold Spender ran (but failed) as the Liberal candidate in the by-election of Bow and Bromley – he was labelled a friend of the enemy by his opposition.[2]

By November Massingham's new policy had aroused the ire of the proprietors, headed by Frank Lloyd. It is difficult to separate the two issues – drop in circulation and revenue, and editorial policy toward the war – but the matter of principle is what was talked about. Massingham in a letter to Bryce explained it quite simply: 'I only resigned when I was peremptorily required to maintain absolute silence on the policy of the Government in South Africa until after the conclusion of the war. That was impossible.'[3]

Massingham's resignation was always explained in those terms. Spender wrote some years later: 'There was to be no more criticism of the Government as long as the war lasted. We who opposed the war on Saturday were to support it on Monday. We could not do that.'[4]

In the newspaper world Massingham's enforced departure from the *Chronicle* greatly enhanced his reputation. The Radical press was quite naturally the most eloquent. 'Scrutator' in *Truth*, seemed to have access to the facts. In three and a half columns he held forth. Massingham was 'one of the most brilliant of our journalists and a thorough going radical'. 'In the future I shall merely glance over it [the *Chronicle*] to bring home to myself to what base uses a so-called Liberal journal can be put, under the censorship of a jingo paper manufacturer who owns it.' This article was excerpted in the *St James's Gazette*, which was read by Nevinson now with the British troops under siege at Ladysmith: 'an overwhelming blow for me – all my hopes & position & power gone at once'.[5]

[1] *D.C.*, 23, 25, 26 Sept.; Chūshichi Tsuzuki, *H. M. Hyndman and British Socialism* (Oxford, 1961), 127–8.
[2] *D.C.*, 7 Oct.; Gooch, *Courtney*, 389, 393; Spender, *Campbell-Bannerman*, I, 251.
[3] 5 Dec. 1899, Bryce Papers.
[4] Spender, *Fire of Life*, 97. See also Vaughan Nash, in *H.W.M.*, 293.
[5] *Truth*, 30 Nov. 1899; *St James's Gazette*, 6 Dec. 1899; N.D., 17 Jan. 1900.

Another strong tribute came from Hammond's Radical *Speaker:*

When we recall Mr. Massingham's brilliant gifts, Mr. Harold Spender's 'House and Lobby' articles . . . and Mr. Vaughan Nash's very special knowledge . . . we realize that the proprietors are paying a very heavy price for . . . silencing the chief morning critic of the Government's blunders.[1]

Keir Hardie, hardly a close friend, called on Massingham in his Grosvenor Road home. And he wrote in the *Labour Leader*: 'Mr. Massingham is a brick', but 'the *Daily Chronicle* sinks quietly to the ooze which buried the *Daily Mail*'. Even *Justice* and the *Methodist Times*, very often at odds with the *Daily Chronicle*, had words of evident sincere regret.[2] And there was a word by Shaw: 'We . . . congratulate our friend on having refused to shout with the mob when the mob was shouting its loudest.'[3]

One of the most gratifying of the tributes must have been in the letter from E. T. Cook of the rival *Daily News*. 'In the present matter, your courage in asserting and maintaining the most honourable traditions of our profession will, I am sure, command the admiration of every journalist. They certainly command mine.'[4] The *Outlook*, a Conservative organ, was equally generous: Mr Massingham's departure is 'an indubitable loss to London journalists'. 'If he never again sat in an editor's chair, Mr. Massingham's resignation . . . would mark an epoch in British journalism. He was the first editor to give literature and art their proper place in daily journalism.'[5]

It remained for Hobson to return to reality and appreciate the irony of the situation – that Massingham and the *Daily Chronicle* had accepted British policy in South Africa before the final crisis in the Transvaal. Hobson in the *Speaker* for 9 December wrote of 'a period of rapid decay' in which the press now found itself, resulting from a 'false and artificial unanimity'. And, the interesting fact was, he continued, that before the outbreak of the war, the *Daily Chronicle* itself had participated in that 'artificial unanimity'.

---

[1] *Speaker*, 2 Dec. 1899. In unsigned articles in the *Speaker* on 'The Daily Press' throughout December, Hobson made frequent reference to the Massingham Case.
[2] 'Marxian' in *Labour Leader*, 2 Dec.; *Justice*, 2 Dec.; *Methodist Times*, 7 Dec., p. 848.
[3] Draft of a letter, undated, G.B.S.P., Add. MS. 50513/245–6.
[4] J. Saxon Mills, *Sir Edward Cook, K.B.E.: A Biography* (London, 1921), 216.
[5] *Outlook*, 2 Dec., 563–4.

In certain respects the *Daily Chronicle* years are the most representative of Massingham's characteristics and achievements as a journalist. He was S. K. Ratcliffe's 'journalist adventurer', carrying forward a paper, already transformed by Fletcher, into one of the most widely read and most influential of the London dailies. He was the Webbs' 'mercurial Massingham', a man of strong but unstable convictions. He was in and out of the Fabian Society, hot and cold towards the Webbs; he elevated Rosebery and he 'savaged' him. It was a turbulent period – a break with his editor, Fletcher, and alternate agreement and disagreement with his own assistant, Henry Norman. But in these respect Massingham is not unique as an editor, only more arresting than some of the others. He was as consistent as many of his fellow editors, notably W. T. Stead. 'Liberalism' itself was full of contradictions; as its leadership differed and quarrelled so did the so-called 'Liberal press' – the *Chronicle*, the *Daily News*, *Westminster Gazette*, the *Manchester Guardian*, the *Speaker*, and the rest. As to internal crises on the *Chronicle* staff, Norman had as much claim to the label 'Liberal' in 1896 as Massingham, and Harold Spender as much before the outbreak of the Boer War. The idea of Massingham's papers always speaking with one voice – the editor's – does not hold up. But it would seem that the *Chronicle* was most effective as a moulder of opinion when the staff *was* in agreement, as in the Venezuelan Crisis or in the break with the proprietor in November 1899. It was least effective when the staff was divided – when Rosebery was Prime Minister, and in response to the developing crisis in the Transvaal. But Massingham never loosened his hold on the helm; when this was threatened, he resigned.

It may be remembered that when Massingham became chief editor in 1895 he wrote Stead that as a journalist he preferred to write 'behind the scenes and in the dark'. This role to a large degree he played. Interesting, perhaps, but it underlines the shadowy and transitory character of the *Chronicle* years. In histories of English journalism, only as an exponent and practitioner of the 'New Journalism' is the Massingham of these years given any clear or satisfactory recognition. But what of controversies? Massingham's *Chronicle* was significant in the Venezuelan Case. This is now almost completely forgotten. Historical scholarship has brought forward Massingham's role in the rise and decline of Lord Rosebery and later in the resignation of Harcourt as

Liberal leader, but without great interest and almost with an air of disbelief. Massingham leaders on the Eastern Question – Armenia, Crete and Greece – have often been interpreted as disastrous for the cause, without recognising that they influenced the attitudes of tens of thousands of daily readers, unaware of Salisbury's despatches. In support of social legislation, the *Daily Chronicle* was of more assistance to Tory democracy than was much of the Conservative press. Massingham's 'finest hour', or so it is usually represented, came in November 1899 when he resigned rather than end his criticism of the Government. This is, of course, accurate in itself but it knows nothing of the 'flexible imperialism' reflected in hasty *Chronicle* leaders, nor of sharp differences within the staff, nor of Massingham's own mercurial mind. And while the *Daily Chronicle* often led, sometimes it followed. There was not always a clear goal. Thus it was as well with Party politics; the difference is that journalism is the more temporal and transitory, and sooner forgotten.

'Manchester Guardian', 'Daily News', 'Speaker' (1900–1907)

Massingham's reputation as a reporter and commentator reached its height during the only period of considerable length in his career when he was out of an editor's chair. This was the interval, 1900–7, between his *Daily Chronicle* and his *Nation*. He did not then indulge his preference for writing 'behind the scenes'. But he was able to give full rein to that 'quality of recklessness' which 'defied caution and deference to precedent' – as Winston Churchill put it.[1] Everything he wrote in these years, or nearly everything, can be identified – his portion of the 'London Letter' and a few 'Sketches from Parliament' in the *Manchester Guardian* in 1900, his 'Pictures in Parliament' in the *Daily News*, from 1901 to 1907; and his contributions to the *Speaker*, from 1902 to 1907. His significant writing also included articles in periodicals and 'Letters to the Editor', particularly in *The Times*. From time to time he wrote a weekly letter for the *Eastern Daily Press* in Norwich. Now in his forties he had arrived as a powerful political reporter and John Morley could remark to Hirst that while he considered J. A. Spender as the most influential of all the journalists, he regarded him 'as less brilliant and interesting than Massingham'.[2]

The beginning, however, was not auspicious. After the abrupt break with the *Daily Chronicle*, Massingham's spirit was revived by plans for a new paper, under his editorship, which would take prominent position among Liberal organs critical of Government policy in South Africa. He discussed the project, optimistically, with Dilke and Morley; he sought the aid of Bryce and approached Shaw. With Hobson's assistance he drew up a 'Prospectus' which set forth that the paper would require at least £200,000 capital. Purchase of the *Daily Chronicle* itself was suggested. In the end the matter of finance seemed insur-

[1] *Daily News*, 11 Mar. 1907.
[2] Hirst, *In the Golden Days*, 226.

mountable – Stead understood that only £40,000 was in sight by February. In spite of widespread interest, including the warm support of Liberal M.P.s such as Sir John Brunner and Corrie Grant, the idea was soon abandoned.[1]

But Massingham, Harold Spender and Vaughan Nash were promptly attached to the *Manchester Guardian*. The editor, C. P. Scott, and his chief leader-writer, L. T. Hobhouse, both confirmed opponents of official policy in South Africa, were greatly disturbed now that London was left without a strong daily paper to represent their views. They felt obligation bearing heavily on the *Guardian* and were anxious to 'get into London'. Nash was to be sent to India to investigate the problem of famine – he went at once and his articles, reprinted as *The Great Famine*, won wide attention. And they had no difficulty in agreeing on Spender to whom indeed an offer had been made the previous August – very likely because of Spender's restlessness with *Chronicle* policy at just that time. Now, in mid-December 1899, he was engaged to do 'Sketches from Parliament' (later called 'Sketches from Westminster'), a signed article.

About Massingham, Scott at first had some misgivings. While he 'is an able, versatile fellow', he wrote Hobhouse (30 November), 'his ideas of how a paper should be written are not exactly ours & he would I expect be an awkward horse to drive in harness.' It is of some interest that Scott was quite unfamiliar with Massingham's professional history before he joined the *Chronicle*, so much 'behind the scenes' had he been when with the *Star*. And he and Hobhouse had learned from Spender something of Massingham's vacillation on South Africa. One member of Scott's staff, Dibblee, opposed the Massingham appointment – he thought that Nash, while 'not such an able penman as Massingham . . . [had] more in him'. But the chief proprietor, John Taylor, favoured Massingham to do the 'London Letter', 'even at a cost of £500 a year'. His appointment began on 5 March and by April Taylor was saying to Scott that Massingham 'had certainly raised the

---

1 Morley to Harcourt, 3 Dec. 1899, Gardiner, *Harcourt*, II, 613; Massingham to Bryce, 5 Dec. 1899, Bryce Papers; Hammond to Hobhouse, 5 Dec. 1899, J.L.H.P.; *Review of Reviews*, 23 (15 Feb. 1901), 152. The Gilbert Murray Papers have relevant correspondence.

level of the London Letter and I hope before long he may enlist some useful contributors. We still want lightness and variety'.

Massingham's engagement continued until 15 January 1901. His chief assignment was the political portion of the 'London Letter', usually headed 'Our London Correspondence', a composite from several contributors. For a brief period, from 3 April to 10 April 1900, he did the 'Sketches from Parliament' in place of Spender. No Massingham comment on his *Manchester Guardian* assignment has come down to us, which in itself would indicate no great enthusiasm. And when he left in January 1901 to go to the *Daily News*, Taylor wrote to Scott that while Massingham 'really improved the London Letter . . . his loss is not irreparable'. Massingham left at the first good opportunity. He could not have relished playing second fiddle to Harold Spender. Nor did his own assignment bring out his talents. As one reads day by day the unsigned 'Our London Correspondence', one has little sense of Massingham's presence. The sections which one assigns to Massingham, while often of interest, are usually written blandly and lack what Margot Asquith referred to as his 'bitter-almond flavour'.[1]

We find more of the real Massingham elsewhere. Quite naturally, upon leaving the *Chronicle*, his mind dwelt upon dissent. Almost at once appeared in the *Speaker*, 2 December 1899, his 'The Duty of Speech'. He remarked that in eighty per cent of the Liberal Party there has been no 'factious opposition', as often charged. Instead the Liberals had been both 'prudent and patriotic'. But the Government in labelling all the opposition as 'pro-Boer' seemed to seek the very abnegation of Liberalism. And Liberals would continue to speak 'until the principles and practices of Liberal statesmanship are again applied to the situation in South Africa'.

In an even stronger presentation in the *National Review* for April 1900, on 'The Ethics of Editing', Massingham declared, in a melancholy tone, that the prosperity of the great daily papers was increasingly dependent on advertising rather than on literary qualities or editorial policy. He was inclined to believe that the editor as critic was on his

---

[1] For the *Manchester Guardian* engagement, see the C. P. Scott Papers, Guardian office, Manchester. See especially Scott–Hobhouse, and Scott–Taylor correspondence. Margot Asquith's phrase is in *Autobiography*, II, 258.

way out though he did find a hopeful sign in the increasing practice of the signed article providing the writer with independence. The signed article was to be Massingham's own salvation in the years that followed.

It is often said that the Liberal Party in its attitude towards the Boer War in 1900 was divided three ways – a considerable number of Liberal Imperialists, led by Lord Rosebury, as war-minded as the Government, a middle group critical of the Government but which reluctantly supported the war, and a smaller number of outright pro-Boers. But this distribution suggests a static situation. Except for a few of the more committed pro-Boers, attitudes were constantly shifting. And so it is not surprising that Massingham's position is not always consistent; indeed it does not always clearly emerge. In December 1899 he told a reporter from the *Outlook* that he resented the label 'pro-Boer'. On the other hand, a month later John Burns reports a conversation in which Massingham was 'confident of England losing.'[1] But such statements have full meaning only in context. Burns himself was an ardent pro-Boer, and the Massingham remark to him was made in the midst of a series of defeats in the field for Britain.

However, Massingham was uniformly critical of the jingoism and complacency which dominated the press and which seemed to him to be motivating Conservative policy. So he joined the 'International Union', formed by W. T. Stead to combat jingoism, though there is no evidence that his militancy went as far as Stead's. During the sieges in South Africa in the winter months and the hard fighting of the spring he reacted angrily to atrocity charges – such as firing on hospitals – against the Boers. In several letters to *The Times* he pointed out that the excitement of war increased the possibility of inaccurate observation and deduction, and thought it improper to argue general inhumanity from a few isolated cases of bad conduct.[2]

In the *Manchester Guardian* 'London Letter' Massingham remarked on the low esteem in which Rhodes was now held, he commented favourably on the South African side of a pre-war correspondence between the presidents of the Republics and Lord Salisbury, and was

---

[1] *Outlook*, 2 Dec. 1899, p. 564; B.P., Add. MS. 46318/5, Burns Diary, 30 Jan. 1900.
[2] Whyte, *Stead*, II, 173; *The Times*, 21 Mar. 1900, p. 12; 27 Mar. 1900, p. 13; 2 Apr. 1900, p. 2.

of the opinion that the Nottingham meeting (March 1900) of the N.L.F. did not reveal strength in the Imperialist wing of the Party – these remarks dissociate him entirely from the Imperialists of the party. So one cannot give much weight to a chance comment of F. W. Hirst on a dinner party given by John Morley which turned into a conference on 'What would be the reply to Chamberlain's Annexation policy?' Hirst notes that to his surprise Massingham was 'mealy mouthed about annexation'.[1] Possibly Massingham did not care to share the ardently pro-Boer sentiments of the others – Morley, Hirst, Lloyd George, J. L. Hammond, R. C. Lehmann.

But his respect for and confidence in the Liberal Party was at a new low ebb. The most caustic language was reserved for Rosebery who had 'made himself impossible' by his excursions into politics since 1896,[2] but others of the Party were treated almost as severely. In the *Contemporary Review* (February 1900) he wrote that the nation, 'if it is to better its ways', must recognise 'a serious falling off in the ability of its statesmen and administrators'. By June 1900 he was ready to admit that the 'Liberal Party no longer possesses the power to do what it pretends to do, namely to provide an alternative Government to the present Tory–Liberal–Unionist combination'. This was clearly evidenced in a vote on 25 July; on a motion hostile to the Government the Liberals split three ways. Thirty-five joined Campbell-Bannerman in abstaining, 31 voted for the motion, and 40 Liberal Imperialists voted with the Government. This outcome shocked Massingham.[3]

A few days later Nevinson returned from South Africa. He records in his diary that Massingham was very depressed and bitter but had taken refuge in Leo Tolstoi and was writing an essay called 'The Philosophy of a Saint'. This appeared in the *Contemporary Review* in December. Massingham, Nevinson said, 'was hardly the old editor . . . [and was] inclined to run off on side issues & to despair of the country.'[4]

By mid-September 1900 Massingham was absorbed in the 'khaki

[1] *Manchester Guardian*, 'Our London Correspondence', 7, 14, 20, 30 Mar. 1900; Hirst, *In the Golden Days*, 208.
[2] *Nineteenth Century*, XLVI (Nov. 1899), 729–33.
[3] 'Decline of Liberalism', *National Review*, 35 (June 1900), 560–8; *Manchester Guardian*, 'Our London Correspondence', 25, 26 July 1900.
[4] N.D., July 1900; 3 Aug., 16 Sept. 1900. Ten years later Massingham wrote 'Prophet and Seer – Tolstoi and his Generation', *Morning Leader*, 12 Sept. 1910.

election', the General Election which came in October. He was now a pro-Boer, or very close to it. He talked to Nevinson about 'peace at any price' and said that people were beginning to see the error of their ways. He remarked that he would not operate 'on the old D.C. lines again',[1] possibly a reference to his 'flexible imperialism' before the war. He wrote a series of articles for *Echo*, which ran from 19 September to 8 October. But his letters to *The Times* were more relevant to the immediate situation. Soon after the dissolution of Parliament (18 September) he wrote that the two major questions which divided Conservatives from Liberals were the war and Irish Home Rule. Yet, he pointed out, two prominent Liberals, H. H. Asquith and Herbert Gladstone, had virtually eliminated these matters from the Election. They represented only one section of the Party and ignored Radicals such as John Morley and John Bryce who favoured a settlement which would guarantee autonomy to the South African Republics. These Radicals, he said, constituted the fighting strength of the Party. Massingham was answered by a leader in the *Pall Mall Gazette* emphasising the divisions in the Liberal Party.[2]

Throughout November and December Massingham's letters to the editor retained prominent place in *The Times* and drew a small host of replies. Much of his ammunition was directed at the Liberal Imperialists. From one of them, Sir Edward Grey, this provoked a protest to C.B. that the 'name and action [of the Liberal Imperialists] are the natural result of men like Labouchere, Massingham and the 'Speaker' group claiming to be the only true Liberals'. For his part Massingham insisted that the Election results did not strengthen Rosebery's chances of returning to Party leadership. Massingham seemed almost unaware of the note in Rosebery's Glasgow speech (16 November) about 'national efficiency', stressing the need for modernisation of imperial institutions, linking 'true imperialism' with social reform, and emphasising Britain's obligation now that she found herself 'the foster-mother of nations and the source of united empires'. This was the approach which attracted Fabians like Shaw and the Webbs, which aroused politicians like Grey and Haldane to ecstatic enthusiasm, but which left journalists like Massingham unmoved.[3]

[1] N.D., 16 Sept. 1900.   [2] *The Times*, 20 Sept. p. 8; *Pall Mall Gazette*, 20 Sept. 1900.
[3] *The Times*, Oct.–Nov., *passim*; Wilson, *CB: A Life of Sir Henry Campbell-Bannerman*,

Massingham himself was about to move to greener pastures. In January 1901 came to fruition the idea of acquiring a daily which would be critical of Government policy in South Africa. The *Daily News* which had staunchly supported Conservative policy was purchased by a proprietary group of Liberal persuasion, including George Cadbury, R. C. Lehmann and J. P. Thomasson. Much of the prodding came from Lloyd George. An initial suggestion that Massingham become editor with John Morley as 'consulting political director' came to nothing. The new staff included Lehmann as editor, Harold Spender as assistant editor, Herbert Paul as literary editor, and Massingham as parliamentary correspondent. Now John Morley could remark to Hirst and Hammond that the *Daily News* was returning to the main stream.[1]

But the reconstructed *Daily News* had a stormy start with friction between Lehmann and D. Edwards, the financial manager, who, according to the most reliable version of the episode, wished to control editorial policy. Lehmann was eased out. Massingham sympathised with him but decided to remain. A. G. Gardiner, a young journalist, aged thirty-six, who had been with the *Daily Telegraph* in Blackburn, was appointed the new editor in February 1902, with a staff including Massingham, Harold Spender and Hammond and some younger men – C. F. G. Masterman, H. N. Brailsford, R. C. K. Ensor – all to be closely associated later with the *Nation*. But the literary editor, Herbert Paul, was soon abruptly dismissed under circumstances which elude re-examination but which Massingham called 'shocking', and the future of the paper did not look bright. Massingham somewhat doubted whether the *News* 'would ever rise to much'; he advised Nevinson, when offered the post of literary editor, to decline it, and he thought of the possibility of a twopenny independent weekly of his own.[2]

339; Bentley B. Gilbert, *The Evolution of National Insurance in Great Britain* (London, 1966), 72–3. Massingham never took 'national efficiency' seriously. See G. R. Searle, *The Quest for National Efficiency* (Berkeley, Cal., 1971), I, 169–70.

[1] The most complete account is by W. T. Stead: 'The Reconversion of the "Daily News" ', *Review of Reviews*, XXIII (15 Feb. 1901), 147–53. See also Spender, *Fire of Life*, 109, and Hirst, *In the Golden Days*, 214.

[2] *Review of Reviews*, XXIV (14 Sept. 1901), 244, and XXV (10 Mar. 1902), 227–8; Massingham to R. C. Lehmann [n.d.] (courtesy of John Lehmann); N.D., Feb.–March and 1 and 8 Apr. 1902.

If such treatment of Massingham in 1901–2 lacks something in coherence, this merely reflects his own uncertainties about the future. As it worked out he remained with the *Daily News* until February 1907 and, as a parliamentary correspondent, added to the reputation he had established with the *Daily Chronicle*. It was H. W. Massingham who was quoted, not just the *Daily News*. According to W. T. Stead he was given 'general oversight' of the parliamentary leaders. But 'Pictures in Parliament', beginning on 15 February 1901 was his great contribution. In it, he proposed, he tells us, to report what people say in Parliament, to estimate its impact, and to comment on its character (tone, appeal, intelligence, success or failure). Just how significant he was is a matter of opinion – some years later Masterman went so far as to say that Massingham's 'influence was certainly greater than that of most of the Ministers and ex-Cabinet Ministers of the time'. Masterman delineated his quality – 'a complete fearlessness, a brilliance of phrasing, a disinterestedness, and that sudden seizing of the effect of events at the moment, with all their implications, which make the difference between a first-class and second-class journalist in the extraordinarily rapid hour-by-hour changes in the discussions of parliament'.

Massingham's connection with the *Daily News* began brilliantly with his account (3 February 1901) of Victoria's funeral at Windsor. He inaugurated 'Pictures in Parliament' with a fine description, three columns in length, of the opening of the new Parliament. One might single out as well the article in the issue for 21 July 1904 describing a twenty-four hour session of the Commons. Night after night, when Parliament was in session, he wrote his sketch – one, two, often three columns – and A. G. Gardiner's famous profiles of 'Men of the Day', appeared alongside. Many voices echo Masterman's remark that everyone around Westminster who mattered read Massingham and many who knew nothing of the actual debate very largely took their opinions from him. On his death, the *Daily News* referred to 'Pictures in Parliament' as 'admittedly in its force and originality the best example of its kind that has ever appeared'.[1]

During the *Daily News* phase Massingham was also writing regularly for the *Speaker*. Established in 1890 as a Home Rule Liberal

[1] Stead in *Review of Reviews*, XXIII (15 Feb. 1901), 153; Masterman in *Nation*, 28 Apr., 1923, pp. 110–12; *Daily News*, 29 Aug. 1924.

paper to balance the *Spectator*, in 1899 it came under the editorship of J. L. Hammond and became dominated by anti-Imperial and pro-Boer Liberals, including F. W. Hirst. On its literary staff were Desmond MacCarthy and Hilaire Belloc. Its circulation was small (about 3,000 according to MacCarthy) but it was highly respected and widely read in political and literary circles. Beginning in 1900 Massingham wrote for it occasionally and his profile of Joseph Chamberlain in the issue of 12 July 1902 inaugurates a series, 'Characters in Outline' which he continued fairly regularly throughout 1902 and less frequently thereafter. In due course he assessed all the major political figures and, as one reads them today, his 'characters' stand up well.

In the summer of 1902 he was seriously considered as the *Speaker*'s editor, partly because it was thought he would bring an increase in capital. But the *Speaker* remained under Hammond. In December 1902, Massingham proposed to Lehmann, one of the proprietors, a weekly commentary on politics:

This is not done anywhere and might be a good thing . . . for it enables the writer to give the inside as well as the outside view & to sum up events in the way they are seldom done in this country. I would suggest about 1500 words which I should be willing to do for you for three guineas a week.

Lehmann highly approved and instructed Hammond to proceed.[1] 'Politics and Persons' begins on 24 January 1903, changing to 'Persons and Politics' in the next issue and continuing with short breaks now and then until March 1907 when the *Speaker* became Massingham's *Nation*. It provides us with a continuous commentary, broader in scope than the parliamentary article for the *Daily News* and of particular value in presenting Massingham's opinions when Parliament is not in session. Furthermore, in the *Speaker*, he seems to write with even greater freedom than in the *News*. In both, his comment and criticism led to lively controversy in the columns devoted to 'letters to the editor'.

But as one reads over 'Pictures in Parliament' and 'Characters in Outline' day by day, month by month, in 1901 and 1902, one is at first surprised and even disappointed. Massingham seems to lack drive, his attitudes are tentative, his over-all objectives ill-defined; he was on the

---

[1] J.L.H.P., Hammond to Hobhouse, 19 and 28 Aug. 1902. Massingham to Lehmann, 20 Dec. [1902]; R. C. L[ehmann] to Hammond, 21 Dec. 1902 (courtesy John Lehmann).

defensive. But these are the very qualities which make him credible, for these are years when politics and Government revolved around personalities and reputations rather than issues. Massingham's penetrating remark in the *Daily News*, on 13 March 1901, that 'nothing is more curious to watch than the personal currents which run athwart policy in the House of Commons', is a comment which, under ordinary circumstances, would sound conventional; in 1901–2 it has special relevance.

Another Massingham remark helps us to understand his writing during this period. At the dinner tendered him in 1907 he responded: 'I make no extravagant pretensions. I am not an idealist; I am rather an opportunist.'[1] It may seem surprising to find Massingham protesting that he was an 'opportunist' but as we have seen, his Liberalism, always expressed in general, even vague, terms, required situations, circumstances, and opportunities for expression. As the South African War was grinding to a halt there were not many opportunities to take the initiative on behalf of a weak Opposition divided against itself. But if it took time for the Liberal Party to rehabilitate itself so it took time for politicians like Campbell-Bannerman and journalists like Massingham to find firm ground on which they could stand with confidence. It is indicative of Massingham's own distance from reality that after the Election of 1900 he refused to take seriously the Liberal Imperialist wing of his Party.

Liberal leadership – old faces and new

The Liberal Party was of course struggling for its very life. The history of the 1900 Parliament 'shows to what straits a party may be reduced' writes a historian of the time. Massingham, like Campbell-Bannerman, was strongly influenced by the changing character of the war late in 1900 and in 1901 when the Boers, defeated in pitched battles, resorted to guerilla tactics and the British retaliated with systematic farm-burning and internment of Boers where resistance persisted. As early as November 1900 Massingham took the position that if the war could be continued only by such methods it should be terminated by a negotiated peace and he engaged with Lloyd George, Hammond, Hobhouse, Courtney and Bryce in preparing a memorial to present

[1] *Daily News*, 11 Mar. 1907.

evidence of the new British tactics. Campbell-Bannerman moved somewhat more slowly. While pleased with the transfer, in January 1901, of the *Daily News* to Radical control he counselled moderation in attacks on the Government.[1] But in June 1901 he left his middle-of-the-road position; after his 'methods of barbarism' speech he was a 'pro-Boer'. The Liberals now indulged in 'the war to the knife and the fork' with a series of dinners highlighted by attacks and counterattacks. Though Campbell-Bannerman won a unanimous vote of confidence on the the floor of the Commons, the party was demoralised. The low point was perhaps the session of 2 August which extended through the night until adjournment at 5.15 a.m. – at times a disorderly session if ever there was one – with Radical against Liberal Imperialist, and Irish Nationalist against nearly everyone. Sir Edward Grey was not permitted a hearing by his own party. And on Labouchere's motion to reduce Chamberlain's salary, the Liberal Front Bench walked out rather than vote. Somehow Massingham got his copy to the *Daily News*:

The night marked the last stage of humiliation for the Liberal Party. Deserted and enfeebled, its great traditions either misstated or misunderstood, it has, indeed, suffered a terrible eclipse. And over its failure Mr. Chamberlain celebrates his vulgar triumph.[2]

So fascinated was Massingham by this scene that he returned to it in his column on 6 August. He dwelt on the contrast in Chamberlain's moods – during Labouchere's bitter attack 'he looked steadily at the ceiling, his features fixed as if they were cast in stone', and a few minutes later during a temperate discussion of Malta, he was 'so smooth, so affable, so tolerant'. As to the Liberals, it was monstrous that after the whole party had sworn fealty to its chief, Campbell-Bannerman should be deserted. Why did not Grey and others mark their hostility to the Government by a hostile vote, Massingham asked? There were only two cures: '(1) the constituencies should force the hands of the members, (2) the rise of a determined and united Radical Party'.

---

[1] James F. Hope, *A History of the 1900 Parliament*, I (London, 1908), 208; J.L.H.P., Hammond to Hobhouse, 6 Nov. 1900; Spender, *Campbell-Bannerman*, I, 317–18.
[2] Hansard, *Parliamentary Debates*, Fourth Series, vol. XCVIII, cols. 1,094–224; *Daily News*, 3 Aug. 1901. In his *History of the 1900 Parliament*, Hope's only quotation from a journalist (I, 275) is the first sentence of Massingham's comment.

Liberal leaders, save Campbell-Bannerman, found no comfort in such comment from 'the Liberal press'. In December, in reporting on the conference of the N.L.F. at Derby, the secretary, Robert Hudson, wrote to Herbert Gladstone that no credence should be given the impressions recorded in the *Daily Chronicle* or the *Daily News*: 'Really the temporary suppression of both of these organs would be a great boon.'[1]

Massingham returned the hostility in full measure. He practically laughed on paper at *The Times*' remark that Rosebery could restore Liberal unity under 'the banner of imperialism'. 'Can it be seriously contended that the regular general should disband his army and seek service under the new commander especially when he learns that this is the course recommended by his enemies?'[2]

Nor did he have much more confidence in Asquith, in 1902 a vice-president of the Liberal League. His friends had watched in vain 'to see the familiar figure of the lawyer in politics develop into the statesman'. After Asquith's direct clash with Campbell-Bannerman in 1901 Massingham wrote that for Asquith to take Cabinet office would 'open a breach with the Radicals, the anti-war Liberals and the Labour Party'. And a year later, Massingham said Asquith 'wanted moral courage' when he turned over to Lloyd George the leadership of Nonconformity against the Education Bill.[3]

Concerning his old friend, Haldane, another 'Limp',

he pursues . . . an infinitely complicated series of manoeuvres for the undermining of the Liberal leadership and the substitution for existing Liberalism of Lord Rosebery and a party undistinguishable in ideas and policy from that now in power. . . His delusion is that he is supplying an alternative to the Government, when in truth he is part of the reaction.[4]

As for another vice-president of the Liberal League, Sir Edward Grey, as a Party spokesman on foreign policy he was disappointing. In the expansionist policy pursued by the Tories, where should Liberalism call 'Enough'? 'It is safe to say it will never intervene if it is in the hands of men like Grey, who identify patriotism with an uncritical temper and an unimaginative acceptance of the accomplished fact.'[5]

---

1 Mallet, *Herbert Gladstone*, 183.
2 *The Times*, 2 Jan. 1902.
3 *The Times*, 18 Oct. 1901, p. 8; *Speaker*, 1 Nov. 1902.
4 *Speaker*, 11 Oct. 1902.
5 *Ibid.*, 27 Sept. 1902.

It must have been a relief for Massingham – it certainly is for his readers – when he turned occasionally to Campbell-Bannerman for whom he had much good will. In contrast to his castigation of the president and vice-presidents of the Liberal League, he emphasised C.-B., the man who had 'simple shrewdness and definite political views'. Such a man, he said, would gather around him the elements of future power.[1] Where would these elements be found? In time Massingham had the answer. 'The centrepoint of Liberal power and activity' was, he said in 1905, 'in the young men below the gangway, especially David Lloyd George, Winston Churchill, Reginald McKenna and Walter Runciman.'[2]

In February 1901, shortly after the death of Queen Victoria and the assembly of the new Parliament, and as it so happened, just as Massingham was launching 'Pictures in Parliament' in the *Daily News*, Lloyd George, Radical member for the Caernarvon Boroughs since 1890, and Churchill, aged twenty-six, newly elected Conservative member for Oldham, shared the spotlight in the Commons and in the press. On 18 February Lloyd George made a bitter attack on methods of warfare in South Africa, and Churchill's maiden speech was in response. Massingham's comment is more often quoted than that of any other journalist. First he expressed admiration for 'Mr. George' who 'never speaks now without drawing a house'. He has 'a pleasing face, animated and expressive, with the natural refinement of the Celt . . . the power of continuous narrative and sustained argument, and above all the true Parliamentary style, simple, easy and clear'. Then Massingham turned to Churchill whose response was 'in very striking contrast'.

Mr. George has many natural advantages; Mr. Churchill has many disadvantages. . . [He] does not inherit his father's voice – save for the slight lisp – or his father's manner. Address, accent, appearance do not help him.
But he has one quality – intellect. He has an eye – and he can judge and think for himself. . . Such remarks as the impossibility of the country returning to prosperity under military government, and the picture of the Old Boers – more squires than peasants – ordered about by boy subalterns, the appeal for easy and honourable terms of surrender, showed that this young man has kept his critical faculty through the glamour of association with our arms.

[1] *The Times*, 6 Mar. 1902, p. 7; *Speaker*, 18 Oct. 1902.
[2] *Speaker*, 12 Aug. 1905.

Here was a Radical journalist admiring a Conservative M.P. and his attitude towards the war. As to Chamberlain's remarks which followed, Massingham commented: 'an able piece of debating – but . . . utterly without elevation – and in insight and breadth of treatment it was far inferior to Mr. Churchill's'. Later in the evening, we are told, Lloyd George and Churchill met for the first time.[1]

Less than a month later, Churchill again made headlines in a debate on a motion for an inquiry into the Colville Case – the conduct of a military commander. With his insistence that 'the right to select, promote and dismiss' must be left to the military authorities he saved the War Secretary and the Cabinet considerable embarrassment. Massingham was all admiration:

> To their rescue came Mr. Winston Churchill in what was certainly the ablest speech he has made since his entry into the House. . . Nothing could be more remarkable than the way in which this youth has slipped into the Parliamentary manner and has flung himself as it were straight into the mid-current of the thoughts and prejudices of the House of Commons. . . He chose on this occasion to act as the 'bonnet' of the Government, the man who should lead them out of a dangerous pass. And he did it to perfection.

Churchill wrote to his mother: 'If you read the *Daily News* or *Daily Chronicle* you will see that my intervention was by no means ineffective.'[2]

But the climax of his first session and the climactic comment of 'his faithful troubadour Massingham', came two months later when he chose to challenge proposals from his own Party made by the War Secretary for an extensive and expensive enlargement of the army. For an hour Churchill held the House in spell. Massingham called it 'uncompromising, most daring, challenging'.

> In its elevation of purpose, its broad conception of national policy, and in the noble and delicate movement of its closing sentences, I recall nothing like it since Gladstone died. And I will make two criticisms of it. The first is that it is a speech that should long ago have been delivered from our own

---

1 'Pictures in Parliament', *Daily News*, 19 Feb. 1901, in Randolph S. Churchill, *Winston S. Churchill*, companion volume 2 (3 parts, Boston, 1969), pt 1, 11–12; Violet Bonham-Carter, *Winston Churchill as I Knew Him* (London, 1965), 85. For Churchill's earlier association with the *Chronicle*, see Randolph S. Churchill, *Winston S. Churchill*, companion volume 1 (2 parts, Boston, 1967), pt. 1, 673 and pt. 2, 880.

2 *Daily News*, 13 Mar. 1901, in Bonham-Carter, *Winston Churchill as I Knew Him*, 86–7; Churchill, *Winston S. Churchill* vol. 2, 15.

benches. The second is that in the years to come its author should be Prime Minister – I hope Liberal Prime Minister – of England.[1]

Such praise was matched only by similar enthusiasm for Lloyd George who in 1902 became the champion of Nonconformity in the Commons' debates over the Education Bill. Of his speech on 8 May during a four-day debate on the second reading, Massingham's comment is often quoted. We must turn again to W. T. Stead. 'The ablest chronicler of our parliamentary debates', wrote Stead, composed a passage 'which illustrates his own powers of expression as well as the importance of the occasion in the career of Lloyd George.' Massingham wrote:

[Lloyd George's] speech was not only the most powerful he has ever delivered, but it had the high interest of being a complete and sincere self-revelation. Here was the Nonconformist attitude in its strength and its weakness. Here was an authentic voice, worthy in its way of the traditions associated with the great names of Bright and Spurgeon.

Such performances inspired Massingham's profile on Lloyd George in the *Daily News*, on 8 November 1902. He could not recall a committee debater, save Gladstone, as effective. He

resembles a figure in a well-made play; he comes upon the stage at the apt, the critical moment... Mr. George's appearance and the revival of below the gangway Radicalism... have supplied a new outlook to the dreary sameness of English politics since Mr. Gladstone's death.

When Chamberlain, in the Commons debate of 22 May 1903, linked old-age pensions to tariff reform – a review of the fiscal system would determine whether old-age pensions were possible – Lloyd George took on the Colonial Secretary directly. Massingham spoke out:

Mr. Chamberlain will not soon forget the dressing-down which Mr. Lloyd George administered to him this afternoon. And I do not think he will forget the unfeigned delight with which the majority of the House witnessed his punishment... Today he got his fall – one of the heaviest of his career. He got it from the one member of the Opposition who has never been afraid of him, and who told him the truth in words that burned through the tolerably thick covering of his self-approval and pierced him to the quick.[2]

---

[1] *Daily News*, 14 May 1901, in Bonham-Carter, *Winston Churchill as I Knew Him*, 92.
[2] *Review of Reviews*, October 1904, p. 377, for Massingham's accounts in *Daily News*, 9 May 1902 and 23 May 1903.

And soon after, Massingham urged the Liberal Party to take Lloyd George into its inner councils.[1]

'The Wearing Down of Arthur Balfour'

Meanwhile, Lord Salisbury had been succeeded as Prime Minister in June 1902 by Arthur Balfour, who promptly became a fresh target for Massingham's barbs. It would be difficult to find people more unlike than Balfour and Massingham. Balfour was above all an intellectual, worldly in outlook, a dilettante in public affairs but a shrewd politician, a man of wide interests and broad sympathies but few convictions. On the other hand, Massingham was essentially a social critic – a moralist, a crusader, intolerant of those who differed from him, with no talent for politics. Robertson Nicoll once suggested that Massingham publish his parliamentary sketches in the *News* for 1902–5 under the title 'The Wearing Down of Arthur Balfour'.[2] In the *Speaker*, however, appear the more venomous shafts. Massingham savaged Balfour as he had no one else, save Rosebery.

Just as Balfour became Prime Minister Massingham commented:

Remove Mr. Balfour from his fascinating exercises in apologetics in the House of Commons and he hardly presents himself as a political figure of definite quality and achievement. . . [He has] a dispassionate and essentially fair intellect. Only it is a mind at play, rather than at tight grips with its subject. . . [Where he] is really wanting is in practical training and in fitness for supervising a great machine, like Government by Cabinet.

With the emergence of the tariff controversy in 1903 among the Conservatives Massingham could 'remember nothing like the sudden decline in public confidence which has beset Mr. Balfour's administration'. Massingham found the Government entirely bankrupt. And by 1904, 'I see in Mr. Balfour the worst of all our prime ministers. . . Certainly he is unfit to govern the House of Commons.'[3]

But for Massingham, the opportunist, the turning-point of the Unionist Government came with Chamberlain's spectacular pronouncement, in Birmingham on 15 May, in support of import duties on food and preferential treatment for colonial trade. The controversy over Free Trade had begun. A year before when Chamberlain had

[1] *Speaker*, 30 May 1903.
[2] Lord Riddell, *More Pages from My Diary, 1908–1914* (London, 1934), 14.
[3] *Speaker*, 19 July 1902, 16 May 1903, 11 Apr. 1903, 2 Apr. and 6 Aug. 1904.

prophesied disasters 'if we do not take every chance in our power to keep British trade in British hands', Massingham commented: 'Let us, therefore, surrender our hold upon the markets of the world and drop two-thirds of our foreign trade for the sake of one-third. . . Such are the infatuate counsels that come to us from the Town Hall of Birmingham.'[1] But now Chamberlain spoke of Food Taxes, and divisions at once appeared in the Unionist ranks which the Liberal press promptly exploited. Of the Commons debate on 28 May Massingham wrote in the *Daily News*, 'Mr. Chamberlain spoke more like a Monarch than a Minister. . . It seems to me that Mr. Balfour might as well resign out of hand, and let his fearsome colleague walk straight into the Premiership.' And Massingham was electrified when Churchill and Hugh Cecil, both Conservatives, spoke out against the Colonial Secretary. But Massingham turned on the 'Limps' as well. He wrote to *The Times* that 'their desertion of Chamberlain is simply an admission that the only alternative to his policy is that of Little Englandism'. Protection, he said, was a necessary consequence of Imperialism, whether it be Conservative or Liberal.[2]

In summer of 1903 he organised a symposium of articles on Free Trade. It was to be written 'from the point of the workman as consumer and wage earner' – so he explained to Leonard Courtney whom he asked to write an introductory essay 'on the general moral, economic and political consequences of the protective system, as it affects workmen'. But Massingham wrote the seventeen-page preface himself. He insisted that Protection was directly hostile to labour and Chamberlain's only answer 'was the old and false Protectionist suggestion that high prices bring high wages in their train'. Massingham declared that both theory and practice were against such a proposition for 'no addition to the share of labour in the reward of production can come from a system which reduces the total output'. There was special interest in George Jacob Holyoake's article 'In the Days of Protection' – a working-class leader, born in 1817, Holyoake wrote this essay from his own experience.[3]

[1] Alfred M. Gollin, *Balfour's Burden: Arthur Balfour and Imperial Preference* (London, 1965), 25–6, quoting *Speaker*, 24 May 1902.
[2] Gollin, *Balfour's Burden*, 61; Massingham, 26 May, in *The Times*, 28 May 1903, p. 5.
[3] Massingham to Courtney, 15 July 1903, Courtney Papers, IX/9–10, B.L.P.E.S.; H. W. Massingham (ed.), *Labour and Protection* (London, 1903).

J. A. Spender produced for the *Fortnightly Review* (September 1903) an answer to J. L. Garvin's massive support for Chamberlain in the same periodical. About this time Massingham wrote to Spender: 'I feel impelled to write you a line to congratulate you on the really remarkable success of your Free Trade propaganda.' C.-B. himself bided his time in the Commons, avoiding divisions which would surely have gone against him and content to let time and the Chamberlain proposals divide the Conservatives. The Liberal journalists had been particularly eager for debate and attack in Parliament, but, by September, C.-B. could write: 'even . . . that fire-eater Massingham at least modified his ardour when he came to see the real bearings'.[1]

Whether modified or not, Massingham's approach was to exploit the breach in Conservative ranks. In September he was writing: 'I have never looked for any issue but the débâcle of Unionism which has actually occurred.'[2] With prospects of a General Election Massingham and Herbert Gladstone, the Liberal Whip, were again on speaking terms. At the end of October Massingham reported that he had learned by 'direct' communication that a few of the Unionist 'Free Fooders' planned to seek re-election on the issue of Free Trade alone. They could be elected, was Massingham's opinion, only with Liberal support. He considered it a risky business but felt they must be supported since their defeat would remove from the Commons strong Unionist criticism of Chamberlain. A few days later Gladstone discussed the matter with Massingham and noted that they were in agreement.[3]

The resignation from the Cabinet of the titular head of the Unionists, the Duke of Devonshire, and the strength of the Free Food League (initially some fifty-four Unionists) aroused hope of bringing together all Free Traders – Unionist and Liberal. Massingham was Churchill's source of information when he reported to Lord Hugh Cecil, a Unionist Free Trader, that the Liberals, dependent on Irish support, would accept for a time a Government under the Duke of Devonshire.[4]

[1] Spender, *Life, Journalism and Politics*, I, 112; Spender, *Campbell-Bannerman*, II, 110.
[2] *Speaker*, 26 Sept. See also 17 Oct. 1903.
[3] H.G.P., Massingham to Gladstone, 'Private', 20 Oct. [1903], Add. MS. 46042/60–3, and Gladstone Diary, 2 Nov. 1903, Add. MS. 46484/56.
[4] *Speaker*, 28 Nov. 1903. Churchill, *Winston S. Churchill*, companion volume 2, pt 1, 272.

Though these developments suggest something like political strategy, Massingham's approach to politics was generally uncompromising. Thus soon after his discussion of 'practical' politics with Gladstone and Churchill we find him writing an article, 'The Need for a Radical Party' in which he raised the issue of land reform to counter Chamberlain's cry for a protective tariff. The Radical group in the Commons, he wrote, small as it is (about a dozen) 'is the chief formative influence in English politics, and is clearly called on to mark out the line of advance'.[1]

Sometimes his inflexibility is a source of strength, as in the by-election for North East Lanark in September 1901. The local Liberal association, controlled by Liberal Imperialists, chose to run Cecil Harmsworth, owner of the Imperialist Glasgow *Daily Record*, in opposition to Robert Smillie, chairman of the Scottish miners – and this despite much protest from Liberals in Parliament and in the Press. The strong Liberal vote was split, and the Conservative candidate got in.

Massingham struck out in an oft-quoted comment:

The sooner Mr. Herbert Gladstone and his friends understand that so long as Harmsworth candidates are put in the field, they will be fought by Radical and independent candidates the better will be the prospect of averting the ruin of the Liberal Party... A few more Harmsworth candidates and Radicalism all over England, Scotland and Wales will be in flaming revolt.[2]

But Massingham never pushed Lib.-Lab. collaboration very far. To be sure in 1900 Keir Hardie sought through Massingham to secure John Burns' support for a Labour group in the Commons – nothing came of it. Massingham knew of the electoral understanding reached in 1903 between MacDonald for the Labour Representation Committee (L.R.C.) – to be the Labour Party in 1906 – and Gladstone for the Liberals whereby some thirty-five seats were to be set aside for the L.R.C. undisturbed by Liberal candidates. He was enthusiastic about the election of Will Crooks at Woolwich in March 1903, 'a dramatic conversion of a great industrial constituency to labour politics from a very tight and not over-scrupulous Conservative and capitalist

---

[1] *Contemporary Review*, 85 (Jan. 1904), 12–23.
[2] 'A Word to Parliament Street', *New Age*, 26 Sept. 1901, p. 61. See also *The Times*, 4 Oct. 1901, p. 9.

influence'. And he added: 'it ought to be the guarantee of a Labour Party in the next Parliament numbering from twenty to twenty-five members'. Little but good would come of a Socialist Party in the House of Commons. The prospect might possibly be menacing to the Liberal Party, 'but not to that more important entity, the life and ideas of Liberalism'. But in practical politics this philosophical attitude was counterbalanced by his lack of confidence in Keir Hardie and Ramsay MacDonald. Hardie, in particular, seemed irreconcilable to Liberalism.[1]

A by-election in January 1904 in Norwich, where Massingham still had close ties, offers a good opportunity for examining his attitude toward Lib.-Lab. politics. Norwich, with two seats both won by Conservatives in 1900, had been easily arranged in the Lib.-Lab. understanding of early 1903 – in the next General Election one seat would be contested by Labour, the other by a Liberal. A Norwich Liberal, A. Cozens-Hardy, wrote to Massingham that the Liberal candidate in this by-election, Louis Tillett (grandson of Massingham's old patron), had almost insisted upon this understanding as a condition of his candidacy. The Liberals hoped Labour would not contest the by-election, but Hardie wished to fight no matter what, and the local I.L.P. in Norwich insisted on running a candidate despite MacDonald's advice against it.

Massingham set forth his views in the *Daily News* for 29 December. He argued that if Liberals and Labourites quarrelled in Norwich, both sides would lose. Labour must look to a Government of Liberals and Radicals if there is to be an effective restoration of the right of combination (a reference to the Taff Vale decision). Cozens-Hardy wrote to Massingham approvingly and proposed that Tillett run unopposed by Labour in Norwich, and in return the Labour candidate at Gateshead (another by-election in January) be unopposed by a Liberal. Massingham took the letter to Jesse Herbert who sent it on to Gladstone.[2]

---

[1] Philip P. Poirier, *The Advent of the British Labour Party* (New York, 1958), 153 n. 5, 191; Frank Bealey and Henry Pelling, *Labour and Politics, 1900–1906* (London, 1958), 141; *Speaker*, 21 Mar, 18 Apr., 2 May 1903

[2] H.G.P., A. Cozens-Hardy to Massingham, 29 Dec. 1903 and Jesse Herbert to Gladstone, 30 Dec. 1903, Add. MS. 46042/40–43, 64. Bealey and Pelling, *Labour and Politics*, 241–2. At Gateshead, there was no Labour candidate; the Liberal won.

Liberal headquarters sought vainly to secure the withdrawal of the I.L.P. candidate – the Norwich by-election was regarded as very significant and Gladstone kept Campbell-Bannerman informed. Massingham, writing in the *Speaker*, held the I.L.P. responsible, emphasised the Liberal assurance that only one seat would be contested in the coming General Election, and cautioned that any serious breach between Liberals and Labour would permit the Chamberlainites to win a dozen seats or more. In the polling the Liberal candidate won a surprisingly easy victory with the Labourite a poor third. In the *Speaker*, Massingham called the result 'most satisfactory' and declared that a Liberal defeat at Norwich might have brought Lib.-Lab. war all around which would have been disastrous for Labour.[1] At the same time he had misgivings about the future of the advanced wing of Liberalism – this he voiced in the *Labour Leader* immediately after the poll in Norwich. If the Radicals lost confidence in Liberalism they would have to look to Labour, he said. But neither Keir Hardie nor Philip Snowden took this gesture very seriously – they had long known Massingham's hostility to working-class politics – and they argued that 'the Labour Movement' should go its own way.[2]

At this time, in February 1904, Massingham was approached as a prospective parliamentary candidate by the Liberals of Dundee – a unique experience for him. He reported to Gladstone that he was not particularly interested.[3] We can only wish we had knowledge of their several conferences. So far as we know he did not confer with Hardie or MacDonald. He continued to see a great deal of Burns, now more independent of Labour than ever.

The 'New Liberalism'

For the immediate future Massingham found cause for optimism not in Labour or Lib.-Lab. politics but in a revival of Liberalism. And so he turned with a new sense of purpose to the session of Parliament which opened in February 1904. It would seem that he was never happier than when looking down from the Press Gallery in the House

---

[1] Gladstone to Campbell-Bannerman, 3 Jan. 1904, Campbell-Bannerman Papers, Add. MS. 41217/73. *Speaker*, 2, 9 and 23 Jan. 1904.
[2] *Labour Leader*, 30 Jan., 6, 13, 20 Feb. 1904.
[3] H.G.P., Gladstone's Diary, Add. MSS. 46485/23 and 46484/53, 56, 59.

of Commons. His great themes now were contempt for the Conservatives, confidence in the Liberals. He commented on the opening session: 'I never saw such a woe-begone Treasury Bench as in Mr. Balfour's absence confronted the House of Commons – eloquent of the new relationship which the great Chamberlain adventure had brought about.' And Campbell-Bannerman's speech was 'perhaps the ablest and most entirely successful speech he has ever delivered'.[1] As to Chamberlain 'he has brought nothing but loss and ruin to his party'. By-elections (especially North East Lanark) reinforced, he said, the discouragement of the Protectionists. And when the parliamentary session came to an end (August) he expressed disgust with the Government – 'what with hugger-mugger in both houses and closure in one, the entire function of Parliament has this year been in abeyance'.

But the Liberal Party: 'has reorganized itself, it has attracted new recruits . . . and practically formed a new party. The outside event that has most stimulated it has been Mr. Churchill's adhesion'.[2]

To Massingham, Churchill's parting with Toryism came with his speech on 10 February 1904, in which he supported John Morley's Free Trade amendment to the Address from the Throne. Churchill declared that the distinguishing mark of a Conservative would become the willingness to work for the Chamberlain fiscal policy.' 'Some of us, will not take his terms, now or ever.' Massingham wrote in the *News* (11 February):

I have heard perhaps one or two more brilliant speeches from him in the House, but none which gave more evidence of the qualities which at such a crisis the country wants in its representatives – character, power of decision, power to see through deceptions, power to stand for a conception of what is truth, power to strike at the centre of a gross fallacy.

Then came the dramatic moment in the Commons on 29 March when some seventy or eighty Tories 'stole out . . . one by one' in the train of the Prime Minister who left abruptly when Churchill began to speak. So it seems rather anticlimactic when Massingham, in reporting the events of 31 May 1904, remarked that 'Mr. Churchill contributed the sensation by transferring his seat for an hour or so to the Liberal

[1] *Daily News*, 3 Feb. 1904.
[2] *Daily News*, 28 July and 13 Aug. 1904; *Speaker*, 13 Aug. 1904.

side.' Several months later in a full length character sketch in the *Speaker* Massingham declared that now Churchill was 'practically a confessed Radical'.[1]

With the parliamentary session opening in February 1905 Massingham spoke with confidence of a Liberal victory in a General Election which seemed imminent. 'The Government is like a rolling stone poised over a precipice.' The great stimulant in the Liberal revival, according to Massingham, was Radicalism, an idea of some excitement to him. In the next Parliament there were sure to be members hostile to local Liberal associations and critical of conventional parliamentary procedure. 'The great question is: What will the next Government attempt?' As to Labour, while it should serve as a thorn in the side of a Liberal Government, he had now even less confidence in the L.R.C., since the resolution at the Newcastle Conference of 1903 restrained all officials and endorsed candidates from identifying themselves in any way with either the Liberal or the Conservative Party.[2]

As 1905 progressed both the attack on Balfour and support for Campbell-Bannerman were stepped up. In an article on 'An Unconstitutional Minister' Massingham said that Balfour had exalted the Executive at the expense of Parliament and was governing against 'the real, if partially veiled opinion of the House of Commons and the unquestioned opinion of the country'. In another connection he asserted the Opposition would have destroyed the Conservative Government long since, had not Campbell-Bannerman often been quite alone; where, for example, had Asquith and Grey been?[3] The biographer of 'C.-B.' cites a letter of early October 1905 in which Campbell-Bannerman says, 'making the necessary discount for the kindliness of the writer', a certain article by Massingham 'contained more of what he hoped was the truth about himself than anything he had ever seen in print'.[4] In the *Speaker*, for 23 September Massingham had written:

As to the Liberal Premiership, it is no secret at all that the claims of the Leader in the Commons are now uncontested. . .

---

[1] *Daily News*, 1 June 1904; *Speaker*, 27 Aug. 1904.
[2] *Daily News*, 16 and 22 Feb. 1905; *Speaker*, Jan.-Feb. and Apr. 1905.
[3] *Contemporary Review*, 88 (July 1905), 118–29; *Speaker*, 22 July, 19 Aug. 1905.
[4] Spender, *Campbell-Bannerman*, II, 398–9.

As for the Liberal Party, it has had no other figure consistently presented to it during the last five years as its champion against the powerful enemies who now lie at his feet... [C.-B.] never sought the leadership; it came to him through the voluntary withdrawal of the only other possible candidate. When it fell to him, there fell with it one of the hardest tasks that ever confronted an English statesman. No one who has not watched what C.-B. had to endure in the House of Commons at the hands of two of its most insolent speakers and from a section of his own friends and followers can understand what the ordeal was. He has come out from it with greatly enhanced powers and authority, and with the field clear of rivals for whose removal he has never raised a finger.

Campbell-Bannerman became Prime Minister on 5 December.

Massingham's professional life was entirely apart from his personal life. And so it is necessary to break context completely to record as important an event as any in his life – the death in March 1905 of his wife, Emma. On 5 March John Burns, Massingham's closest friend, was informed by telegram of her death which came shortly after the birth of her sixth child. From the diaries of Burns and Nevinson we know something of the shattering effect of this sad event. We do not have the letters, including one from Churchill, which Massingham received but we do have a few of his replies. There is a note to Beatrice Webb, begging forgiveness for any unkind remarks he may have made about her husband's work. And a few lines to A. G. Gardiner, ending, 'I shall never raise my head again.'[1]

John Burns was his chief source of consolation. Thanks to Burns' diary we know something of Massingham's life in these years outside the newspaper office. Burns was a frequent visitor at the Massingham home, and took an interest in the children. He and Massingham occasionally went to the theatre together (to *Major Barbara*, for example, in January 1906). Massingham had even more occasion to consult him when he became president of the Local Government Board in the Liberal Cabinet. And in 1906 we find them in company with John Morley dining with Churchill to meet William Jennings Bryan from America.[2]

[1] B.P., Burns Diary, 5, 6, 7, 8 March, Add. MS. 46323/10; P.P., Massingham to Beatrice Webb [1905]; Massingham to Gardiner [1905], Gardiner Papers; personal knowledge of Miss G. M. Cross.
[2] B.P., Burns Diary, 1905: 19 Mar. 14 Nov., 30 Dec. 1906; 19 Jan., 7 Feb., 12, 23 Oct., 9 Nov., 21 Dec. Add. MSS. 46323 and 46324.

In October 1905, Campbell-Bannerman, writing from Marienbad to Gladstone, noted that 'Massingham has gone out [to South Africa] for the *Daily News*.' On the 14th his children and a few friends (Nevinson, Masterman, Vaughan Nash and others) had seen him off at Waterloo. He returned to London early in January.

Under any circumstances it would have been an interesting assignment. In Massingham's case he had had previous contact with Boer leaders. In October 1902, the Boer generals (Botha, de la Rey and de Wet) were in London searching for means to secure better terms than those in the formal settlement at the end of hostilities. Among those they consulted were Massingham and Burns who advised them to return home, from where they could work more effectively. Massingham, along with Lloyd George, attended a dinner for them. And we know that the *Speaker* reached General Smuts in South Africa.[1]

On his visit Massingham apparently expressed his views candidly; he was well received by the Liberal Association, not so well by other political groups. He wrote to his daughter, Dorothy, from Bloemfontein, that the two papers there were at odds about him, one editor writing a leading article on his visit, and another editor warning him not to have anything to do with such people as the first editor.[2] And in Cape Town, the *Cape Times* referred to Massingham as 'an ambassador to the Chinese on the Rand'. One episode had repercussions at home. In his remarks at a farewell dinner given him by the African Liberal Association he said he saw no reason why self-government should not at once be granted, with South Africa enjoying status similar to that of Canada or Australia. In response J. H. Hofmeyr, leader of the Cape Dutch Afrikander Bond, referring to Massingham's 'honest journalism', advised caution so that self-government would be 'a blessing and not a curse' through tyranny of the majority. His remarks were passed on in London by the Imperial South African Association to *The Times* which treated them as a matter of great controversy between Hofmeyr and Massingham. Massingham replied in *The Times* that there was no difference between their positions.[3]

[1] H.G.P., Campbell-Bannerman to Gladstone, 20 Oct. 1905, Add. MS. 45988/193; N.D., 14 Oct. 1905; B.P., Burns Diary, 28 Oct. 1902, Add. MS. 46320/45; W. K. Hancock and Jean Van der Poel (eds.), *Selections from the Smuts Papers* (Cambridge, 1966), II, 46; F. V. Engelenburg, *General Louis Botha* (London, 1929), 111.
[2] Massingham to Dorothy Massingham, 11 Nov. [1905], courtesy Mrs Betty Massingham.
[3] *Cape Times*, 14 Dec. 1905; *The Times*, 9 and 10 Jan. 1906.

Massingham had written to his daughter, 'I see both sides... I have piles of notes, and quite dread having to put them on paper.' But he did so in a series of twelve articles which appeared in the *Daily News* from 2 January to 30 January 1906. They are impressive in manifesting Massingham's powers of observation under pressure of time. The first article was descriptive: 'As It Looks to a Stranger: Life in Johannesburg.' Other articles treated various phases of the South African problem: the Dutch, the Blacks, the Chinese, and the labour problem generally. There were, he said, two gospels, that for the black or yellow man – the gospel of 'the dignity of labour', and the gospel for the white man – 'the dignity of doing nothing, or of working, if he must, with his head rather than with his hands'. The concluding article was 'The Call for Self-Government'. He returned to England depressed by his experience.[1] For some weeks his views appeared extensively in *The Times*.

At a memorable Cabinet meeting, on 8 February, Britain was committed to self-government for the Boer states. Massingham was not unassociated. When the Liberal Government was formed General Smuts went promptly to London. There he profoundly influenced Campbell-Bannerman and reinforced his case in interviews with others – including Hobson, Courtney, Massingham. Some years later Massingham tells us of his breakfast meeting with the new Prime Minister: 'I had seen nearly all the leaders of Dutch and British opinion there [in South Africa], but long before I finished my account of their perfect ability and readiness to work self-government, I divined there was no call to persuade "C.-B." of or to anything.'[2]

Massingham returned from South Africa in time to enjoy the fruits of the Liberal victory in the General Election of January 1906. For him it signified not only the defeat of proposals for a protective tariff but the establishment of 'a Liberal-Radical Government in full command and independently equipped for its task'. He was even enthusiastic about the Labour Party with its twenty-nine M.P.s 'whose advent every right-thinking Liberal who is sure of his principles should

[1] B.P., Burns Diary, 30 Dec. 1905, Add. MS. 46323/53.
[2] Smuts to Gardiner, 16 Jan. 1906, Gardiner Papers; Massingham in *Nation*, 21 May 1921, p. 282. Massingham wrote an article on the 'South African Constitution' for *World's Work*, December 1906.

welcome'. Of the congratulatory dinner to the new Prime Minister at the National Liberal Club, on 14 February, Massingham remarked that since the days of Gladstone, 'I have never seen [there] such tumultuous and overflowing enthusiasm.' Then his language ran away with him. He found 'practically but one party' in the new Parliament, which 'is Radical right through; and the only difficulty I can see for the Government is that with all the will in the world it may not be able to keep pace with its impatient spirit'. Before long he was referring to Campbell-Bannerman as 'the first Radical prime minister'. About many new recruits in Parliament he was enthusiastic, particularly G. P. Gooch (and his selection as Parliamentary Secretary to James Bryce, the new Irish Secretary) and journalists such as C. F. G. Masterman, Hilaire Belloc and R. C. Lehmann, though he expressed concern over the effect of 'the intolerable ennui' of Commons' life upon them.[1]

Churchill, as the new Under Secretary for the Colonies, Massingham found to be 'the most observed of Ministers after the head of the Government. Here at least every man discovers a star whose course he cannot predict with certainty, while it attracts him by its light'. On taking office Churchill consulted various individuals with special knowledge of the South African situation, including Massingham, General Smuts and others.[2] Even Sir Edward Grey came in for a kind word from Massingham. He was one of those who have at once 'attained a position of great authority in the new House of Commons'. This friendliness from Massingham must have startled Grey – as late as 1904 he dismissed the idea of a Radical Government: 'What a futile thing it would be – all froth.' When the honours list in June included a peerage for Courtney, Massingham wrote to Mrs Courtney that her husband was 'almost too good for the House of Lords'.[3]

It is never easy to generalise about Massingham's attitudes and ideas. But concerning his writing in the *Daily News*, in the *Speaker* and in frequent periodical articles, in the first year of the new Liberal Government, two characteristics seem fairly prominent. One is the commitment he feels to the Liberal Party, based on the mandate, as he interprets it, of the General Election. This leads him to write with enthusi-

[1] *Speaker*, 1906: 6, 13, 20 Jan.; 3, 17, 24 Feb.; 18 Aug.; 29 Dec.
[2] *Speaker*, 18 Aug. 1906; Churchill, *Winston S. Churchill*, companion volume 2, pt 1, 523.
[3] *Speaker*, 12 May 1906; Keith Robbins, *Sir Edward Grey* (London, 1971), 114–15; Gooch, *Courtney*, 513.

asm and zest of the general goals, but also with impatience at controversy and delay, and at the intransigence of the Opposition. So he picks
up the themes which he had developed lugubriously and in reverse a
few years before. Then he had been concerned with decline and failure
of democratic processes through Parliament. Now he is concerned with
the 'Revival of Parliament' and 'The Success of the New Government'.
Progressive opinion, he said, called for action on education, temperance, land, poor law reform, unemployment and trade. He construed
the 1906 victory as a triumph of forces favouring 'a policy of constructive reform which is now thoroughly ripe for execution'.[1]

The other characteristic is suggested by a comment of John Burns
in December 1906 – that it was 'impossible to advise Massingham
because he takes a 5 minute view of every subject'.[2] Haste in composition, the constant shift in subject matter, day by day, the change of
direction or of objective give Massingham's writing a note of urgency,
very often a tone of great conviction, but at the same time an uneven-
ness in the disciplined quality of his writing, a tentativeness in its
relevancy, sometimes an inconsistency in its logic. He does not find it
easy to shift from the role of critic to that of advocate.

Massingham's remarks on the South African problem have special
point. He is still at his verbal best when leading an attack. So when
Milner admitted, on 26 February, permitting corporal punishment of
Chinese labourers in the mines, Massingham wrote:

It is good for a nation to see clearly who are the authors of its misfortunes. It
is better still for those men to show themselves for what they are... What
struck me chiefly about Milner was his essentially un-English character...
Men with him are things to be compressed within formulae and to be hated
and driven, if they won't be compressed.

And later, when the Lords (29 March) carried a resolution exonerating
Milner, with the press generally echoing a sentiment of approval voiced
by the Archbishop of Canterbury, Massingham delivered a blast:

Lord Milner is nothing if not the embodiment of the spirit of intolerant,
unsympathetic ... ascendancy. This is why Society has taken him up after

---

[1] These statements are based on various articles in the *Contemporary Review*: vol. 89
(Feb. 1906), 267–73; (Mar. 1906), 305–12; (June 1906), 867–75. See also *Speaker*, 11 Aug.
1906, pp. 433–4; 29 Dec. 1906, p. 374.
[2] B.P., Burns Diary, Add. MS. 46324/52.

the politicians deserted him. Let such a statesman plunge his country deep in the mire and mischief, and Society will forgive, so long as he speaks the same smug language of this narrow creed. And the Church is never unwilling to pronounce its unctious benison on such a type of Englishman.[1]

Massingham felt rather frustrated over interpretation of the Aliens Act, strictly controlling immigration, legislated in 1905 by the Conservatives and then supported by many Liberals representing working-class constituencies which favoured the measure because it protected against an influx of sweated labour. Massingham had taken a dim view of Liberal support and now he was dissatisfied with the limited steps by which the Home Secretary, Herbert Gladstone, proposed to ease its application, particularly with respect to political refugees. He declared that these measures had not satisfied his party, that the Home Secretary had confessed his powerlessness over the Immigration Boards and had not even hinted at a possible repeal of the extra-criminal provisions of the act. Gladstone must have remonstrated against so strong a statement, for Massingham addressed him, putting his position in more acceptable language. A new bill designed to forbid immigration of aliens who would replace native workmen during a trade dispute, passed by the House, was defeated in the Lords. But Massingham was satisfied when the Government dropped the matter.[2] Other areas in which he was at odds with the Government were the Plural Voting Bill – he was doubtful of some of its details – and old-age pensions on which he felt the Cabinet should be prodded into action.[3]

On the new Education Bill (1906), Massingham fought the battle in the columns of the *Speaker* and his comments called attention to the divisions within his own party, almost as serious as those which divided Liberal from Conservative. His own divergence came with his insistence that denominationalism of whatever character be kept out of religious instruction in the schools. He soon found the Commons'

---

[1] *Speaker*, 27 Feb. 1906; *Daily News*, 30 Mar., as quoted in Alfred M. Gollin, *Proconsul in Politics* (London 1964), 95.
[2] *Speaker*, 6 May 1905 and 26 May 1906; *Daily News*, 6 Mar. 1907; H.G.P., Massingham to Gladstone, 23 Mar. [1906], Add. MS. 40042/65–6.
[3] *Speaker*, 9 June and 8 Sept. 1906.

debates insufferable – a 'politico-religious squabble which we dignify by calling it the problem of education'.[1]

The House of Lords issue was a simpler matter. Massingham had spoken out irrevocably in September 1893 after the Lords voted down the Second Home Rule Bill by 441 votes to 419.

> The farce is played . . . Preposterous in theory, foolish in fact, an obstacle to every measure of popular justice, an organized band of the mercenaries of class and privilege, they exist only to debase the moral currency and to falsify the national standard of value. Down with the House of Lords – it is no use mincing words.

In 1906 he was at first incredulous that the Lords might through amendments in effect destroy the Education Bill. In the autumn session, day after day 'Pictures in Parliament' set forth the magnitude of the impossible demands of the Lords, the 'disorderly' debates, preposterous in length, and the 'chaos' of the Bill, and painted a scene of the 'Lords between Fear and Effrontery'. Then, hard upon the crushing action on the Education Bill came the rejection of the Plural Voting Bill by the Lords, after only two hours' debate.[2]

On the constitutional issue of the Lords he was never of two minds. He wrote in February 1906: 'Let us hope the House of Lords will bow to the verdict of 1906 and give the new democracy a fair chance. If it does not . . .' By December his position is well summed up in his article 'The Coming Battle with the Lords'. In action on the Education Bill the Lords had exceeded the constitutional limits assigned to them and had become 'a standing challenge to Liberalism. One force or the other must go down'.[3]

A toast to 'H.W.M.'

In February 1907 Massingham left the staff of the *Daily News* to become the first editor of the *Nation*. With the *Star* and the *Daily Chronicle* he had made a great impact on journalism; with the *Daily*

[1] *Speaker*, 1906: 7, 14 April, 2 June, 7 July, 4 Aug. Peter Rowland, *The Last Liberal Governments: The Promised Land, 1905–1910* (London, 1968), 350, for Massingham's discussion of the Education Bill with Herbert Gladstone.

[2] Massingham's leader in 1893 as quoted in E. C. Bentley, *Those Days* (London, 1940), 229. *Daily News*, 27 Oct. to 11 Dec. 1906, *passim*. *Speaker*, 1906: 27 Oct., 8 Dec.

[3] *Contemporary Review*, 89 (Feb. 1906), 267–73; *Independent Review*, XI (Dec. 1906), 254–62.

News he made a great impact on public opinion. He was now 'H.W.M.', the initials used to identify his pieces in the *Daily News* and the *Speaker* and which would be appended to most of his signed articles henceforth. The initials stood for a strong personality, a great talent, an absolute independence; as 'H.W.M.' he was now known to his family, his friends, his associates, and much of the reading public.

And so H.W.M. was 'the toast of the evening', on Saturday, 9 March 1907, when the staff of the *Daily News* supported by men of affairs and men of letters celebrated his career with a complimentary dinner at the National Liberal Club.[1] A. G. Gardiner, the editor, presided. From the Prime Minister, unable to attend, came this greeting:

I am very sorry not to be able to be with you to-night and bear my share in honouring our friend Massingham. We all know how incisive his pen is, how shrewd his judgment, how brilliant his descriptive powers. But even more admirable is his staunch advocacy of the true principles which form the only solid ground work of Liberal policy. We are deeply his debtors for the past; we confidently anticipate a splendid and useful career in his new enterprise.

On hand to represent the Liberal Government were Lloyd George, Winston Churchill and John Burns. Others present included Lord Courtney, George Bernard Shaw, Sir Henry Norman, R. C. Lehmann, William Robertson Nicoll, C. F. G. Masterman, Leo Chiozza Money, Vaughan Nash, F. W. Hirst, H. W. Nevinson, J. L. Hammond and Clement Shorter. From John Morley, Augustine Birrell, Sir Charles Dilke, George Cadbury, Joseph Rowntree and J. A. Spender came regrets and best wishes. Like all such affairs much of the oratory was sentiment or flattery but here and there was depth and imagination. Gardiner praised Massingham's courage and independence; Burns his rectitude; Norman his sympathy and intuitive insight; Shaw his 'magnificent dramatic criticism of the House of Commons'. Churchill acknowledged his personal debt to Massingham and added:

Dark days, has he passed through – days when his views and his personality were the objects of bitter attack; yet he comes out at the end of the day...
In this somewhat shoddy age in which we live we do admire most in our guest to-night the quality of recklessness which he possesses, which is of superb value in an age when everyone is always enjoining caution and deference to precedent.

[1] This account is from the *Daily News*, 11 Mar. 1907, pp. 7–8.

It was causes for which Massingham laboured, said Churchill, 'regardless of the interest of his newspaper, regardless of the interest of the party, regardless of the interest of his country, utterly regardless on all occasions of his own interest'. Churchill was talking about Massingham, the journalist adventurer.

The year 1907 – like 1883 when he left Norwich, or 1888 when he joined the staff of the *Star*, 1895 when he became editor of the *Daily Chronicle*, and 1901 when he became columnist for the *Daily News* – was a milestone. He now left daily journalism for weekly, the Press Gallery of the House of Commons for the editor's chair. The change had its light touches. Miss Cross, Massingham's last secretary, recalls the tale that Massingham at first turned up at the office of the *Nation* at 5 p.m. as though his schedule would be similar to that of a morning daily.

He was to stay in weekly journalism for the rest of his life, but with excursions on the side. From November 1909 his articles, usually once a week, on subjects of his own choosing with no general head, about a column in length, appeared in the *Morning Leader*. His piece continued when the *Daily News* and *Morning Leader* merged in May 1912; his final article appeared on 22 January 1915.

In 1907, as well, came (in May) his second marriage – to Ellen Snowdon, his deceased wife's sister, who since 1905 had been housekeeper for his large family. The ceremony took place on the Island of Guernsey, since at that time the law of the United Kingdom did not permit such a union.

CHAPTER 7

Editing the 'Nation' (1907–1923)

'Next week a new issue of *The Speaker* will appear under the title of "The Nation", edited by Mr. H. W. Massingham.' Thus reads a 'Notice' in the *Speaker* for 23 February 1907.

Even under J. L. Hammond's aggressive and intelligent leadership the *Speaker* had had its problems, not the least of which was its appearance. Frank Swinnerton recalled that it simply 'looked dull' – he had in mind that it was largely political in character. Edward Garnett, its chief literary contributor, repeatedly confided his despair to Galsworthy. 'There isn't room for a mouse to turn around, after the regular dull contributions – Social Policy, Massingham, etc., are inserted.'[1] Not much room for Garnett, he meant. For his taste, Hammond's idealism had limits.

Both Hammond, who required additional funds, and the *Speaker* Publishing Company, Ltd, controlled and subsidised by the Joseph Rowntree Social Service Trust, were unhappy over the paper's fortunes. Changes came in the summer of 1906, with the *Speaker*, somewhat popularised, continuing without formal editorship, to reduce expense.[2]

Not until January 1907, according to the evidence, does Massingham come into the story. But on 23 January, at a conference with the *Speaker* committee of the Rowntree Trust at the Rowntree Cocoa Works in York, he accepted appointment as editor of the *Speaker* at an annual salary of £1,000. The editor was to control staff and policy, subject to the approval of the directors of the *Speaker* Publishing Company. The Trust gave assurances that it would provide necessary funds for from three to five years. Massingham negotiated his release from the *Daily News* through George Cadbury. In reporting these developments to the *News'* editor, A. G. Gardiner, Massingham added

[1] Frank Swinnerton, *Background with Chorus* (London, 1956), 116; Edward Garnett (ed.), *Letters from John Galsworthy, 1900–1932* (London, 1934), esp. 54, 59.
[2] Hirst, *In the Golden Days*, 205; J.L.H.P. and Gilbert Murray Papers for January and February 1907 have much correspondence on J. L. Hammond's situation.

that the paper would not suffer by his departure. 'I have seen too much of the House, & a fresher eye & style will be a good change. . . I find also that fatigues of the session fall on me more than formerly.'[1] Clement Shorter tells us that he suggested the new title, the *Nation*.[2]

Its advent was hailed enthusiastically by Liberals and by the Liberal press. Massingham was interviewed by Jane T. Stoddart of Robertson Nicoll's free church *British Weekly*. She found him in his new office, a flat of three rooms at 12 Henrietta Street, near Covent Garden, just above the offices vacated by the *Speaker*. Massingham outlined the format of the new paper – on the front outside page, 'Notes', which would be a blend of news and criticism; then three or four unsigned leaders generally political in character; 'middles' on current topics and then a fully-organised literary department which would be designed 'for the general body of thoughtful, intelligent readers' and not for experts alone. Correspondence from readers would be encouraged. But 'full of ideas' the new editor had no hard or fixed rules about 'make-up'. The *Nation* was to have a minimum of thirty-six pages.[3]

The first issues of the *Nation* gave evidence that it would indeed be livelier and more comprehensive than the *Speaker*, and perhaps more controversial as well. The feature article for the first issue, on 2 March, was written by the Prime Minister, Campbell-Bannerman, on 'The Hague Conference and the Limitation of Armaments', and at once the new periodical became known outside Britain. 'The Diary of the Week', largely written by the editor, commented on current events – Massingham's more personal 'A London Diary', signed 'Wayfarer', came years later, beginning with the issue of 7 December 1912. The department 'Open Questions' began on 9 March with Winston Churchill's 'A Smooth Way with the Peers' and was accompanied by comment, probably written by Massingham. 'Open Questions' for 16 March carried Lord Courtney's 'Devolution in Ireland', and correspondence with readers began at once. With the issue for 23 March came 'Present Day Problems', providing space for letters written by the editor or for signed letters by members of the staff – a frequent practice.

---

1 Minute, 4 Mar. 1907, Joseph Rowntree Social Service Trust, Rowntree Papers; Massingham to Gardiner, 26 Jan. 1907, Gardiner Papers.
2 Bullock (ed.), *C. K. S., An Autobiography*, 49.
3 *British Weekly*, 21 Feb. 1907, p. 543. See also 31 Jan. 1907.

Massingham reached back to the *Daily Chronicle* to attach to his staff Eduard Bernstein, the German Socialist, who tells us that it was only through the *Nation* that he became known in England outside Socialist circles. The *Nation*, he said, 'is read in all the political clubs'. The opening issue carried his 'New Reichstag and its Visions', and the issue for 6 April his 'Germany and the Limitation of Armaments' – the latter inspired by Campbell-Bannerman. Thereafter, Bernstein's letters are frequent, sometimes with a Berlin date-line and sometimes not. His first attendance at a *Nation* Lunch, according to Nevinson, was in December 1910.[1]

G. P. Gooch remarked that no other editor could boast such a staff as that which Massingham gathered around him. Much the same comment has been made about A. R. Orage's *New Age*, John St Loe Strachey's *Spectator* and Clifford Sharp's *New Statesman*. As Leonard Woolf once remarked to the author, writers, political and literary, had to make a living and they published wherever they could.[2] And the staffs very much overlapped. Massingham's own group was in part inherited from the *Star*, the *Daily Chronicle*, the *Speaker* and the *Daily News* – but there were new faces as well. Thus, the issue of 19 March 1910, described by Nevinson as 'very strong', contained contributions by Galsworthy and Brailsford as well as by Shaw, Nevinson and Massingham himself.[3] In point of fact, the regular staff was small, but with unsigned leaders and middles the reader of the *Nation* was led, as was intended, to regard the paper as having a large staff.

J. L. Hammond is commonly referred to as an original member of the *Nation* staff but during the first two years no signed article bears his name. After that he is a regular contributor. In 1913 we find him saying that with difficulty he has time to work on his *Town Labourer, 1760–1832* (eventually published in 1917), for 'as soon as one gets into it, it is time to write for the *Nation* and earn my living'. He remained at Massingham's right hand, and his tribute after Massingham's death is an entirely genuine and very moving document.[4]

[1] *My Years of Exile*, 252–3; N.D., 27 Dec. 1910.
[2] Hearnshaw (ed.), *Edwardian England*, 22; author's interview with Leonard Woolf, 12 Jan. 1965.
[3] N.D., 19 Mar. 1910.
[4] Hammond to Rothenstein, 16 Nov, 1913, Rothenstein Papers, Houghton. Hammond's tribute is in the *Nation*, 6 Sept. 1924, reprinted in *H.W.M.*, 19–22.

But it was H. N. Brailsford, a newcomer to Massingham's circle, who wrote most of the leaders on foreign affairs in the pre-war years. While unintentional, this resulted in a tone rather more favourable to Germany than to France.[1] It is difficult to assess his immediate impact since he had only one signed article in the first two years. But he wrote and spoke with great authority and figures prominently in the 'violent discussions' at the *Nation* Lunches.

C. F. G. Masterman, Massingham's associate on the *Daily News* and a close personal friend, was at once invited to contribute to the *Nation*. As a member of the Government, from 1908, he brought practical experience and personal knowledge of Government policy. His articles are generally, perhaps always, signed. His significant *Condition of England* (1909) was first published in part in the *Nation*. L. T. Hobhouse, leader-writer for the *Manchester Guardian* and a person absorbed in manifold interests – politics, philosophy, journalism, literature (too many conflicting interests, thought Nevinson[2]) – was a frequent contributor, beginning with his 'The Career of Fabianism', on 30 March 1907, and a regular attendant at the Lunch.

Of J. A. Hobson, Brailsford has written that his influence on current affairs, in its most important aspect, came from his *Nation* articles and reviews; from the outset these appear in a steady stream. Brailsford emphasises Hobson's talent for irony and satire and points out his gift for giving to discussions at the weekly Lunch startling changes in direction. Hobson's *Dips into the Near Future* (1919) brings together eight war-time sketches in the *Nation* written over the pen name, 'Lucian'.[3] F. W. Hirst, from September 1907 editor of *The Economist*, wrote for the *Nation* on financial issues. An old-fashioned Liberal, apparently uninfluenced by the twentieth century, he was of a breed different from the others. He had no strong interest in social change nor did he share Massingham's admiration for Lloyd George and Churchill, but he constituted an important link with Liberal Party officialdom, particularly Sir John Brunner. The Rev. W. D. Morrison

---

[1] This was called to my attention by A. J. P. Taylor, *The Trouble Makers* (London, 1957), 112. In October 1914 Hammond wrote Bertrand Russell that he had never associated himself with the *Nation*'s foreign policy. *Autobiography of Bertrand Russell*, II (London, 1968), 47.

[2] N.D., 4 June 1907 and 23 Apr. 1907 on Brailsford and Hobhouse.

[3] H. N. Brailsford, *The Life and Work of J. A. Hobson* (London, 1948), 4.

was carried over from the *Daily Chronicle* – his special concern remained prison reform. Though some, like Nevinson, found him a bit of a bore, Massingham himself was always appreciative: in the 'Diary of the Week', of 15 February 1908, there is praise for Morrison, just appointed to the crown living of Marylebone in London.[1]

Then there were occasional contributors like Arthur Ponsonby, Radical M.P., soon recognised as the leading parliamentary critic of British foreign policy. An ardent pacifist, son of Victoria's Private Secretary, Sir Henry Ponsonby, he had an unusual knowledge of the royal family. Thus he was invited by Massingham to write an article on Edward VII and the Prince of Wales as Edward's life came to a close. The article, 'The Two Sovereigns – By One Who has Known Them', appeared on 14 May 1910. In a different vein was his 'Our Old and New Nobility' (24 September 1910), also unsigned, which Massingham referred to as 'a first rate piece of slanging'.[2]

Who was to be literary editor? Not Edward Garnett, the chief literary writer for the *Speaker*. He was carried over, but as a book reviewer without general responsibility for the literary pages. Just before the *Speaker–Nation* change-over Massingham sent Garnett a batch of novels 'to be dealt with briefly'. And he added by way of guidance that he had no objection to harsh comments about 'a bad book by a writer who ought to do better work, or who has a swollen reputation for working well when he is really working ill.' The first issue of the *Nation* carried Garnett's review (unsigned) of Galsworthy's *The Country House*; Galsworthy found the review 'exhilarating and delightful' and added that 'the *Nation* looks like prosperity. I hope to goodness it succeeds and gives you the chance you ought to have'.[3]

But judging from a file of letters from Massingham to Garnett (unfortunately we do not have the Garnett side of the correspondence) their relationship was not altogether compatible. Garnett's 'militant' anti-puritanism, particularly on matters of sex, disturbed Massingham who asked for 'a *little* more tolerance for the better kind of conven-

---

[1] On Hirst, Mary Agnes Hamilton, *Remembering My Good Friends* (London, 1944), 82–3. On Morrison, N.D., 23 Apr. 1907 and 18 May 1909.

[2] Massingham to Ponsonby, 5 May [1910]; 19 Sept. 1910. Ponsonby Papers.

[3] Massingham to Garnett, 18 Feb. 1907 (U. of Texas). Galsworthy to Garnett, 7 Mar. 1907, Garnett, *Letters from John Galsworthy*, 139.

tional art in fiction, or we shall be regarded as too "sniffy" altogether'. In 1912 Massingham remarked that reviewing fiction was too much for one man and suggested an article every other week,[1] and Garnett's pieces thereafter are less frequent.

Lytton Strachey and Desmond MacCarthy were not continued from the *Speaker*. MacCarthy had been the drama critic and Massingham is said to have remarked later that not holding on to him was his biggest mistake. One wonders what was said when, in March 1907, Strachey visited the MacCarthys near Bury St Edmunds and they talked about 'whether the *Nation* was better than the *Speaker*'.[2] Garnett's contributions attracted W. H. Hudson to the *Nation*; in June 1907 he was reading Garnett's articles 'with pleasure and profit', Massingham's 'with a grin'. Hudson confided to Garnett that he cared little for Galsworthy's first sketches in the *Nation* – 'there is a certain something of sermonizing about them, and I prefer him when he conceals that part of his mind.'[3] In the *Nation*'s columns Garnett welcomed E. M. Forster's arrival as an important novelist.[4]

As 'literary editor', there may have been a possibility of Holbrook Jackson soon after he left the *New Age*. In January 1908 Shaw drafted a letter to Massingham:

Do you happen to want for the *Nation* one of those amazing people, like Robertson Nicoll or Clement Shorter, who have an incalculable appetite for books and authors and publishers? ... If so, please take on Holbrook Jackson... [His] infatuation for literature is such that he is actually giving up a comfortable position ... on the chance of realizing a wild ambition to be edited by you, and to have a page in your paper for booknews.

If Massingham received this letter it came to nothing. Over the years, there was occasionally, as in the first issue, a separate 'literary supplement', but the usual practice was to include the literary pages with the regular sections. 'The World of Books' or 'Books in Brief', containing news items and brief notes about writers, appears, with occasional

---

[1] Massingham to Garnett, letters for the most part undated (U. of Texas).
[2] Desmond MacCarthy, *Humanities* (London, 1953), 16 n.; Michael Holroyd, *Lytton Strachey*, I (London, 1967), 308, 371–2. Nothing signed by MacCarthy appears in the *Nation* before 1910.
[3] Edward Garnett (ed.), *Letters from W. H. Hudson, 1901–1922* (New York, 1923), 126–7, 134, 162–3, 197–8, 259, 294.
[4] *Nation*, 12 Nov. 1910, pp. 282–4.

lapses, throughout Massingham's editorship. Quite early, this page was the responsibility of A. W. ('Penguin') Evans; in time he was regarded as assistant editor.[1]

But it is Henry W. Nevinson who dominated the literary side of the *Nation* in its first years. His diary is our chief source of knowledge about the *Nation* Group; like a kaleidoscope, it provides enormous detail, constantly shifting in context and personalities. Highly subjective, sometimes warm and sometimes cold on the same individual, it has the merit of candour and immediacy. From it we often gain our initial impression of a situation, an issue, a controversy.[2] But Nevinson now had a literary reputation of his own, particularly with his essays *Plea of Pan* (1901) and *Modern Slavery* (1906), the latter an account of his long visit to Angola in 1904–5, the last years of outright slavery in the Portuguese colony. Of *Modern Slavery*, Galsworthy wrote to Garnett: 'With the exception of Hudson there is no one can write like that – so direct, so genuine, so insightful, and ironical.' Comment in this vein also comes from Massingham. On one occasion he identified for Sir Charles Dilke an article by Nevinson 'who at his best and on his subject has no equal, I think, for color and interest among contemporary writers'.[3]

On 26 January 1907 Nevinson returned from a trip to Russia – this one including Georgia and the Caucasus. A few days later, in his account, he met Massingham at the National Liberal Club and 'gladly accepted his offer to write regularly' for the *Nation* 'at good pay'. But somewhat to his disappointment his assignment was not to be leaders on foreign affairs but 'middles'. Massingham, by no means always successful in handling people, understood Nevinson and appreciated him as well. Of his first contribution, 'The Kindling of the Flame' (23 March 1907) concerning the *Fors Clavigera* of Ruskin, Massingham wrote to him that it was 'about the most perfect thing I have ever read'. And of 'The Drama of Freedom' (30 March), a comment on Aeschylus'

---

[1] G.B.S.P., Add. MS. 50558/52. On Evans, see Henry W. Nevinson, *More Changes, More Chances* (London, 1925), 220. When Massingham became editor in 1907, R. Mudie Smith was designated sub-editor at £5 a week (Minute, 4 Mar. 1907, Rowntree Papers.) According to Nevinson, he resigned in August 1907 (N.S., 27 Aug. 1907).
[2] Nevinson's diary is the basis of his autobiographical works: *Changes and Chances* (1923); *More Changes, More Chances* (1925) and *Last Changes, Last Chances* (1928).
[3] Garnett, *Letters from John Galsworthy*, New Year's Eve, 1907, p. 160. Massingham to Dilke, 3 Nov. [1908?], D.P., Add. MS. 43920/153–4.

The Persians, as performed at the Literary Theatre Society, Massingham wrote him 'The article is delightful; I know of no such distinction of writing in English journalism. It's much the best thing in this number as the Ruskin article was ... in last week's.'[1]

Occasionally Nevinson wrote a signed article for 'Open Questions' (e.g., his 'The Rights of Subject Races', in the issue for 20 April 1907) and now and again a 'Letter to the Editor' on some special concern. He tried his hand at poetry but generally he stuck to 'middles', for though belittling them he was proud of them all the same, and they became a valued feature of the paper.[2] Among early pieces which became celebrated were 'The Passing of the Horse' (12 September 1908) and 'The Scholar's Melancholy' (26 September 1908). For sixteen years, from 1907 to 1923, except when Nevinson was absent from London, the 'middles' appeared. Brailsford, quite familiar with Nevinson's habits, tells us:

Usually it was Massingham ... who found his subject for him. When his theme was set, Nevinson would retire from the world for twenty-four hours, browse among his books, sleep on his camp-bed among his shelves, rise early and then write, with intense concentration, an essay always ready to the last comma by noon.[3]

Nevinson's *Nation* 'middles' were reprinted in book form: *Essays in Freedom* (1909), *Essays in Rebellion* (1913) and *Essays in Freedom and Rebellion* (1923). The first was dedicated to Massingham with an elaborate tribute, part of which reads:

The battle of freedom is never done, and the field never quiet... From my place among the camp followers I have watched you upon that field, flashing and flickering in the van of the turmoil, smiting the foul swarms of the enemy, charging them full in front, hanging on their flanks, often defeated but always heartening your men.

'It is really most kind,' wrote Massingham to Nevinson, 'but you shouldn't have done it... You should not have mixed up my journal-

---

[1] N.D., 31 Jan., 22, 26 Mar. 1907. Massingham's letters, 26 Mar. [1907]; 22 Aug. [1907] are in Nevinson Papers.
[2] E.g., N.D., 12 and 29 Sept. 1908.
[3] Nevinson, *More Changes, More Chances*, 214–15. H. N. Brailsford (ed.), *Essays, Poems and Tales of Henry W. Nevinson* (London, 1948), 12.

ism with your literature.'¹ In the diary Nevinson brings out all sides of their relationship – praise and mutual loyalty, but also annoyance and rage. There was the occasion (*Nation*, 9 December 1911) when Massingham tempered Nevinson's attack on public officials because Hobson had praised them in a preceding article. And of his unsigned middle, 'The Satire of Rage' (10 May 1913) Nevinson noted that his editor had probably ruined it by toning down his reference to a Dyson cartoon in the *Daily Herald*. And so it went, this 'gentle creature', Nevinson, who 'would have terrific passionate outbursts' – Felix Frankfurter's language. Nevinson, at one time or another feuded with nearly everyone – Brailsford, Masterman, Hirst, Hobhouse, Morrison, Shorter. His causes, his convictions and his vanities will appear as we proceed. He tells us that it was St Loe Strachey who coupled him with E. D. Morel as the two 'knights-errant' of the day, a reference which he protested to be nonsense but one on which he liked to ruminate nevertheless. E. D. Morel, to whom Nevinson refers and who had written occasionally for the *Daily Chronicle*, was now absorbed in the activities of the Congo Reform Association. In 1904 Morel along with Mrs Richard Stopford Green had secured assistance from Massingham in selecting the official sponsors. At that time, of the London dailies, only the *Morning Post* gave active support and Morel had written to Massingham, 'I wish you would start a real Liberal paper!'²

The 'Nation' Lunch

Outside the *Nation*'s pages we turn to the weekly *Nation* Lunch for manifestations of the talent, the interests and the controversies of the *Nation* Group. C. F. G. Masterman records that just before the first issue Massingham told him that he had in mind

running that paper not entirely as a one-man show, but to hold a meeting every week, of which he would be chairman indeed, but in the midst of a gathering that would include not only his regular contributors, but visitors [as well] ... where conversation would be entirely free, entirely reckless, entirely secret, in which we would hammer out together ideas suitable for the paper to advocate.

¹ Massingham to Nevinson, 20 May [1909], Nevinson Papers. Nevinson also dedicated *More Changes, More Chances* to Massingham.
² Phillips (ed.), *Felix Frankfurter Reminisces*, 93; *More Changes, More Chances*, 291; N.D., 12 Dec. 1911; B.L.P.E.S., Morel Papers, Morel to Massingham, 12, 24, 29 Feb. and 10 May 1904 (Copies).

In his invitation in June 1908 to Arthur Ponsonby, just elected to replace Campbell-Bannerman as M.P. for Stirling Burghs, Massingham put it this way:

I wonder whether you would care to join the weekly informal lunches at which we discuss the policy of 'The Nation'? . . . We should often like to have your voice and opinion and, on the other hand, attendance would not at all imply obligation to write. We discuss politics and other things in a free way, and come to the sort of conclusion about them which you see in 'The Nation'.

We turn again to Masterman for representative comment of the significance of this institution: 'I can assert that the *Nation* lunch, with Mr. Massingham in the chair, represented something so unique and exhilarating that one would sweep away all other engagements in order to attend.[1]

In eulogy of Massingham's career, after his death, it was commonly remarked that no matter how varied the writers and their points of view the paper seemed the expression of one great mind. Nevinson says that somehow Massingham kept order by 'driving that mixed and unruly team . . . with so light and steady a hand, holding them to the centre of the road and preventing them from kicking over the traces or even kicking each other'. This of course is an idealised version of a mixed reality. But no doubt, as Masterman said, at the Lunch 'the real centre and core . . . was the Editor. He would break up small groups which would generate in corners, dragging men into the main stream of conversation'. But Brailsford recalled that Massingham declared his own views 'hotly, vehemently, in jerky, explosive sentences, full of hearty abuse of his foes, expressed in language of whimsical and unprintable violence'. Hobson refers to the 'frank utterance of men representing wide divergencies of mentality and political opinions, yet holding the common title of Liberal'.[2]

The Lunch began in March or April 1907 (Nevinson's first attendance was on 16 April); for years it was held, generally on Tuesdays, but in 1918 it was changed to Mondays. A large round table at the National

---

[1] *Nation*, 28 Apr. 1923 (much of this article is in Lucy Masterman, *C. F. G. Masterman*, London, 1939, 78–80). Massingham to Ponsonby, 25 June 1908, Ponsonby Papers.
[2] Nevinson, *More Changes, More Chances*, 216; N.D., 16 July 1907; Brailsford in *New Leader*, 5 Sept. 1924; J. A. Hobson, *Confessions of an Economic Heretic* (New York, 1938), 82–3.

Liberal Club was the normal setting. Around it would gather the editor and several regulars of the staff with the occasional contributors attending from time to time, and usually one or two or more visitors, 'men of all classes and creeds from Prime Ministers downwards'. This included, Masterman continued, 'every kind of genius or freak'.

Mr. Nevinson would bring romantic copper-coloured chiefs to tell us of some iniquity. . . Mr. Brailsford would introduce strange figures with heads shaped like eggs, bald-headed with long beards, who, we would only casually learn, had spent the best part of their lives in prison . . . and who have subsequently become Prime Ministers, or members of high office in that strange land which we term, for want of a better title, Eastern Europe.

Masterman escorted Lloyd George there, and 'literary men were accounted as common as silver in the days of King Solomon'. Lord Courtney attended and wrote to Massingham afterwards, 'may its disputatiousness increase'.[1]

For names of other guests one consults Nevinson's diary. In 1910, there was Booker T. Washington, 'a fine brown person, full of drama & vitality', and George Harvey, journalist, later to be American Ambassador to Great Britain; in 1913, Mohammed Ali, the deposed Shah of Persia, and thereafter C. P. Scott, Gilbert Murray, Lowes Dickinson, Sir Edwin Pears, Israel Zangwill, Philip Morrell, Paul Miliukoff, Cunninghame-Graham, H. G. Wells, John Simon – to name a few at random. Occasionally there was one of the Rowntrees or E. Richard Cross, their solicitor. After the war came almost a stream of Americans. In 1919 there were Justice Brandeis and Felix Frankfurter. In 1920 Vachel Lindsay recited some of his poems 'with immense gestures and variety of voice' and in 1921, Sinclair Lewis 'talked brilliantly'. In 1922 came Herbert Croly, editor of the *New Republic*. The comment of the American, Thomas B. Wells of Harpers, was characteristic – there was, he said, no such gathering to be found in the United States.[2]

In matters of finance, the Joseph Rowntree Social Service Trust is central to our story. In Massingham's time, 1907–23, the Trust contributed some £60,000 and without this subsidy the *Nation* would have

[1] Masterman in *Nation*, 28 Apr. 1923. Courtney to Massingham, 21 Sept. 1914, M.P.
[2] N.D., *passim*, e.g., 30 Aug. 1910; 21 Oct. 1913; 18 Aug. 1919; 11 Oct. 1920; 20 June 1921, 27 June 1921; 20 May, 1913.

collapsed. Particularly during the early years the Committee of the Trust in charge of *Nation* affairs followed carefully its fortunes, meeting frequently with the editor either in York or in London. Of the first four issues, about 20,000 free copies were mailed to prospective subscribers. This raised direct subscribers from 374 to 1,136. At the end of seven months, circulation stood at 4,200 with direct subscribers numbering 1,248, both figures well up on those of the *Speaker*. By 1909 net circulation was about 5,000 with direct subscribers rising to 2,100. In October 1907 Massingham discussed with the Trust Committee a proposal to reduce the price of the paper from 6*d*. to 3*d*. but the proposal was discarded as unwise. During the first year the subsidy from the Trust amounted to £6,500 and then the figure declined, never rising again above £5,000 a year.

From the start, the directors of the Trust praised the quality of the paper and generally approved its editorial policy. However, a recurring comment was that the paper did not have sufficient coverage of religious issues. Massingham pointed out that satisfactory articles on religion, constructive in outlook, were hard to come by but religious writers were canvassed. The articles by R. J. Glover of St John's College, Cambridge, in 1908–09 attracted attention. The directors also favoured more attention to areas of local government and applied science. With the death in 1911 of Sir Percy Bunting, editor of the *Contemporary Review*, there was some possibility that Massingham might add its editorship to his duties, with Evans as his assistant – such an arrangement, it was urged, would strengthen the staff of the *Nation*. The directors concluded that it was inadvisable for the Trust to have the controlling interest in the *Review* with the responsibilities that would entail. However, they voted an annual supplement of £200, in addition to his regular salary, to Massingham in recognition of his services.

Consideration of the *Contemporary Review* called attention to Massingham's health. The directors expressed concern over his frequent absence from the office, particularly a prolonged period (some thirteen weeks) late in 1911. Massingham's health became a regular factor in the Trust's occasional review of the fortunes of the *Nation*. Note was taken that circulation and general financial condition suffered in 1909 and again in 1911 when the *Nation* took an unpopular stand on the navy and on labour questions.[1] But prior to 1914 the circulation of the *Nation* remained higher than that of the *New Age*, its chief competitor.[2]

'Men of letters'

Massingham's *Nation*, as his *Star* and his *Daily Chronicle*, was an important vehicle for the 'man of letters'. Though the term had lost much of its original austerity and primacy,[3] the literary world which it then still suggested in the broadest sense – the writer, the artist, the critic, the literary journalist, the populariser, or whatever – found in the New Journalism of the later Victorian years and of the Edwardian period ever-widening outlets through which to influence the ideas and the tastes of society. And the artist and the critic were confronted to their mutual benefit. They stretch through the pages of the *Nation* – Shaw, Bennett, Galsworthy, Rothenstein, etc. – and also Garnett, Nevinson, Archer, Masterman, Roger Fry, Tomlinson, Murry and the rest. Without them, the *Nation* would have been as 'dull' as the *Speaker*, would have narrowed its appeal, and could hardly have survived.

The *Nation*'s history often runs parallel to that of other weeklies. Two months after the birth of the *Nation*, the *New Age*, founded in 1894, after vicissitudes, financial as well as editorial, came under the joint editorship of A. R. Orage and Holbrook Jackson and entered on a new life as 'An Independent Socialist Review of Politics, Literature and Art'. By January 1908 Orage was alone in the editorial chair where he remained until 1922. Like the *Nation*, the *New Age* was something of a literary club, but even more informal, with casual gatherings for tea on Monday afternoons in the basement of the A.B.C. in Chancery Lane, where galley proofs were read, politics argued and the arts discussed.[4]

When the *New Age* went over to Guild Socialism in 1912, Shaw and

---

1 This account of the relation to the Joseph Rowntree Social Service Trust is based on the 'Minutes' of the Directors from 1907 to 1914, Rowntree Papers. The discussion of the *Contemporary Review* is in the 'Minute' for 5 Sept. 1911.
2 Wallace Martin, '*The New Age*' under Orage (Manchester, 1967), 10.
3 John J. Gross, *The Rise and Fall of the Man of Letters* (London, 1969), xiii.
4 Paul Selver, *Orage and The New Age Circle* (London, 1959); Philip Mairet, *A. R. Orage, A Memoir* (London, 1936); Martin, '*The New Age*' under Orage.

Webb established the *New Statesman* with Clifford Sharp as editor – he had been a director of the *New Age* and a contributor. Since the *New Age* and the *New Statesman*, both more inclined toward doctrinaire Socialism than the *Nation*, competed for the same audience, Orage was infuriated. When he read the first issue of the *New Statesman*, he exclaimed, 'Worse than the *Nation* – damnation.' Mrs Webb, perhaps somewhat on the defensive, recorded at the time that the *Nation* Group predicted that the new venture would fail.[1]

From the start there was friction. In its opening issue (12 April 1913) the *New Statesman* pronounced: 'We shall strive to face and examine social and political issues in the same spirit in which the chemist or biologist faces and examines his test-tubes or his specimens.' Massingham was unmoved. Several months before, he wrote that Mr and Mrs Sidney Webb bring out their 'new collectivist weekly' in the coming year but collectivism 'on the old Fabian lines'. The papers differed more in tone than in attitude.[2] Desmond MacCarthy remarked that while the two periodicals often advocated the same views, '*The Nation* supplied arguments which encouraged its readers to feel that they were the salt of the earth and the tone of the *Statesman* in arguing the same point would be, "if you *want* to escape being a short-sighted fool, this is the line you must take".'[3]

Providing commentary on current events and criticism of all the arts in their contemporary expression, the *Nation*, the *New Age*, and the *New Statesman* had much in common. And each had its passionate admirers. In 1908 Arnold Bennett considered 'the *Nation* out of sight the ablest weekly' (he was then also writing for the *New Age*), and Shaw is said to have referred to Orage as 'the most brilliant editor of the twentieth century'.[4]

During the Massingham years the *Nation* published most of England's significant writers: poets, novelists, dramatists, essayists, critics. From the start the editor made a bid for the best. Back in the nineties Massingham was one of the few who foresaw that ultimately

---

[1] Mairet, *A. R. Orage, A Memoir*, 71. *Beatrice Webb's Diaries, 1912–1924*, ed. Margaret I. Cole (London, 1952), 11.
[2] 'Wayfarer' in *Nation*, 14 Dec. 1912.
[3] MacCarthy, *Humanities*, 19–20.
[4] Bennett to Garnett, 29 Nov. 1908, in *The Letters of Arnold Bennett*, ed. James Hepburn, II (London, 1968), 236; Gross, *The Rise and Fall of the Man of Letters*, 230.

Thomas Hardy would be ranked higher even than Meredith.[1] And now in the very first issue of the *Nation* appeared Hardy's poem 'A Latter-Day Chorus'. But this association did not hold, perhaps, as Harold Massingham suggests, because his father 'was no countryman'. Even after years of acquaintance, on an occasion when Massingham was Hardy's guest for lunch at Max Gate, they did not get 'beyond an interchange of courtesies'. But Massingham's admiration remained undiminished. In 1910 when Hardy was awarded an 'O.M.' Massingham declared (*Nation*, 16 July 1910) that 'Mr. Hardy is now the one great classical novelist left to us, his works representing . . . the greatest imaginative achievement in modern English literature by a living author.' Ten years later (*Nation*, 5 June 1920). Massingham wrote: 'Thomas Hardy's eightieth birthday finds him securely fixed in his right place as the greatest literary figure of our time, perhaps of all our English times since Shakespeare.' In 1922 Massingham wrote a sensitive comment on Hardy's *Late Lyrics*, and in 1924 accompanied Clement Shorter and Archibald Henderson (Shaw's biographer) to Dorchester to see Hardy's *The Famous Tragedy of the Queen of Cornwall*.[2]

But in 1907 Massingham sought a poet who would contribute regularly. Nevinson suggested Francis Thompson; in reporting this conversation to the Meynells (Alice and Wilfrid) Nevinson tells us, 'a chill fell over us all' for Mrs Meynell at first thought she was to be suggested. Thompson's poem 'The Fair Inconstant' appeared in the issue for 6 April 1907. Massingham, referring to the old *Daily Chronicle* days, sought further contributions: 'I have always retained the utmost admiration for your poetic genius, and regard with much warmth its association with a paper like the *Nation*.' But Thompson died in November. A tribute, unsigned, in the *Nation* for 23 November, was written by Alice Meynell.[3]

Bernard Shaw is as closely associated with Massingham's *Nation* as with his *Chronicle*. The issue for 28 August 1910 carried his celebrated

[1] Sassoon, *Meredith*, 230. Massingham reviewed Hardy's *Tess of the D'Urbervilles* in the *D.C.*, 28 Dec. 1891.
[2] Carl J. and Clara Weber (eds.), *Thomas Hardy's Correspondence at Max Gate* (Waterville, Me., 1968), Nos. 2280, 2283, 2757; *H.W.M.*, 176–80, for the review of *Late Lyrics*. On the 1924 visit, see Archibald Henderson, 'Mr. Hardy Achieves a Second Immortality', *International Book Review* (April 1924)
[3] N.D., 21 Mar. 1907; Meynell, *Life of Francis Thompson*, 336–7, 216.

review of Chesterton's *George Bernard Shaw* – 'the best work of literary art I have yet provoked'. When Shaw's mother died in 1913, H.W.M. referred to her son 'whose wit, clear, good humoured, derisive judgment of the ways of the world, descended in no small degree from her'.[1] But Shaw's presence in the *Nation*'s columns usually means controversy. Thus he is in the midst of the discussion over censorship and licensing of plays. In 1907 the censor refused to license Granville Barker's *Waste* and Shaw was aroused. In 1909 two short plays of his own – *Press Cuttings* and *The Shewing-up of Blanco Posnet* – were banned from the stage; the issues were discussed in the *Nation* (June and July) along with comments from Shaw. All of which grew out of discussion between Shaw and Massingham. In June, well before formal statements were drafted, Shaw outlined to Massingham, in rough form, proposals for the position of the theatre managers: freedom of managers to produce what they pleased; immunity from all censorship except by a public prosecutor; in the event that theatres were placed under a licensing authority, decisions to be made by the whole body and not by an individual or a committee; all complaints brought to the licensing authority to be communicated to the manager and the lessee concerned before any action was taken. Such proposals were debated before the joint select committee appointed in June in Parliament. When its report was issued in November, Massingham sought an article of comment for the *Nation* but Shaw pleaded a schedule so crowded that it was impossible.[2] For censorship the outcome was a decided improvement in procedures; licensing continued, but upon application, the producer could learn in advance of production whether or not the play was licensed. Massingham, as is so often the case, is not a part of the recognised 'history' of the controversy. As usual he was behind the scenes. Yet he is there, close to the action, in communication with a leading participant, discussing issues with him, influencing his judgment. And the *Nation* publicised the course of events and appraised the results.

---

[1] *Nation*, 1 Mar. 1913, p. 882. Some of Shaw's pieces in *Nation*, 1909–18, are collected in *Pen Portraits and Reviews*.

[2] *Nation*, 26 Oct. p. 117, and 16 Nov. 1907, p. 237; 8 Feb. 1909. Shaw to Massingham (draft), 30 June, 1909 (U. of Texas). Shaw to Massingham (draft), n.d., G.B.S.P., Add. MS. 50559/313–14. This last letter can be dated by context and on location in the MS., as between 11 and 13 Nov. 1909.

Surviving correspondence between Massingham and Frank Harris adds to our knowledge of the well-known Shaw–Harris controversy over Shakespeare's sonnets. Harris had charged Shaw with stealing from him the identification of Mary Fitton as the 'Dark Lady' – Shaw used this in his interlude, *The Dark Lady of the Sonnets*, produced in 1910. In his hilarious manner Shaw responded that the Mary Fitton theory did not originate with Harris, but went back to Thomas Tyler – this answer Shaw set forth in his review of Harris' play, *Shakespeare and his Love*, produced in November 1910. The Shaw review, with the title 'Mr. Frank Harris's Shakespeare' is in the *Nation* for 24 December 1910 and concludes: 'Mr Harris's theory of Shakespeare as a man with his heart broken by a love affair will not wash.'

The rest of the story is best followed in a Massingham–Harris exchange of letters hitherto unknown.[1] Harris, in Nice, did not see the Shaw review until mid-January, 1911. Thereupon he wrote to Massingham as follows:

2 Square Gambetta
NICE

January 20th/10 [1911]

Dear Massingham,

I have only just seen Shaw's pretended review of my play in *The Nation*. I do not object to any criticism, but he has evolved Shakespeare out of his own consciousness, and I would like to show that it is ludicrous. Secondly in the guise of a review he has attacked me, and I want to answer him in a good-natured way, just to warn him that he must do better than this, or that one will not need to answer him in the future. I think you will give me the same hospitality, you have accorded to him and so I send you my reply. It is nearly as long as his attack, but I cannot help it. I have tried to make it of at least equal importance. If for any reason you cannot use it, please let me have it back at once to the above address.

I never see *The Nation*, you do not send it to me, or I should have answered this when it first appeared. The Shakespeare subject is of perennial interest it seems, and Shaw allowed a month to elapse before he answered me. By the way, I wish you had done the play yourself instead of letting Shaw do it.

The weather here is wonderful, and I am working hard.

Yours sincerely,
[Signed] Frank Harris

P.S. Could you let me see a proof of this? By the way, read my Carlyle article in the February issue of *The English Review*.

[1] M.P.

We do not have the Harris 'reply', mentioned – it did not appear in the *Nation*. Nor did Massingham comment on the Shaw review. But we do have Massingham's answer (in draft form) to Harris:

24th January 1911

My dear Harris,

You and Shaw between you will slay 'The Nation'. I gave up rather over five mortal columns to Shaw's review of your book – which really was a very kind and handsome review – and now you send me between six and seven columns of your answer to Shaw. This is to usher in a deluge of authors, to the drowning out of my poor politics, art, literature and the rest of the show. On the personal point, too, I am bound to say I think Shaw is right. I complain of you, as all your friends complain, that you have not done enough literary work, especially considering the kind of work which it is always in your power to give us. You are always read, and get an audience, so I find myself a little prejudiced against you upon a point on which I think you feel rather agrieved [sic]. Why not, therefore, write a shorter and milder reply, (you are unnecessarily savage about Shaw) making your really good and interesting Shakespearian criticism the main point of your article instead of a quite subordinate feature.

Yours very truly,

Frank Harris Esq.

Harris, in writing to Massingham, it may be noted, remarked: 'I wish you had done the play yourself instead of letting Shaw do it.' Massingham had indeed established his own reputation as a dramatic critic. So Shaw had declared at the *Daily News* testimonial dinner in March 1907, and a year later in a letter to Massingham himself, lingered over the same idea. Years later, J. L. Garvin of the *Observer* spoke of Massingham's Hazlitt touch.[1]

Massingham's old friend, William Archer, wrote dramatic criticism fairly regularly for the *Nation* between 1908 and 1910, a fact which E. R. Cross reported on enthusiastically to the directors of the Rowntree Trust. But, we are told, a difference of opinion developed between Archer and the editor over use of the space available[2] and Massingham became to a considerable degree his own dramatic critic. His reviews and articles often appear for weeks in succession. Examination of a

[1] *Daily News*, 11 Mar. 1907; G.B.S.P. (draft), Add. MS. 50558/52; *Observer*, 31 Aug. 1924.
[2] Rowntree Papers, Minute, 21 Jan. 1909; C. Archer, *William Archer: Life, Work and Friendship* (New Haven, 1931), 314.

random year – 1 April 1911 to 30 March 1912 – reveals eleven reviews of plays staged, two book reviews on dramas, and three other articles about the theatre. He assisted with the creation of 'The Everyman Theatre' in Hampstead and expressed repeated interest in a 'national theatre'. His review of G. K. Chesterton's *Magic* was considered by Harold Massingham as 'the most direct, subtle and triumphant piece of dramatic criticism' his father ever wrote.[1]

Massingham, indeed, attended the theatre at every opportunity – Nevinson's diary keeps us informed. In September 1913 H.W.M. reviewed for the *Nation* a performance of Shaw's *Androcles and the Lion*. It 'is a fable, and will, I suppose, succeed as a farce', Massingham wrote; to Nevinson he remarked that he didn't care for it – 'too burlesque'.[2] A few months earlier Massingham had reviewed *Caesar and Cleopatra*, a production which received a shower of attention. But, said Shaw, 'only two critics, Mr. Massingham and Mr. Desmond MacCarthy knew that what they were looking at was a chapter of Mommsen and a page of Plutarch'.[3]

Shaw's respect for Massingham's judgment and talent as a dramatic critic was manifest many times over. In 1895 he had been host at a private reading of *Candida*. In 1917 he was present for a trial reading of *Heartbreak House* which was not published until 1919 and not produced until 1921. On the afternoon of 8 June 1917, at Charlotte Shaw's invitation, he was one of 'a select few' – Sir Sydney Olivier, Gilbert Murray and Lady Kathleen Scott (widow of the explorer) were the others – who gathered at the Shaw home above the *Nation* office. As Lady Scott tells the story Shaw was in his best form as he read all the roles of *Heartbreak House*. To the end of his life, on occasion, Massingham discussed Shaw's work with him. In May 1924 Shaw sent a copy of *St Joan*, just published, to Massingham for his birthday and correspondence followed on Shaw's handling of his characters on the stage.[4]

---

[1] *H.W.M.*, 227–30; 'Wanted: An After War Theatre', *Nation*, 12 Jan. 1918, p. 486; 'Organized Art: A State Theatre', *Morning Leader*, 11 Dec. 1911.
[2] *Nation*, 6 Sept. 1913, p. 843 and N.D., 1 Sept. 1913.
[3] *Nation*, 19 Apr. 1913 (also in *H.W.M.*, 243–5); Shaw in *New Statesman*, 3 May, 1913.
[4] Shaw to Massingham, 7 June 1924, M.P. (Copy); Stanley Weintraub, *Journey to Heartbreak: The Crucible Years of Bernard Shaw, 1914–1918* (New York, 1971), 243–4.

John Galsworthy's fame had been assured by 1906 with *Man of Property* and *The Silver Box*. Of the latter an early issue of the *Nation* (13 April 1907) pronounced: 'No modern play running at a London theatre has any place beside it for significance, for artistic and intellectual power.' Galsworthy's first piece in the *Nation* was 'The Lost Dog' in the issue for 4 May 1907; other sketches followed promptly to be gathered together and published in 1908 as *A Commentary*. A smaller group made up *A Motley* (1910). When *The Patrician* was published in March 1911, Nevinson prided himself that he was the prototype for 'Courtier' and Galsworthy wrote that in fact 'your figure stood bang in my path'.[1] As the *Nation* reviewer of *The Patrician* Galsworthy requested Masterman. The unsigned review found Galsworthy 'in a new phase, as a political philosopher'.[2]

On 20 July 1910, Winston Churchill, now Home Secretary, made a major statement of policy on prison reform to the Commons. He went out of his way to remark that solitary confinement 'has been brought before our notice by various able writers in the Press, and by exponents of the drama who have with force and feeling brought home to the general public the pangs which prisoners may suffer in long months of solitude'. The *Nation*'s 'Diary of the Week', in the issue of 23 July, referred to Churchill's 'large and bold scheme of prison reform'. He had exhorted his hearers to 'a tireless effort towards the discovery of some regenerative process. . . This is the note that Liberals like to hear from their leaders'. Soon after (30 July) Churchill wrote Galsworthy:

I am very much obliged to you . . . for the excellent valuable support you have given me in the public Press. There can be no question that your admirable play bore a most important part in creating that atmosphere of sympathy and interest which is so noticeable upon this subject at the present time.[3]

In the immediate background of Churchill's prison reforms are Galsworthy's pieces in the *Nation* – first his 'The House of Silence' (19 October 1907) and 'Order' (2 May 1908); these were inspired by a

[1] N.D., 4 and 11 Apr. 1911; H. B. Marrot, *The Life and Letters of John Galsworthy* (New York, 1936), 314–15.

[2] *Nation*, 25 Mar. 1911; Marrot, *Life and Letters of John Galsworthy*, 311.

[3] *Hansard*, Commons, 20 July 1909, 5th ser., vol. XIX, col. 1,349. Churchill, *Winston S. Churchill*, companion volume 2, pt 2, 1,189–91.

visit to Dartmoor Prison and announce his concern over solitary confinement. On 9 March 1909, *Strife* had its first performance at the Duke of York's Theatre. Included in the chorus of praise was Archer's extensive notice in the *Nation* (13 March 1909), 'Mr Galsworthy Arrives'. In the audience were three members of the *Nation* staff – Nevinson, Brailsford and Masterman.[1] Soon after (1 and 8 May) the *Nation* ran Galsworthy's 'Open Letter' to the Home Secretary on 'Solitary Confinement', with editorial comment in the 'Diary of the Week'. In the issue for 12 June is another Galsworthy article, 'The Prisoner'. These came to the attention of Churchill, then at the Board of Trade, who wrote to Galsworthy of his great admiration for *Strife* and his sympathetic interest in the problem. Discussions ensued among Churchill, Lord Crewe (Colonial Office), Haldane (War Office) along with Gladstone and Samuel (Home Office). By September Galsworthy himself was in touch with Gladstone who announced his intention of reducing the length of solitary confinement.[2]

With Churchill moving to the Home Office in February 1910, Galsworthy's association became even closer. *Justice* was produced the same month – Churchill attended a performance – and Archer in the *Nation* (26 February) spoke of the 'dynamic' three-minute scene in the solitary cell – daring, unforgettable'. At lunch on Tuesday, 5 April (almost certainly the *Nation* Lunch) Masterman, now Under Secretary at the Home Office, told Galsworthy 'he had turned the Home Office upside down with *Justice*'. On 12 July Galsworthy called on Churchill and Masterman who outlined the projected reforms which were presented to the Commons by Churchill eight days later.[3]

Two groups of Galsworthy sketches in the *Nation* having proved successful, Massingham sought more. In September 1910, Galsworthy wrote to him:

Alas! Yes, still silent. . . If I do burst out again into studies or sketches, I think they will not be social, but working towards a book that might express what of reverence there may be in me. I find it hopeless to hunt about for

[1] N.D., 9 Mar. 1909.
[2] See Marrot, *Life and Letters of John Galsworthy* for much of the Churchill–Galsworthy correspondence, the whole of which is in the Galsworthy Papers, U. of Birmingham, which also has the correspondence with Crewe, Haldane and Gladstone.
[3] Churchill, *Winston S. Churchill*, companion volume 2, pt 2, 1,148–53, 1,187–8; Marrot, *Life and Letters of John Galsworthy*, 261, 281, 283.

subjects. I must express a mood, and the lived through moods which remain within one's consciousness are so rare.

Ten days later, he wrote again 'I have in my head a book of studies, sketches, impressions of moods which I would group under the heading, "At the Inn of Tranquility". Perhaps you might care to print say one a month.' In his diary he noted that he was planning this volume 'to consist of nature and life sketches which should bring out the side of one which acquiesces and is serene'. They duly appeared, though hardly one a month (in 1911, he wrote to Massingham 'I have failed lamentably to sustain my sketches') but over a period of two years – 'Evolution', 'Sheep-shearing', 'Riding in the Mist', 'Threshing' and the rest. They composed, in collected form, The Inn of Tranquility (1912). Other Nation pieces were incorporated in The Little Man (1915).[1]

But it was the Galsworthy interested in correcting social evils who most attracted Massingham. A Galsworthy letter to The Times, on 28 February 1914, concerning sweated labour, poor housing, treatment of pauper lunatics, cruelty to animals, inspired the comment in the Nation that Galsworthy represents 'more than anybody else the indignation with the wrongs ... of our civilization'.[2]

In July 1913, the Galsworthys took up town residence in a flat at 1A Adelphi Terrace, neighbouring the Nation office, where they remained some five years. There were 'jolly' dinners at Romano's and the Automobile Club with Barrie, Conrad, Massingham and others. Hugh Massingham tells the story that his father, who liked good food and good wine, went off to the Galsworthys to celebrate the appearance of The Stoic (1917) and returned to mutter: 'tough mutton and 3s. 6d. Burgundy'. When the Galsworthys in November 1918 moved from Adelphi Terrace to Grove Lodge in Hampstead early dinner guests included Barrie, Arnold Bennett, Max Beerbohm, Hugh Walpole and the Massinghams.[3]

In December 1913, the Galsworthys and the Massinghams, finding themselves on the same boat out of Marseilles, joined up for an Egyp-

[1] Galsworthy to Massingham, 3 and 10 Sept. 1910, M.P.; Marrot, Life and Letters of John Galsworthy, 305, 697.
[2] Nation, 7 Mar. 1914, unsigned leader, 'Our Present Discontents' and p. 923.
[3] Robertson-Scott, 'We' and Me, 161; Marrot, Life and Letters of John Galsworthy, 433–4, 445.

tian tour, with a stay together at the Palace Hotel at Heliopolis and an eleven-day trip into the desert from Luxor. On their return Massingham wrote 'The Last of the Pharaohs', a comment on the Kitchener regime.[1] The Galsworthy–Massingham friendship continued until the end of Massingham's life. When *The Skin Game* was produced in 1920, H.W.M. wrote Galsworthy

> I saw 'The Skin Game' last night; it left me in a continued state of excitement... I can't imagine a finer or more important play. The worst of it is those accursed critics (including the 'Nation' one) didn't seem to have a notion what you were driving at. However, the play is in for a glorious run; and let's hope some of it will penetrate. A thousand congratulations.[2]

Of *Loyalties*, produced in 1922, 'Wayfarer' remarks: 'Mr. Galsworthy is, of all dramatists, the one who keeps most closely in touch with the social history of his time.' And a year later, on receipt of a copy of *Captures*, Massingham wrote to Galsworthy: 'It seems to me to have heaps of fine workmanship in it.' The final item in the record is in March 1924 when 'Wayfarer' asked for a revision of the initial, unfavourable, verdict of the critics on the play, *The Forest*.[3]

On 26 November 1909 Arnold Bennett recorded in his journal: 'H. W. Massingham wrote me yesterday inviting me to contribute to the *Nation*... He said he considered *The Old Wives' Tale* to be one of the one or two great novels of the past thirty years.' In the issue of 24 September 1910 an admiring *Nation* review of *Clayhanger*, one and a half columns in length, was much appreciated by Bennett. Three months later, Bennett wrote in his journal: 'On Saturday appeared in the *Nation* the most striking article on me that has yet been written.' He referred to the *Nation* (10 December) in which an unsigned article, 'The Grey Novel', declared: 'We have at last among us a true and notable realist... When Arnold Bennett wrote the 'Old Wives' Tale' the discerning critic had no hesitation in placing him among the masters, and ranking his novel among the real books of our generation.'[4]

[1] Marrot, *Life and Letters of John Galsworthy*, 385–9; *Nation*, 7 Mar. 1914.
[2] Massingham to Galsworthy, n.d., U. of Birmingham.
[3] *Nation*, 18 Mar. 1922 and *New Statesman*, 29 Mar. 1924; Massingham to Galsworthy, 1 Nov. 1923, U. of Birmingham.
[4] Bennett, *Journal*, I, 347, 401; Bennett, MS. journal, 26 Sept. 1910, Berg. An unsigned review of *Old Wives' Tale* in *Nation*, 21 Nov. 1908 was by Garnett (*Letters of Arnold*

Bennett had long since been a regular reader of the *Nation*. While settled for a time at the Villa des Néfliers, near Fontainebleau, Bennett recorded in his journal (4 May 1908) that among the little things which gave him the 'liveliest pleasure' was 'opening and glancing through the *Athenaeum* and through the *Nation* on Monday mornings, especially the advertisements of new books'. In November he wrote Garnett that he thought the *Nation* was easily the best weekly.[1]

In April 1911 Bennett lunched with Massingham, Shorter and others at the Devonshire Club where he and Massingham made arrangements for a series of articles which appeared in the *Nation* from May to July 1911, under the head 'Life in London'. On Bennett's first appearance at a *Nation* Lunch (2 May) Nevinson set down this description:

Sat next to Arnold Bennett ... young, brown haired, brilliant-eyed ... misshapen mouth and irregular teeth, speaks in high voice with slight impediment, was very agreeable, talking of Galsworthy & Phillpotts & all manner ... Said he would not care to do anything but write ... only regretted that he could never know anything through & through as a writer.[2]

Bennett's writing from 1914 to 1918 was largely journalistic, and this put him in even closer touch with the press and its editors. Association with Massingham developed into friendship. In July 1919 Massingham along with Masterman spent several days with Bennett at Comarques. There was 'much fine wine, much tennis'. Massingham read aloud the first act of Bennett's play, *What the Public Wants*. In recording the event, Bennett observed that Massingham 'showed an all-round highly sensitive appreciation in all the arts'.[3]

There were dinners with Bennett as host; one in 1920 included Barrie, Elgar, Sassoon, Massingham. And luncheons at the Reform Club.[4] On 22 March 1920 Bennett wrote to Hugh Walpole: 'I am having great larks with Massingham & Murry of the *Nation*.' This episode concerned the work of a popular novelist, Charles Garvice, to

Bennett, ed. Hepburn, II, 232–3). Nevinson (N.S., 11 Dec., 1910) assigns the article, 'The Grey Novel', to Brailsford.

[1] *Journal*, I, 296; *Letters of Arnold Bennett*, ed. Hepburn, II, 236.

[2] Bennett, *Journal*, II, 8 (29 Apr. 1911). Of these sketches Galsworthy wrote in praise to Massingham (Marrot, *Life and Letters of John Galsworthy*, 697). N.D., 2 May.

[3] Bennett, *Journal*, II, 288.

[4] *Ibid.*, 297, 320; MS. journal of Bennett, 20 May and 15 June, 1921, Berg.

whose defence Bennett came, referring to the unsympathetic comment of 'Wayfarer' (Massingham) and Murry as 'mischievous and perverse'.[1] But it could hardly have caused much of a rift for soon, over Easter, Massingham spent the week-end with Bennett and Frank Swinnerton on the *Marie Marguerite* off Dover. Massingham read the first two acts of Bennett's new play, to be called 'The Bright Island' and Bennett agreed that the third act would be 'a hell of a job' .[2]

H. G. Wells' connection with the *Nation* was less significant, at least before the war. Wells hoped for *Nation* serialisation in 1907 of his new novel *Tono-Bungay*. He sent Massingham a copy which was read with 'great interest and sympathy'. On 13 June 1907 Massingham gave his answer:

it is with very great regret, and much hesitation, that I decide that your very powerful and interesting book cannot well be published by us. . . It would spoil your book, unless we could publish it in tolerably big instalments. . . This we could not do.[3]

So serialisation in the *Nation* of a Wells novel had to await the war.[4]

Chesterton likewise was never close to the *Nation* Group though he had connections with the Liberal press through the *Speaker* and the *Daily News*. Nevinson mentions that he attended one of the first *Nation* Lunches, but it was no place for his 'delightful paradoxes and epigrams' and 'I think he never came again'.[5] But Chesterton was published in the first month of the *Nation* and until the war his pieces are frequent. On a political matter – the control of politics by the Cabinet – there are lively Chesterton letters in January and February 1911. Massingham's attitude towards Chesterton was usually caustic, reminding the author of *Magic*: 'the Middle Ages do not merely seem to be over; they are over' (*Nation*, 15 November 1913).

'If you want to understand my father', remarked Hugh Massingham, 'you must read Mark Rutherford, especially *The Revolution in Tanner's*

---

[1] *Letters of Arnold Bennett*, ed. Hepburn, III, 123–6; *Nation* for Mar.-Apr., 1920.
[2] Bennett, MS. journal, 6 Apr. 1920, Berg. Swinnerton describes this week-end in *Swinnerton: An Autobiography* (London, 1937), 255–6.
[3] Wells' engagement book, 10 Mar. 1907; Massingham to Wells, 16 May 1907 and 13 June [1907]. Wells' Papers, U. of Illinois.
[4] *Tono-Bungay* was serialised in the *English Review* beginning Dec. 1908.
[5] Nevinson, *More Changes, More Chances*, 216–17.

Lane.' And to a friend, H. W. Massingham himself often suggested a reading of *The Autobiography* and *Deliverance*. 'If you've ever been sad for a longish time, they will come with a kind of healing touch that doesn't soon go away.'[1]

Upon the death of William Hale White (his pen name was Mark Rutherford) in 1913, Massingham remarked that 'literary London hardly knew him or noted him'. But Hale White's life had always been a part of Massingham's own – from those days of his early apprenticeship in Norwich when he read proofs of the 'London Letter'. It was appropriate that at the moment of Massingham's greatest personal sorrow (the death of his first wife in 1905) Hale White called upon Massingham in London.[2]

Wilfred Stone has written: 'nearly every word that William Hale White wrote was the product of a self-confessional impulse, or at least the reflection of a deep intellectual or emotional engagement'. This might as easily have been written of Massingham. The parallel goes further – the deepest influence on each was that of Nonconformist religion, for Hale White that of Bedford, for Massingham that of Norwich, both strongholds in Victorian England of Puritan dissent. On going to London each left behind orthodox religious faith and Massingham, like Hale White, 'spent the rest of his life trying to find some substitute in the world of men for the community of belief he had known in his provincial birthplace'.[3]

Mark Rutherford is 'the only great modern English writer sufficiently interested in provincial dissent, and knowing enough about it, to give it a serious place in fiction' – thus Massingham described him in the 'Memorial Introduction' to *The Autobiography*.[4] And in another connection Massingham wrote that Hale White

lays bare 'shy neighborhoods,' like out-of-the-way London or out of the way Eastern Midlands, studying the life ... of the obscure, lower, middle

---

[1] Author's conversation with Hugh Massingham; *H.W.M.*, 171.

[2] 'London Diary', *Nation*, 22 Mar. 1913. Massingham's letter to Hale White's son, n.d., Public Library, Bedford, 'You may remember coming to my house in Grosvenor Road on a sad occasion eight years ago.' It is unlikely that the son went alone.

[3] Wilfred Stone, *Religion and Art of William Hale White* (New York, 1967), 3–4.

[4] Quoted in Stone, *ibid.*, 128. See also Massingham's article in *New Leader*, 5 Oct. 1923, reproduced in *H.W.M.*, 165, and his article on Hale White in the *Dictionary of National Biography*.

people who built our country chapels and carried on the Puritan tradition. . .
He makes their lives shine with sympathetic genius.[1]

With similar traditions behind them, Massingham along with William Robertson Nicoll, the editor of the *British Weekly* and of the *Bookman*, were largely responsible for providing for Mark Rutherford a prominent place among minor novelists. 'I am an old and profound admirer', wrote Massingham to the family upon Hale White's death.[2] The writings of Mark Rutherford during the last years of his life, largely published in the *Nation*, were a substantial part of the collection, *Last Pages from a Journal* (1915) – one of its pieces, 'The Love of Woman', published after the author's death, owes its title to Massingham. And his comment was a significant element in the discussion of the relation of *The Autobiography* and *Deliverance* of Mark Rutherford to the life of William Hale White himself. Massingham remarked in 1924 that *The Groombridge Diary* of Dorothy V. White and *Letters to Three Friends* present the 'closest revelation' of Hale White we are likely to have.[3]

Massingham's admiration for Mark Rutherford was passed on to others. To Lady Ottoline Morrell he suggested the comparison with Rousseau. William Rothenstein, very likely led to Mark Rutherford through the columns of the *Nation*, found in him 'a provincial flavor . . . an imaginative quality' akin to English painting. It was after reading *Deliverance*, probably at Massingham's suggestion, that Arnold Bennett noted: 'The man had no notion of fiction. But a work not easily forgotten. Full of wisdom and high things.' And through Bennett, André Gide's interest developed into enthusiasm.[4]

In 1924 Massingham sent Shaw a copy of the new Memorial Edition of *The Autobiography*. We have Shaw's comment in a letter to Massingham, hitherto unknown.

[1] 'London Diary', *Nation*, 22 Mar. 1913. See also the comment in *Daily News and Leader*, 22 Sept. 1913.
[2] The letter, n.d., is in Public Library, Bedford.
[3] Catherine Macdonald Maclean, *Mark Rutherford: A Biography of William Hale White* (London, 1955), 397; *Nation*, 26 Feb. 1916, pp. 758–9; 'Wayfarer' in *New Statesman*, 31 May 1924.
[4] Robert Gathorne-Hardy (ed.), *Ottoline: Memoirs of Lady Ottoline Morrell* (New York, 1964), 157. For Rothenstein, see *Men and Memories*, II (New York, 1932), 219. On Bennett, see journal, 19 Feb. 1914 and 30 Sept. 1923, Berg. On Gide, see Justin O'Brien (trans.), *Journals of André Gide* (2 vols., New York, 1947–51), 2 (1915–16), *passim*.

I read this at a single sitting: I don't know why. It is valuable as a document of unmistakable authenticity describing what Dissent really is. These dull religious sects and the minister getting light from Wordsworth (like John Stuart Mill) but having only brains enough to break out into spots, mostly irritable and angry, makes desperate but readable reading. It was really his struggle with his ignorance; for with a reasonable amount of knowledge and culture he would have been at no disadvantage.[1]

One wonders at Massingham's thoughts in response.

Associated with the *Nation* is a host of other writers. When Augustus Jessopp died in 1914 he was generally remembered for his historical scholarship but to Massingham he was always the schoolmaster at Norwich. Jessopp did leave, in 1879, to become rector of Scarning in Norfolk. One letter to Massingham, dated 26 July 1906, survives – praise for Massingham's writing and amusing details of problems back in Norwich. He occasionally wrote book reviews for the *Nation* and it was a matter of general knowledge that Massingham proposed to Campbell-Bannerman the Deanery of Norwich for Jessopp, but in vain.[2]

Of William Rothenstein, lithographer and painter, Roger Fry wrote in the *Nation* that he was 'one of our very few real draughtsmen'. With Rothenstein Massingham was on informal terms, an association which may have reached back to 1893 when the *Daily Chronicle* announced the serial publication of his 'Oxford Characters'. Roger Fry brought to the attention of *Nation* readers the great exhibitions. When Eric Gill first exhibited his sculpture at the Chenil Gallery, Chelsea, in January 1911, Fry found it 'an astonishing phenomenon'. His articles in 1912 on the Post-Impressionist Exhibition at the Grafton Gallery attracted special attention.[3]

It was through Rothenstein that Massingham met Rabindranath Tagore in 1913, the year in which Tagore received the Nobel prize. Massingham wrote to Rothenstein:

[1] 7 June, 1924. Copy in M.P.
[2] M.P. See also Miss Cross to the author, 6 Apr. 1965.
[3] *Nation*, 10 June 1911 and 11 June 1910; *D.C.*, 14 June 1893. Letters from Massingham to Rothenstein, Houghton. The Fry articles are in *Nation*, 28 Jan. 1911; 20 April and 9 Nov. 1912.

I am deeply indebted for the suggestion about Mr. Tagore's work, and I welcome the idea of his making 'The Nation' its general means of expression . . . His teaching is of the utmost importance to our time and people. . . Nothing like 'Gitanjali' has ever appeared in an English dress since Wordsworth.

Soon after, Massingham heard Tagore read one of his dramas. 'One could not but feel that here was the voice of the East, after a silence of centuries, again speaking in parables and spiritual songs to the hard and coarsened ear of the west.' Massingham proposed that every fortnight for a time, a poem be published. This series appeared from 28 June to 20 September 1913. And Massingham wrote 'Would he [Tagore] consider three guineas for the little group of poems adequate? If not I would gladly increase the amount a little.' Rothenstein brought Tagore to a *Nation* Lunch. And later – 1914, 1915, 1916, 1920 – other Tagore poems were published.[1]

R. C. Lehmann introduced Alfred Noyes to Massingham and the first of Noyes' poems in the *Nation* appeared on 27 April 1907. In Dublin Noyes met Francis Meynell who wrote to him about young Irish poets. 'There is James Stephens . . . who writes some strangely fine verse. . . If you read *The Nation* every week you will be very familiar with his poetry for Massingham has taken a great fancy to it'.[2] R. C. K. Ensor's sketch, 'A Village Character' is in the *Nation*, 1 June 1907. Massingham wrote to him: 'If you could give us two or three studies of town life on the lines of your very remarkable study of village life, I should be grateful. I thought the latter touched with extreme power and reserve of style.' Subsequent articles by Ensor, unsigned, cannot be identified. In 1909 when Ensor turned to social criticism, we have this rather surprising letter from Massingham. 'I return your article because, brilliant as it is, it is a rather more violent assault on our delightful social order than so sedulously moderate a paper as the *Nation* ought to print. I wish it were otherwise.'[3]

Massingham attended a dinner in honour of Anatole France, and spoke of him as 'the greatest living artist in letters'.[4] How he rated the celebrated literary figures in England other than Hardy is indicated by

[1] *Nation*, 14 June 1913, pp. 413–14; Massingham to Rothenstein, n.d., and 7 Oct. 1913, Houghton; N.D., 2 Sept. 1913.
[2] Alfred Noyes, *Two Worlds for Memory* (London, 1953), 24, 72.
[3] Ensor Papers, Corpus Christi College, Oxford. Professor Stephen Koss called these to my attention.
[4] *Nation*, 13 Dec. 1913, p. 479.

his comment in the *Nation*, 7 January, 1922, when J. M. Barrie was granted an O.M. After words of praise for Barrie, he said he should put him behind Kipling and Shaw and even outside a second group composed of Wells, Galsworthy, Conrad, Bennett and George Moore. In particular he thought it would have been 'fitting and gracious' to have granted the O.M. to Kipling. A few days later a letter from Lord Stamfordham advised Massingham that the king had proposed the O.M. for Kipling who had declined it. Back in 1900 Massingham had referred to Kipling as 'the uncrowned laureate' of the English people.[1]

The *Nation*, like the *Speaker*, provided a beginning for many talented, eager young writers. For 'a young man of great promise called Padraic Colum' Yeats besought Garnett of the *Speaker* staff for some reviewing assignments. This work was continued with the *Nation*. Nearly sixty years later Colum recalled a letter Massingham had written him on publishing his short story, 'Maelshaughlinn at the Fair' (*Nation*, 30 May 1908) – 'his praise of the humour of the story heartened me'. Massingham had written 'I am sure our readers must have been delighted with your short story which was quite perfect in its way. . . It was full of color and movement. I shall be glad to have fresh work from you in this line of production.' Thereafter Colum's work appeared frequently. On 10 March 1910 the writer of the 'World of Books' remarked that since the death of Synge 'perhaps the dramatist of most promise of the young Irish School' is Colum.[2] Massingham's special interest in Ireland probably stemmed from his enthusiasm for Gladstone and Home Rule. In 1909 he lectured at Trinity College, Dublin, on 'The Duty of the Press to the People'.[3] James Joyce's *Chamber Music* was first reviewed in the *Nation*, 22 June 1907 – by Arthur Symons. And the first review in England of Joyce's *A Portrait of the Artist as a Young Man* was by H. G. Wells in the *Nation*, 24 February 1917. From Zurich Joyce wrote to Wells: 'I am sure if the book has any success it will be due in great measure to your friendly recommendation.'[4]

---

[1] *Nation*, 7 Jan. 1922; *Speaker*, 23 Mar. 1900, p. 674. Stamfordham's letter, 9 Jan. 1922 is in M.P.
[2] Carolyn G. Heilbrun, *The Garnett Family* (London, 1961), 99 n.; Colum to the author, 22 May and 23 June 1966; Massingham to Colum, 2 June 1908, Berg.
[3] Résumé of lecture in *The Times*, 20 Jan. 1909, p. 6.
[4] S. Gilbert (ed.), *Letters of James Joyce* (New York, 1966), 100.

Then there was R. H. Mottram. In his early twenties, he was a
protégé of the Galsworthys. With the beginning of the *Nation*, Galsworthy advised Mottram that here was his chance. 'You mustn't throw
it away.' The first poem appeared 9 March 1907 and others thereafter,
in 1907 and 1908, all under the pseudonym of 'J. Marjoram'. And
Galsworthy wrote to Mottram, 'Very glad H.W.M. is keen. I thought
he was from what he said to me.' With further assistance from Galsworthy, Mottram's poem 'Bucolic' appeared (unsigned) in the *Nation*,
on 25 June 1910.[1]

W. H. Davies, poet and 'super tramp', was published fairly regularly for some years in the *Nation*; a 'discovery' of Shaw's, this fact
may have brought him to Massingham's attention.[2] For Edward
Thomas there is more of a story. Through Nevinson and Garnett he
became one of the book reviewers for the *Nation* – from 1905 to 1912
his livelihood came from some 100 reviews for various publications
he wrote each year. His first original piece in the *Nation*, on 5 June
1909, was 'A Late Adventure', based on his experience during a year's
tramp through the south of England. His essays and stories then became frequent. His final piece, 'This England', in the *Nation*, on 7
November 1914, came from a visit to midland cities.

But Thomas found it impossible to place his poetry. His verse made
the rounds – the *English Review*, *Blackwood's*, the *Nation*, and so on,
but in vain. In January 1917 Garnett took Thomas' 'Home' and 'The
Owl' (re-entitled 'Those Others') to the *Nation* office but they were
soon returned with Massingham's regrets. Four months later Thomas
was killed in action.[3] He had, it seems, been able to do more for his
American friend, Robert Frost, than for himself. For *A Boy's Will*,
Thomas helped set the reviewers' response by his notice (anonymous)
in *The New Weekly*, 5 April 1913 and this was followed by a favourable
notice in the *Nation*, 20 September 1913. A full-length review of
Frost's *North of Boston* by Lascelles Abercrombie, headed 'A New

---

[1] Galsworthy to Mottram, 6 Mar. 1907; 23 Aug. 1907, U. of Birmingham; R. H. Mottram,
For Some We Loved: An Intimate Portrait of Ada and John Galsworthy (London, 1956),
68.

[2] Archibald Henderson, *Bernard Shaw, Playboy and Prophet* (London, 1932), 742.

[3] R. George Thomas, *Letters from Edward Thomas to Gordon Bottomley* (London, 1968),
209. R. P. Eckert, *Edward Thomas* (New York, 1939), 19, 58–9, 112; Eleanor Farjeon,
Edward Thomas, The Last Four Years (London, 1958), 69, 123–4, 213.

Voice', came in the *Nation*, on 13 June 1914. Such reviews heralded the recognition that was soon to come to Frost in America.[1]

To appreciate more fully Massingham's extraordinary energy, his astonishingly well-stocked mind, and the versatility of his pen, observe his calendar, his concerns, his writing at any given time – for example, in September 1913. His attention was fixed on the naval Estimates, on the complexities of the Irish Question, on the details of the Balkan problem, on the latest incidents of suffragette militancy. He went to see Shaw's new play, *Androcles and the Lion*; he became engrossed in the writing of Tagore and hosted him and Rothenstein at a *Nation* Lunch. Of all this and much more he wrote week after week in the *Nation*. And somehow he found time to write a remarkable article, 'Caricature or Art? – Some Recent Appeals to the Public Taste', for the *Daily News* and *Leader* (22 September) with informed references to Mark Rutherford, Tolstoi and Tagore, as well as to examples of 'bad art'.

For the celebrated men of letters, for those not so successful and for the young aspiring to fame, Massingham's role was very significant – he encouraged, he criticised, he opened up the columns of the *Nation*, he gave them all place and made them known. When Shaw in 1910 made special reference to Massingham's 'editorial services to literature'[2] he was merely expressing the thought of countless others.

[1] Lawrance Thompson, *Robert Frost, The Early Years, 1874–1915* (New York, 1966), 451–2.
[2] Laurence (ed.), *Bernard Shaw, Collected Letters*, vol. 2, *1898–1910*, 936.

CHAPTER 8

The 'Nation' and Radical Politics
(1907–1914)

On its appearance in 1907, the *Nation* was greeted by *The Economist* as 'the new weekly organ of the united Liberal Party'. And the *British Weekly* pronounced: 'it will not be surprising if the *Nation* becomes the authoritative organ of the Liberal Party'.[1]

Such comments proved far wide of the mark. Indeed there is little indication that Massingham ever aspired to speak with authority for the Liberal Party, no evidence whatsoever that he ever found himself doing so. Those at this time who knew Massingham best emphasised as his chief virtue and the nature of his contribution, his independence from any faction, from any party. He once said that 'a paper can't head a party'. We will look in vain for evidence that the *Nation* Group ever stood for a Liberal or even a Radical 'consensus' with Massingham as the moderator and compromiser among conflicting views. The files of the *Liberal Magazine*, which record the history of the party for the years 1907–14 have but a single reference to Massingham and the *Nation*.[2]

Massingham's role was indeed first and last that of the critic, but often more than a touch of the troublemaker and wrecker as well. He was given to distinguishing between Party philosophy and Party practice. Thus, writing in 1911, he declared that his function was 'to interrogate the Government', not necessarily to support it. Liberalism, he said, 'is the general temper of those who vote Radical and Labor'. Ministerialism, on the other hand, he found well represented by the *Westminster Gazette*, orthodox Liberal, and its editor, J. A. Spender. Said Massingham:

I always turn to the *Westminster Gazette* with the utmost interest – first

---

[1] *The Economist*, 9 Mar. 1907; *British Weekly*, 21 Feb. 1907.
[2] *Daily News*, 11 Mar. 1907, 7–8; N.D., 8 Dec. 1900; *Liberal Magazine*, Apr. 1908 (pp. 168–71) where Massingham's views on the Licensing Bill are outlined with approval.

because I always meet an admirable mind, very alert and very fully equipped with arguments for its famous position that all is for the best; and secondly, because I always find myself in disagreement with it.

'Criticism', he said on another occasion, 'is . . . the one condition of efficiency in the public service, and it is therefore, a duty which journalism owes to the community.'[1] We are thus more amused than surprised when we find Shaw in 1913 referring to Massingham, who 'in the *Nation* . . . supports the Government only on condition that he is not to be let in or trifled with', or when G. K. Chesterton complains to A. G. Gardiner that if Massingham has the right 'week after week, to damn and blast the Liberal Party to infinity', why should he not be accorded a similar privilege.[2]

When, in Massingham's judgment, fellow journalists compromised, hedged, prevaricated or appeased, they won his scorn as well as his indignation. The examples are numerous. Take his series of articles, 'The Harmsworth Brand', in 1908, from 18 July to 28 August, inspired by Lord Northcliffe's acquisition of *The Times*. The theme was the constantly shifting ground of Northcliffe's *Daily Mail* on the tariff issue since 1903. In the first article, Massingham wrote: 'The "Times" under Lord Northcliffe may be amusing . . . or . . . successful; it cannot well possess any moral or intellectual force.' And later, of the Harmsworth press: 'What are the views? . . . It has no views, and all views. It can be Liberal and Conservative'. For the record, it may be pointed out that some years later, in 1913, Massingham was writing that the 'new *Times*' under Northcliffe after he had assumed larger control was better than the old.[3]

A frequent target is Garvin. With the failure of the Constitutional Conference in November 1910, the *Observer* shifted abruptly from the federalist position on Home Rule and its talk of 'a quieter Ireland', to an aggressive attack on Redmond and the Irish Nationalists. Blasts came from the Liberal press with Massingham setting the pace with his 'Garvinism' (*Nation*, 19 November). Tailor-made for Massingham's

[1] 'Liberalism and Ministerialism', *Morning Leader*, 13 Mar. 1911; *Daily News and Leader*, 11 July 1913.
[2] *New Statesman*, 12 Apr. 1913, p. 6, unsigned but attributed to Shaw; Chesterton to Gardiner, n.d., Gardiner Papers.
[3] *Nation*, 18 July 1908, p. 567 and 22 Aug. 1908, p. 734. The articles, unsigned, were, by all indications, written by Massingham. *Daily News and Leader*, 13 Oct. 1913.

exploitation was Garvin's 'A Review of Events' in the *Fortnightly Review*, written earlier but published at the same time as his attack on Redmond in the *Observer*, 13 November. Massingham points it all up: For the *Fortnightly*, Mr Garvin needs 'the existence of a mild and sweetly reasonable Mr. Redmond... The Mr. Garvin of the "Observer" requires a ruthless Mr. Redmond, arch-corruptor, Empire-wrecker, content with nothing short of separation.'[1]

When Massingham and his associates wished to define themselves with some precision they were usually 'Radicals'; shortly before the First World War, it was frequently 'New Radicals'. When they wished to be ecumenical they would speak for 'Liberalism'. But this made them uncomfortable and as often as not it became 'New Liberalism' and sometimes 'Radical Liberalism'. One might expect that such terms would have been explicated for readers of the *Nation* in a declaration of faith, an explanation of purpose. There is none. For if we seek anything approaching a dogma in the tone, style and point of view of the *Nation* we shall not find it. Nor shall we necessarily find agreement within the staff, and to quote the *Nation* anonymously, as is common practice, can be quite misleading. In 1912 (*Daily News and Leader*, 17 June) Massingham writes of 'those who believe in Liberalism – that is to say in the principles of political liberty and social progress on the lines of democracy'. It is safe to say that nowhere in Massingham's writings will one find a definition any more precise. When the Conservatives in 1911 accused the Liberals of 'party tyranny' in forcing the limitation of the Lords' veto Massingham observed (*Morning Leader*, 27 March 1911): 'Liberalism is no extreme creed. It represents rather an opportunistic attitude towards politics. The true resources of moderation are the prevailing temperament both of our people and of their leaders'. Such a philosophy somehow held the *Nation* staff together.

Principles are broadly stated with application depending on circumstances. In foreign affairs there should be no dangerous adventures abroad; the essence of British policy should be the maintenance of peace. Consequently the Radical took no Liberal pledge in the Election of 1906 more seriously than that to reduce expenditure on arms.

[1] Gollin, *The Observer and J. L. Garvin*, 241–4.

Political and social policy of the Liberal Party was not, according to Massingham, something carved out, established and revered from afar. Rather 'it has been a slow, secret, many-sided, obscure growth within the party', he wrote in 1909. It was also unstructured. Writing in 1908 Massingham was intrigued with the metaphor of 'the kaleidoscope of politics' – a multitude of details, tumbling over one another as they cross the stage.

From education to the Lords, from the Lords to the land, from the land to temperance, from temperance to old-age pensions, from pensions to women's 'suffrage . . . before any of these questions is well on the way, the kaleidoscope has moved and another is before us.[1]

The figure has further relevance. The general context, the relation of component parts, is constantly changing, each part affecting the whole in a manner different from a moment before.

When Radicals attacked domestic problems they made up in eloquence for any deficiency in precision. It was abundantly clear to them that any action in domestic policy awaited the subordination of the Lords to the Commons. Then a solution could be found for Ireland; then the temperance problem met; then unemployment conquered and provision made for old-age pensions; then the land could be put to uses for the common good. A sign of the times was Asquith's Budget of 1907 – a reformed fiscal policy would finance social reform. As to women, it was no longer a question of whether or not they would be enfranchised, but how.

Leaders in early issues of the *Nation* set forth these matters, becoming increasingly strident. In October 1907 we read:

For the first time in the history of English Liberalism, leaders, with a powerful support of the rank and file, have committed themselves with zeal and even passionate conviction to promote a series of practical measures which . . . have the common result of increasing the powers and resources of the State for the improvement of the material and moral condition of the people.

By 'radicalism' Massingham signified that element in Liberalism which kept alive this spirit.[2]

[1] *Nation*, 27 Nov. 1909, 'The Social Policy of Liberalism', from context almost certainly written by Massingham; *Nation*, 23 May 1908, 'The Government and the Suffrage', by Massingham as we know from N.D., 23 May.
[2] *Nation*, 12 Oct. 1907 ('Socialism in Liberalism').

The function of this chapter is to examine the political and social outlook of Massingham and the *Nation* Group during the pre-war years in the context of 'Liberalism' and 'Radicalism' and in relation to the policies of the Liberal Government.

The Hague Conference – the Entente with Russia

That foreign policy would be an area in which Radicalism and official Liberalism might be difficult to accommodate was at once revealed in the Hague Conference and the Anglo-Russian Entente, both in the summer of 1907. As it happened these episodes coincided with the crystallisation of policy within the British Foreign Office towards France and Germany – best expressed in the famous Memorandum of Eyre Crowe, Senior Clerk, submitted 1 January 1907, emphasising the grave dangers, as Crowe saw them, arising from German ambitions, and the necessity for British naval supremacy and the maintenance of the balance of power. This Memorandum, though it attracted little notice in the Foreign Office at the time, was in fact a statement of the position which Grey, in the course of events and not altogether consciously, had come to adopt as his own.

The stance of the Liberal press, particularly that which could be called Radical (*Manchester Guardian, Daily News, Morning Leader, The Economist* and the *Nation*), was quite different – their columns set forth the goals of peace, warned against jingoism, and opposed large armament. To be sure the *entente* which the Conservative Government had negotiated with France had been welcomed; after all it had eliminated sources of friction between Britain and her chief rival, France.[1]

As to the Liberal Cabinet, Campbell-Bannerman's attitude had always been clear. Back in 1905, for example, he had called for a reduction in armaments and Massingham attacked *The Times* for refusing to treat his remarks seriously. After the Liberal victory of 1906 the Prime Minister was even more vigorous. On 23 July he welcomed, in French, the delegates to the Inter-Parliamentary Union Conference in London; Massingham commented (*Daily News*, 24 July): 'The Prime Minister's speech is the sensation of the hour... I do not think that

---

[1] Massingham's enthusiasm was somewhat tempered by statements in the French press that Britain had offered France military aid against Germany, but these statements he believed to be untrue. H. S. Weinroth, 'The British Radicals and the Balance of Power, 1902–1914', *Historical Journal*, XIII, 4 (1970), 659–60.

any public man of great responsibility has ever gone so far in denouncing war and all its works.' Towards Grey, Radical opinion abruptly changed in his favour once he became Foreign Secretary. In May 1906, in an important statement, he declared that British expenditures on armaments could be safely reduced and he anticipated that the larger question of a reduction of arms by international agreement would be raised at the Hague Conference in 1907. It was, said Massingham, 'an historic declaration'. Reduction of arms would be proposed at the Hague! 'Here . . . is a great and definite advancement in world policy.'[1]

It must have been, therefore, with considerable pride that Massingham published in the inaugural issue of the *Nation* (2 March 1907) the Prime Minister's article, 'The Hague Conference and the Limitation of Armaments'. The purpose of the article seems clear: to allay uneasiness in the British mind about the consequences of a reduction in arms. With guarantees of peace, armaments could be safely reduced. What is not so clear is why Campbell-Bannerman chose to have it published by Massingham – hardly the most representative voice in the Liberal press – and what effect he anticipated abroad.

Massingham's own satisfaction seemed unbounded. In the issue of 16 March, we find him saying: 'The Prime Minister has, we think, every reason to be satisfied with the moral and material effect of his declaration in this paper in favour of international disarmament'. Again, C.-B. was proclaimed as 'the first radical Prime Minister'.[2]

The source of Massingham's elation is a mystery since outside the *Nation*'s columns there was no strong support. So far as the Powers were concerned, Campbell-Bannerman's remarks seemed ill-timed. A Russian statement in January had, with the approval of the Powers, barred such discussion of arms limitation. The proposal was received with misgivings by France and Russia and with outright opposition by Germany and Austria.[3] In England King Edward was disgusted at

---

[1] *The Times*, 23 Jan. 1905, p. 14 c; *Hansard, Commons*, 4th ser., vol. CLVI, cols. 1,411–15; *Speaker*, 12 May 1906. Wilson, *CB: A Life of Sir Henry Campbell-Bannerman*, 536.

[2] 'The Prime Minister and Peace', almost certainly by 'H.W.M.' See also *Nation*, 9 Mar. 1907, p. 55 and 29 June 1907, p. 663.

[3] *Documents diplomatiques français, 1871–1914*, 2nd ser., X (Paris, 1948), 685, 769; Johannes Lepsius, Albrecht Mendelssohn Bartholdy and Friedrich Thimme (eds.), *Die Grosse Politik der europäischen Kabinette, 1871–1914*, XXIII (Berlin, 1925), Nr. 7781, pp. 43–4; G. P. Gooch and Harold Temperley (eds.), *British Documents on the Origins of the War, 1898–1914*, VI (London, 1930), 15–16; VIII (London, 1932), 213–15.

the 'woolly' tone of the article; the Cabinet refused to discuss it in Parliament. The *Manchester Guardian* emphasised the unfavourable response from France; *The Economist* declared that the article had been received abroad with suspicion.[1] The end result was that at the Hague the British proposal on the armaments question, even when toned down, failed to get serious consideration.

In the *Nation*, before and during the Conference, comment is uneven, and it is obvious that various hands are at work in unsigned leaders. 'The Causes of German Isolation' (4 May), which sounds like Brailsford, speaks of the growing suspicion in Germany that she is faced with secret diplomacy seeking to encompass her, and emphasises the profound differences between Britain and Germany which 'for many a year to come ... are likely to be the decisive fact in European history'. Compare the substance and tone of the leader (1 June), 'The Policy of Penning In', attributed to Hammond, which, while pointing out the dangers of continued isolation of Germany from the *entente* powers, holds Germany responsible for that isolation: 'The isolation of Germany was a moral before it became a diplomatic fact. Other Powers offend against the better conscience of the civilised world. No other Power so steadfastly ignores that conscience.' But just before the conference convened optimism is expressed in 'Hopes for the Hague Conference' (15 June), which sounds much like Massingham; the writer speaks cheerfully of Campbell-Bannerman's article as 'an act of Faith', and 'let us hope for the best'. On the other hand, 'Our Correspondent in the Hague' (either Brailsford or Nevinson – both were there) reported 'an atmosphere of suspicion and secrecy'. With sessions under way, Nevinson's unsigned leader is headed 'The War Conference'. Repeated postponement of consideration of the armaments questions brought disappointment, and opposition of the British delegation to the proposal that private property other than contraband of war be immune from seizure at sea by belligerents brought dismay. Still the *Nation* found some satisfaction in the plan for establishing an international prize court and in support of the principle of arbitration of international disputes, and

---

[1] Philip Magnus, *King Edward the Seventh* (London, 1964), 390; Hansard, *Commons*, 4th ser., vol. CLXXI, cols. 462, 1,496; *The Economist*, 9 Mar. 1907; *Manchester Guardian*, 16 Mar. 1907.

managed to conclude that the Conference had not been entirely fruitless.[1]

What can we make of it? Grey and the Foreign Office had seen the Prime Minister's article and agreed to its publication. Was it originally suggested by Massingham? We do not know. Perhaps the most sensible contemporary comment is found in a leader in the *Daily News* (2 March 1907) which treated the Campbell-Bannerman article not as a serious move in British policy but merely as an episode in Massingham's career and in Liberalism's creed. It was not quickly forgotten though now diplomatic historians hardly mention it. Perhaps it was merely Massingham 'the journalistic adventurer' on the move again. But as J. A. Spender remarked later: 'no adventure seemed less promising or more dangerous in those days than the endeavour to promote peace by disarmament'.[2]

Parallel with the sessions of the Hague Conference is the final phase of the negotiation of the Anglo-Russian *Entente*, signed in August 1907 and published in September. Though in time British policy towards Russia was to be a general target for *Nation* attack, in 1907 the attitude of its staff again reflects a varied opinion. Nevinson's position was strong and clear – as a member of the 'Friends of Russian Freedom' he passionately opposed any development which might strengthen the Czarist regime. In 1906 he had carried to Russia a memorial expressing sympathy over the dissolution (July 1906) of the First Duma; a deputation had been proposed but failed for lack of sufficient support from the Liberal press (Massingham, Donald, Spender and Gardiner).[3]

In the spring of 1907, the sharpest clash was between Nevinson and Hirst, with Brailsford, writing the leaders, somewhere in between. Massingham, possibly because he was loath to attack the Government just when he hoped for progress on disarmament, often sided with Hirst. But Massingham was also news-conscious and readily granted space to Maxim Gorki, in London in May attending the Fifth Congress

[1] *Nation*, 22 June 1907, p. 631; July-August 1907, *passim*; 28 Sept. 1907. N.D., 18 and 23 July 1907. Taylor, *The Trouble Makers*, 112, attributes the 1 June leader to Hammond.
[2] Wilson, *CB: A Life of Sir Henry Campbell-Bannerman*, 539–40; Spender, *Life, Journalism and Politics*, II, 181. For details of this episode see A. J. A. Morris, 'The English Radicals' Campaign for Disarmament and the Hague Conference of 1907', *Journal of Modern History*, 43 (Sept. 1971), 367–93.
N.D., Sept.-Oct. 1906, *passim*.

of the Social Democratic Labour Party, for a letter declaring that any alliance with Czarist Russia would not embrace the real Russia. There was no editorial comment.[1]

Editorial statement in the *Nation*, as negotiations progressed, does not reflect a decisive mind; indeed there is an uncommon moderation. Brailsford's leaders are rather bland, stressing the possibility that Britain might, through an *entente*, exercise a decisive influence towards constitutionalism for Russia. Perhaps a diplomatic agreement should be postponed until freedom for the Russian people seemed assured.[2] Massingham himself remarked that while the views expressed at a Trafalgar Square protest meeting, on 14 July, were 'extreme views', the Government 'cannot be ignorant of the very strong objections to the Russian alliance'. The leaders became more critical as negotiations progressed – publication of the text had 'allayed few of the disquietudes which have perplexed Liberals in this country'. However, Massingham himself was almost noncommittal; 'the general tendency', he said, 'is to welcome the agreement as an instrument toward peace'. But *The Economist*, now with Hirst as editor, supported the *entente* as a boon for India. Nevinson clashed with Hirst, drafted a letter to the *Westminster Gazette* renouncing membership in the Liberal Party, and in early October 1907 set forth for India.[3] The epilogue to this episode came the following May when Gopal Krishna Gokhale, the Indian leader, was in London. In arranging hospitality Nevinson encountered difficulties with Massingham. Massingham in the 'Diary of the Week' made no reference to Gokhale's presence. The *Nation* for 9 May carried a mild leader (unsigned) declaring that views of men like Gokhale formed a link between Morley at the Indian Office and the Indian Native movement. The leader was written by Nevinson but he mentioned in his diary that to his disgust 'H. W. M. almost completely rewrote it'.[4]

---

[1] N.D., 14, 24, 27 May and 4 June 1907; *Nation*, 22 June 1907.
[2] 'The Second Duma', 2 Mar. 1907, unsigned but clearly by Brailsford as indicated in N.D., 6 Feb. 1907. See also *Nation*, 27 Apr. 1907, p. 338 and 8 June 1907, pp. 552–3.
[3] *Nation*: 20 July 1907, p. 751; 7 Sept. 1907 ('The Price of the Russian Agreement'); 28 Sept. 1907 ('The Anglo-Russian Convention'); 7 and 28 Sept. ('Diary of the Week'). *The Economist*, 28 Sept. 1907; N.D., 24 Sept. 1907; Nevinson, *More Changes, More Chances*, 284.
[4] N.D., May 1908.

The shift from Campbell-Bannerman to Asquith in April 1908 brought reassessment of men and measures by the *Nation* staff. With Campbell-Bannerman in poor health for some months, Asquith seemed the logical successor but there had been conjectures about Grey, now Massingham's man of 'character'.[1] It is therefore difficult to evaluate a remark in a letter by J. A. Spender to Churchill (travelling in Africa) in November 1907. He mentions as Asquith's only possible rival, Grey 'who steadily refuses to emerge from the F.O., and the Radicals led by Massingham in the *Nation*, appear to be planning an attack on him and Haldane'. There is no 'attack' in the *Nation*, though an article on 'Mr. Haldane's Ideas' asks with a doubtful air, 'Are [they] Liberal and Radical ideas?' and misgivings are expressed over the increase in navy Estimates.[2] Asquith's succession, in the *Nation* columns, was taken for granted and when it came was greeted with approval, though in no extravagant terms.

Among journalists Radical opposition to Asquith, such as it was, seems to have come from C. P. Scott and Leonard Hobhouse. We find Hobhouse writing to Scott: 'You ought . . . to understand that we are at present practically alone. We had it out at the *Nation* lunch today and they were all against me; though I made a little impression on Massingham.'[3] It was probably this Lunch (11 February 1908) which led to Masterman's comment: 'We all mourned over the Government and prophesied a gloomy future.' But we have no evidence of extensive analysis of Asquith's claims to leadership. Hobhouse apparently took it to heart for, according to Nevinson, he stopped attending the *Nation* Lunch 'for rage against Asquith'.[4]

Hobhouse and Scott, and Massingham as well, turned to the reconstructed Cabinet. They all deplored the retention of John Burns at the Local Government Board for he had been signally ineffective. For Massingham, still a personal friend of Burns, the situation was unhappy.

[1] E.g., 'H. W. M.' in *Daily News*, 14 Feb. 1907: 'The Secretary for Foreign Affairs . . . is the supreme instance of the extent to which character, as distinct from principles or opinions, tells in public life.'

[2] J. A. Spender to Churchill, 23 Nov. 1907, Churchill, *Winston S. Churchill*, companion volume 2, pt 2, 707–8. *Nation*: 21 Dec. 1907.

[3] N.d., Scott Papers, Manchester. Scott's notation, 'L. J. H. (Asquith)', indicates the context. Scott was also in touch with Lloyd George and Loreburn. Lloyd George to Scott, 6 Feb. and 6 Mar. 1908, Scott Papers, Manchester.

[4] Masterman, *C. F. G. Masterman*, 97; N.D., 24 Mar. 1908.

In 1908 the issue was the Housing and Town Planning Bill, now being boggled by the Local Government Board. When the *Nation* (25 January 1908) was sharply critical, Burns called it a 'nasty' article, holding Masterman and Nash responsible. Massingham admitted that Burns should have left office and by August was writing to Ponsonby: 'The *fou furieux* of this Government is John Burns. He'll ruin everything. I think he must have a gentle warning'.[1] It was much happier for Massingham to regard Asquith's new appointments: Lloyd George to the Exchequer, Churchill to the Board of Trade, Runciman to the Board of Education, McKenna to the Admiralty and Masterman to the Local Government Board as Parliamentary Under Secretary. The future of Lloyd George, Massingham found, was fascinating to think on; their acquaintance clearly grows. But at this juncture Massingham's strongest passion was for Churchill for he sponsored proposals which ordinarily would have emanated from the Local Government Board. He had written for the second number of the *Nation* 'A Smooth Way for the Peers' – a mild proposal for summoning privy councillors to the Lords.[2] In the *Nation* for 8 June 1907, an unsigned leader, with strong evidence as the work of Massingham, takes a long and admiring look at 'Mr. Churchill's Career'. 'Humanity and intelligence, joined to the political instinct, are the gifts that Mr. Churchill brings to the party with which his fortunes are necessarily bound.' In the issue of 7 March 1908 appears a letter from Churchill entitled 'The Untrodden Field in Politics', written by way of congratulation as the *Nation* began its second year. 'The *Nation*', he writes, 'has maintained a position of sober but unflinching Radicalism, and has steadily acquired a true political significance.' Then he sketches the social reforms to which Liberalism must give itself. He concludes: 'It is because the influence of the *Nation* may be powerful to aid and further these causes, that I send you my good wishes and congratulations today.' This article along with public addresses delivered early in 1908 and a celebrated letter to Asquith, of 14 March, suggest in Churchill a dedication to social reform as Radical as any programme espoused within the *Nation* Group.

[1] B.P., Burns Diary, 2 and 25 Jan. and 14 Apr. 1908, Add. MS. 46326; P.P., Massingham to Mrs Webb, 16 May [1908]; Ponsonby Papers, Massingham to Ponsonby, 10 Aug. 1908.

[2] F. E. Smith, in argument with Churchill in the Commons, referred to this article. Hansard, *Commons*, 27 June 1907, 4th ser., vol. CLXXVIII, cols. 1,440–1.

For Lloyd George and Churchill represent, to the *Nation*, the Radical opportunist wing of the Liberal Party. Over the years it was Massingham's concern to discover just how Radical and just how opportunist. He was not unaware of the problem, even from the beginning. Ponsonby in a letter to the editor (*Nation*, 15 August 1908) stated it this way: 'To fight Socialism which cannot be detached from Independent Labor, which, in its turn, cannot be detached from Trade Union Labor and Radicalism will produce a rift widening in time to a chasm right through the party of progress.' And 'H.W.M.' adds a note: 'We cannot too strongly express our complete agreement.' Doubts about Churchill are behind Ponsonby's article. Massingham wrote to him on 10 August:

Churchill can't be such a fool as to go in with the Whigs. If so there's an end to him. But I always found he appreciated this position vis-á-vis to Socialism and his article in the 'Nation' ['The Untrodden Field'] showed this pretty clearly, I fancy. But I'll give him one of my gentle warnings.'[1]

But to all appearances Churchill was in the Radical fold. There was his memorandum to the Cabinet (11 December 1908) on Insurance and Labour Exchanges, and his speech in the House of Commons, on 19 May 1909, introducing the Bill on Labour Exchanges. Twenty-one of his speeches between 1906 and 1909 are gathered together in *Liberalism and the Social Problem*, published in 1909. Massingham contributed the preface, dated 26 October 1909 – at about that time he and Churchill conferred.[2] Like most prefaces to other people's books it is incidental, and it is too bland to be regarded as one of Massingham's important statements.

The material of these speeches is of great importance to the future of democracy in this country. . . [They have] a unity and sincerity of thought which give them a place above mere party dialectics. . . The main purpose of these speeches [is] to show that Liberalism has a message of the utmost consequence to our times.

Then followed more of the same, quite proper as preface to a collection of speeches on diverse subjects, but we learn very little.

At a *Nation* Lunch, soon after formation of the Asquith Government, 'the future position and meaning of Liberalism' was discussed –

---

1 Ponsonby Papers.
2 Churchill, *Winston S. Churchill*, companion volume 2, pt 2, 914.

'equal opportunity, equal education, opportunism vs. dogmatic socialism, the individual with a fair start'.[1] In the *Nation* we find 'The Vision of Liberalism' (2 May 1908) – a vague statement that each generation of Liberals must reinterpret the ideal of 'equality of opportunity' for all and must translate new needs and aspirations into facts. Such verbalisation of Liberalism and Radicalism will continue, but without much depth except as directed at a particular issue.

1908–1911 – Dreadnoughts, House of Lords, Votes for Women

On 10 February 1906 the first Dreadnought was launched at Portsmouth. In the same month Massingham wrote: 'No question of her [German] rivalry need disturb the present generation of British statesmen.' Even a year later scrutiny of the naval Estimates for 1907 brought no apprehension. Massingham, first in the *Speaker* and then in the *Nation*, was under the spell of Sir Edward Grey and the forthcoming Hague Conference.[2] But the Estimates for 1908–9 announced in December 1907, incorporating new expenditures to meet the German programme, touched off Radical protests against the naval establishment which continued until 1914.

On 16 January 1908, Massingham wrote to Arthur Ponsonby that the new expenditure proposed for the Navy was 'monstrous' and unjustified, since the German programme would not affect the comparative strength of the British fleet for some years. And he drew on Lord Eversley, once an official in the Admiralty, for a signed article opposing the increase; Eversley's trump card was a statement that Fisher, First Sea Lord, had told him that Admiral Tirpitz of the German Navy, in a confidential report to the emperor, had declared the British Navy four times as strong as the German.[3]

The Cabinet decision to reduce the Estimates (without affecting new construction) was hailed as a victory for 'Liberal intervention',

---

[1] N.D., 28 Apr. 1908. The general position of the *Nation* is well set forth in Weiler, 'Liberal Social Theory in Great Britain,' which directed me to the more significant articles.

[2] 'Victory and What to do about it', *Contemporary Review* (Feb. 1906); *Speaker*, 12 May 1906; *Nation*, 2 Mar. 1907, p. 2 and 13 July 1907 ('The Truth about the Navy').

[3] Massingham to Ponsonby, 16 Jan. 1908, Ponsonby Papers; *Nation*, 25 Jan. 1908 ('The Anglo-German War of Armaments'). Fisher complained that Eversley had passed on to Massingham 'my private conversation'. See Arthur J. Marder (ed.), *Fear God and Dread Nought* . . . II (London, 1956), 194.

but the *Nation*, alone in the Liberal press, remained dissatisfied with Asquith's reaffirmation of the two-Power standard. However, Massingham was reassured by Grey's declaration in the Commons, 27 July 1908, that Britain had no intention of isolating Germany and that co-operation with France and Russia was not motivated by selfish aims. This speech, said Massingham (*Nation*, 1 August) was thoroughly 'permeated with the Liberal spirit'.

But this is merely the beginning of a long and tortuous story. McKenna, now First Lord of the Admiralty, under pressure from the Board agreed to four new Dreadnoughts (six, if necessary by 1909) with Lloyd George and Churchill insisting that four were ample and Grey prepared to resign if provision were not made for six. Eversley continued to speak for the *Nation*, regretting the jingoistic tone of much of the press, and emphasising 'useless' expenditure.[1]

Much more acute was the crisis in 1909, with the Admiralty recommending six new Dreadnoughts, and then to satisfy the Sea Lords, raising the figure to eight. Radical politicians (especially Lloyd George and Churchill) urged restraint while the Radical press (especially the *Nation* and the *Daily News*) warned that Liberal Party unity was at stake. The showdown came in February. On the evening of 22 February Masterman consulted with Massingham who 'thinks [it] may come to resignation; perhaps afterwards if we win – J.[ohn] M.[orley] Prime Minister.' The next day at the *Nation* Lunch 'a chorus of condemnation swept the Government'.[2] But on 24 February the Cabinet accepted Asquith's proposal of four new Dreadnoughts the ensuing year and four more, if necessary, laid down by 1 April 1910. Massingham seemed well instructed – very possibly his informant was Churchill – and Gardiner passed on to Nevinson a conversation with McKenna. The programme as adopted was cautiously received by the *Nation* – 'little room for excessive congratulations' – with Admiral Fisher one of its readers.[3]

Translation of the Asquith solution into Estimates produced further Cabinet controversy and a notable debate in the Commons, beginning on 16 March. Remarks by Sir Charles Dilke, a 'Big Navy' man, urging

[1] *Nation*, 1 Aug. and 5 Sept. 1908.
[2] Masterman, *C. F. G. Masterman*, 123–5.
[3] *Nation*, 27 Feb. 1909, p. 808; N.D., 18 Mar. 1909; Marder (ed.), *Fear God and Dread Nought*, II, 225.

restraint brought Massingham's praise. He wrote Dilke that his was 'the only speech that a statesman whatever his precise view . . . ought to make'. Nevinson records that the Lunch of 23 March was 'stirring' and Massingham 'magnificent' in denunciation of the Navy scare.[1] On a vote of censure proposed by the Conservatives after Asquith's refusal to guarantee the four additional Dreadnoughts, the principal speech for the Government was made by Grey. He declared that the Navy should not be treated in a partisan manner, urging exchange of information between the German and British Admiralties and warning against an armament race, and this speech won the *Nation*'s respectful attention. It also prompted a personal letter from Massingham to Grey. After praising the 'broad' conception of policy which Grey's remarks represented, Massingham urged his attention to 'outside forces in democracy', such as Socialism and extreme Radicalism, which might succeed in forcing disarmament. A good deal would depend, he added, on the attitude of statesmanship whether these forces became revolutionary or reforming agencies. The next day Grey answered that he had seriously considered including just such ideas in his speech but did not wish to 'overload' his argument. He suggested a meeting the week following to pursue the idea further.[2] It hardly seems likely that Massingham gave up such an opportunity, but we know nothing of any such meeting.

On 24 June 1907 the Commons approved by 432 votes to 147, a resolution,

That, in order to give effect to the will of the people as expressed by their elected representatives, it is necessary that the power of the other House to alter or reject bills passed by this House should be so restricted by law as to secure that within the limits of a single Parliament the final decision of the Commons shall prevail.

Thereafter 'the House of Lords issue' had priority in Radical thought. In his final contributions to the *Speaker* Massingham had so viewed it. The rejection of the Education Bill by the Lords had caught the Liberals unprepared; it was the consequence of 'an open conspiracy,

---

[1] *Nation*, 28 Mar. 1909, p. 949; Massingham to Dilke, 26 Mar. [1909], D.P., 43921/63–4.
[2] *Nation*, 3 Apr. 1909, pp. 4–7; Massingham to Grey, 30 Mar. [1909] and Grey to Massingham (Copy), 1 Apr. 1909, P.R.O., F.O. 800/108.

engineered by Mr. Balfour in concert with Lord Lansdowne'.[1] The resolution of 24 June set the course which the Government must follow to its logical end. So in the *Nation*. And similarly, by Massingham, in the *Contemporary Review* for July 1907.

However, Campbell-Bannerman was unprepared to act upon this resolution, and for some time Asquith was as well, despite prodding from Radicals in the Government (especially Lloyd George and Churchill)[2] and in the press. The titles of *Nation* leaders indicate a restless urgency: 'The Point of Controversy over the Lords' (4 May 1907) is the constitutional relation with the Commons; 'The Only Way with the Lords' (22 June 1907) is found in the Commons' resolution; then 'Back to the Lords' (16 May 1908). The question constantly returns, should not the Commons seek an unqualified victory over the Lords?

During 1908, when parliamentary achievement seemed meagre indeed, Radical impatience increased. Culmination of frustration came in November with the defeat of the Licensing Bill in the Lords (by 272 votes to 96), approved in the Commons (by 350 votes to 113). Massingham wrote: 'The House of Lords has thus declared itself, both in form and effect, to be a mere branch of the Tory Party' and Nevinson records a doleful Lunch, with a depressing analysis of the fortunes of the Liberals who in Masterman's words 'have turned every cheek in their bodies'. While Massingham took heart from Asquith's declaration at the National Liberal Club, on 11 December, that the Lords' veto was now 'the dominating issue in politics', it was soon evident that Liberalism was divided against itself.[3]

The immediate problem was one of tactics. Should not the resolution of June 1907 be implemented, and direct and immediate attack be made upon the legislative power of the Lords? – this was the issue. The role of the *Nation* can be followed through Churchill, now president of the Board of Trade and propagandising for social legislation. He wrote to Asquith that 'the general situation does not easily lend itself to a fighting speech' and in an address in Birmingham (13 January 1909) opposed an assault on the Lords at that time. The *Nation* expressed

[1] *Speaker*, 5 and 19 Jan. 1907.
[2] Churchill to Massingham, 22 Jan. 1909 (Copy), Churchill, *Winston S. Churchill*, companion volume 2, pt 2, 872–3.
[3] *Nation*, 5 Dec. 1908, p. 361 and 19 Dec. 1908; N.D., 8 Dec. 1908.

great disappointment in finding 'the dominating issue not dominant'.[1]

Liberals wished to be led against the Lords and not fed with excuses for fleeing from them. These remarks may have been written by Nevinson, as his diary suggests. Massingham was in Dublin. On his return he urged Ponsonby, M.P., to come to the Lunch, for the matter must be discussed 'if any kind of tonic to the complete flabbiness of the party is to be administered'. Ponsonby must talk with a group of M.P.s whom they would select. 'I suppose Winston will be wild with me. But his speech is that of a mere wild ass; he must be tamed and driven, or he'll be more than useless.'

Now Massingham was privy to certain Cabinet discussions[2] and he responded directly to Churchill. In 'Diary of the Week' for 23 January, he declared that the Cabinet was divided, with Haldane and Crewe taking a tougher line than Churchill who was suggesting a dissolution of Parliament if the Lords rejected the Budget. With this proposal Massingham was much exercised – the Lords, he said, must not be allowed to dictate the circumstances of the parliamentary dissolution.

Either in answer to these statements (the *Nation* for 23 January may have been available to Churchill the day before) or to a letter we do not have, Churchill responded in a 'Private & Confidential' letter to Massingham, of 22 January:

To attack the Lords upon the constitutional question alone is to court defeat. The constitutional attack, however vigorous, must be backed by some substantial political or social demand which the majority of the nation mean to have and which the Lords cannot or will not give. Unless or until that conjunction is created . . . a Lords' Reform Bill would only be a forlorn prelude to a disastrous election.

The Licensing Bill was so generally unpopular that in rejecting it the Lords gained strength with the electorate, he wrote. And he pleaded for *Nation* support for measures in preparation – measures which had popular support.

I am where I was when I wrote you 'The Untrodden Paths of Politics' [*sic*]. For the first time some of those with whom for a long time you have liked to work, have got some power. Very large plans are being industriously

[1] Churchill to Asquith, 12 Jan. 1909, Churchill, *Winston S. Churchill*, companion volume 2, pt 2, 872. *Nation*, 16 Jan. 1909, p. 596.
[2] 21 and 23 Jan. [1909], Ponsonby Papers.

and laboriously shaped. . . Two complete sessions will be needed to produce them and to finance them. . . I do not think the Lords will interfere with any of them. . . There is no reason why controversial political bills should not meanwhile move forward to the climax *together* . . . in the last weeks of 1910. Then indeed – life or death, but with a chance of victory. . . You ought to be with us in all this.[1]

In the *Nation* for 30 January there is no indication that Churchill had won over Massingham. Rather, Massingham gave support to Ponsonby who at Stirling Burghs (6 February) declared that the prompt handling of the issue of the Lords would decide the 'credit' of Liberalism. It was time for action, he said. Massingham commented that 'when this spirit gets firm hold of the party, it will make short work of the calculations and plans of delays'. With Parliament reopening on 16 February Massingham urged on Ponsonby a resolution the Government would not dare ignore completely.[2]

On 22 February came Ponsonby's amendment to the Address – behind his action were the *Nation* Lunches, his conversations and correspondence with Massingham. The amendment called for legislation that session to implement the Commons' Resolution of 1907. The Ponsonby amendment was defeated by 226 votes to 47, but 'there was really nothing brave about the Government but its speeches', pronounced Massingham.[3]

Massingham, the opportunist, soon found in the Lloyd George Budget, introduced on 29 April 1909, inspiration for a revival of zeal and enthusiasm – enthusiasm which mounted week by week. The Budget represented 'adaptive, constructive and prospective statesmanship' and the chancellor was 'a man of genius'. Churchill's proposals for labour exchanges and unemployment insurance were 'the natural corollaries of the Budget'. Lloyd George came to a *Nation* Lunch (27 July).[4] On 9 July Massingham attended a conference of Liberal press editors and the executive committee of the Budget League, held at 12 Downing Street. The League was headed by Haldane as president, Churchill as chairman, and Sir Henry Norman, secretary. When his

---

1 (Copy), Churchill, *Winston S. Churchill*, companion volume 2, pt 2, 872–3.
2 *Nation*, 6 Feb. 1909, p. 698; Massingham to Ponsonby, 23 Jan. [1909], Ponsonby Papers.
3 Hansard, *Commons*, 22 Feb. 1909, 5th series, vol. I, cols. 443, 456ff.; *Nation*, 27 Feb. 1909, p. 806.
4 *Nation*, 1, 8, 29 May, 1909; N.D., 27 July 1909.

turn came Massingham emphasised the importance of the weekly press as reaching countless hundreds, outside of cities, who never read the daily press. And he strongly supported the proposal that editors be provided with 'points' and arguments which they might use in a variety of ways, thus avoiding the uniformity of articles and speeches prepared at headquarters.[1] In August he was quick to exploit the admission of the *Daily Mail* that the Budget had enhanced the attraction of the Liberal programme.[2]

In October the *Nation* Lunch was still absorbed with the Budget and the Lords. A strong article in the *Nation*, on 9 October ('The King, the Lords and the Budget') emphasised the constitutional issue. Lloyd George himself contributed a powerful statement, moral in tone, in the 30 October issue – an article widely quoted. He associated the Budget with a comprehensive programme of social reform. 'The Crisis and How to Meet It' (*Nation*, 6 November) called on the Liberal press to instruct the country on the issue and the struggle ahead which would determine where ultimate power in the community resided.[3]

As the crisis came to a climax – overwhelming passage of the Budget in the Commons (4 November) and even more overwhelming rejection in the Lords (30 November) – we are blessed with a remarkable series of articles in the *Nation* signed 'H.W.M.' which far surpass in strength of thought and power of expression the unsigned leaders. And further, just at this juncture Massingham joined the staff of the Radical daily, the *Morning Leader*, with his column appearing henceforth, with an occasional break, each week. Now in three articles – 'The Battle Joined' (22 November), 'From the Seat of War' (29 November) and 'The Cockpit of the Fight' (6 December) – in these and in his *Nation* articles he reproduced the unfolding drama at Westminster. For

[1] Notes of the Conference, Norman Papers (courtesy of Dr Cameron Hazlehurst).

[2] Gollin, *The Observer and J. L. Garvin*, 107.

[3] *Nation* for 27 Nov. contained a letter to the editor, entitled, 'How to Deal with the Lords', from Arthur Chamberlain, brother of Joseph Chamberlain. His proposal – creation of peers in numbers sufficient to overcome opposition to the Budget – had been discussed in the previous issue. See also Arthur Chamberlain to Massingham, 24 Nov. 1909, M.P. Upon Arthur Chamberlain's death, Massingham wrote; 'I have often heard Mr. Arthur Chamberlain described as the ablest member of his family with a talent which quarried rather deeper into affairs than his great brother.' *Nation*, 25 Oct. 1913, p. 167.

Massingham had returned to the Press Galleries in the Commons and in the Lords.

Of his thought and language we can reproduce but a limited selection. As usual he is more facile in criticism than in praise. An excellent example is in *Nation*, on 6 November. While the concluding speeches in the Commons of the Prime Minister and the Chancellor of the Exchequer were 'brilliant', a pedestrian word, the final remarks of Balfour were '*piano*' – it was only a journalist like Massingham who would have thought of that word. And he observed: 'In this state of enfeeblement and doubt, therefore, is the great Tory Party and its leader going to their *débâcle*.'

Lansdowne gave notice in the Lords (16 November) that when the Budget came up for its second reading he would move 'that this House is not justified in giving its assent to this Bill until it has been submitted to the judgment of the country', and Massingham (*Nation*, 20 November) shouted: 'If the seventeenth century peers had submitted a similar resolution to Puritan democracy, they would have answered for it with their heads.' Massingham heard Rosebery in the Lords, 24 November and remarked, 'Through the ironical medium of his speech . . . one sees the fatal perturbations of the party that he has more than half-led to its doom' (*Nation*, 27 November).

H.W.M. was in the Lords for the final debate. His article 'In the Kingdom of the Blind' (*Nation*, 4 December) is shot through with brilliance – one can see and hear Lord Curzon 'royally patronizing Lord Lansdowne and nobly shielding him from Radical slander'. And back in the Commons, his comment (*Nation*, 4 December) on Asquith's 'magnificent oration' on his motion (2 December) 'that the action of the House of Lords . . . is a breach of the constitution and a usurpation of the rights of the Commons', an oration 'acclaimed with a passion that only Gladstone's greatest utterances evoked'. The aftermath – Lloyd George's speech at the National Liberal Club, on 3 December: 'I have never known a more wonderful piece of combative oratory. . . Such a leader will flash through the country with a force rarely known in our politics' (*Morning Leader*, 6 December). These articles written under great pressure of time are Massingham at his best at what he did best – parliamentary reporting. To appreciate his quality one has only to compare his writing with Nevinson's 'It Can Never Happen Again'

(*Nation*, 27 November) – a good piece but as he says (diary, 24 November), 'a little high-pitched' – and the other unsigned leaders on the Lords' issue which crowd the *Nation* in November 1909.

The *Nation* staff, like the Liberal Party, was divided on Women's Suffrage – hardly any other concern so engaged emotions as well as reason. Nevinson and Brailsford were ardent supporters and through their own crusading enthusiasm, augmented by their militant wives, became at once strategists, propagandisers and demonstrators. But others of the *Nation* Group shared their zeal only to a degree and were opposed to militancy and violence. To Massingham the issue always seemed clear and simple – Women's Suffrage should come, but through the orderly legislative process. Illegal demonstrations would only weaken the cause and postpone parliamentary action. Masterman, now holder of office in the Government, found himself in a delicate position when sparring with *Nation* colleagues.

Irritations are first noticeable in the argument of Nevinson with Morrison and Hirst over suffragette action in the by-election at Peckham in March 1908. A little later at a dinner party at the Imperial Nevinson clashed with Massingham and Lloyd George over the role of the Women's Social and Political Union (W.S.P.U.). Massingham went out of his way to dissociate 'the opinion of the paper' from articles in the *Nation* (in June) by Nevinson on a suffragette demonstration in Hyde Park and by Evelyn Sharp on the Annual Congress of Women's Cooperative Guilds at Newport, Monmouthshire.[1]

Then, on 14 November, the *Nation* carried an article (unsigned, but clearly by Massingham) 'Suffragists and Suffragettes' praising the efforts of the National Union of Women's Suffrage Societies to set aside the tactics (opposing all Liberal causes) of the W.S.P.U. And he adds:

The historic business of Liberalism has been to disentangle causes where elements of justice and right existed . . . from factors of violence or unreason. There is nothing in the Suffragettes' onslaught on law to qualify this duty of discrimination and of action.

'Hideously bad' is Nevinson's comment on this article, and he spent

[1] N.D., 24 and 31 Mar. and 13 May 1908; *Nation*, 27 June 1908, p. 454.

a morning on a 'Letter to the Editor' in total disagreement. Several weeks later (5 December) when Lloyd George addressed a mass meeting at the Albert Hall, demonstrating suffragettes were ejected, and Nevinson as well after he had joined in heckling the speaker. In the next issue of the *Nation*, the 'Diary of the Week' (normally written by Massingham) commented unfavourably on the demonstration.[1] And so it continues, with Nevinson attacking Hirst at a Lunch (30 March 1909) – Hirst 'who sat sneering at the suffragettes' – with Nevinson writing 'A Letter to the Editor' (3 April) criticising the methods of dealing with women demonstrators in the Commons.

By September 1909 the movement was in a new phase – hunger strikes and forcible feeding – and controversy within the *Nation* staff mounted. Nevinson and Masterman ceased speaking. According to Nevinson Massingham admitted 'indifference on the whole subject'. But not quite, for Massingham (from Nevinson's diary it was clearly he) wrote in the *Nation* (25 September) that 'the tactics of violence' had lost the women's movement most of its support in the Commons. When Gardiner of the *Daily News* did not oppose forcible feeding, both Nevinson and Brailsford announced publicly (*The Times*, 5 October) resignation from his staff. Massingham, briefly in Italy, on reading the statement in *The Times*, was able to provide a lighter touch – for him in such a matter rather unusual. He wrote Nevinson a letter of 'comic abuse' (Nevinson's phrase), concluding: 'Never leave a ship as long as there is a plank left in her.'[2] When Massingham returned to London, about mid-October, he was much moved, says Nevinson, by Mrs Leigh's plight – she was the first prisoner subjected to forcible feeding. The *Nation*'s 'Diary of the Week' regrets such measures but on Women's Suffrage holds to the principle that 'bad tactics prejudice a good cause'.[3]

In the provenance of the first Conciliation Bill (1910) is some other *Nation* history. The issue for 9 October 1909 carried a leader, 'The Suffragist Deadlock: A Suggestion', urging amnesty to all imprisoned suffragettes, suspension of violence and assurances from the Government that if a clearly-pledged majority for Women's Suffrage were

[1] N.D., 14, 17, 18 Nov. and 5 Dec. 1908.
[2] N.D., Sept.-Oct. 1909, *passim*; Massingham to Nevinson [October, 1909], Nevinson Papers.
[3] N.D., 12 Oct. 1909; *Nation*, 16 Oct. 1909, p. 106; 23 Oct. 1909, p. 143.

elected to the next Parliament a legislative proposal would be incorporated in a Franchise Bill. Nevinson's entry of 6 October suggests that Brailsford wrote this leader. But this proposal did not bring peace at the *Nation* Lunch. On 16 November, when Masterman turned up, conversation ceased – Masterman, now Under Secretary at the Home Office, accepted forcible feeding. The entry in Nevinson's diary for 7 December must be reported at length.

At Nation lunch. Got letter from J. E. M. [Mrs Brailsford] saying HWM had requested HNB [Brailsford] not to come to lunch at present after last week's outburst. She trusted to me to carry on the fighting. I opened the attack quite calmly . . . though Hobson lost his temper over the torture & Hobhouse was alarmed and silent throughout. Morrison is the worst opponent but very stupid. HWM hinted at knowledge of dark & bloody designs of WSPU. Morrison prated of Tory gold, Hammond scoffed at limited bill.

The controversy proceeded in the columns of the *Nation*. Brailsford, in a letter to the editor, attacked forcible feeding as 'cold and deliberate malice' on the part of the Government; Massingham added editorial comment questioning that a policy of forcible feeding, designed to save life, was vindictive in intent. At the Lunch on 4 January 1910 Masterman said he 'wished all the leaders of the women's movement were drowned' to which Nevinson responded: 'drowned with a fire hose, I suppose – a true tyrant's recourse. . . So the contest raged, HWM trying in vain to quiet it'.[1]

With Massingham's assistance Brailsford, seeking an agreement, approached Herbert Gladstone, Home Secretary, in November 1909. There was a deputation to the Home Office and much correspondence, with Massingham not directly involved, perhaps by choice and perhaps also because those days he was in the parliamentary gallery listening to the final debates on the Lloyd George Budget. Brailsford found it difficult to believe that the Government really sought a solution while Gladstone said flatly (in letters to Massingham and to Brailsford) that there would be no negotiation as long as there was defiance of the law and that an interview with Brailsford did not imply formal proposals. The frenzied correspondence usually found Massingham in the middle.[2]

But after the General Election in January 1910, a Non-Party

---

[1] *Nation*, 18 Dec. 1909; N.D., 4 Jan. 1910.
[2] H.G.P., 46068/8, 15; 46042/67-8; N.D., 3 Nov. and 17 Dec. 1909.

Parliamentary Committee prepared a Conciliation Bill. The Lunch of 18 January was relaxed – 'much laughter over my proposal to write on the Element of Calm in the midst of it all', notes Nevinson. But the staff did not agree on the merits of the Conciliation Bill – Hammond and Hobhouse in favour argued with Masterman and Morrison in opposition. The measure passed its second reading only to be shelved in July by the Cabinet. This time Nevinson was in agreement with Massingham whose signed article, 'The House and the Women', deplored the outcome which demonstrated that the Party system could not solve the problem, with Liberals refusing to follow Asquith, the Tories overthrowing Balfour, and the Radicals rejecting Lloyd George and Churchill.[1]

But at the end of 1909 – despite the urgency of the naval question, the pressure of suffragettes on Cabinet and Parliament, and the debate over social reform – the 'dominant' issue was still the future of the House of Lords. The General Election, set for January 1910, would clear the atmosphere – so it was thought in Radical circles. Ponsonby, in the *Nation*, 11 December, 1909, all but warned the Prime Minister that he must not fail to do battle against 'the block veto'. In acknowledging receipt of this article, Massingham wrote to Ponsonby: 'I've written Asquith on your lines, after much hesitation. I daresay he will misunderstand, but at all events he is warned.'[2] However, Asquith addressing some 10,000 in the Albert Hall, on 10 December, officially opening the Election campaign, was reassuring in his insistence that 'the will of the people, as deliberately expressed by their elected representatives, must, within the limits of a single parliament, be made effective'. Massingham in the *Nation*'s 'Diary of the Week' (18 December) lauded Asquith's remarks as 'a bold, explicit and deeply impressive statement of the party's unalterable policy on the veto'. And in an article dated 1 January 1910, Massingham called for a written constitution which would secure 'undivided supremacy for the Commons in finance and reasonable superiority in legislation'.[3]

As the campaign opened his tone reflected confidence. He wrote in the *Morning Leader* (13 December) of his heroes:

[1] N.D., 18 Jan. 31 May, 1910; *Nation*, 16 July 1910. Churchill, *Winston S. Churchill*, companion volume 2, pt 3, 1,427–54, for Brailsford's interviews and correspondence with Churchill in 1910.
[2] 6 Dec. [1909], Ponsonby Papers.   [3] *Putnam's Magazine*, VII (Mar. 1910).

Mr. Churchill is regarded as having made Lancashire safe by the most wonderful series of argumentative and oratorical efforts I think I have ever read. As for Mr. Lloyd George's progress to North Wales and his reception there, some . . . tell me that in the whole history of electioneering they have seen nothing approaching it.

When the results confirmed the Liberals in office, the *Nation* was ecstatic with satisfaction and anticipation. In the *Morning Leader* Massingham called for an unequivocal statement of policy. He found no problem with the King and ignored the dependence of the Government after the Election, on Labour and Irish support.[1]

But the Cabinet was divided – Lloyd George favoured immediate abolition of the Lords' veto; Churchill urged reform of the composition of the Lords first; Grey, Haldane and Morley were for reform but not for abolition of the veto. Very likely the *Nation* Group was kept well informed by Hobhouse, Ponsonby and Hobson with whom C. P. Scott discussed the 'crisis' at length. Ponsonby expressed the concern of the *Nation* over going to the country on the issue of 'reform' with no assurance that if the Liberals were again returned a measure limiting the veto would be enacted.[2] By the time the new Parliament convened (21 February), the *Nation* had (on 19 February) sounded the alarm. 'We see no obstacle to the tactic of the Veto First', it declared without qualification. As the weeks pass, Massingham's articles in the *Morning Leader* reflected shifting despair, enthusiasm, doubts and hopes. At the *Nation* Lunches Hobhouse and Hirst disputed at length, to the dismay of the others.[3]

On 26 February, the *Nation* had a solution. 'If a Veto Bill or Resolution passes the House of Commons it should be made a subject of a Referendum'. Massingham's role in this proposal, Hobhouse tells us, was central. He reported to Scott that Churchill had persuaded Massingham to advance and support the referendum proposal, in spite of considerable distaste for the idea. And the *Manchester Guardian* gave it support. But soon Hobhouse, after a discussion with Massingham and Gardiner, was able to report to Scott that Massingham was satisfied

---

[1] *Morning Leader*, 31 Jan. and 7 Feb. 1910.
[2] Scott Papers, Manchester: C. P. Scott to Hobhouse, 27 Jan. 1910; Ponsonby to Scott, n.d.
[3] N.D., 15 and 22 Feb. 1910.

that Asquith and Lloyd George were meeting the situation satis-
factorily.[1]

On 28 February, the Prime Minister declared that the Government
would deal first with the veto, through resolutions, and then with
reform. Massingham in the *Nation* 'Diary of the Week' (5 March)
announced the end of the crisis. And in a signed article he asserted
that 'this week the Liberal Party has plucked its leaders from the pit'.

The Referendum proposal lingered on. Churchill wrote to Scott
that since Massingham had incurred considerable risk in pressing it,
the proposal should be further explored. Massingham himself discussed
the matter in the *Morning Leader* (21 March) and in the *Nation* (26
March) insisting that another General Election was unnecessary for
legislation against the Lords' veto since a Referendum could bring the
same result. Then he wrote to Runciman that he was impenitent and
that attempts to reform the Lords would merely divide the party.[2]

But the issue within the Liberal Party was settled, and the rest of
the story may be quickly told. Asquith's resolution formed the basis
of a legislative bill, excluding the Lords from financial legislation,
strictly limiting the Lords' veto on other legislation, and extending
the life of a Parliament to five years. It brought a rising crescendo of
applause in the *Nation* and in Massingham's column in the *Morning
Leader*. The acceptance of this resolution by the Commons indicated
a dramatic change in the spirit of Liberalism; this was the characteristic
comment. The *Nation*'s own optimism was only slightly dimmed by
misgivings over the party constitutional conference which followed
King Edward's death in May. In the *Morning Leader* (5 September),
Massingham wrote: 'It is well for our leaders to recognize that the
Conference is unpopular with rank and file. They don't like it and they
don't believe in it.' The Liberal victory in December, in the second
General Election of the year, was acclaimed in the *Nation* (31 December) by Ponsonby. In the *Morning Leader* (20 February 1911) Massingham rang the bell for Liberalism. It was again 'a vital factor in our
politics, and large and deep differences of opinion and of conduct

[1] Hobhouse to Scott, 18 and 24 Feb. 1910, and 'Thursday' [1910], Scott Papers, Manchester. As early as 29 June 1907, J. A. Hobson writes in the *Nation* arguing for the
Referendum.
[2] Churchill to Scott, 2 Mar. 1910, Scott Papers, Manchester; Massingham to Runciman,
24 Mar. [1910], Runciman Papers.

emerge, threatening a real reconstruction of society... Change is wanted. Change must come'.

In the course of events which led to the enactment of the Parliament Act in August 1911, the headings of Massingham's *Morning Leader* column reflect the confidence and the satisfaction of the Radicals: 'Root and Branch' (6 March 1911), 'Nearing the End – The Fate of the Lords' (27 March 1911); and a leader in the *Nation*, 12 August 1911 – 'The End and the Beginning'.

In the *Nation* for 18 December 1909 appeared an unsigned article, 'The Motive Force of War' – a review of Norman Angell's *The Optical Illusion* – which spoke of 'a new and brilliant writer' who has produced 'one of the most original pieces of pamphleteering which has appeared for many years'. But neither book nor review attracted much attention and Angell requested Massingham's opinion whether or not the book was of any consequence. Massingham's response was a further review of the reissue of Angell's book, now called *The Great Illusion*, in the *Nation* for 3 December 1910. This review, entitled 'The Psychology of War', written by Brailsford – or so Angell always understood it – led to correspondence in the *Nation*, and was in considerable part responsible for the widespread notice of the book in Europe and America. Joseph Rowntree was so impressed that he sought means for making *The Great Illusion* more widely known within 'the powerful classes'. Such means were pursued with the aid of Hobson and Baron de Forest, a wealthy Liberal M.P.[1]

Angell came down hard on one point – economically, armaments and war do not pay. That this approach influenced Massingham is evident. In the article 'A Parliament of Peace: The Great War Game' (*Morning Leader*, 30 May 1910) he wrote of the loss of faith in war. 'The reign of International Law is no longer a phase – it is a fact.' And again (*Morning Leader*, 8 August 1910) he wrote of 'the world movement against armament'. Two years later (*Morning Leader*, 1 July 1912) *The Great Illusion* was still one of 'Two Books that Matter'. *The Great Illusion* mattered to Massingham and the *Nation* Group not so

---

[1] Norman Angell, *After All* (New York, 1952), 148; Angell Papers: Massingham to Angell, 21 Apr. [1911]; Angell to Massingham (copy), 4 June, 1911; Angell to Hobson (copy), Sept. 1911.

much for its economic arguments – Massingham seldom discussed them and Brailsford used Angell's material to support his own 'conspiracy' view ('finance capitalism') of the origin of war with which Angell sharply disagreed – as for its support of the Radical philosophy that peace was to be had for the asking and that the Liberal 'peace policy' would bring limitation of armaments and thus reduce the possibility of war.[1]

But was the Government taking the road toward peace? That was the question. Towards Grey and the Foreign Office Massingham's attitude seems constantly in the process of change, in the manner of journalists, in his own manner. This was in part because Grey himself changed course, or at least modified his tone, according to circumstance. So, by mid-summer 1910, Massingham's lack of confidence in Grey returns.[2] Now, with the German Question relatively quiet, Massingham's attention focuses on Anglo-Russian policy and the implications of the *entente* with the Tsarist regime which was itself a violation of liberal democratic principles. There was Finland, for example. When her autonomy as a duchy was threatened early in 1910 the *Nation* urged British support against Russian pressure. Ponsonby reported that Grey would not approve a parliamentary petition to the Duma.[3] In September Nevinson was in Finland with other journalists and his description of the Finnish Diet in session, receiving a message from the Tsar recalling the Diet, was published in the *Nation* on 24 September, as 'A Scene from the Finnish Tragedy'.

But Persia presented graver problems. By October 1910 the *Nation* was saying: 'The meaning of the Anglo-Russian Convention is clear. It leads straight to partition.'[4] And in larger terms, the problem of Persia was the problem of Germany. In an article 'Steps to Anglo-German Peace' the *Nation* (17 December 1910) declared: 'We have seen our policy linked in an unnatural alliance with Russia.' What was required was an understanding with Germany. 'To succeed is probably to end the dread of war forever in Europe.' This was the article which

---

[1] A. J. Dorey, 'Radical Liberal Criticism of British Foreign Policy, 1906–1914' (Ph.D. Thesis, Pembroke College, Oxford, 1964), 13, 16, 128, 370–6. Dr Dorey is a reliable guide through the files of the *Nation* for examination of Massingham's attitudes.
[2] *Morning Leader*, 25 July and 8 Aug. 1910.
[3] N.D., 12 Apr. 1910.
[4] *Nation*, 29 Oct. 1910, pp. 186–8.

prompted a letter dated 3 January 1911 from Sir Arthur Nicolson, Under Secretary in the Foreign Office, to Buchanan, the British Ambassador in St Petersburg:

If you get an opportunity you might impress on Sazonov [Russian Foreign Minister] that certain articles which have appeared both in the 'Daily News' and 'The Nation' in no way represent the views of the Government and that neither paper enjoys the reputation which, for some reason or another, appears to be attributed to it abroad.

Buchanan carried out his instructions.[1]

But in 1910 Massingham's quarrel was not with the Foreign Office but with the Admiralty. Under pressure from the Board of Admiralty, McKenna's revised programme submitted to the Cabinet in January 1910 called for an increase in capital ships from four to six. Lloyd George and Churchill were pitted against Grey and McKenna and resignations from the Cabinet seemed possible. A compromise on four new Dreadnoughts and one cruiser brought new Estimates, presented 9 March, calling for an increase of five and a half million pounds. The *Nation* alone with the *Manchester Guardian* and the *Daily News* denounced these requests, with Massingham emphasising that, in the face of a Government pledge to reduce the naval programme, here was McKenna appealing over Parliament to 'the experts'.[2] A debate in the Commons in July on the Navy Votes brought Massingham to the fray once again. Thus in the *Morning Leader* (18 July) in 'The Naval Scare: The Forces Behind It', he referred to the political power of admirals, the jingo press, the military association with France. *Nation* leaders spoke of a Foreign Office which evaded the check of parliamentary debate ('Light on the Naval Rivalry', 23 July 1910) and declared that the price of continued Anglo-German naval rivalry would be the defeat of the programme of social reconstruction ('From Old to New Liberalism', 20 August 1910).

Massingham's attack brought an answer in the *New Age*. In the issue for 4 August 1910 S. Verdad labelled Massingham's article 'What Shall We Do with Sir Edward Grey?' (*Morning Leader*, 25 July) as 'absurd, ill-informed and pernicious'. Verdad referred to Massingham as

---

[1] Gooch and Temperley, *British Documents on the Origins of the War, 1898–1914*, X, pt I, 599–601, 608.　　[2] *Nation*, 9 Mar. 1910 ('A New Style of Leadership').

a well-meaning journalist, who, led astray by a partisan bias and a distorted perspective has written a superficial article on a subject of which he does not even know the alphabet. Come down from your watch tower, Mr. Massingham; come down and go about the world for a time.

On the other hand the Unionist paper, the *Morning Post*, not very often in agreement with Massingham, in its issue for 9 August 1910 criticised McKenna and cited the *Nation* as support. Fisher wrote to McKenna of 'the unholy alliance' of Massingham and Fabian Ware (editor of the *Post*).[1]

By September the Big Navy party was clamouring for at least six new capital ships in 1911–12 – the Radicals called this 'a recrudescence of scare'.[2] Massingham wrote a letter to the *New South Wales Daily News* (31 October 1910)

I believe that deep dissatisfaction exists in the Liberal Party concerning these speeches and estimates [of McKenna]. . . It is the character, the tradition and the resources of Liberalism that these speeches have so gravely compromised.[3]

It is worth noting that McKenna preserved this newspaper cutting. When the Estimates were debated in the New Year what attracts our attention is Massingham's renewed fascination with Grey. Though supporting McKenna in his programme and his Estimates, he spoke eloquently in the Commons debate of the necessity of law rather than force in international relations, welcoming American suggestions for arbitration of disputes and expressing the fear that an arms race might end in revolution of the masses against excessive taxation for war. This last concern is reminiscent of his correspondence with Massingham two years before. Grey wins good marks from Massingham and is now 'The Apostle of Peace'. Such praise stands in sharp contrast to Massingham's condemnation of the service Estimates themselves.[4]

Agadir, 1911, and reassessment

Though Agadir came out of the blue in July 1911, it revived and

---

[1] Fisher to McKenna, 11 Aug. 1910, McKenna Papers. When Fabian Ware left the editorship of the *Morning Post* in 1911, Massingham referred to 'his honourable independence of party ties where they conflicted with the journalist's sense of honour and intellectual consistency'. *Nation*, 17 June 1911.

[2] Arthur J. Marder, *From the Dreadnought to Scapa Flow*, I (London, 1961), 216.

[3] News cutting, McKenna Papers.

[4] *Morning Leader*, 20 Mar. 1911; *Nation*, 18 and 25 Mar. 1911.

confirmed the Radical conviction that Anglo-German relations constituted the key to the limitation of armament and the maintenance of international peace. But the pages of the *Nation* again reflect a varied response to particular circumstance. Just before Agadir, Hobhouse, in an article called 'The Harvest of Pessimism', asserted that the Dreadnought scare was manufactured by interested parties. Perhaps it was also Hobhouse who wrote 'The Sequel of Agadir': 'The curious spectator who has read Mr. Norman Angell's brilliant pamphlet will ask himself whether the whole play was mere illusion.' Not so to Massingham. And unlike other Radical editors he did not support Britain's right of intervention. In his 'Diary of the Week' he found Lloyd George's Mansion House speech 'disquieting' – a word which reflects his response to events week after week.[1] An understanding with Germany was urgent. But first cordial relations must be re-established to dispel the suspicion and hostility on both sides – this in an unsigned article 'A Liberal Policy Towards Germany' (14 October). Massingham's concern was manifest in the headings of his articles in the *Morning Leader*: 'Our Allies: The "Concert" of Europe' (16 October); 'Secret Diplomacy: The Silence of Sir Edward Grey' (20 October) and 'A Reckoning: Plain Words about Sir Edward Grey' (6 November 1911).

The Radical voice was insistent elsewhere. Early in November Courtney, Massingham, C. P. Scott and Noel Buxton consulted and this meeting seems associated with a memorial to the Prime Minister of 10 November, signed by about eighty M.P.s, asking the Government to dispel German notions of British hostility. Also at a public meeting, on 14 November, Courtney was in the chair, Ponsonby gave the address, and Hobhouse, Hobson and Noel Buxton were there. When Sir John Brunner in his inaugural address as president of the National Liberal Federation, at Bath on 24 November, welcomed gestures of friendliness between Britain and Germany, Massingham pronounced the Bath session 'a powerful and enthusiastic demonstration in favor of an understanding with Germany'.[2]

Grey, generally unaffected by public criticism, was well aware of

---

[1] *Nation*: 1 July 1911; 29 July 1911; 2 Sept. 1911.
[2] Koss, *Sir John Brunner*, 240, 245; Dorey, 'Radical Liberal Criticism of British Foreign Policy', 293–4.

the attacks in the Radical press. On 27 November he rose in the Commons to answer his critics. He attempted too much: to defend his policy, to reassure France, to cultivate Germany and to silence the Radicals. But he did make clear that the relation with France was the cornerstone of British policy. He won approval from the *Westminster Gazette* and the *Daily Chronicle* but sharp criticism from the Radical press. A *Nation* leader bitterly attacked Grey 'who believes in the anti-German alliance into which in effect he has moulded the *Entente*'. At the *Nation* Lunch on 28 November, the Grey statement was roundly condemned. When the debate continued in the Lords, Lord Courtney's remarks calling for an Anglo-German agreement similar to the *ententes* with France and Russia, were, in the *Nation*'s view, of the most significance.[1] Massingham was disenchanted. In the *Morning Leader* (4 December) he flatly declared that Grey's policy 'binds us absolutely to France; last September this led us to the brink of war'.

Massingham informally revealed even greater despair. To Nevinson he 'spoke much against Lloyd George, especially for his war scare speech and his general gassy ways'. With his old friend John Burns, still at the Local Government Board, Massingham would unburden himself as to no one else. And so on 9 October, while lunching together at the Devonshire Club, Burns found Massingham greatly agitated over the political situation, especially disturbed at the recent hostile attitude of 'the dauntless two [Lloyd George and Churchill] and sceptical of what they had advocated and the Government had accomplished'.[2]

At the end of a year which produced the Parliament Act, the Agadir Crisis and (in October) important Cabinet changes, Massingham reassessed Liberal leadership. First he took a long look at Lloyd George and Churchill. 'It would be hard to imagine two men more unlike in their origin and upbringing.' They are still of the 'star' class and 'remain the rising hopes of the party and its main guarantee against a Tory reaction'. From 1908 to 1911 they had stood staunchly for 'old Radicalism' and had sought to limit Britain's commitments abroad and hold armament expenditures within bounds. 'But now?'

[1] *Nation*, 2 Dec. 1911; N.D., 28 Nov. 1911, Zara S. Steiner, *The Foreign Office and Foreign Policy, 1898–1914* (Cambridge, 1969), 190–1.
[2] N.D., 16 Oct. 1911; Burns Diary, B.P., Add. MS. 46333/177.

Lloyd George, continued Massingham, was 'the most interesting figure in British politics – no career . . . has marched so fast since the days of Pitt; and none has seemed so lightly planted in the soil from which it has made such astonishing growth.' The high point of his career was the evening his Budget became law. But his Mansion House speech, a direct breach with Liberal tradition, was a puzzle. 'What will he do next?' Massingham is friendly and admiring but also disquieted.[1]

He was even more uncertain about Churchill. It was but two years since the *Nation* had heaped praise on his labours leading to the Labour Exchanges Act and the Trade Boards Act. Then in 1910, as Home Secretary, his commitment to prison reform, his attitude towards law and order, his opportunism and courage deepened Massingham's admiration and warmed his heart. Churchill had made 'a searching and brilliant report' to the Commons on mining accidents in June 1910. His role in the 'Siege of Sidney Street' of January 1911, when a gang of thieves found temporary refuge after killing three policemen, revealed a spirit kindred to Massingham's. They were both at the scene. Though Churchill's presence and conduct were widely criticised he was supported by the *Nation*, which said he should not be held accountable for errors of the police.[2]

But these matters retreated into the shadows with Agadir, and then, in October 1911, came the appointment of Churchill to the Admiralty; he traded posts with McKenna. Churchill had already rendered great service to Liberalism, remarked the *Nation*. But now had come an even greater opportuntity. 'We cannot doubt that when . . . [he] surveys the naval force he will control he will tell his colleagues that nothing which he contemplates need prevent an early rapprochment with Germany.' But naïveté was foreign to Massingham. He was not at all sure that Churchill's early experience transformed his Tory democracy into philosophical liberalism. Could he detach himself from the class into which he was born? 'What kind of political interest will two or three years at the Admiralty develop?'[3]

Then on to Grey. Of course Massingham admired him; only a year

[1] 'The Position of Lloyd George', *Nation*, 6 Jan. 1912.
[2] On mining accidents, *Nation*, 8 June 1910, p. 407. On the Sidney Street episode, N.D., 3 Jan. 1911; *Nation*, 'Diary of the Week', 7, 14 and 21 Jan. 1911 and unsigned leader, 7 Jan.
[3] *Nation*, 28 Oct. 1911, pp. 152–3; 'Mr. Churchill's Career', *Nation*, 13 Jan. 1912.

before he had been 'The Apostle of Peace'. Grey never fell short on the moral side, but his intellect and his judgment – these were other matters. He took refuge, said Massingham, in the eighteenth-century doctrine that British power could not be maintained apart from continental allies. To be sure he sought peace, but *peace in the panoply of war*, peace that went to the razor edge of strife at Agadir, a non-British interest'.[1]

Asquith was in a dilemma. Here was a Party leader who had permitted full play to Liberal principles in social and economic legislation but who had favoured the Imperialist wing of his Party in foreign policy, and could not here expect the Party loyalty he enjoyed in the constitutional clash with the Lords. As to Women's Suffrage, now that the issue was no longer a matter of Party politics, he would render no judgment, take no initiative, accept no responsibility. In sum, Asquith as a politician was critical and orderly but not originative.[2]

Massingham noted that under Campbell-Bannerman, the inner Government had been divided between the Liberal-Radical group and the Imperialist group. Now, Massingham remarked, the Cabinet contained one 'definite' Radical (Lloyd George), two Gladstonian Liberals (Morley and Harcourt), and Burns 'who is a little difficult to classify'. Foreign policy, dominated by former Liberal Leaguers, had become 'pure imperialism', far beyond 'Lord Lansdowne's cautious approach to Continental engagements'. The consequence – 'the standing conflict with Germany . . . darkens the whole European sky'. But, Massingham quickly reminded himself, Liberal Imperialism had moved ahead since 1905; it had recognised social issues and the role of labour, had accepted the Budget of 1909 and stood by Home Rule. Liberalism still had both measures and men, and this was in contrast to the Tories who possessed no programme, no leaders, no future.[3]

Massingham found in social reform and its accomplishments, year by year, the unifying element in Liberal leadership, in the parliamentary party, and in the press. Thus in these pre-war years of the Asquith administration there was in Massingham's writing, parallel with the unfolding story of Liberal Imperialist foreign policy and commented

1 'The Personality of Sir Edward Grey', *Nation*, 20 Jan. 1912.
2 'The Task of the Prime Minister', *Nation*, 27 Jan. 1912.
3 'The New Cabinet and the Party', *Nation*, 15 June 1912; 'The Past and the Future: Liberal Unity', *Morning Leader*, 11 Mar. 1912.

on with sombre apprehension, the narrative of a domestic programme of social legislation – its aspirations, its proposals and its achievements – reported with enthusiasm and pressed forward with zeal. At the end of 1911 the *Nation* hailed the Parliament Act as 'a great liberating agent' and the parliamentary session of 1911 as attesting 'the power and vitality' of Liberalism. Massingham put out of his mind the Mansion House speech and wrote with spirit: 'All Radicals must rejoice to see Mr. Lloyd George back again in social reform rather than disporting himself in the arid desert of diplomacy.'[1] In 1911 the National Insurance Bill loomed above other measures in interest, and its introduction in May 1911 attracted far more public attention than the Parliament Bill. When Lloyd George presented the measure, Massingham in the *Morning Leader* of 27 May greeted it as 'a great social experiment'; the Bill, he said, 'should pass . . . with benisons on its head'. The voice of the *Nation* was important in its legislative fortunes. In the concluding debate (December 1911), just before passage, Massingham observed:

Whatever be the judgment on the Bill, the feat of the Chancellor in devising and passing within a single year a measure of such vast complication, and involving such infinitely delicate social adjustments, must stand as one of the greatest *tours de force* in modern politics.[2]

Once the measure was enacted a battle ensued with the British Medical Association over the implementation of the health service sections. In July 1912, Masterman set forth the political problem in one of the best of his *Nation* articles. In August and September, the *Nation* ran a series of four-page 'Medical Supplements', with articles by medical experts. And in the *Nation* Lloyd George himself answered his critics.

After the National Insurance Act, what next? Writing in March on 'What the Liberals Must do', Massingham designated 'completion of national education' and 'restoration of the people to the land' as the two most urgent tasks. In the Cabinet, Haldane, now Lord Chancellor, along with the president of the Board of Education advocated educational reform, including raising the school-leaving age to fourteen. Here Massingham and Haldane were on common ground. It is pleasant

---

[1] *Nation*, 23 Dec. 1911, pp. 502–3; *Morning Leader*, 1 Jan. 1912.
[2] Gilbert, *Evolution of National Insurance in Great Britain*, 376–7; *Nation*, 9 Dec. 1911, p. 399, and Masterman's important article, 'The Case for the Insurance Bill'.

to find their friendly correspondence renewed and in the issue of the *Nation* for 12 April 1913 Haldane's article urging full state responsibility for secondary education. A flutter of letters to the editor followed, as well as numerous references to 'the coming Education Bill', but there was no such measure until the end of the war.[1]

Lloyd George's commitment to social change ensured Massingham's support and admiration down to the war. The Marconi Case, of 1912–13, is sometimes mentioned as marking their estrangement. Indeed Frances Stevenson records that in November 1914 Lloyd George told her that he would never forgive Massingham 'for deserting him' at the time of Marconi.[2] It is true that the *Nation*, almost alone in the Liberal press, remained objective in an episode its staff found distasteful. After the majority report of the Committee of Inquiry in the Commons had exonerated Lloyd George and other Cabinet members, the *Nation* (14 June 1913) in a much quoted passage pronounced:

For the Liberal Party in Parliament, we can only express two hopes for the future. The first is that the watchword will be 'Everything into the light' instead of 'As much in the dark as can be trusted not to come out'. . . . Our second hope is that as this matter has now touched the Achilles' heel of Liberalism, which is the secret Party Fund, the Party will proceed resolutely to a reform of the system.

It is not likely that Massingham wrote this leader (the second in the issue) for its tone is at variance with statements for which he was more directly responsible. During the parliamentary investigation he cautioned against hasty judgment and called on Leo Maxse, editor of the *National Review*, to produce 'facts', not just 'strong grounds for suspicion'. Massingham acclaimed the Budget speech in April 1913 and very likely he and the Chancellor conferred at that time.[3] Lloyd George's manner and words in the Commons' debate over the report of the Committee of Inquiry elicited only praise. Lloyd George's speech, said Massingham, 'was a great success; it was human and frank . . . and it completely turned the current of Liberal feeling, and to a lesser extent, but still a notable extent, that of the whole House'. And

[1] *Daily News and Leader*, 3 Mar. 1913; Haldane to Massingham, 10 Feb. [1913], M.P.
[2] *H.W.M.*, 97, 101; A. J. P. Taylor (ed.), *Lloyd George: A Diary by Frances Stevenson* (London, 1971), 14, 24.
[3] *Nation*, 1 Mar. 1913, p. 891; 26 Apr. 1913, p. 133; *Daily News and Leader*, 31 Mar. 1913. Telegram to Lloyd George, 24 Mar. 1913, L.G.P.

to the Chancellor's more informal remarks at the National Liberal Club, on 1 July, Massingham's quiet observation was that Lloyd George should now show that he possesses 'the moral force to rise above his errors and his opponents misuse of them'.[1]

In sum Massingham, while generally moderate in his criticism, stood aside from the Liberal chorus which exculpated the members of the Cabinet associated with the scandal. An exchange of letters between Massingham and Chiozza Money in the *Daily News and Leader* in July reflects official irritation with the *Nation*.[2] Lloyd George took the Marconi episode very hard, and apparently regarded the *Nation*'s position as 'treachery', but to this reaction, Massingham, judging from his conduct in the year following, was oblivious.

Once the National Insurance Bill became law, the Chancellor turned to land – the breaking up of great estates, the encouragement of small holdings and tenant farming, and the safeguarding of tenants' interests. Massingham embraced the cause wholeheartedly. In the *Daily News and Leader* for 24 June 1912 he sets forth 'the task of Liberalism' presented by the plight of the farm worker. The agricultural labourer, he says, wants land, he wants a decent lodging, he wants better wages, because these will give him independence. In a signed leader in the *Nation* for 6 July 1912 he poses the basic question: how can the land once taken from the people by enclosures be returned to them? The correspondence columns are thrown open for discussion and for the next two years he rings the changes on these themes.

The *Nation* was proud to publish the *Report of the Land Inquiry Committee* (vol. I, *Rural*) in three issues beginning on 18 October 1913. It acclaimed Lloyd George's address to a great concourse at Swindon (22 October), setting forth 'at last' (as the *Annual Register* put it) a definite Government proposal for land reform. Massingham accompanied Lloyd George all the way. Just before the Land Committee made its first report Massingham was invited by the Chancellor to a 'Land Breakfast'.[3] Later he wrote to Lloyd George in ecstatic praise of his speeches at the Holloway Empire (20 November 1913) and at

[1] *Nation*: 21 June 1913; 5 July 1913.
[2] *Daily News and Leader*, 14 and 15 July.
[3] Massingham to Lloyd George, 19 Sept. [1913], L.G.P.

Glasgow (4 February 1914), speeches which ranked with Limehouse, he said, than which no greater accolade could be accorded.[1]

When Lloyd George was interviewed in January 1914 by the *Daily Chronicle*, he said Liberalism should at once strive for retrenchment in armaments; for twenty years there had been no more favourable moment. He spoke of the Liberal programme of social reform as only a Radical could. The *Nation* was impressed and gratified. Massingham was on holiday in the Mediterranean or no doubt he would have capitalised on the statement even more, for until the war Lloyd George remained Massingham's hero, even if slightly tarnished, and the great hope of Radical Liberalism.

Hard on the end of the Party truce in November 1910 came a revival of militancy in the Women's Suffrage Movement and thereafter a depressing procession of unhappy episodes and abortive efforts at legislation. At the end of February 1911 a Memorandum from the Parliamentary Committee on Reconciliation supporting a request for investigation of police methods against demonstrators brought sharp criticism in the *Nation* from the editor. The next week came Brailsford's answer and to it was appended further remarks by Massingham extending the argument. A mere reading of this exchange brings a start and a shiver and confirms the atmosphere provided by Nevinson. He and Brailsford put their heads together and were reminded of divisions within the *Daily Chronicle* staff in pre-Boer War days. As then, they hoped the staff might be won over, but the storm continued. Brailsford wrote to Massingham renouncing all friendship, a letter which Massingham called 'insolent'. And he supported Churchill against charges that as Home Secretary he had given orders to harass the women demonstrators.[2]

In May 1911 the second Conciliation Bill passed its second reading overwhelmingly though, rather ominously, after a listless debate. Engrossed with the Parliament Bill the Cabinet put the Conciliation Bill aside but declared, with emphasis, that the following year a week or more would be provided for its consideration. This seemed reassuring. Nevinson wrote in his diary 'the end of worst' and Massing-

---

[1] Massingham to Lloyd George, 1 Dec. [1913] and 8 March [1914], L.G.P.
[2] *Nation*, 24 Feb. 1911, pp. 858–9 and 4 Mar. 1911, p. 909; N.D., Feb.-Mar. 1911.

ham wrote a leader (24 June), 'The Women's Victory', declaring the battle at an end; now, he said, the Commons could translate their convictions into a statute.[1] Cause for satisfaction was short-lived. A new Conciliation Bill, on its second reading in March 1912, was defeated in the Commons. Massingham was sure where the fault lay. In an article on 'The New Terrorism', he spoke out bluntly:

Were it not for the fact that some very fine people have engaged themselves to the extreme Suffragette movement one would be inclined to say that the Suffragettes had done nothing but harm to the country, their cause and themselves. . . What is to be done? Well, nothing can be done. . . All that one hopes is that fate will be kinder to them than they deserve.

Nevinson labelled it 'a horrible article . . . showing great ignorance'.[2]

The Franchise and Registration Bill, which could be amended by the Commons, if it so wished, to include women, was introduced by the Government in June 1912; the *Nation* optimistically followed its movement through legislative channels. Then came the bombshell from the Speaker, January 1913, that according to Commons' rules an amendment on Women's Suffrage would be out of order.

Constructive measures having failed, Massingham's feud with Nevinson and Brailsford was renewed. In 'War on Everybody' (*Daily News and Leader*, 24 February) Massingham declared that 'the real remedy for suffragettism is to grant the suffrage and that is what the suffragettes make so hard'. Two days later, Nevinson gave answer: 'In my opinion that sentence far surpasses any incitement that Mrs. Pankhurst may have uttered and I wish to protest against it.' Nevinson termed 'fantastic . . . foolish and dangerous' Massingham's proposals for local option on women's suffrage in each constituency, a proposal which he set forth in the *Pall Mall Gazette* as well as in the *Nation* and the *Daily News and Leader*.[3]

In the circumstances of the ensuing year we find no variation in Massingham's general stance on his support for votes for women, his interest in local option as a viable procedure, and his opposition to militancy. He was not surprised that the 'Cat and Mouse Act' failed (he had so predicted) and he hoped the militants would take as an object

---

[1] N.D., 19 June 24.
[2] *Daily News and Leader*, 22 July 1912; N.D., 22 July.
[3] N.D., 25 Feb.-4 Mar. 1913.

lesson the orderly and impressive Hyde Park demonstration in July 1913 by the Woman's Freedom League.[1] In June 1914 Asquith declared that Women's Suffrage, if it came, must be a democratic measure on the same terms as male suffrage, a statement greeted by the *Nation* as perhaps opening 'a new departure and a new chapter of hope'. It inspired a Massingham letter to Grey. We have Grey's answer:

I had not seen the Prime Minister's statement about Women's Suffrage until I got your letter. I have now looked it up, but I have no time to draw up any communication of my own at present and I think I shall defer making any new statement till I can do it to my constituents.[2]

But the 'new chapter' was postponed.

In April 1912, with the introduction of the third Home Rule Bill, the Irish question assumed great urgency. There had never been any question of the *Nation*'s support of the principle of Home Rule, of its loyalty to Liberalism on the issue or its appreciation of the leadership of Augustine Birrell, Irish Secretary, 1907–16.

Coming on strong the *Nation* was at once involved in controversy, this time with such quite different persons as W. H. Hudson and J. L. Garvin. Hudson wrote to Edward Garnett:

Massingham and others of his party who are shrieking at their leaders just now on account of foreign policy may presently make the discovery that Ulster is nearer to us than Persia and Tripoli and Morocco. Their cry should be 'hands off' in Ireland as well as in Asia and Africa.[3]

With Garvin the confrontation was head on. Now editor of the *Pall Mall Gazette* as well as the *Observer*, Garvin employed both papers in a campaign to demoralise the Commons and to persuade the Liberals that Unionists would not permit enactment of the Home Rule Bill without another General Election. 'A disciplined storm', wrote Garvin, 'should be maintained day in and day out in the Commons and thus bring the Government to a standstill.' Massingham greeted this with disdain. Garvin, he said, was trying to persuade the public that the Tories possessed 'some sort of intellectual and moral right' to turn out

1 *Nation*, 26 July, 1913, p. 633.
2 *Nation*, 27 June 1914, p. 478; Grey to Massingham, 27 June 1914, M.P.
3 21 Jan. 1912. Garnett (ed.), *Letters from W. H. Hudson*, pp. 167–8.

the Government. His 'rapid hocus-pocus of incantation' was reminiscent of Disraeli. But it wouldn't work, this 'sensational apparatus of Counter Revolution'. In this attack Massingham is at his best in thought and expression.[1]

But generally the *Nation* was surprisingly patient and optimistic of amicable solution. Little notice was taken when the Lords rejected in January 1913 the Commons' Home Rule measure. In June there was reference to Birrell's 'brilliant and impressive sketch of the new, united Ireland which was springing up on the ruins of the old divisions'. Loreburn's plea in *The Times*, September 1913, for a Party conference was hailed. It would, said Massingham, at first win little attention.

> But sooner or later, out of the Liberal difficulty of coercing Ireland, and out of the Tory fear of an unreconciled Ireland, out of the prudent fears of Belfast merchants and traders, out of the form and spirit of the time, and the instinct of statesmen to feel for the path of safety, a true and full Irish settlement will come. And this ought, I am convinced, to be the faith of Liberalism.[2]

In March 1914 'the Mutiny at the Curragh' leading to the resignation of the War Secretary and others was treated by 'Wayfarer' in the *Nation* as a blunder revealing 'a certain slackness in Cabinet methods'. But in the *Daily News and Leader* Massingham showed more objectivity. Coercion in Ulster, he said, must be tempered with justice. And 'The Plot against Parliament' will have to be resolved by the nation, not the Cabinet. When Asquith himself assumed the post of War Secretary it was 'a grand stroke'. In the months before August 1914 the *Nation* warmly commended efforts at conciliation through Party conference.[3]

Balance of power or concert of Europe? (1912–1914)

In August 1912 Churchill proposed a Civil C.B. for Massingham, a notion which Asquith rejected out of hand. In this statement we have epitomised Massingham's relation to the Liberal Party and the Liberal Government in the years of the New Liberalism, 1906–14.

Churchill, now First Lord of the Admiralty, wrote to the Prime Minister of a suggestion from Northcliffe that the Liberal Party had

---

[1] Gollin, *The Observer and J. L. Garvin*, pp. 394, 401. The leader for 30 Mar. is signed by Massingham; the one for 22 June, unsigned, is almost certainly his.
[2] *Nation*, 14 June 1913, p. 406; *Daily News and Leader*, 15 Sept. 1913.
[3] *Nation*, 28 Mar. 1914, pp. 1,064–5; *Daily News and Leader*, 23 and 30 Mar. 1914.

many distinguished journalists – C. P. Scott, Massingham, J. A. Spender, Robert Donald (*Daily Chronicle*) and Drysdale (*Yorkshire Daily Observer*) – and that it was a matter of some comment in newspaper circles that the Liberals had failed to reward the profession in a manner comparable to that of the Conservatives when they were in office.

Churchill, much impressed, added his own opinion that journalists should receive something of the attention shown to the military, to civil servants, or members of the House of Commons.

This is a time when we ought to consolidate and encourage all our forces, and when we have need of all the help we can get. . . I therefore venture to suggest that on the next occasion you should consider Spender for a Privy Councillorship, Massingham and Scott for Civil CB's, and Donald and Drysdale for knighthoods.

Asquith in reply wasted no words. 'No party', he wrote, 'was ever worse served than ours by its Press'. Spender stood by himself and in due time would have anything he desired. But he had reason to believe that neither Scott nor Donald would accept such recognition. 'And to Massingham I shall certainly not offer it.'[1]

Churchill made the proposal just as the Radicals were preparing their strongest assault on foreign policy and just as Massingham's own attacks on Churchill were in crescendo. For surely Massingham at the time had no intelligence of the Churchill proposal of honours. On 9 September 1912 Massingham wrote in the *Daily News and Leader* of 'A New Churchill since 1909'.

He has gone very wrong indeed. He has broken from his close association with the Chancellor in the fight for moderate expenditures and peaceful policy. . . Why did his change of view coincide so sharply and so instantly with his transfer to the Admiralty? Why did he become the champion of an aggressive anti-Germanism? . . .
What will he do to reestablish his place in the hopes of Liberalism? . . . Let him choose wisely and in time. But he cannot make another false step.

These remarks reflect the atmosphere of Radical thought in the autumn of 1912. The confidence in a more liberal Reichstag had come to nought. Grey, though flexible and reputed to favour an Anglo-

1 Churchill to Asquith (Draft), 12 Aug. 1912 and Asquith to Churchill, 16 Aug. 1912. Churchill, *Winston S. Churchill*, companion volume 2, pt 3, 1,627–9.

German understanding, had again disappointed. The Haldane mission to Berlin in February 1912, though at first sending hopes aloft, had failed. Again it was Churchill, this time by his celebrated remark, while Haldane was in Berlin, that the German fleet was 'in the nature of a luxury fleet', who jolted Massingham.[1] Early in 1912 Morrell and Ponsonby, with support from Massingham, came down hard on Russian movements in North Persia rendering Persian independence precarious. Support for Russia was essential to Grey's reliance on the balance of power, a policy 'fundamentally ruinous and unsuited to our position in Europe',[2] according to Massingham. Then Brailsford and Hobson contributed to the debate on foreign policy with a series of articles in the *Nation* for May and June 1912, reflecting Hobson's well-known conclusion that Imperialist rivalry resulted from capitalist competition overseas. Their conclusion: the problem of naval rivalry with Germany could be settled by a comprehensive agreement on colonial issues.[3]

Churchill's naval Estimates for 1912 (presented 18 March) keeping pace with the German programme seemed to the *Nation* merely to raise again a question of general policy. But in July Churchill's presentation of his Mediterranean strategy, calling for three additional battleships, brought alarm and consternation; there was now

a virtual naval alliance between France and ourselves with Russia as a third (and slippery) partner. It seems to make an Anglo-German *rapprochement* impossible, and to open up a fresh and indefinite war of building programs and counter-programmes.

Massingham seemed well-informed. He reported to Hirst on the Cabinet crisis, with a break-up including Lloyd George's resignation threatened. He urged an emergency meeting of the N.L.F. The compromise in the Cabinet which moderated the Churchill programme somewhat allayed Massingham's agitation. He wrote to Ponsonby on 15 July: 'I hear tonight there are to be no more ships proposed now. The Jingoes have been beaten; Churchill perhaps not quite so much to blame in this instance as others.' And in the *Nation* he reported with

---

[1] *Nation*: 10 Feb. 1912, pp. 764–6; 17 Feb. 1912 ('Diary of the Week').
[2] *Nation*: 24 Feb. 1912, p. 836 and 'Persia and Our Foreign Engagements'; 20 Apr. 1912, pp. 81–1.
[3] Taylor, *The Trouble Makers*, 122, 124.

guarded optimism.[1] But he spoke out more vigorously in the *Daily News and Leader* (15 July), reviving the cry 'To Your Tents, Oh Israel!' He declared that Asquith 'cannot keep the soul and mind of his party in chains to such a conception of European policy as that on which the Admirals and the Generals and the Committee of Defense, and, I am afraid I must add, the First Lord of the Admiralty are now embarked'. If Asquith persisted, Massingham added, he would lose the Chancellor along with 'nine-tenths of the thinkers of Liberalism.'

Churchill's presentation on 22 July of supplementary Estimates was greeted as 'an alarming restatement of Anglo-German Naval rivalry', perhaps intentional, with Haldane scoring an extra point.[2] In the *Daily News and Leader* (29 July) Massingham called for 'an Independent Radical Party' to muster votes and sentiment against the naval Estimates. For such a group a leader was at hand in Ponsonby – honest, able, informed, courageous'. Altogether, it was a hectic time for statesmen, politicians, journalists alike. Sometime in September Masterman scribbled a few lines in a letter:

Treasury work, haircut, shopping, hell, clothes etc. Had lunch with Gardiner, who was quite cheerful and cursing Winston's speeches. Dined with Massingham, also cursing Winston. Afterwards with him to 'Everywoman' at Drury Lane, which was such deplorable *muck* that we came out before the end.

One of Massingham's articles (it is impossible to determine which) was reported by the German Embassy in London to the German Chancellor, von Bethmann Hollweg. The Massingham article was cited as an example of Radical reaction to the new British policy in the Mediterranean. The Kaiser annotated this document – 'von der sagt Grey: "I never read The Nation" ',[3] hardly an accurate comment.

The approaching annual meeting of the N.L.F. at Nottingham (in November) seemed to offer an opportunity for influencing the Government. Here the impetus came from Hirst, adviser to Sir John Brunner, supported by Massingham. In July Hirst had urged Brunner to write to Asquith in protest against the Churchill programme, adding that it

---

[1] Koss, *Sir John Brunner*, 253–4; Massingham to Ponsonby, 15 July [1912], Ponsonby Papers. *Nation*, 20 July 1912, p. 568.
[2] *Nation*, 27 July 1912, p. 605.
[3] Masterman, *C. F. G. Masterman*, 244; Lepsius *et al.* (eds.), *Die Grosse Politik*, XXXI, Nr. 11595, p. 546.

would be just as well not to mention his name or that of Massingham·
In September Hirst declared that both he and Massingham were
'determined not to let this dangerous naval expansion and friction with
Germany continue any longer' and proposed an 'appeal' to be despatched to Liberal Association chairmen for signatures. Also strong
resolutions should be brought before the annual meeting at Nottingham. Hirst emphasised Massingham's remark that Churchill's silence
about the Navy indicated his fear of Liberal sentiment in his own constituency. Altogether it was 'a golden opportunity which should not on
any account be lost'.[1] Brunner's letter (dated 15 October) to each of
the Liberal associations brought Massingham's blessing. 'Open protest
has been forced upon us and let us pray heaven it will avail.' At the
Nottingham meeting (21–2 November) Brunner put his case 'with
great power'. Massingham warned the Liberals that they must close
their ranks over foreign policy, lest the Tories secure a majority at the
next election, form a Government, force Protection upon the nation
and repeal the Parliament Act.[2]

In the autumn of 1912, the Radical press, the Radicals in Parliament and
the leadership of the N.L.F. were all in sharp confrontation with the
Government on foreign policy, in particular on Anglo-German policy.
Yet, in a few months, the atmosphere was transformed. In February
1913 we find Massingham writing:

I think we are all surprised to find Germany speaking so early and so clearly
against a further extension of her Fleet Law. But the betterment of the
general relations of the two countries was no secret, and has been going on
ever since the Morocco incident closed.

In the same issue, a leader declared that 'an active Anglo-German cooperation has replaced an active Anglo-German rivalry'. Also in the
Daily News and Leader (10 February) Massingham wrote: 'Could there
be much better news than the new German declarations on naval
armaments and Anglo-German relationships? Now is the time to go
further and have a real understanding with Germany.' Haldane, let it
be noted, wrote to Massingham in appreciation of this article. And by

[1] Hirst to Brunner, 15, 23 Sept., Brunner Papers, courtesy of Stephen Koss. See his
Sir John Brunner, 254ff. for more extended treatment.
[2] Nation, 19 Oct. and 23 Nov. Daily News and Leader, 21 Oct. and 25 Nov.

the end of 1913 the *Nation* was able to declare: 'Nothing more than a memory is left of the old Anglo-German antagonism.'[1]

In this change of attitude the decisive factor was the British role in the Balkan Wars. Even during the concerted attack on Grey in October and November 1912, Massingham's emphasis in his *Daily News and Leader* weekly column was on the Balkans. Peace negotiations at the London Conference in January, with Britain and Germany leading the way, in Massingham's words, 'converted him [Grey] into a strong worker for a definite European settlement, based on but not of course dependent only on an understanding on armaments. If he achieves this, his Foreign Secretaryship becomes the most distinguished of his time'. And as successful negotiations proceeded the *Nation* assigned credit to Grey and to the German representatives who have at last found 'a consciousness of their common duties'. When peace was established between Turkey and the Balkan league Massingham wrote 'I remember no act of foreign policy which has been received with more universal approbation than Grey's summons to the delegates of the Balkan states to sign the draft treaty or go'. The Balance of Power, so the Radical press concluded, had been replaced by the Concert of Europe, and although the Second Balkan War revealed that exclusion of the Turk would not bring peace to the Balkans, confidence in Grey continued. Massingham seemed undisturbed by Bernstein's articles, emphasising the continued hold of militarism in Germany, and by a personal letter from Bernstein which cast doubt on any change in direction of German naval policy.[2]

With Anglo-German relations remaining much improved, Radical attention turned to other issues, including compulsory military training. Periodically brought forward since 1903, it reappeared early in 1913, in the campaign staged by Earl Roberts, as an imminent threat. At the start Massingham could not take it seriously; he thought the Liberals would not dare support it and that the Roberts' campaign was dangerous only in an atmosphere of Anglo-German hostility. But soon the issue became a reality with the Cabinet divided. The *Nation* came

---

[1] *Nation*, 15 Feb. 1913, p. 808, 894; 13 Dec. 1913, p. 483. Haldane to Massingham, 19 [Feb.] 1913, M.P.
[2] *Nation*, 15 Feb. 1913 ('Wayfarer'); 10 May 1913, p. 216; 31 May 1913 ('Wayfarer'). Bernstein's 'Letters from Abroad' are in *Nation*, 15 Mar. and 5 Apr.; Bernstein to Massingham, 6 Mar. 1913 is in M.P.

out with a blast, 'The War Office and the Military Conspiracy' (19 April), declaring that the attitude of Colonel Seely (the War Secretary) in its obscurity and evasion, was supporting 'a covert conspiracy to militarize this country, and to undermine the civil liberties of its people'.

An angry Churchill reacted at once. According to Riddell he remarked

I think I shall write in reply, pointing out that Massingham . . . has fallen foul of almost every member of the Government. The Prime Minister who has accomplished practically all he set out to do; Sir Edward Grey, who has prevented a European conflagration; the Chancellor of the Exchequer, who has done more for the working classes than any other statesman; the first Lord of the Admiralty, who has tried, however inefficiently, to do his duty, and now Seely, who is endeavouring in a courageous, able manner to deal with a most difficult situation.

Though there was only much talk and little prospect of action, Massingham advocated a strict watch, for many Liberals were still shaking their heads over certain ministerial speeches, notably by Colonel Seely. Very likely this was the topic of conversation when Massingham was closeted with Runciman for two hours on 29 April.[1]

But the more comprehensive issue of arms and preparations for war dominated the Radical complaint in 1913. It was a major concern with Massingham in the *Daily News and Leader* from his 'Pitfall of Militarism' (10 March) to his 'Cutting Down Armaments' (8 December). He had been optimistic about reduction of naval expenditures, but Churchill's speeches, to Massingham's consternation, foreshadowed increased spending; the 'naval holiday' was now slated for 1915, not 1914. Churchill's statement at the Guildhall banquet in November 1913 that naval Estimates in 1914 would be substantially higher were referred to as 'deliberately whipping up the old German antagonism. . .'. The Cabinet Crisis early in 1914 over Churchill's naval programme came during Massingham's holiday in the Mediterranean but he was back when the Estimates were introduced in the Commons and he very likely wrote the comment that Churchill's latest figures, involving a new policy never submitted to Parliament, rendered him guilty of 'a grave breach of trust'.[2]

---

[1] Lord Riddell, *More Pages from My Diary*, 140–1 (19 Apr. 1913); Massingham to Runciman, 25 Apr. [1913] and Runciman's notation, Runciman Papers.
[2] *Nation*, 15 Nov. 1913, p. 309 and 7 Mar. 1915, p. 921.

It has been remarked that in 1913 and 1914 the Radical outlook was essentially optimistic. (It is true that with the Irish Question being the most insistent issue, the Radicals had no intention of putting great pressure on the Government for they did not wish to bring it down.) But the same observer comments that on foreign affairs the Radical voice 'was rarely clear and frequently discordant'.[1] This is quite apparent as Anglo-German tension diminished. And so we find Brailsford in *The War of Steel and Gold*, published in March 1914, saying: 'The dangers which forced our ancestors into European coalitions and continental wars have gone never to return... My own belief is that there will be no more wars among the six great Powers.'[2]

Compare this with such statements, ominous, as in the doubt expressed: 'whether the sinister policy of the Balance of Power has ever more fatally involved European statesmanship than at this moment. The leadership is with Russia, but our complicity is evident'; and in the observation: 'our responsibility and our share is direct and heavy in the rivalries which are in progress and in the conflict which they might by chance unchain'.[3] But no one saw any danger immediately ahead. Massingham himself was off guard. When the tenth anniversary of the *Entente Cordiale* was celebrated in April 1914 in Paris, Grey accompanying the king (Grey's first departure from the British Isles since he became Foreign Minister), Massingham accepted Grey's words that there was no intent to develop the *entente* into an alliance.[4]

In point of fact it was the Russian *entente* which just now aroused concern in the Radical press and this because of new developments in the Persian Question and because of rumours of an Anglo-Russian naval agreement. Joseph King, a Radical M.P., put a question (11 June) in the Commons to Grey who responded that there was no agreement with Russia which would hamper Britain's decision as to war or peace. In 'Events of the Week' in the next *Nation*, Massingham suggested that King ask two additional questions 'whether any convention exists, short of a binding alliance, and if so whether its effect will be communicated to Parliament'. King at once wrote to Massingham that after conversation with Acland, the Parliamentary Under

[1] Dorey, 'Radical Liberal Criticism of British Foreign Policy', 392–3, 474.
[2] As quoted in Taylor, *The Trouble Makers*, 122–3.
[3] *Nation*, 6 June 1914, p. 366; 20 June 1914, p. 442.
[4] *Nation*, 25 Apr. 1914, p. 125.

Secretary for Foreign Affairs, he feared such a question might be mis-interpreted as referring to some understanding about exchange of information, which was not an agreement 'in the ordinary sense'. In reply Massingham suggested a more direct approach, namely, that King inquire whether there had been communication with Russia con-cerning 'the new naval arrangements in the Mediterranean or whether any request has been made by the Russian Government to His Majesty's Government to facilitate the passage of Russian ships into the Mediter-ranean, or to a concerted naval action in these waters'. Since Russian naval talks on these matters had in fact been sanctioned by the Cabinet, Massingham was well informed.[1]

The journalist of Fleet Street is the only Massingham we can recover in any detail and present with any assurance. When we venture into his family life, we are without the details which family correspondence and records usually supply. Even the memories of his sons and of his daughters-in-law are dim.

We cannot as a start establish with any exactitude the location and dates of family residence. It was probably in 1909 that the family moved from 34 Grosvenor Road, Westminster, to 'Mayertorne Manor' at Wendover in Buckinghamshire some twenty-five or thirty miles from Paddington. A few years later the family was established at 21 Bedford Square, Bloomsbury. Of numerous holidays – in England, in Ireland, and on the Continent – we have details for only one, the Mediterra-nean and Egyptian trip of December-January 1913–14, already narrated.

We are startled to learn that Massingham was known as 'Harry' in the family circle; the only person, apparently, outside that circle who thus addressed him (as 'arry) was John Burns. To all others he was 'H.W.M.' or 'Mr Massingham.' His children attest to their unhappy family life. Their most vivid memories are of such matters as their father at table addressing the dog ('Nick, would you like to hear a story Shaw told me today') rather than the family, or, if by chance he were home of an evening, of a silent parlour with their father in a corner busily sketching out his next article. On the other hand, in one of the

[1] Samuel R. Williamson, Jr, *The Politics of Grand Strategy: Britain and France Prepare for War, 1904–1914* (Cambridge, Mass., 1969), 338–9; *Nation*, 13 June 1914, p. 402. King to Massingham, 16 June 1914, and Massingham to King, 19 June 1914 ('Copy'), M.P.

very few informal letters which have survived from this period, we find Massingham writing to Nevinson in May 1909; 'My life is often hateful and tedious to me, & except for my children and a little fun, I have little joy in it.' Though usually regarded as 'a loner', Massingham was one of the forty original members of 'The Other Club', organised in 1911 by Churchill and F. E. Smith as a non-partisan club whose sole purpose was to dine – always a matter of interest to Massingham. He was one of two journalists (the other was Garvin) included.[1] Massingham was not only more complex but perhaps more human than we know.

As we move toward the Great War we cannot give to Radical journalism a touch of the dramatic it does not possess. But Westminster, no more than Fleet Street, anticipated the course of events. However, Massingham at this time does pause to re-examine Liberalism as a social philosophy. This was in part inspired by the appearance of the *New Statesman*, in April 1913. To Fabianism Massingham had given answer long before. Now he dismissed it with the observation that whenever he became convinced that 'Liberalism cannot provide the State and the people with all that is good in Socialism, and cannot at the same time preserve the idea and the practice of liberty' he would quit Liberalism and seek shelter elsewhere. Liberalism, he continued, had been fortified by its principles of government: Home Rule or national autonomy, Free Trade, voluntary military service. But Liberalism had also stood for social progress, for fulfilment of the principle of democracy, for an end to poverty. And he concluded, 'By the way, Mr. Shaw and Mr. Webb, tell me, *en bons comarades*, what you propose to put in its place?'[2]

But this was Massingham merely standing his ground. The prospect for the future was not bright. In August 1913 Nevinson found Massingham 'maddened at the condition of all politics and thought and parties'. An unsigned leader pointed out that with the passage of Irish Home Rule and Welsh Disestablishment old Liberalism would have about

1 Author's conversations with Mrs H. J. Massingham, Mrs Madge Massingham, Godfrey Massingham and Hugh Massingham. Massingham to Nevinson, 20 May [1909], Nevinson Papers. *H.W.M.*, 214, 216. Colin R. Coote, *The Other Club* (London, 1971), 20–2.
2 'The Claims of Liberalism', *Daily News and Leader*, 14 Apr. 1913.

completed its mission. 'What is to emerge as the new moral basis?' Liberalism could not stand still – 'another Session like the present would kill it'. And late in the year Massingham wrote to Lady Courtney that his mind often turned towards 'change in this wretched party system'; still, though the Liberals grumbled 'because we don't follow them through the mud of party politics', he thought it important to keep them in power as long as possible.[1]

As we approach 1914 we find Massingham at his peak as writer and editor. In the years since the Boer War Massingham's political and social philosophy, opportunistic yet passionately evangelical, had inspired one of the more strident voices in Fleet Street, yet one which was seldom ignored. The impact of journalism can seldom be measured but we can assert that Radical politics – the careers of Lloyd George and Churchill especially – would not have been the same without Massingham. Radical journalism – nowhere better exemplified than in the *Nation* – challenged the foreign policy of the Liberal Imperialists, and kept it in public view, and also popularised the domestic policy of the New Liberalism. Chiozza Money was referring to the Marconi Affair when he said that many of Massingham's friends consider that he had developed 'an abnormal capacity for giving his own side out',[2] but it is a particularly appropriate remark as we turn to Massingham's response to the First World War.

[1] N.D., 17 July 1913; *Nation*, 2 Aug. 1913, pp. 665–6; Massingham to Lady Courtney [Dec.?] 1913, Courtney Papers, X, f. 117, B.L.P.E.S.
[2] Letter to Editor, *Daily News and Leader*, 14 July 1913. Thus it is difficult to accommodate Massingham to many of the judgments of Howard Weinroth in 'Left Wing Opposition to Naval Armaments in Britain before 1914', *Journal of Contemporary History*, VI, No. 4 (1971), 93–120.

CHAPTER 9

Mr Massingham sees it through
(1914–1918)

The Great War of 1914–18 was for Massingham, as for H. G. Wells' fictional character, 'Mr. Britling', a crisis of mind and spirit. Just as we move from illusion to disillusion in *Mr. Brittling Sees It Through*, which appeared serially in the *Nation* from May to October 1916, so may we watch Massingham's dedicated conscience and mercurial mind confront the changing fortunes of war and peace. The *Nation* now represented, on the issues of foreign policy and the war, a fractured Radicalism, not only reflecting the editor's support of British entrance into the war but providing equally for those who refused to condone Government policy in early August as well as for those who un-equivocally opposed the war. Similarly, on policy towards neutrals, on British war aims, and on the merits of a negotiated peace, conflicting and constantly shifting positions are presented. Thus, and the point deserves emphasis, during the war years, and more especially before 1917, it is of little consequence merely to quote the *Nation*, since varying positions may be found in 'The Diary of the Week', the leaders, 'Wayfarer's' column, and letters to the editor from staff members.

So, while the *Nation* perforce forsook much of the consistency which generally characterised the Radical press before the war, it now served, and equally impressively, as a clearing house for the whole spectrum of the Liberal point of view. It is this character as a forum which explains the invariable mention of the *Nation* as one of the significant Liberal journals during the war and its frequent citation as the leading Radical paper. L. W. Martin in his *Peace without Victory: Woodrow Wilson and the British Liberals* (1958) relied heavily on the *Nation* as a fairly accurate gauge of 'the swings of Liberal opinion' in general and of the direction of Radical thought in particular. When Albert J. Beveridge, the American Progressive, was in London in

March 1915 on a hunt for news and opinion, he was advised by William Archer to see Massingham who not only represented 'advanced Liberal opinion ... but ... perhaps brings it to a focus better than anyone else'.[1]

In October 1915 Bernard Shaw told the Webbs that the *Nation* was 'doing the war far better than the *New Statesman*', for it was 'getting in more criticism of the Government'. Perhaps Shaw meant more *varied* criticism, for his own views were not only expressed in the columns of the *Nation* but as often attacked there. His 'Common Sense About the War' (*New Statesman*, 14 November 1914) brought the comment (*Nation*, 21 November) that while 'marred by many of his defects as a political writer', the article was nonetheless very significant in making English people realise 'that militarism is as great a danger here as elsewhere'. And Shaw's 'Open Letter to the President of the United States', soliciting American influence towards getting the belligerents out of Belgium, was published (7 November 1914) without hesitation by Massingham; but he added in an editorial note that 'an Irish mind', in ignoring the large issue of Prussian militarism, 'puts the case with an indifference we cannot pretend'. To Massingham's thinking on the coming of war the Belgian issue was crucial. Shaw dismissed it; 'neutrality' he wrote in a letter to the *Nation* (20 February 1915) 'is utter humbug'. After Shaw broke with the *New Statesman* in 1915, his most important pronouncements appeared in the *Nation*, on which, he repeatedly noted, he became largely dependent; Massingham, he said, 'though he felt as a very English Englishman about the war, carried on with extraordinary courage and independence ... refusing any kind of censorship'.[2]

The *Nation*'s circulation remained limited, but, as often remarked at the time, it reached a highly select reading public.

'What We are Fighting For'

As the war opened, Massingham was no longer a 'Radical', if that was

[1] Martin, *Peace without Victory*, 218; Archer to Beveridge, 11 Mar. 1915, Beveridge Papers, Library of Congress. Caroline E. Playne in *Society at War, 1914–1916* (Boston, 1931) and *Britain Holds on, 1917–1918* (London, 1933) found the *Nation* 'indispensable'. See also Maccoby, *English Radicalism: The End?*

[2] Weintraub, *Journey to Heartbreak*, 116; Bernard Shaw, *What I Really Wrote About the War* (New York, 1931), 119.

now defined as one who dissented from the majority position in the Liberal Party concerning the war and its causes.[1] The Radicals did still include *Nation* veterans (Hammond, Hobson, Brailsford, Hirst and Ponsonby) as well as relative newcomers (C. R. Buxton, Noel Buxton, G. Lowes Dickinson, Norman Angell). The term also embraced James Ramsay MacDonald, Bertrand Russell, Charles Trevelyan, E. D. Morel, Philip Morrell and John Burns – all of whom contributed to the *Nation*. But Massingham, Nevinson, Morrison, Masterman, Hobhouse were not now Radicals, for they did not interpret the advent of the war in the light of their pre-war opinions on British foreign policy. In October 1914 Emily Hobhouse referred to the *Nation* as 'now ... lost to Liberalism'.[2] Massingham readily opened his columns to the Bryce Group and to the Union of Democratic Control (U.D.C.) for their dissent from official policy, but he never identified himself with them. 'We know little of the work of the U.D.C.', he remarked (*Nation*, 4 December 1915).

The great reversal of the Liberal press on British intervention in Europe in August 1914 is well known. Massingham was no exception. In the *Nation* for 1 August, the initial sentence reads: 'It is safe to say that there has been no crisis in which the public opinion of the English people has been so definitely opposed to war as it is at this moment.' A week later, in a paragraph certainly written by Massingham we read:

There are great masses of opinion ... which hoped ... that this country might have avoided intervention. But the feeling is unanimous that the struggle must now be carried on with the utmost energy ... until a German aggression is defeated and a German militarism broken.

The *Nation*, like Britain generally, had been slow to awaken to the possibility of a general war – in the *Nation* for 25 July there is only brief reference to the Austrian-Servian Crisis. Massingham, and this is a factor of some importance, was ill and largely confined to his home from 21 to 31 July where, however, he managed to do some writing from his sick bed. But his weekly article is absent from the *Daily News and Leader* on 20 and 27 July and 3 August, and Hammond was largely responsible for the *Nation* for 1 August.[3]

[1] Martin, *Peace without Victory*, 54.
[2] Marvin Swartz, *The Union of Democratic Control in British Politics During the First World War* (Oxford, 1971), 99.
[3] N.D., 21, 31 July; Hammond to G. Murray, 28 July 1914, J.L.H.P.

On Sunday 2 August Massingham attended the peace rally in Trafalgar Square and he and Hammond, in argument with the Webbs, denied that violation of Belgium neutrality would require British intervention. On Monday morning, 3 August, Hobson wrote to C. P. Scott that Massingham 'intends to commit the *Nation* to opposition policy' and would like to have the *Guardian*'s cooperation in securing common action with the Labour Party.[1]

It was not Grey's speech that Monday afternoon in the Commons which changed Massingham's mind, for in a letter dated 3 August and published in *The Times* on 4 August, he argued that Russia by mobilisation had taken the first fatal step, that treaty obligations with Belgium did not cover strategic passage of German troops and that support for France could best be expressed by holding the power of the British fleet in reserve.

At the *Nation* Lunch the next day (4 August) Bertrand Russell found Massingham enthusiastically receptive to the offer of an article in opposition to British intervention. On this day of the ultimatum to Germany we catch glimpses of Massingham – in the lobby of the Commons awaiting news and looking 'miserable', and on the steps of the German Embassy. But we have no evidence of the processes of his mind. At 11 p.m. Britain was at war. Overnight, apparently, Massingham had second thoughts, for on the 5th he wrote to Russell, 'Today is not yesterday' and sought to avoid publishing the Russell article.[2]

But for several days Massingham was under great strain – he was looking both ways. He promptly addressed the two Cabinet members who resigned rather than approve entrance into the war. His letter to John Burns dated 6 August begins: 'My dear old Friend: Receive the deepest expression of my affectionate admiration and thanks. You are the noblest Roman of them all.' And about the same time he wrote to Morley, whose reply reads: 'Well may you speak of this hour of grief and despair. To me, personal attachments have made the last few days truly lacerating. It is no small compensation to receive such a letter as yours from a man such as you.'[3] Grey's White Paper, issued 7 August,

[1] *Beatrice Webb's Diaries, 1912–1924*, ed. Cole, 25; Trevor Wilson (ed.), *The Political Diaries of C. P. Scott, 1911–1928* (London, 1970), 94.

[2] Gathorne-Hardy (ed.), *Memoirs of Lady Ottoline Morrell*, 259; *Autobiography of Bertrand Russell*, II, 16–17; Russell to the author, 9 Mar. 1965.

[3] B.P., Add. MS. 46303/59; Morley to Massingham, 6 Aug., M.P.

could not have much influenced the *Nation* for 8 August, obviously thrown together as circumstances were changing and judgments shifting. One leader, 'The War of Fear', refers to Grey's strenuous labours for peace, while another, 'The End of the Balance of Power', declared that 'what has happened now is the fatal consequence of the pursuit of the Balance of Power'. Massingham, as 'Wayfarer', writes moderately:

I suppose this week has altered men's lives and thoughts to a degree with which no previous experience can compare.

One superficial aspect of popular feeling offers a faint consolation. It is a passionless war. No one hates anybody, not we the Germans, or the German us.

Careful study of the White Paper brought stronger convictions. In his *Daily News and Leader* column for 10 August, entitled 'What We are Fighting For', Massingham testified: 'Sir Edward Grey's speech left me unconvinced and hostile on the subject of our individual intervention. But reading the White Paper produced a tremendous revulsion. . . I could not resist the evidence that we were being forced into the war.' And in the *Nation* (15 August) 'Wayfarer' reiterated that the White Paper had persuaded him that Grey had 'left nothing undone to secure the peace'. A. J. P. Taylor concluded that by 1913 Grey had adopted Radical policy on Germany.[1] It is self-evident that with the outbreak of war Massingham accepted the policy of Grey.

Massingham's judgment rapidly became a moral conviction of the justice and rightness of Britain's cause – an attitude characteristic of the English middle classes generally, particularly those with traditions of evangelical Nonconformity behind them, as Professor Noel Fieldhouse reminds me. Like all of Massingham's causes, the war became a crusade which he fought against friends and foes alike. The battleground was the weekly Lunch, the pages of the *Nation* and the *Daily News and Leader*, and occasionally *The Times*, and hence his prompt altercation with Morrell at the Lunch on 11 August.[2] When Russell's article, 'The Rights of the War', protesting against 'our share in the destruction of Germany' and referring to 'the futile horror of the White Paper' appeared in the *Nation* of 11 August, Massingham gave

[1] *The Trouble Makers*, 125–6.
[2] N.D., 11 Aug. J. L. Hammond and Bertrand Russell exchanged letters, with Hammond insisting that *Nation* support of British intervention was not inconsistent with the *Nation*'s pre-war policy. *Autobiography of Bertrand Russell*, II, 45–7.

prompt reply. The controversy continued for some weeks in 'letters to the editor'.

On the one hand we have, by 15 August, *Nation* leaders such as 'Why Britain is Right' which assert that 'German militarism' is the great enemy. And Nevinson, who had been in Germany when war broke out, found no alternative to British intervention. H. G. Wells launched into his theme of the war as 'opportunity' to achieve 'the confederation and collective disarmament of Europe'. In the *Daily News and Leader* (24 August) Massingham pleaded for support of the war and spoke hopefully of a peace based on democratic principles. But Massingham's writings in August and September lack drive and power – he is on the defensive and hardly aware of it. For one thing he was again confined to his home, ill for a week or so after 18 August.[1] When he does write it is to answer his critics or to call attention to stories of German atrocities (suggesting their investigation), to write amiably about recruiting, or to reason that it would be a short war; none of it is inspired.

On the other hand Massingham's comments are vigorously attacked by his friends and associates. In the name of the Union of Democratic Control, Ramsay MacDonald, Charles Trevelyan, Norman Angell, Philip Morrell, E. D. Morel, and Arthur Ponsonby, in a communication in the *Nation*, of 19 September entitled 'Conditions of a Stable Peace', favour increased parliamentary control of foreign policy, advocate a peace which would include universal arms reduction and oppose transfer of any territory without a popular plebiscite. Brailsford, in particular, is the *Nation* spokesman for the redefined Radical cause. In a heady letter (29 August), while admitting that Germany had been heavily in the wrong, he asked 'Is any power in the right?' 'This war has been ten years in the making, and the time that ought to have been used to avert it was spent instead on the struggle for a balance of power'. To his plea for a 'democratic' settlement, Massingham expressed support (he received a letter from Lord Courtney with the plea, 'quench not this spirit') but was doubtful about a negotiated peace. In response to Brailsford he wrote for the *Daily News and Leader* (21 September) a piece 'A Fight to the Finish' (the phrase was taken from Brailsford's article), asserting that a war which ended in a

[1] N.D., 8 Aug. and 8 Sept.

'draw' would settle nothing. Yet the German spirit might yet set Germany free.

Thus, a careful reading of Massingham reveals considerable qualification, uncertainty, hesitation. This was unlike him. Perhaps he was more himself in conversation with Burns (22 September) – doleful about the war and unhappy with Churchill's speech (21 September) that if the German ships did not come out, 'they will be dug out like rats in a hole'. And Burns found his friend 'very upset in having to defend a war which he thought could have been avoided',[1] a revealing observation.

But at this time Massingham's public stance was unqualified support of the Government and the war effort. To Churchill he sent an advanced proof of an article on provision for dependants of service men ('Children of the State', *Nation* 12 September) which Churchill forwarded with approval to Lloyd George. The Chancellor's brilliant address in London on 19 September on the nation at war brought congratulations from Massingham and a request for an appointment. He had nothing but praise for the labours of Grey ('looking care-worn'), nothing but admiration for Asquith ('if you want a tonic ... the thing to do is ... have a look at the Prime Minister'), or for Churchill (his 'magnetic power is unimpaired'), or for Lloyd George (his 'bold and sanguine temper').[2]

For several months, he contributed a signed article each week on the character of the war: for example, 'Why We Came to Help Belgium' (3 October), republished as a pamphlet and reissued from Lausanne in French; 'Idealism and the War' (10 October); 'The Aim of Britain' (17 October) which called for German cooperation in a lasting peace; 'The Ends of British Policy' (19 December), a plea for a new concept of state. His tribute (21 November) to Lord Roberts, who died while on mission in France, was, he told Garvin, deliberately 'strong because I wanted to wake readers up to the coming battle'.[3] The moral tone rises until in January 1915 he is writing of 'the spiritual factor

[1] Burns Diary, 22 Sept. and 16 Oct. 1914, Add. MS. 46336/155, 167, B.P. A few months later (10 January 1915) Burns records a talk with Massingham about the war – Massingham saying he thought Burns' resignation reflected wisdom and courage. Add, MS. 46337/30, B.P.
[2] L.G.P., C/3/16/14 and C/11/2/30. Comments by 'Wayfarer', *Nation*, 21 Nov.
[3] Massingham to Garvin, 4 Dec. [1914], Garvin Papers.

which has governed our intervention and will, we hope, ensure our victory'.[1]

Of divisions within the *Nation* staff we learn, week in and week out, from Nevinson's notes on the Lunches – first on the origins of the war, then on the merits of Shaw's 'Common Sense about the War', and constantly on the nature of the peace. Articles by H. G. Wells reflected his early convictions about the rightness of Britain's cause and his optimism about the war's outcome. These brought such a flood of criticism that on 3 October he announced, 'I will write no more ... I leave the field and return to fiction.' Brailsford continued as the chief apologist for Germany. In the *Nation* (21 November) he raised the question that if Belgian territory is considered inviolable, what about Persia? In an editorial note Massingham responded that the cases were hardly the same. His own article 'A Tragedy of Pride (5 December) asserting that the chief cause of the war was German pride ('a fortified, autocratic Germany rapidly became the enemy of European civilization') brought prompt answer from Brailsford (12 December) that anyone who denied that the Allies shared responsibility was 'the enemy of a better future'. An article submitted at this time by Norman Angell, 'The Menace of English Junkerdom', was rejected by Massingham as not 'quite pertinent', for he found no 'rational comparison of Prussian and English Junkers', as the article suggested.[2]

But to any and all dangers threatening civil liberties, the editor and his staff closed ranks. In October 1914 when the Government ordered internment of all alien 'enemies' (German and Austrian) of military age the *Nation* cautioned against panic and Massingham pleaded for moderation. Apparently he had special knowledge for he reported to Hobhouse Asquith's concern and prompt modification of policy.[3] But internment of some aliens without trial continued. In a leading case, that of Arthur Zadig, German by birth but a naturalised British citizen who was detained because of 'his hostile origin and associations,' Massingham sponsored a Habeas Corpus Defence Fund for legal

---

[1] *Nation*, 9 Jan. 1915, p. 460. See also Massingham in *Atlantic Monthly*, Jan. 1915.
[2] Angell to Massingham, 28 Nov. and 7 Dec. 1914 (Copies); Massingham to Angell, 8 Dec. 1914. Angell Papers.
[3] *Nation*, 24 Oct. p. 103 and 31 Oct. pp. 34–5, 137; Wilson (ed.), *Political Diaries of C. P. Scott*, 109.

assistance. Final appeal in the Lords in 1917 went against Zadig, but the publicity in the case helped bring his release soon after.[1]

No one was more zealous than Massingham in speaking out in support of a free press, 'the right of fair criticism' of the Government even in war time. Thus, at the outbreak of hostilities when British correspondents were barred from within the lines of the Expeditionary Force, he lashed out against 'this crushing blow to the right of free speech and communication'. He was alive to the power given the Press Bureau by the Defence of the Realm Acts. A later example is his letter to *The Times*, 26 April 1916, in which he emphasised 'the social responsibilities of journalism' in the absence of Party government; but how could they be discharged if free criticism of the Executive and the Legislative was suppressed? After the war he asserted that the *Nation* had steadfastly refused to accept the Press Bureau version of the news.[2]

On the delicate problems of neutral shipping and the British blockade Massingham had a special source of knowledge through Runciman at the Board of Trade. Again he disagreed with many of his *Nation* associates. In the controversy with the United States and other neutrals in 1914–15 over the effects of the blockade he thought the British case well established, though he grasped at the interpretation that Britain was making some concessions.[3] When Norman Angell in February 1915 submitted an article, 'America and Sea Power', suggesting that while the United States probably would not greatly embarrass Britain during the war she would at its conclusion demand a great internationalisation of sea power, Massingham refused publication on the grounds that German sympathisers in the United States might use it to the detriment of Anglo-American relations.[4] But he was obviously uncomfortable with his position, and he must have turned with relief to proposals for the prevention of future wars which he discussed with

[1] Francis W. Hirst, *The Consequences of the War to Great Britain* (London, 1934), 109–15; *Nation*, Feb.-Mar. 1916.

[2] Signed article by Massingham, *Nation*, 21 Nov. 1914 ('The Right of Fair Criticism') and 9 Jan. 1915 ('The Case for Liberty'); see also his articles in *Daily News and Leader*, 26 Oct., 8 Dec. 1914 and 11 Jan. 1915. Post-war comment in *Nation*, 5 Apr. 1919 and 21 Feb. 1920.

[3] *Nation*, 14 Nov. 1914, and Jan.-Mar. 1915; Massingham to Runciman, 12 Feb. 1915, Runciman Papers.

[4] Angell to Massingham, 2 Feb. 1915 (Copy) and Massingham to Angell, 2 Feb. 1915. Angell Papers.

Walter Hines Page, the American Ambassador, to whom he was introduced by Lord Bryce.[1]

'Liberalism Beaten to its Corner'

In the opening months of 1915 Massingham's attitude towards the Asquith Government was somewhat ambivalent. His articles for the *Daily News and Leader* in February (his weekly contribution now ends) concern German responsibility for the war. Churchill's survey of the Navy (February) won his good marks. When Grey gave a public accounting of the Foreign Office, 1906–14, renouncing British responsibility for the war, Massingham was present. Grey, he said, 'possesses its ear [that of the country] and its confidence to a degree which no Foreign Minister has attained since Palmerston and it is to his temperament and character that Europe will chiefly turn for an end to her present travail'. A *Nation* leader 'Garbled History' (13 March), attacked the I.L.P. pamphlet 'How the War Came'; Massingham defended Trevelyan and Ponsonby from abuse but underlined his disagreement. At stormy Lunches Hobhouse, Hammond and Morrison attacked Brailsford's position on Germany. An irritated Hobhouse soon deserted the Lunches and wrote little more for the *Nation*.[2]

It is a different Massingham when military conscription becomes a possibility as well as a threat. Its mention (January) brought an emotional appeal on behalf of 'The Case for Liberty'. 'The advocate of conscription . . . does every kind of disservice to his country. He tears up the national unity, puts shackles on the willing mind.' He was shocked and dismayed at Lloyd George's hasty action, in March, in ramming through the legislative process the Defence of the Realm Act No. 2 calling for mobilisation of industrial resources. Such a measure, Massingham remarked, called for 'a higher sense of accountability than now reigns on the Treasury Bench'. An appeal to the country as 'a free nation' would have brought the result sought. When Lloyd George introduced the measure (9 March) Massingham wrote to Runciman: 'Many shakings of heads there must be over L.G.'s speech and the measure it propounded.'[3] Massingham was also distressed by

---

[1] Massingham–Page correspondence, Feb.-Mar. 1915, Houghton.
[2] *Nation*, Feb.-April 1915; N.D. 23 Mar., 13 April and 18 May 1915; J. A. Hobson and Morris Ginsburg, *L. T. Hobhouse: His Life and Work* (London, 1931), 62.
[3] *Nation*, 9 and 16 Jan. 1915; Massingham to Runciman, n.d., Runciman Papers.

the Chancellor's handling of the 'drink problem' among industrial workers, with decline of factory production. The proposal of nationalisation was not the issue; it was supported by Joseph Rowntree and E. R. Cross, and indeed by Massingham – he was one of the Liberal editors who met with Lloyd George and gave their approval, but he was disturbed that only representatives of management had been consulted. He wrote to Runciman: 'I do hope that in whatever steps you take on temperance you will try and carry the workmen with you, before anything drastic is done.' The project itself, in the face of Conservative opposition, soon died.[1]

Massingham was in truth rapidly drawing away from his one-time heroes – Lloyd George and Churchill, the Radicals of the 1906 Liberal Government, for the war was playing havoc with political ties. Of this Massingham seemed well informed. There is the well-known story that on 24 March he told Margot Asquith that Churchill was 'intriguing hard' to replace Grey at the Foreign Office with Balfour and he could prove it. She told her husband at once and he reported it to Lloyd George who, somewhat to the Prime Minister's surprise, said he believed the remark was substantially correct.[2] Next week, in the *Nation*, 'Wayfarer' referred to the rumour of the withdrawal from the Government of both Asquith and Grey, but added that 'the thistledown which was floated down the wind ... has pretty well blown away'. To Runciman Massingham wrote: 'finish this coalition nonsense'.[3]

When the Liberal Government did give way to the Coalition, on 17 May – a change generally accepted, if without enthusiasm, by the Liberal press – the editor of the *Nation* was startled and dismayed. In signed leaders (a procedure reserved for extraordinary occasions) he found no prospect of greater unity; indeed the new Cabinet was 'essentially and inevitably weaker' than its predecessor. In particular he regretted the appointment of Balfour to the Admiralty and the retention of Churchill, even in minor office ('if he was right, he need never have gone; if he was wrong his association with the Cabinet

---

[1] *Nation*, 3 and 10 Apr. 1915; Massingham to Runciman, 8 Apr. [1915], Runciman Papers. H. A. Taylor, *Robert Donald* (London, 1934), 82.
[2] Randolph S. Churchill and Martin Gilbert, *Winston S. Churchill*; vol. 3, *The Challenge of War, 1914–1916* (Boston, 1971), 361–2.
[3] Massingham to Runciman, 8 Apr. [1915], Runciman Papers.

should have ceased'.) The chatter at *Nation* Lunches reflected the distrust of Lloyd George, the opposition to conscription and the rising enthusiasm for Kitchener. Indeed the *Nation* Group was harmonious for a change.[1]

The formation of the Coalition brought Massingham back to Haldane's side. Early in the year the *Nation* with other Liberal journals had defended Haldane against charges of pro-Germanism. Now his shelving brought a personal letter of concern from Massingham who paid tribute in the *Nation* to a man who had brought cultivation and intellect to public office.[2] Massingham sent on to the Foreign Office a letter from Eduard Bernstein in Germany commenting on the German version of the Haldane Mission of 1912 in the *Norddeutsche Allgemeine*, a comment which inspired Massingham's remark that the German Chancellor was responsible for the article. When Grey drafted a White Paper (31 August) with the British version of the Haldane Mission he had in hand Bernstein's letter and Massingham's comment.[3] As to Haldane, he contributed 'Democracy and Ideas' to the *Nation* (7 August) in answer to a piece by Wells (24 July) on the weakness of democracy. The three of them – Massingham, Haldane and Wells – dined together a few months later and the following year Massingham read a draft of Haldane's 'diary-biography' of the previous decade, eventually published as *Before the War* (1920).[4]

For Massingham the shift to the Coalition marked an important stage in his alienation from Lloyd George. Early in May in an address at Manchester Lloyd George approved in principle both military and industrial conscription. Outraged, Massingham in the first sentence of the *Nation* for 5 June declared that just as Joseph Chamberlain had forced the Government's hand on protection in 1903 so now Lloyd George was doing the same on compulsory service. Chamberlain, he added, did not get protection, but did break up the Government.[5] Then

[1] *Nation*, 22 and 29 May 1915; N.D., 1 June.
[2] *Nation*, 29 June, p. 282; Massingham to Haldane [26 May 1915], H.P. 5911/121–2.
[3] Massingham–Drummond correspondence in P.R.O., F.O. 80c/108; Bernstein to Massingham, 12 Aug. 1915, M.P.; *Nation*, 21 Aug. 1915, p. 667. A more complete account is in Stephen E. Koss, *Lord Haldane, Scapegoat for Liberalism* (New York, 1969), 90–4.
[4] Haldane to Massingham, 11 Aug. 1915, M.P. Haldane to his mother, 5 Nov. 1915, H.P.; Massingham to Haldane, 10 June 1916, H.P. 3913/20–1.
[5] *Nation*, 12 June, for comment from Miss Frances Stevenson (Lloyd George's secretary) and Massingham's response.

a few weeks later Massingham suffered additional shock when Lloyd George not only failed to come to the aid of Kitchener under attack in the Commons but turned on Haldane who did. Massingham, Burns recorded: 'at last sees the dangerous structure he helped to build and too late saw the mistake he made in his early subservience to the most dangerous man that in the name of the people has played reaction's game.'[1]

Conscription, more than any other issue, brought Massingham's return to the Radical fold, for in compulsory military service his concept of the war as a crusade was destroyed. During the second half of 1915 the threat of compulsion dominated the *Nation*'s columns. But Massingham did not then anticipate that military conscription would come. He seized upon the Derby Scheme (October) as the way out and was soon in controversy with *The Times*. When the *Nation* welcomed the suggestion that the Derby Plan would indeed meet recruiting needs, Lord Derby himself was so exercised over this 'erroneous statement . . . [which] if repeated in other papers would probably do his movement serious injury' that he enlisted Lord Riddell's aid in drafting a contradiction for the press.[2]

When the first Conscription Law came in January 1916 Massingham could hardly find language adequate to describe 'this historic reversal of Liberalism and democracy'. The action, he said, was arbitrary: 'No proof has been given of the necessity of conscription, and no attempt made to secure a general assent to it.' Unreason seized him. He declared that only 30 of the 200 Liberals known to be against the measure had voted their convictions, only to be answered that had the others done so, Asquith would have resigned to be replaced by Lloyd George, something Massingham himself had said should be avoided.[3]

In the Cabinet Runciman and McKenna had opposed conscription – but to Massingham's disappointment they did not resign. To McKenna he wrote at once that a firm stand, with resignation if necessary, would be a great aid to the revival (some day) of Liberalism. By April he was

---

[1] Burns Diary, 5 June 1915 (see also 25 May, 5 July), B.P., Add. MS. 46337.
[2] *The Times*, 23 Oct. 1915, p. 7; 25 Oct. 1915, p. 9; 26 Oct. 1915, p. 9; *Lord Riddell's War Diary, 1914–1918* (London [1933]), 132.
[3] *Nation*, 1 and 22 Jan. 1916; Trevor Wilson, *The Downfall of the Liberal Party, 1914–1935* (Ithaca, New York, 1966), 40.

also urging immediate resignation on Runciman: 'What ground can you now stand on? The Liberal coalition outside will now become more and more formidable, and from it the party of the future will be formed. Surely your place is with it.'[1]

What attitude to take toward Asquith? He felt sympathy for the Prime Minister's position – a crisis over conscription precipitated chiefly by Lloyd George, and now under pressure from his Cabinet and victimised by 'the personal vendetta' of *The Times*. Massingham (*Nation*, 20 April) urged Asquith to take the country into his confidence and assert his authority. The phrase 'personal vendetta' annoyed Northcliffe and he remonstrated. The great problem, he wrote Massingham, was 'the scientific utilization of the men recruited'.

The Government brings about its own difficulties. You have great influence with them. Why not urge them to send out one or two shrewd men of business to go through our lines and insist upon the military utilizing to the full the force already enlisted.

Massingham answered apologetically, saying he judged Asquith more harshly than did Northcliffe and had in fact given up on the Coalition. But he used Northcliffe's admonition as the basis for a paragraph (*Nation*, 29 April), suggesting shifting younger men from non-combatant jobs to the front and filling their places with older men.[2]

With the second conscription measure in May, which was no surprise, Massingham returned to the theme of 'loss of soul and freedom'. Politically, all was a shambles. 'The old coalition was Liberal-Tory with Liberalism uppermost. The new coalition is Tory, with Liberalism beaten to its corner.'[3]

With the first conscription measure came protest from conscientious objectors – the *Nation* declared that 'the Government in drafting this Bill have shown no comprehension of this problem' and its columns came alive with correspondence. In a characteristic mixture of irony and rage Massingham, in a letter to *The Times* on 15 February 1916,

---

[1] Massingham to McKenna, 1 Jan. 1916, McKenna Papers; Massingham to Runciman, 28 April [1916], Runciman Papers.

[2] Northcliffe to Massingham, 25 April 1916 (Copy); Massingham to Northcliffe, 27 April [1916], Northcliffe Papers.

[3] 'Wayfarer', *Nation*, 6 May. From N.D., 6 May, we know that Massingham also wrote the powerful leader, 'The Defeat of Liberalism'.

denounced interference with Quaker meetings. In the *Nation* he provided space for Shaw whom other papers brushed aside. And though, as usual, no joiner himself, Massingham was in touch with members of the No Conscription Fellowship. At the end of May he was at Garsington, at the home of Ottoline and Philip Morrell, in 'a nest of rebels' along with Philip Snowden, Bertrand Russell, Lytton Strachey and Maynard Keynes. At another gathering at Garsington on 9 July, Clifford Allen who was chairman of the No Conscription Fellowship awaited Massingham and his help in drafting a public statement. For some reason he failed to get there.[1]

Russell's writing for the Fellowship in 1916 brought conviction for violation of the Defence of the Realm Act. Then his dismissal from his lectureship by the Council of Trinity College, Cambridge, brought Massingham's challenge and a hurried correspondence with Russell, Runciman and Gilbert Murray. Russell's prohibition, by a military edict, from entering certain areas was termed by Massingham in a letter to *The Times* (5 September) 'a gross libel and an advertisement that the administration of the Defence of the Realm Regulations is in the hands of men who do not understand their business'. This article was called to Lloyd George's attention by his secretary.[2]

In April 1916 Massingham had referred in the *Nation* to 'a distinguished friend of conscription'. This was Lord Northcliffe to whom Massingham had been drawn by their common hostility to the Coalition. Massingham's shift of attitude toward Northcliffe was characteristically abrupt. Well through October 1915, 'Wayfarer' (Massingham), taking seriously the Derby Plan as an alternative to conscription, was outraged by *The Times*' continued attack on Asquith and the *Daily Mail*'s abuse of Grey. An unsigned leader (*Nation*, 16 October 1915) on 'The Peril Within' declared: 'If the Harmsworth journalism is in the last resort brainless, it is clever enough to lead the weak and to impose on the ignorant. It has destroyed one Government and now threatens another. But the real attack is on the spirit of the nation.'

But six weeks later Massingham was defending *The Times* and the *Daily Mail*. When the Commons spent seven hours (on 30 Novem-

---

[1] John Rae, *Conscience and Politics* (London, 1970), 50; Roy Harrod, *Life of John Maynard Keynes* (London, 1951), 212; Holroyd, *Strachey*, II, 196–7; B. Russell to Lady Constance Malleson, n.d. (courtesy Lady Malleson).
Nation, 22 July 1916; *The Times*, 5 Sept. 1916; L.G.P., E/1/4/7.

ber) debating the influence of the Northcliffe press, 'however un-
wittingly ... in encouraging the enemy, in disconcerting our Allies,
in hardening neutral opinion against us', Massingham remarked that
somehow public attention had drifted away from the fundamental
facts – 'the dragging of the war, the absence of freshness of ideas from
the high command'.[1] He and Northcliffe were soon meeting on friendly
terms. After a talk on 23 December, Massingham wrote impulsively:

I should like to say that I think you have not had justice done you in respect
to the present motives of your action considering all the facts you have
known or the impression they were bound to make on you in view of the
traditional policy of the 'Times' in war. I hope you won't consider this
insincere or intrusive. I only say what I feel.

Northcliffe responded with a copy of a confidential and somewhat
sensational report on the Dardanelles by an Australian observer, Keith
Murdoch. In acknowledging it Massingham wrote: 'If it were read out
in the House of Commons it would close the life of the Government of
which (for different reasons) you and I think equally little.'

They agreed there was really no Prime Minister making decisions as
to service requirements and giving the country and the press a lead.
They discussed the financial problems of the Government. At Northcliffe's suggestion, Massingham responded with articles in the *Nation*
and wrote to the Chancellor of the Exchequer (McKenna) urging 'compulsory thrift' on the nation, and suggesting his consultation with
Northcliffe. Such was the mutual confidence which developed between
Massingham and Northcliffe that soon they arranged for a round of
golf.[2]

Because of common distaste for the Coalition Massingham and
another of his villains of the piece before the war, Lord Fisher, were
brought together. When Nevinson returned (October 1915) from an
assignment in the Dardanelles he found the *Nation* Group registering
'a general sense of disaster and despair about the Near East' with

---

[1] Hansard, *Commons*, 30 Nov. 1915; *Nation* ('Wayfarer'), 4 December 1915. In the
debate Sir John Simon, Home Secretary, was taxed with 'indiscretions' in Liberal papers,
e.g. a statement in the *Nation* by 'a very well known writer' that it would be better to
lose the war than lose voluntary service. Massingham, in a letter to *The Times* denied
that either he or the *Nation* had ever made such a statement. *The Times*, 2, 3, 4 Dec.
[2] Massingham–Northcliffe correspondence, Dec. 1915–Jan. 1916 is in Northcliffe Papers.
Massingham to McKenna [January 1915], McKenna Papers.

Massingham supporting a pull-out.[1] Eventually a *Nation* leader (20 November) indicted Churchill for the failure in the Dardanelles and for ignoring Fisher's advice – this was by way of commentary on Churchill's attack in the Commons on Fisher. The latter's five-sentence reply in the Lords was referred to by 'Wayfarer' as a 'brilliant flash of silence'.

All this caught the eye of Captain Crease, Fisher's naval assistant, who reported to Fisher that the *Nation* article on Churchill was 'the best on the subject' and passed along Massingham's request for a meeting. At once they were in touch, Massingham sending Fisher a copy of the *Nation* article (4 December) which proposed his appointment to the War Committee, an action which he urged on McKenna and Runciman. Then he sent to Jellicoe an extract from the *Nation* of 24 December urging Fisher's return to the Admiralty. During the early months of 1916, a movement in the press, including the *Nation*, the *Manchester Guardian* and the *Observer*, backed Fisher's bid for return to government service.[2]

Churchill also hoped to resume office, but knew he would need a favourable press. Lord Rothermere (brother of Northcliffe and a personal friend of Churchill) remarked that if he did return he would be treated 'unmercifully' by Massingham and other Liberal editors. Churchill even joined the chorus for Fisher's recall but his testimony before the War Committee was ineffectual. Still fascinated by the editor of the *Nation*, Fisher, in his first communication to Crease in June after news of Jutland, inquired, 'Tell me what Massingham thinks of it all!'[3]

Peace by negotiation

Far more significant was that by mid-1916 Massingham's attitude towards the prospect of peace by negotiation and his interpretation of the role of the United States in the war had changed. As early as 19 September, 1914 Massingham (as 'Wayfarer') had confidently expected American intervention in the war and with her aid a peace which would

[1] N.D., 12, 19, 28 Oct. 1915.
[2] Extensive Crease–Fisher and Massingham–Fisher correspondence is in Fisher Papers; Fisher to Massingham, n.d., M.P.
[3] 'H' to Master of Elibank, 4 Mar. 1916, National Library of Scotland; Marder (ed.), *Fear God and Dread Nought*, III, 353.

destroy Prussian militarism.[1] Assuming the moral support of the United States straightaway or at least a benevolent neutrality, for the better part of a year he was disappointed. President Wilson's speech 'We are Too Proud to Fight' (10 May 1915) after the sinking of the *Lusitania*, was to Massingham only a reflection of American pacifism and isolation. Then when an important American note (21 July) denied that violations of neutral rights by Britain justified the use of the submarine by Germany, the *Nation*, almost alone in the press, was unimpressed; the significant element, it said, was Wilson's recognition that maritime law might be revised.[2]

Throughout 1915, differences within the *Nation* staff on the merits of a 'punitive peace' as against a 'negotiated peace' are apparent. Hobson's communication, 'Approaches to Peace', in the *Nation* on 16 October, sought a statement of Britain's war aims and for the next two months the correspondence columns carried the views, often conflicting, of G. Lowes Dickinson, Masterman, C. R. Buxton, Ponsonby and others. Massingham's own mind was uncertain. When Lord Courtney declared (November) that the deadlock in fighting called for peace by negotiation, Massingham, who had listened to the 'all-is-lost debate' in the Lords, remarked in the *Nation* (13 November) that what was needed was 'a new Chatham' and he wrote to Courtney that the circumstances of the demands of Prussian militarism and of Britain's undertaking to make peace only in cooperation with her allies would hardly make possible a negotiated peace at that time.[3] However, to Northcliffe in January 1916 Massingham expressed doubts that a victory with power to impose 'real conqueror's terms' could be won.[4] But when Brailsford's letter (*Nation*, 1 January 1916) pointed out the German interests involved in any peace settlement Massingham returned to the theme that Germany menaced European security. And the *Nation* (29 January) backed Grey's statement that the blockade would continue to prevent enemy trade through neutral countries. As late as October 1916, Massingham, in a review of E. D. Morel's *Truth*

[1] See also Massingham, 'The Distrust of Germany', *Daily News and Leader*, 5 Oct. 1914.
[2] Armin Rappaport, *The British Press and Wilsonian Neutrality* (London, 1951), 36–7, 48. See also Massingham, 'Open letter to the American People', *Atlantic Monthly* (May 1915).
[3] Massingham to Courtney, Friday [12 Nov. 1915], Courtney Papers, B.L.P.E.S.
[4] Massingham to Northcliffe, 18 Jan. [1916], Northcliffe Papers.

and the War, reiterated his conviction that Germany's role was the governing and finally determinant factor in the outbreak of war.

But as 1916 progressed, there was a change in tone; the *Nation* supported the Radical attack on proposals for maintaining Imperial preference in trade and for commercial discrimination against Germany after the war. Massingham's own voice became stronger and more consistent. He may have been influenced by Joseph Caillaux, for Massingham was in Paris in mid-March and he talked with Caillaux, by then a pacifist working for an immediate peace.[1] Massingham renounced for England any territorial gain or commercial advantage. He was in the Commons, on 24 May, when MacDonald and Ponsonby raised the question of immediate peace negotiations in consequence of remarks by the German Chancellor and by Sir Edward Grey which seemed to render reconcilable the war aims of the belligerents. He was alarmed by proposals of the allied Economic Conference at Paris in June – proposals for limiting enemy commerce after the war – and he claimed knowledge of the measures anticipated.[2]

In following Massingham's change of attitude towards the United States we begin with his comment (*Nation*, 26 February 1916):

Colonel House's visit to us, which has just come to an end, stands I think, for a landmark in the war. What is the issue? Nothing perhaps immediately decisive. . . A harvest of that kind must needs take some time to ripen. But will not all the world rejoice when America thinks the hour has come to put in the sickle?

Massingham of course knew nothing of the memorandum drawn up by Colonel E. M. House, President Wilson's personal representative, and Sir Edward Grey, which misled Wilson into assuming that Britain would welcome American mediation for peace. It was with enthusiasm and considerable confidence that the *Nation* (3 June) welcomed Wilson's offer (27 May) suggesting American mediation to end the war and participation in a post-war association of nations. Wilson's speech, wrote Massingham, 'opens to Europe and to us the first clear prospect of hope since the war began'. Apparently Massingham thought that

---

[1] Martin, *Peace without Victory*, 32, 70–1. T. P. O'Connor said later that it was Caillaux's influence which 'drove Massingham into pacifism'. *Sunday Times*, 7 Sept. 1924.

[2] 'The Sort of Peace We Want', *Nation*, 15 Apr. 1916; *Nation*, 27 May 1916, pp. 243–4, 249. For the Paris Economic Conference, see Massingham's review (*Nation*, 14 Oct. 1916) of E. D. Morel, *Truth and the War*, published in London in July 1916.

sentiment within and without Government circles was gathering for a move towards peace. So he remarked to Hobson. The Rowntrees urged C. P. Scott to call radical journalists together 'to discuss peace terms and to take action.' While Lloyd George called for 'a knock out blow', Grey's remarks to the Foreign Press Association (23 October) stating the allied case in moderate terms brought British policy back to 'the region of statesmanship'.[1] Well before the end of the year Massingham was one of the 'Radicals' along with Gardiner, Trevelyan and Noel Buxton whose views were frequently canvassed and presented to Colonel House for President Wilson's information. On 24 November William H. Buckler, a special agent of the State Department attached to the American Embassy in London, reported to Colonel House that Massingham of the *Nation* had now 'come around in favor of "peace by negotiation" '. Shortly before that, in September 1916, he resigned membership of the Liberal Club, when the Club acquiesced in Government appropriation of its premises for a recruiting office. Soon he joined the Reform Club in its stead.[2]

Massingham always had a multitude of matters on his mind – among them, in 1916, Ireland. The policy of the Government after the Easter Rebellion in Dublin brought from him expressions of dismay, anger and lack of confidence in the Coalition. He was annoyed at the scarcity of accurate news reports, he considered Birrell's resignation as Irish Secretary a tragedy (Massingham wrote Birrell a note of personal appreciation) and he hoped in vain that Britain would show magnanimity and humanity in abstaining from reprisals. His absorption in the Irish problem took him (in May) to Dublin and in the *Nation* he pleaded for Home Rule straightaway with complete independence promised for the future. Lloyd George labelled 'probably mischievous' the *Nation* remark that his assignment to find an Irish settlement 'almost puts the premiership in Commission'. Massingham was in Ireland again the next month attending the session (25 June) of the Belfast convention of Nationalists which voted for exclusion from a

[1] N.D., 1 Sept. 1916; *Nation*, 30 Sept., 28 Oct. 1916; Wilson (ed.), *Political Diaries of C. P. Scott*, 227.
[2] Buckler to House, 24 Nov. 1916, Buckler Papers; membership registers of the Liberal Club and the Reform Club.

Home Rule Ireland.[1] Massingham considered Roger Casement legally guilty of treason but urged reprieve from the death sentence. He associated himself with an informal committee (including Shaw, Nevinson and Mrs Stopford Green) which circulated a petition among the distinguished and influential.

To combat the charges of homosexuality against Casement, which the committee at first considered false, Massingham investigated at Scotland Yard. He reported that the 'black' diaries of Casement substantiated the charges. Though repelled he applauded (*Nation*, 5 August) *The Times* for rebuking officials for allowing knowledge of the diaries to filter through to the public to the prejudice of the accused charged with treason.[2] A few months later, in the *Atlantic Monthly* for December, Massingham expressed hope of a future when England and Ireland would be equals in the new Imperial Federation.

Throughout 1916 the *Nation*'s comments on the Coalition Government reflected helplessness, for there seemed no alternative. Massingham was not anxious to anticipate Lloyd George's further rise to power. With Kitchener's death, he considered Lloyd George's elevation to the War Department as impossible – for one thing, Margot Asquith seemed 'dead against it'. Still, he wrote Haldane, 'the P.M. may be driven to it'. We can only be curious about a conversation at the National Liberal Club between Scott, Hirst, Sydney Olivier and Massingham. Runciman, still in the Cabinet, wrote at length to Massingham at the end of July. He concluded: 'How do you stand it all?'[3] Nevinson thought Massingham was bent on 'overturning Asquith and the coalition', but Massingham would merely say in the *Nation* (29 July) that the Coalition would remain in power on the basis of what it accomplished, not by virtue of enjoying the confidence of the Commons. But for War Secretary Lloyd George's interview (28 September) with an American journalist: 'the fight must be to the finish – to a knock out blow', Massingham had no such moderate language. The interview he, wrote to Runciman, was a 'compendium of vulgarity, folly, and

---

[1] Birrell to Massingham, 14 May 1916, M.P.; *Nation*, 6, 13, 20, 27 May and 1 July 1916; *Lord Riddell's War Diary*, 184. In 1918 Birrell wrote literary articles for the *Nation*.

[2] N.D. gives the story in some detail. In 1927 Charlotte Shaw wrote T. E. Lawrence that Massingham was shown the Casement Diaries at Scotland Yard. Dunbar, *Mrs. G.B.S.*, p. 256. See also Weintraub, *Journey to Heartbreak*, 168.

[3] Massingham to Haldane, 10 June 1916, H.P.; Memorandum, Scott Papers, Add. MS. 50902/103; Runciman to Massingham, 27 July 1916, M.P.; N.D., 3 Aug.

callousness. It will, I think, do more than anything he has said to convince people that he's unsafe and intellectually inadequate to his job'. The year 1916 was strenuous for the editor of the *Nation*. One is not surprised that Galsworthy on meeting Massingham by chance in Devon in mid-July should have noted that Massingham 'looks pale and worn and wants air'.[1]

On 6 December 1916 Lloyd George replaced Asquith as Prime Minister. Nine days before, the *Nation* Lunch discussed 'the probable overthrow of the Government by Lloyd George and Carson'. A leader in the *Nation*, on 2 December, very probably by Massingham, asked the questions: Would any Government in sight (under Lloyd George or Carson) provide 'a strong or a united Cabinet? . . . A well-ordered plan of campaign? A good peace? A contented Alliance? A resettled Europe?' The answer: 'There is no prospect.'

These weeks of the change of government and uncertainty over the reception of 'peace notes' from Germany and the United States were a time of trial. From 5 December to 18 December Massingham was out of the office much of the time, ill with influenza. Nevertheless he most certainly wrote the well-known leader in *Nation* for 9 December, 'A Leap in the Dark', cited by Asquith himself at the time as providing an understanding of 'the inner history of events'.[2] It constituted a blistering attack on Lloyd George's political techniques and an expression of grave misgivings for the future. And 'Wayfarer' referred to the 'random dictatorship . . . likely to suffer early separation, from incompatibilities of temper'. Massingham's alienation from Lloyd George and his defection from organized Liberal politics were soon complete.

The response to the American note of 18 December suggesting an exchange of peace terms by the belligerents made this abundantly clear. While British opinion, including most of the Liberal press, was cool and often hostile, the *Manchester Guardian* and the *Nation* were 'admirable'. This was the report to Colonel House who was sent Massingham's article (30 December) hailing 'this first definite step' by

---

[1] 30 Sept. [1916], Runciman Papers; Marrot, *Life and Letters of John Galsworthy*, 421.
[2] N.D., 28 Nov. 1916; *H.H.A.*, *Letters of the Earl of Oxford and Asquith to a Friend*, ed. Desmond MacCarthy (London, 1933), I, 12–13.

Wilson as a peace maker.[1] But Massingham, the opportunist and the moralist, also appealed directly to the new Prime Minister. On 22 December, while at the Reform Club, he wrote a simple letter: 'You will not expect to have a word from me, and the estrangement between us has gone far,' he began. Then he pledged his support if the Prime Minister decided to accept 'the American offer of mediation [for so Massingham termed it], the best news since Bethlehem'.

The world is now offered a way of escape from its impending ruin. Now that America has spoken, it is in my humble view possible for European statesmanship to act.

God has put this . . . power in your hands. May you use it!

On Christmas Day, Massingham wrote to the Prime Minister again, more deliberately, but with equal fervour. He pointed out that since Lloyd George shared little of the responsibility for the coming of the war, he enjoyed great opportunity for securing 'a real peace', a peace by negotiation based on mutual understanding between Germany and Britain. 'It may not be possible to get to this end publicly. But surely it can be approached privately, or through American mediation.' He concluded with an impassioned appeal to Lloyd George to respond to this opportunity to serve mankind. 'I hope you will not misunderstand this. It has no purpose beyond which its words imply.' He said he expected no reply; the records disclose none.[2]

These letters expressed Massingham's feelings. To Runciman, just dropped from the Board of Trade, he wrote his mind on 26 December. Disappointed in the Liberal response to the America note, Massingham declared flatly that the Liberal Party must develop a policy or be smothered under Lloyd George's initiative; Liberalism must lead the movement for ending the war or 'expire of inanition and division'. Curiously enough, at just this time Massingham received an invitation from Haig to visit the Somme sector – facetiously he remarked to Nevinson that obviously it was a Lloyd George trick – and it is likely his letters to the Prime Minister prompted the invitiation.[3] In the second week of January he visited the Somme; his report, 'A Visit to the Front', in the *Nation* of 20 January, overflowed with sympathy for

1 Buckler to House, 30 Dec. 1916, Buckler Papers.
2 L.G.P., F/94/1/41–4.
3 Runciman Papers; N.D., 1 Jan. 1917.

the soldier's lot. 'If the politicians contrive a peace, the fighting men will keep it and make it lasting.'

Though the American note of 18 December and Wilson's 'Peace without Victory' address to the United States Senate, on 22 January, met with polite indifference from the British Government they were embraced by the Radicals as a representation of their own views, indeed as the *Nation* (27 January) put it, as 'an endorsement of the true case of the Allies'. The *Nation* Group, save Masterman, feared a prolongation of the war with a very heavy expenditure of lives – and to no purpose. House continued to receive cuttings from the *Nation* and in Washington he was visited by S. K. Ratcliffe, one of Massingham's contributors. Unrestricted submarine warfare and American severance of diplomatic relations with Germany heralded the approach of a new phase in the war. Noel Buxton who dined with Lloyd George and other officials on 5 February and lunched with the *Nation* staff on the 6th, drew up a Memorandum on 'Views held of American Entrance into the war', dated 8 February which Buckler sent on to House. 'The writers of the *Nation* are a good microcosm of Radical views', noted Buxton, and he reported that most of the staff was 'strongly pro' American entrance into the war as a moderating influence on allied policy, though a few thought that the absence of a strong neutral power was 'dangerous'. After receiving these reports, House wrote to Buckler (25 February): 'I wish you would tell Mr. Massingham, Noel Buxton, A. G. Gardiner . . . how much their support heartens us here.' And he added, 'Do not let our Liberal friends be fearful of the President's attitude. You can assure them that when the time comes for action, they will find him on the right side.'[1] Writing on 21 February in a symposium of Liberal opinion (German, French, Russian and English) on 'The Allies' Terms of Peace' which appeared in the New York *Evening Post* and was reprinted in the New York *Nation*, 12 April 1917, Massingham declared that the close identity between American and British Liberalism governed the British view of possible American intervention in the war. The formal entrance of the United States was greeted in the *Nation* (5 April) with his leader: 'American Liberalism comes into Action.' His claims for the role of Radicalism were justified.

---

[1] Buckler letters are in Buckler Papers: House Diary, 27 Jan. 1917 and House to Buckler, 25 Feb. 1917, in House Papers.

'Dam – Nation'[1]

On 29 March 1917 the *Nation* received notice from the War Department that its overseas circulation was henceforth prohibited on the grounds that certain of its statements had been used by the enemy as propaganda. Massingham made this matter public in a letter to *The Times* on 7 April. 'Mr. George's Government has now added British Liberalism to its list of prohibited exports,' he wrote.

On occasion Lloyd George had sought the intervention of the Rowntree Trust in the *Nation*'s policy. In April 1916 E. R. Cross, solicitor for the Trust and chairman of the Directors of the *Nation* responded with assurances of his own loyalty to Lloyd George and that of Seebohm Rowntree, now on the staff of the Ministry of Munitions. Cross pointed out Massingham's own services to Lloyd George in the past and felt that any present differences were due not to 'malignancy' but to 'misunderstanding and temperament'. While it was not 'in the power of men' to alter the latter, he would try to remove the misunderstandings. Soon after, Christopher Addison, Lloyd George's Parliamentary Secretary, and Seebohm Rowntree lunched with Massingham and sought to moderate his attitude towards Lloyd George. Then again in September 1916, when Lloyd George returned from France, his secretary, Sir William Sutherland, reported that both Massingham and Gardiner were 'bitter' about the Government's closing of the Liberal Club and using its premises, as the *Nation* said, 'as a recruiting office (under conscription!)' and he enclosed cuttings from articles in the *Nation* and *Daily News*. He suggested that Arnold Rowntree see to it that the new chairman of the *Nation* board (Cross had just died) was friendly to the Government. 'It is time that he [Rowntree] really dealt with this nuisance.'[2]

In December 1916, two weeks after Lloyd George became Prime Minister, the Directors of the Rowntree Trust held 'a special meeting' to consider the policy of the *Nation* towards the new Government. Massingham came off well. When Seebohm Rowntree emphasised Lloyd George's concern that a paper owned by those friendly to him

---

[1] This heading in *John Bull* is cited in *Nation*, 20 Oct. 1917.
[2] Cross to Lloyd George, 7 Apr. 1916 ('Confidential'), L.G.P. Christopher Addison, *Four and a Half Years* (London, 1934), I, 194; Sutherland to Lloyd George [Sept. 1916], L.G.P., E/1/4/7.

should be constantly 'abusing' him and making 'incorrect' assertions about him, Arnold Rowntree replied that Lloyd George was of course a very controversial figure; and quite naturally desired 'a good press'. When Seebohm Rowntree responded that Lloyd George objected not to criticism but to personal attacks, J. Stephen Rowntree declared that he did not know of a single offensive sentence in the *Nation*. It was finally agreed that Massingham should be urged to avoid personalities and Seebohm Rowntree, perhaps at his own suggestion, undertook to look in at the *Nation* office regularly. Lloyd George also complained to Herbert Samuel that week after week he was attacked in the *Nation* and in the *Daily News* and not one of his colleagues protested – indeed, he said, McKenna for one, 'had spread the poison'. Samuel could only sympathise by saying that he too had been abused by the *Nation*.[1]

There is no evidence that any remonstrances from the Rowntrees influenced Massingham. With the creation of the Council of Five and the Cabinet Secretariat, Massingham charged Lloyd George with 'separating the premiership from the Commons' and weakening the control of Parliament over the Executive.[2] In March 1917 Massingham was greatly disturbed when the Liberals in the Commons refused to vote against Lloyd George on the increase of import duties on cotton goods entering India. 'By refusing to fight now, the Liberal Party has prepared for itself other and larger surrenders in the future,' said the *Nation* on 17 March. And 'Wayfarer' remarked: 'Had Asquith raised his hand . . . the Government would have been lost', and suggested that a Government under Bonar Law might restore unity.

But, as to the overseas ban, statements in the *Nation* on the course of the war and the peace to come – positions to which Massingham had fully committed himself only by December 1916 – brought official action. In *The Times* for 8 December 1916, Massingham called attention to a quotation from the *Nation* on 2 December, republished in the German press, that forces in England desiring 'a speedy, moder-

[1] Minutes, Rowntree Trust, 22 Dec. 1916, Rowntree Papers; Herbert Samuel, *Grooves of Change* (London, 1946), 154–5. Samuel may have had in mind a remark in the *Nation*, 4 Mar. 1916, suggesting that Samuel had German connections. In response to Samuel's request, Massingham placed a note in the next *Nation* that it had been informed that Samuel had no enemy connection by blood, marriage or business. Samuel to Massingham, 9 Mar. 1916, M.P.

[2] *Nation*, 24 Feb. 1917. For American readers Massingham developed this theme in *Yale Review*, July 1917, 'Lloyd George and his Government'.

ate, honourable peace' were gaining over the forces which were committed to an indefinite conflict. Massingham was then stressing the failures of the Admiralty, the successes of German submarine warfare and the difficulties in getting adequate supplies to Britain. Again he publicly urged the recall to service of Fisher and privately remarked that Balfour's administration at the Admiralty might lose the war; these matters he talked over with Fisher and with Runciman. By mid-January Massingham was urging Northcliffe to publicise the success of the German submarines.[1]

The immediate occasion of the War Department's action against the *Nation* was its comment (3 March 1917) on the great retreat of German forces on the western front in February, 1917:

If we could judge the war dispassionately we should be compelled to confess that Germany is still the master of surprises. . . The events towards which our efforts had been directed for almost five months have at length come to pass; but it has found our soldiers wanting. The greatest retreat on the West since the Marne has taken place; but in this case almost all the honors go to the enemy.

On 5 March *The Times*, at the request of the Government Press Bureau, published a letter, 'The Temper of the "Nation" ', which abstracted statements in the *Nation* for the previous three weeks, including that of 3 March, which were critical of the conduct of the war. To this Massingham responded in *The Times* of 6 March, that no deprecation of the Army was intended. On 10 March, *The Times* reported that the *Cologne Gazette* under the heading 'The Man Who Acts Without Thinking' made play with a *Nation* article for 16 February and from it drew the conclusion 'that until Lloyd George has either been set aside or made harmless as a minister no real disposition for peace will arise in England'.

Now it happened that General Smuts, the South African Minister of Defence, arrived in England on 12 March. Always interested in Radical views on foreign policy and the war, his attention was at once directed to recent articles in the *Nation*. On 24 March he met with the Prime Ministers and other representatives of the dominions in a session

---

[1] Fisher to Gardiner, 1 Dec. 1916 and Fisher to Northcliffe, 17 Jan. 1917, Marder (ed.), *Fear God and Dread Nought*, III, 398–9, 420; Fisher to McKenna, 1 Dec. 1916, McKenna Papers; Massingham to Fisher; 17 Jan. [1917], Fisher Papers; Massingham to G. Murray, 22 Jan. [1917], G. Murray Papers.

of the newly formed Imperial War Cabinet. On Smuts' initiative the possibility and advisability of an early peace, even if that meant some modification of demands, was discussed at length; the general reaction was negative – the war should be pursued with all strength. Thus, the official record. But Sir Maurice Hankey, secretary of the War Cabinet, tells us more. Smuts, he records,

made a long, courageous, and interesting speech on the lines adopted by Massingham in the National Review [sic:], advocating the idea that it is impossible to crush Germany and that we adopt a more modest programme and conform our policy and strategy thereto. A very logical and interesting case, I thought, but the others downed him, and were all for jingoism.[1]

The War Cabinet, itself, when it reviewed on 16 April the case against the *Nation*, fully supported the War Department's action of 29 March, banning overseas distribution. Derby, the War Secretary, reported that the action had been taken with the concurrence of the Foreign Office and Home Office, had been contemplated for some months, and was taken only after it was clear that the *Nation* was harming Britain's cause. Lloyd George said that the *Nation*'s articles would be taken as speaking for Liberals and would encourage the enemy. He added that the matter was of such importance that he was prepared to defend the action, himself, in the Commons.[2]

He did so, the very next day, in one of his rare appearances as wartime Prime Minister. Massingham was also there, in the Press Gallery, and remarked later to Nevinson that Lloyd George was 'venomous' and Churchill 'excellent'. The Prime Minister declared that the action against the *Nation* was not taken because of attacks on the Government but had been done as an 'ordinary course of action' following previous precedents. He himself, he said, had not been a party to the action, but he supported it fully. He declared that the *Nation* article of 3 March which 'found our soldiers wanting' was represented as British Liberalism but in fact discouraged the British forces and encouraged the enemy. After speaking he left the chamber at once and so did not hear

---

[1] Hancock and Van der Poel (eds.), *Selections from the Smuts Papers*, III, 464; Imperial War Cabinet, 24 Mar. 1917, CAB 23/40, P.R.O.; Stephen Roskill, (ed.), *Hankey, Man of Secrets*, I (London, 1970), 372. Hankey dates his entry 23 March but this is obviously in error.

[2] War Cabinet, Minute 119 (24), 16 April 1917, P.R.O.

the reply from Churchill who declared it a great fuss about nothing, that the article of 3 March was 'absolutely immaterial and innocent' and not as alarmist as words spoken by Government officials including the Prime Minister. Only the Front Bench supported the Government's action. Liberal backbenchers seized their opportunity. Herbert Samuel was astounded at the weak case of the Prime Minister and Sir Henry Dalziel thought 'we ought to do justice even to Mr. Massingham'. In May there was a repeat of this performance with only official spokesmen for the Government supporting the War Department. In the Lords, Derby said that the *Nation* had violated principles which publications circulating abroad should respect, but the Marquess of Crewe called the War Department action a 'blunder' and Lord Courtney called out 'Hear, Hear!'[1]

Other repercussions were no less interesting. On 17 April as he left the Commons after speaking, Lloyd George encountered David Davies and asked: 'Well, what did you think of it?' Davies replied: 'A very fine speech on a very bad case.' Lloyd George: 'Oh – go to Hell.' A couple of weeks later, the Prime Minister complained of widespread criticism of his Guildhall speech in which he approved Imperial preference in trade. Of course, he exclaimed, 'nobody cared what the "Daily News" or the "Nation" said because they made it their business to find fault'.[2]

The *Nation* (14 and 21 April) reported developments at length, printing Churchill's speech in full and excerpting some of the thirty-three letters from M.P.s protesting against the ban. McKenna referred to the action as 'a wrong to the individual and to the state' and Runciman declared: 'The treatment of a journal that is, in my opinion, so admirably conducted in the national and public interest, is an outrage.' Shaw tells us that since the *Nation* 'had stood by me so courageously, I was moved to strike a blow for my friend Massingham' and he did so in a letter hilarious, devastating and persuasive. From other writers – including Wells, Bennett, Chesterton, Galsworthy – and journalists – including J. A. Spender and Robertson Nicoll – some thirty-nine in all, came written protests. Bennett wrote to J. C. Squire

---

[1] Hansard: *Commons*, 17 April, 1 May, 9 May 1917; *Lords*, 24 April 1917.
[2] Thomas Jones, *Whitehall Diary*, ed. Keith Middlemas, I (London, 1969), 31; C. P. Scott Papers, B.M., Add. MS. 50904, Diary, Wed. [2 May 1917].

that the action would not have been taken if the War Cabinet 'hadn't previously had their knife into "the Nation" '.[1]

The *Liberal Magazine* for May 1917 reported that the ban received little support in the press generally. Even the *English Review* (May 1917) defended Massingham with whom 'we do not often agree'. And *The Times* (18 April) while denying that the *Nation* represented 'the authentic voice of Liberalism or of any serious party here', called the action 'ill-advised and certain of criticism'. Colonel House in America heard the news from Buckler to whom Runciman had written indignantly and at length. House was much concerned and consulted Northcliffe who promised to do what he could to lift the ban. House's efforts came to Massingham's attention.[2] He himself had opportunities to present his own case. He dined (26 April) with Churchill who expressed his delight with Nevinson's humorous sketch on the Lloyd George breakfasts ('Instances Tyrannus', *Nation*, 21 April). And as Sassoon records a conversation, Massingham said: 'The soldiers are not allowed to express their point of view. In war-time the word patriotism means suppression of truth.' At luncheon and dinner engagements he found himself with Maynard Keynes, G. Lowes Dickinson, T. P. O'Connor, A. G. Gardiner, J. A. Spender and Arnold Bennett.[3]

On 19 October the War Cabinet concurred in Derby's proposal that 'in view of the improved tone and conduct of the "Nation" the embargo on its export might now be removed'.[4] In making the public announcement, the *Nation* said (27 October), 'We are duly grateful to Mr. George for conceding to THE NATION an equal right of entry into America with "John Bull".' The *Nation*'s correspondence columns were thereupon crowded with letters from soldiers, overseas readers and such as McKenna, Samuel, Runciman, Ponsonby, Courtney, Bennett, Galsworthy and J. A. Spender. Shaw gave a dinner for Massingham at Adelphi Terrace (Lady Scott was also there and she tells us about it). Massingham held forth with his account of the ban

[1] Shaw, *What I Really Wrote About the War*, 251–3; Bennett to Squire, 11 April 1917, Berg.
[2] Buckler to House, 13 April 1917, Buckler Papers; House to Buckler, 26 July 1917, House Papers.
[3] N.D., 26 Apr. 1917; Harrod, *Keynes*, 217; Bennett, *Journal*, II, 218–19, 228–9; Siegfried Sassoon, *Memoirs of an Infantry Officer* (New York, 1930), 263–5.
[4] War Cabinet minute 253 (3), 19 Oct. 1917, P.R.O.

with reference to Lloyd George as 'a counter jumper' and to Asquith as 'a drunken pantaloon'. During 1917 the net circulation of the *Nation* rose from about 8,300 to about 11,000.[1]

'Since December last the *Nation* has preached peace by negotiation.' Massingham is apt enough when he says this statement, attributed to the Chief Military Censor in May 1917, summarised the Government's charge against his paper.[2] The fight against the war to the finish, against the 'Never-Endians' (the *Nation*'s phrase), this now remained Massingham's great cause for the remainder of the war. In 1917 the man who only a year before had regarded the war itself as a crusade was reunited with the Radicals and indeed was in the van of those who sought the war's end.

Buckler wrote to House in April 1917 of the bitterness of other journals against the *Nation* 'for its insidious peace-mongering'. He discussed 'the *Nation*'s standpoint' with Brailsford and Noel Buxton and cited (*Nation*, 28 April) the fear that 'the dog-fight spirit' might infect the United States if she were won over to the Lloyd George 'knock out blow' policy. With the ban on the *Nation*'s foreign circulation Buckler saw to it that copies reached House. In June, on the basis of an extended conversation, Buckler reported that the *Nation* editor was troubled that the Allies, instead of cooperating in the task of converting Germany to democracy and Liberalism, were occupied with their own territorial designs and commercial advantages and were thus strengthening the militarists in Germany and alienating the new Russia. Would America 'stop the formidable backstroke of war on liberty?' It was disturbing that Wilson was emphasising the role of Germany in the war, rather than focusing on war aims and the end of hostilities.[3] Hobson's letter in the *Nation* (23 June) on 'An American Victory in 1920' is representative of the *Nation*'s lament in these months. Massingham puts it more subtly for American readers of the *Yale Review*, July 1917:

---

1 Weintraub, *Journey to Heartbreak*, 275. Minutes, Rowntree Trust, 29 June 1917 and 19 Feb. 1918, Rowntree Papers.
2 *Nation*, 13 Oct. 1917. British policy, throughout the war, was directed at total victory and never seriously considered peace by negotiation. V. M. Rothwell, *British War Aims and Peace Diplomacy 1914–1918* (London, 1972).
3 Buckler to House, 20, 27 April, 21, 29 June 1917, Buckler Papers.

Unless the American Liberal idea of the peace ultimately prevails with us and replaces the more official idea of a territorial peace, sustained by armaments, British progress to democracy must suffer arrest... The entry of America into the war is the best hope that offers the return to power of Liberal democracy in Europe.

Inseparable from Massingham's plea for an early conclusion to the war was his demand for an end to the Lloyd George Government. Both concerns were expressed in an exchange of letters with Lord Hugh Cecil whose espousal of a League of Nations stirred Massingham. But Cecil thought that Lloyd George, in the conduct of the war, should be supported and that the conflict would end only when Germany was persuaded of her failure to dominate the world.[1] To General Smuts Massingham probably turned with more confidence – Smuts was not only a rising influence in the councils of state but had retained a sympathetic ear for Radicals. To him Massingham addressed an emotional appeal:

Pray do not leave the centre, on which all depends... The Government cannot last. It is utterly disorganized, if indeed that can be organized which was never organized at all. Then, when the need for a different spirit and method becomes apparent, I am convinced the time will come when all that you have done will be little compared with what you may do for us.[2]

If there was a reply it was not preserved.

In the summer and early autumn of 1917 Massingham found room for optimism in the change to Michaelis as Chancellor of the Reich and the resolution of the Reichstag (19 July) calling for a peace of reconciliation and disclaiming territorial ambitions, in the Papal Peace Note (1 August) and in the speeches of Count Czernin, Austro-Hungarian Foreign Minister, calling for a new world order based on arbitration and disarmament. Massingham told Nevinson in July he believed peace was possible by the autumn, and he wrote to Bryce in August that 'one suggestion after another in the direction of peace, might, I think, be made and tried until we get the right one'.[3]

Now and again Massingham perforce turned his mind from peace-making to the conduct of the war. Throughout 1917 he was one of a varied group of politicians and journalists – including George Lam-

[1] Cecil to Massingham, 21 May [1917], M.P.
[2] Massingham to Smuts, 19 May [1917], Smuts Papers, Capetown.
[3] N.D., 17 July 1917; Massingham to Bryce, 9 Aug. [1917], Bryce Papers.

bert, Rosebery, Churchill, McKenna, Scott, Donald – still working for Lord Fisher's return to some important post. Fisher seemed to bank considerably on Massingham's efforts. We find Garvin writing to Fisher on 26 January: 'It does not help you that Massingham was a persistent little-navy man and pro-German before the war, and is a pacifist now.' In February, after unflattering remarks by Admiral of the Fleet Hedworth Meux concerning Fisher's services as First Sea Lord, 'Wayfarer' took pleasure in pointing out (*Nation*, 3 March 1917) that the presence of one kind of mentor (Meux) and the absence of the other (Fisher) might make the difference between failure and success. And of Meux Massingham wrote Fisher: 'What a worm! I've trodden on him in "The Nation" this week.' Then later in the year, Fisher, always anticipating a return to office, wrote Massingham in delight over 'that delectable little bit of October 27 by that damnable "Wayfarer" '. Massingham had referred to Fisher as a 'Sailor of genius ... genius not being as plentiful as blackberries, his like has not as yet been discovered'.[1]

In November 1917 the military outlook changed drastically with the disaster to the Italian army at Caporetto, and with the Bolshevik Revolution in Russia and her virtual elimination from the war. Massingham was quick to see the widening of the gap between those who sought an early peace through negotiation and those determined to fight to the finish. This was soon appreciated by Colonel House, on a mission to London in November in search of support for Wilson's decision to press for an allied declaration of war aims and peace terms. House found only Radical opinion sympathetic; Massingham was more helpful than C. P. Scott and more useful than Robert Donald (editor of the *Daily Chronicle*) or even General Smuts.[2] That Massingham was quite aware of the direction of American policy is evident in his reaction to the Lansdowne 'Peace Letter' to the *Daily Telegraph* on 29 November, arguing for a negotiated peace. Its significance, declared the *Nation*, was in the aid it provided President Wilson against Lloyd George. 'No utterance of British, or even of European, statesmanship since the war began compares in importance.' Two weeks earlier

---

[1] Marder (ed.), *Fear God and Dread Nought*, III, 410; Massingham to Fisher, n.d., Fisher Papers; Fisher's letters, continuing into January 1918, are in M.P.

[2] Journal of Colonel House, 12 and 13 Nov. 1917, House Papers.

Massingham had set forth in the *Nation* an alternative Cabinet, headed by Lansdowne. Now, to publicise the Lansdowne Letter, the *Nation* solicited, by telegram, response from Members of Parliament and printed the answers of some fifty, both pro and con.[1]

At the same time the *Nation*'s attacks on Lloyd George rose to a new crescendo. In September there was ridicule of the Prime Minister's dependence on the Tories and in October nasty references to the 'Georgian bureaucracy'. On 17 November came Massingham's 'The Impossibility of Mr. George', a brilliant and slashing attack on the Prime Minister's renunciation of military policy for which he shared responsibility and on his proposal for a unified Allied War Council. The growing independence of the Opposition Front Bench was remarked. 'Mr. George commands a raging press; he commands little else.' On reading this issue of the *Nation* Lloyd George remarked to Lord Riddell that Massingham was 'just like a shrieking shrew'. For his part, Massingham would have enjoyed Lloyd George's admission by C. P. Scott that he was caught between Tories who suspected him and Liberals who opposed him. If Massingham heard of renewed complaints by B. Seebohm Rowntree he was unmoved.[2]

But it was a time of shifting policies in the warring nations, and Massingham's moods fluctuated accordingly. So the *Nation* greeted with approval Lloyd George's address, on 5 January 1918, to the man-power conference of the T.U.C., in which he emphasised international cooperation and the sanctity of treaties.[3] Radical satisfaction reached new heights in its enthusiasm for Wilson's 'Fourteen Points'. But Massingham despaired when the Supreme War Council brushed aside peace overtures from Germany and Austria. In turn he was 'almost incoherent with enthusiasm' over Wilson's address to Congress, on 11 February, an indirect rebuke to the War Council.[4]

Massingham was disgusted with Shaw who had written a piece for the *Daily Chronicle*, on 12 January 1918, in which he said that peace aims could not be imposed without victory and Massingham wrote to his friend, 'I hope you will pause once or twice before you join the

[1] *Nation*, 1 and 8 Dec. 1917.
[2] *Lord Riddell's War Diary*, p. 292; Wilson (ed.), *Political Diaries of C. P. Scott*, 325; Minutes, Rowntree Trust, 19 Oct. 1917 and 19 Feb. 1918, Rowntree Papers.
[3] N.D., 7 Jan. 1918.
[4] Buckler to House, 26 Jan., 11, 13 Feb. 1918, Buckler Papers.

chorus of "No Peace but Victory"... All this is the illusion of war. Surely you are not caught in it.' All this must have been debated when Massingham and Lord Hugh Cecil, dinner guests of Sir Ian Hamilton on 15 February, engaged in 'vehement contest' over peace terms.[1]

One problem – Women's Suffrage – came to an end, with the Representation of the People Act, in February 1918. 'Wayfarer' remarked quietly (19 January), 'I watched the Suffrage Movement and came in contact with most of its leaders.' During the war years there was no extension of the wrangling which had marked the discussions of the *Nation* Group and the columns of the *Nation* before 1914. Nevinson and Brailsford remained in the van of the movement, but now wholeheartedly supported by their editor. A leader (13 February 1915) declared that 'the exclusion of women from political life [was] ... a greater injustice in times of war and of great political disturbance than in a period of peace'. In 1916 Massingham became a vice-president of the National Council for Adult Suffrage and participated in its activities. With Asquith's commitment to the cause (August 1916) he considered the issue closed.[2] But there was a final flare-up late in 1917 when the *Nation* published 'black lists' of 'so-called Liberals' who supported the plural voting clauses and the disenfranchisement of conscientious objectors included in the statute.

From Rupert Brooke to Siegfried Sassoon

As we have seen, in the course of 1916 Massingham shifted his position from support of 'a just war' to a commitment to an early negotiated peace. In war poetry we find a parallel transition, from verse which exalted the national achievement and personal valour to poetry of dissent which dwelt on the bestiality of warfare on the western front and the futility of the war generally.

The patriotic phase, in the opening years of the war, is best illustrated in Rupert Brooke. In 1910, when he was twenty-three, he began sending poems to the *Nation*; of the first batch he wrote to his mother: 'The Editor of the *Nation* was so astounded that he has preserved an awe-struck silence ever since.' But it was Nevinson who held up the poems for verbal change in phrases considered 'too strong'. It proved

---

[1] Massingham to Shaw, 10 Feb. Add. MS. 50543/102, G.B.S.P.; N.D., 15 Feb. 1918.
[2] N.D., *passim*, for Massingham's association with Women's Suffrage during the war.

the beginning, so Brooke's biographer tells us, of the difficulty with the 'ugly' poems. Brooke never really caught on with the *Nation* and no more poems were accepted – a matter of considerable disappointment to him. In January 1914 he wrote to his mother

I can't help thinking the *Nation's* a long way better written, both on its literary and political side than *The New Statesman*. I disagree with Massingham on a lot of things, but I think he is very admirably and bravely independent – without being erratic – and consistent with his own views.[1]

Following Brooke's death in the Aegean in 1915 the *Nation* had a part in the myth-making. He became Nevinson's 'dangerously beautiful poet'. Massingham republished (1 May 1915) 'The Goddess in the Wood' with his own comment: 'None of our young poets so caught the imagination of his contemporaries as this brilliant young writer, the darling of his college and University.'

The *Nation's* connection with the poetry of dissent in 1917 and 1918 was much closer. It worked both ways; the *Nation* encouraged poets in uniform who had lost faith in the war to speak out, and they in turn dramatised the cause for which Massingham now stood – a prompt end to the war. In February 1918 a *Nation* article, 'The Joy of Battle', by its title attacked the romantic version of the war and concluded: 'Let poets and writers and artists and all other soldiers of our time be allowed freely to describe the actual truth of war as they have seen it.' After the war, when it became the fashion to 'slang' the war poets, Massingham wrote in their defence: 'They were the first Englishmen of letters to exhibit the war in the dress in which generations of their countrymen will assuredly see it. They and they alone . . . told unthinking, unhearing England what it meant.'[2]

Massingham's relations with the young poets of dissent were characteristic of him – no fuss, no pleas, no nonsense. Nonetheless, two of the poets in particular, Siegfried Sassoon and Osbert Sitwell, liked in later years to recall the association. 'I contributed to the *Nation* and met H. W. M. fairly often at the Reform Club and liked him very much', wrote Sassoon in 1964. And Sitwell in 1965: 'I liked Massing-

---

[1] Christopher Hassall, *Rupert Brooke* (London, 1964), 221; Geoffrey Keynes (ed.), *Letters of Rupert Brooke* (London, 1968), 233, 235, 506, 560.
[2] *Nation*, 8 November 1919. The unsigned article in February 1918 is excerpted in D. S. R. Welland, *Wilfred Owen: A Critical Study* (London, 1969), 28.

ham very much and am grateful for all the help he gave me. . . Massingham was the first person to publish me regularly.'[1]

Sassoon's mind about the war, like Massingham's, changed radically by mid-1917. Only the year before he had remarked to Robert Graves that the war should not be written about realistically. In the *Nation* for 3 March 1917 they both had poems (Graves' 'The Last Post' (June 1916) and Sassoon's 'Died of Wounds') and Sassoon wrote to Graves: 'how jolly . . . to appear [together] as a military duet singing to a pacifist organ'.[2] But soon Sassoon, who had received the Military Cross for heroism in rescuing wounded under fire, made his new position clear. In 'A Soldier's Declaration' in the *Bradford Pioneer* for 27 July 1917 he wrote: 'This war, upon which I entered as a war of defence and liberation, has now become a war of aggression and conquest.' It might well have been a statement from the *Nation* and was in part prompted by his reading of the *Nation*, as recorded in *Memoirs of An Infantry Officer*. In the spring of 1917, in England convalescing from injuries, while riding on a London bus he read some editorial paragraphs of the 'Unconservative Weekly', as he calls it. He wrote to the editor (Markington, as he is referred to), lunched with him – 'a sallow spectacled man with earnest uncompromising eyes and a stretched sort of mouth which looked as if it had ceased to find human follies funny'. The next week, at a conference at the *Nation* office, Sassoon declared he must make a statement 'about how we ought to publish our War Aims, and all that, and the troops not knowing what they're fighting about'. Massingham said it would not be wise for him to publish such a statement – censorship officials were watching him – and the upshot was a letter to Bertrand Russell (Sassoon calls him Thornton Tyrrell), interviews with Russell and the article in the Bradford paper. During the remainder of the war his poems appeared frequently in the *Nation*.[3] His war verse published as *Counter Attack and Other Poems* was reviewed by John Middleton Murry in the *Nation*, on 13 July 1918: 'It is the fact, not the poetry, of Mr. Sassoon, that is important', Murry wrote.

Osbert Sitwell, in the army since 1914, met Massingham through

---

1 Sassoon to the author, 12 Dec. 1964; Sitwell to the author, 28 Feb. 1965.
2 Robert Graves, *Goodbye To All That* (New York, 1930), 213, 304.
3 *Memoirs of An Infantry Officer*, pp. 263–76; Geoffrey Keynes, *Bibliography of Siegfried Sassoon* (London, 1962), 27.

Robert Ross who submitted 'Rhapsode', published on 27 October
1917, the first of Sitwell's satires, signed 'Miles', to appear in the
Nation. Massingham and Nevinson soon introduced him to Shaw –
they were the men at home, 'with their calm protest concerning the
war, and the conduct of it', whom he chiefly admired.[1] His *Collected
Satires and Poems* (1931) was dedicated 'To the Memory of H. W.
Massingham'.

Then there was Wilfred Owen who died at the front in the last
week of the war at the age of twenty-five. Then hardly known, only
four of his poems were published in his life-time, three of them in the
Nation. It was through Sassoon or Ross that he came to Massingham's
attention in 1917 and soon he was also acquainted with Wells, Bennett
and Sitwell. When his first poem in the *Nation* – 'Miners' – appeared,
he sent his mother a copy of the issue (26 January 1918) and commented: 'I am proud of one thing and that's the decent amount of room
they give under the impressive title P O E T R Y.'[2] The *Nation* also
published his 'Futility' and 'Hospital Barge at Cérisy'. When the
collected poems were published in 1920 controversy ensued over their
merit, much of it in the *Nation*'s columns.

'Endians and Never-Endians'

As 1918 developed Massingham was caught up in the rapidly-changing
course of events – Bolshevik revelation of the secret treaties, the
treaty of Brest-Litovsk which left Germany a free hand in Eastern
Europe, the great German offensive in the West in March – these all
affected the issues of war and peace as he saw them. The *Nation* Group,
like other Radicals, felt that unified war aims of Britain and the United
States would keep in check the other Allied nations, would circumvent
the secret treaties and support peace proposals which the Central
Powers would be able to accept.[3]

Here and there we catch glimpses of Massingham himself. In time
of stress always a melancholy man, no doubt the contents of a letter
from Robert Dell in Paris, written on 1 January 1918, weighed heavily
on his spirit; Dell dwelt at length on the low morale of the French.

[1] Osbert Sitwell, *Laughter in the Next Room* (Boston, 1948), 122.
[2] Harold Owen and John Bell (eds.), *Wilfred Owen: Collected Letters* (London, 1967),
529.
[3] Martin, *Peace without Victory*, 167–8.

Massingham devoted the 'London Diary' for 26 January to an analysis of the views of G. K. Chesterton on the war, especially his 'hatred' of the enemy and his desire to see that enemy brought to his knees. According to the Diary, Chesterton ignored the new currents in Germany and Austria – Socialism, Liberalism, Anti-Junkerism, Parliamentarism. Massingham was one of the deputation which waited on Lansdowne with an address commending his efforts for peace. Massingham renewed his wrath at Northcliffe upon his appointment in February as Director of Propaganda in Enemy Countries. Their short-lived harmony had come to an end the November before when *The Times* refused publication of the Lansdowne Letter, though in point of fact, Northcliffe had had nothing to do with that decision. The War Cabinet had again directed its attention to the German use of the British press for propaganda purposes, Milner remarking that the suppression of the *Nation* overseas had been good for it. 'This the P. M. doubted', Jones recorded. The *Nation* staff discussed Northcliffe's 'shameful appointment' and both Shaw and Massingham dealt with it, no doubt as fully as their feelings dictated.[1]

Then early in March came Lansdowne's second letter to the *Daily Telegraph* proposing a peace conference with the enemy without waiting for an armistice, and this Massingham endorsed. On the other hand the jingo press pressed for Japanese invasion of Siberia to destroy Bolshevism. According to Buckler, the Radicals, including Massingham and Gardiner, regarded President Wilson as the chief safeguard against this danger. Arnold Bennett noted that on several occasions he found Massingham in a mood of unrelieved gloom.[2] But he must have found considerable relief of mind and spirit in theatre-going which was perhaps now his chief relaxation, and in the occasional role of drama critic for the *Nation*.

With the great German offensive against the British Fifth Army in the battle-torn area of the Somme, beginning on 21 March, the whole scene, military and civil, changed. On Sunday, 24 March, Massingham was at Garsington when news came of the German breakthrough and the British retreat: Massingham sitting in a deck chair in the warm sun,

---

[1] Dell letter is in M.P.; N.D., 31 Jan. and 18 Feb. 1918; Jones, *Whitehall Diary*, ed. Middlemas, I, 44; *Nation*, 9 Feb. and 9 Mar. 1918.
[2] N.D., 4 and 11 Mar. 1918; Buckler to House, 11 and 19 Mar. 1918, Buckler Papers; Bennett, *Journal*, II, 255, 257.

'ankle deep in newspapers' and with a grey and black checked shawl around his high shoulders – this was Mary Agnes Hamilton's recollection. Massingham sketched out with 'prophetic urgency' the possible consequences – the loss of channel ports and a direct threat to Britain. The next day on a slow war-time train back to Paddington he continued his analysis. At the end of the week the *Nation* (30 March) carried much the same exposition. Soon after, Lucy Masterman encountered Massingham in a distraught state – a son with the Fifth Army had not been heard from for some weeks... Finally came word of his safety.[1]

The first reaction, politically, to the crisis at the front was Lloyd George's new conscription measure, including compulsory service from the Irish coupled with a promise of Home Rule. Massingham was in the Commons Gallery on 9 March when Lloyd George introduced his bill – all dealt with 'very poorly' says the *Nation* for 13 April, an issue largely devoted to the crisis. The issue begins: 'A reckless hand has thrown a flaming torch into the war and the politics of the war.' Lloyd George must go. The call is for Asquith; 'he is bound to answer'. Soon Massingham consulted with Lord Grey, his great hope for the future. All this was spelled out at greater length in two leaders, 'The Responsibility of the Prime Minister' (20 April) and 'The Responsibility of Mr. Asquith' (27 April). 'Mr. Asquith, Lord Grey, Lord Lansdowne and Mr. Henderson ... should be ready to take office tomorrow.' With the enactment of the new Military Service Bill the Irish Nationalist members withdrew from the Commons and Buckler reported to Colonel House Massingham's view that nothing could allay the Irish save the fall of the Government.[2] The Irish question dominated *Nation* Lunches. 'Wayfarer' wrote on 29 June: 'It is shocking to see British policy in Ireland slide back (under a *soi-disant* Liberal) to mere Balfourism. But it is still more shocking to see the coolness with which the Liberal Party takes it all.'

Massingham called repeatedly for a change of Government; on one occasion (18 February) the *Nation* Lunch discussed alternatives to Lloyd George – whether 'any party could or would sweep up Ll. G.'s mess if we drive him out'. However, though Massingham was again

---

[1] Hamilton, *Remembering My Good Friends*, 77–8; Masterman, *C. F. G. Masterman*, 301–2.

[2] N.D., 9 Apr. 1918; Massingham to G. Murray, 20 Apr. [1918], Murray papers; Buckler to House, 25 Apr. 1918, Buckler Papers.

respectful of Asquith's talents – he met him on occasion socially and persuaded him to write (July 1918) an Introduction to *The Idea of Public Right* (London, 1918) incorporating prize essays in a *Nation* essay competition – he had little confidence in a Liberal Party reunion. Respect for Labour, and even confidence in its future, were on the rise, and a combination of Liberalism and Labour might do the trick, he wrote. In October 1917 the *Nation* had proclaimed Labour as 'The Coming Democratic Party', the one quarter from which 'a really fresh and hopeful development can come'. In February 1918, in reporting differences in England on the issues of war and peace Buckler noted that Massingham and others believed that Labour was 'the *deus ex machina* which is alone able to cut this knot'. But at the same time Massingham was writing Villard in the United States: 'The Government does not fall because there is as yet no agreed-on alternative.'[1] This remained his view for the duration of the war.

As the 'decisive battles' (a frequent *Nation* phrase) continue and complicate the question of 'the peace', it is not strange that on occasion Massingham seems to us to have lost his sense of proportion. The Peace of Brest-Litovsk and the offensives in the west had strengthened the bargaining position of Germany but Massingham grasped at statements by her leaders, however ill-supported, which seemed to bring nearer the possibility of peace. When Wilson's statement of 4 July 1918 setting forth general conditions of peace was endorsed by Lloyd George in an address to American troops in France, Massingham (*Nation*, 13 July) was over sensitive in suggesting that *The Times* deliberately played down the Lloyd George speech. This moved the editor of *The Times*, Geoffrey Dawson, equally sensitive, to write Massingham a personal letter in protest against his 'misrepresentation'. In point of fact that very statement of Wilson, in calling for military victory and sanctioning allied intervention in Siberia, greatly discouraged the Radicals. It was just then, on 21 July, that Massingham in an impulsive moment wrote to Arnold Rowntree resigning the editorship of the *Nation*. 'For the first time since the war began I have lost hope of peace. I cannot support the war; it seems that every effort to end it is doomed to fail.' However, attached to the letter is a memorandum that

---

[1] *Nation*, 13 and 20 Oct. 1917; Buckler to House, 11 Feb. 1918, Buckler Papers; Massingham to Villard, 15 Feb. 1918, Villard Papers, Houghton.

Rowntree 'talked H.W.M. around'.[1] One can only conjecture at Massingham's private thoughts, the October following, with the sale of the *Daily Chronicle* to Lloyd George interests and the abrupt dismissal of Robert Donald, its editor since 1902. Massingham's public comment (*Nation*, 12 October) reflected his preoccupation: men will now 'wonder what part of the newspaper world can be made safe from Mr. George's peculiar brand of democracy'.

Since 1914 the *Nation*, in its self-appointed role as a forum for Radical views, had lent its columns generously to movements dedicated to the prevention of future wars. The Rowntrees took the lead in associating with the *Nation* the monthly journal, *War and Peace*, started in 1913 by Norman Angell. From May 1917 until early 1918 it was published as a monthly supplement to the *Nation*, and as such increased its circulation. *War and Peace* drew heavily on the writings of members of the *Nation* Group, notably Brailsford, Hobson and G. Lowes Dickinson, who with others contributed to a symposium, 'Why Not a League Now?' in August and September 1918. The *Nation* itself diverged from many of the opinions expressed in *War and Peace* and from May to September 1918 ran its own series of articles (many written by the editor) on the idea of a league of nations. Besides *War and Peace*, the *Nation* was the only organ to advocate *trusteeship* for native populations in undeveloped lands. In its concept of the 'League of Nations' the *Nation* was well in advance of most Liberal thought – in its repudiation of the League as a mere continuance of the war alliance, in its insistence that Germany be a member, with its emphasis on free trade and an equitable sharing of economic advantage, and above all in its reiteration of the supreme importance of the League as the future safeguard of civilisation.[2]

After the entrance of the United States into the war the best hope of the Radicals for the attainment of their goals rested on President Wilson. Laurence W. Martin in *Peace without Victory* has told the story in detail, using the *Nation* as a guide to Radical opinion. We need not retread the ground but it is important to note that while Massingham had often despaired of the outcome, as the tide of military

[1] Dawson to Massingham, 12 July 1918, M.P.: Massingham to Arnold Rowntree, 21 July 1918, Rowntree Papers.
[2] Henry R. Winkler, *The League of Nations Movement in Great Britain, 1914–1919* (New Brunswick, 1952), 145–7, 150–1.

fortune changed during the summer of 1918 and the war came to an abrupt end in November he was able increasingly to identify Wilson with the Radical crusade. Such doubts as there may have been were put to rest by Wilson himself in his address in New York City on 27 September. The peace, he said, must be one of 'impartial justice in every item of the settlement' and guaranteed by an 'indispensable instrumentality [which] is a League of Nations formed under covenants which will be efficacious'. It was one of his 'greatest orations', said Massingham; 'in the vision of the President' there was hope for the future. This address and the Fourteen Points were regarded as the basis of the armistice agreements, and this further heartened him. 'Peace for Ever' is the first leader of the *Nation*, 16 November. But Massingham was well aware that in peace-making a new struggle lay ahead. Liberalism and reaction were still at grips. But, he asked: 'What is there in the world's history to compare with Mr. Wilson's power?' And so with a degree of optimism he posed the final question: 'What measure of moral force, and therefore of inherent stability, can we attach to the Treaty of Peace?'[1]

[1] Chas. Seymour, *The Intimate Papers of Colonel House*, IV (Boston, 1928), 69–72; *Nation*, 5 Oct. and 9 Nov. 1918.

CHAPTER 10

'Lloyd George for ever and ever?'
(1918–1922)

If the transition from war to peace produced no abrupt change in the major issues confronting the *Nation* – these issues remaining the future of the Lloyd George Coalition and the nature of the peace – without question it affected Massingham's morale, modified his political stance, and determined his role as a journalist for the remainder of his life.

In politics this was soon apparent in the General Election of 14 December 1918. To be sure, an appeal to the country had been anticipated since mid-summer, regardless of the circumstances of the war, and the *Nation*'s first reaction (and that of Massingham) was to regard the election as a challenge which both Liberalism and Labour were prepared to meet. For the Government would be forced to declare itself – on the peace, on military service in peace-time, on Imperialism and Protection, and on measures of reconstruction. It was easy to admonish readers that circumstances required 'some force fit to hold men together, renew and reestablish the industrial order, and save society from despair and from the impatience of revolutionary thought'.[1]

It was another matter to sort out the complexities of political ties and to prognosticate the future. 'What has become of Liberalism?', a Massingham leader (3 August) inquired. The answer was not reassuring: it was now a Party divided, and the effective leadership was associated with a Government in full reaction. Many nurtured in its tradition 'waver in their allegiance or begin to look to some new formation of constructive Radicalism or Democracy in association with Labor'. The N.L.F., in conference in September, missed its opportunity – 'its policy was one of very *piano* criticism' – and took no steps toward an electoral agreement with Labour. On the other hand, Labour, with Radical attachments, had become for Massingham a life-line, and as the war

[1] *Nation*, 27 July and 10 Aug. 1918.

came to an end he played up Labour's decision to withdraw from the Coalition after the dissolution of Parliament.[1]

But he was thrown off balance by Lloyd George's speech to Coalition Liberals on 12 November – references to 'the reign of peace', a settlement 'fundamentally just', the League of Nations 'a reality' – which persuaded Massingham, for the moment, that Lloyd George spoke again as a Radical Liberal. If his 'fair promises' are executed 'he will have done something for the world and incidentally for his own fame'. He had stolen Labour's thunder and Toryism was 'plainly doomed. By degrees it will disappear from the Cabinet until the earlier Liberal predominance is more or less restored'. But, as Trevor Wilson has pointed out, Massingham badly misjudged the situation. Lloyd George's target was neither Labour nor Toryism but the Liberals who refused him their support, as became self-evident with knowledge of the 'coupon' by which Asquithian Liberals were refused endorsement.[2]

Accordingly, the *Nation* for 23 November was a dramatic issue. It begins: 'The Prime Minister has dealt his knock-out blow to the Liberal Party', and the initial leader, certainly by Massingham, concerns 'A Sinister Election': 'It is not with Mr. George's programme that the country has to deal. It is with Mr. George. He has proposed himself as master of Britain. He would make an unspeakably bad one.' 'Wayfarer' called the election a fraud, 'a warning to the thinkers and workers to escape from this confusion to unite, to consolidate, to MAKE A PARTY OF THE FUTURE, and devote to its service every gift of constructive imagination they possess. That is why I, for one, shall VOTE LABOR.' For a time, the *Nation* became a political pamphlet for Labour. In a week Lloyd George had destroyed the great Liberal Party, was its cry, and readers were exhorted to turn to Labour; in time it would sweep Lloyd George from power. The declaration in the Labour Election manifesto, 'to build a new world and build it by constitutional means' would 'furnish the debates and decisions of the next ten years'. With the poll, the Lloyd George victory, unexpected only in its magnitude, was termed by the *Nation* a victory for 'a union of interests, combined by a trick and elected on a minority vote'.[3] But such remarks sound like a man with his back to the wall.

---

[1] *Nation*, August–October 1918 and 16 Nov. 1918.
[2] Wilson, *Downfall of the Liberal Party*, 152.   [3] *Nation*, November and December 1918.

Similarly Massingham's confidence in the peace settlement and his aspirations for the post-war world suffered cruel disappointment, his disillusion the more complete because it was President Wilson himself, on whom had rested his hopes for an 'equitable settlement' implemented by a 'peoples' League of Nations', who failed him. Just as in party politics reality came on him suddenly. To be sure his endemic pessimism led him to dwell after the Election on manifestations of national apathy. So, 'Wayfarer' (21 December): 'not half a dozen people who will be responsible for the peace have the sense to see that a moderate, reasonable settlement, with the League of Nations as its pivot, is the only way out'. But Massingham was able to focus on the American president; his arrival in Britain in December, not the General Election, was the great event. Wilson was 'the great force of rescue and reconciliation . . . and there is no other'. And the League of Nations would be the means. The Paris Peace Conference, under way in January, at first provided little news and Massingham used the interval to develop his concept of the League – not an organisation of representatives of Government which would merely renew 'the old power politics', but a democratic league with deliberative power in an international Parliament to which the executive agencies would be responsible, and consisting of delegates selected by each national parliament on the basis of proportional representation.[1]

This parliamentary assembly now became Massingham's overriding concern. On 29 January he wrote to A. G. Gardiner proposing an address to President Wilson in support of such a League assembly, to be published in the English, French and Italian press. Perhaps 10,000 signatures could be secured, including 100 M.P.s. In England Massingham suggested the *Nation*, *Daily News* and *Manchester Guardian*; in France and Italy, Jean Longuet, the French Socialist, would circulate the petition. How hopeful Massingham was, we cannot say; in his gloomy way, in conversation with Sassoon, he predicted blunders in Paris.[2] Massingham the journalistic adventurer decided not to wait for the slow process of address and petition but to make a direct appeal to President Wilson. He addressed a note to Colonel House in Paris,

---

[1] *Nation*, 14 and 28 Dec. 1918; 11 Jan. 1919.
[2] Massingham to Gardiner, 29 Jan. [1919], Gardiner Papers; Siegfried Sassoon, *Siegfried's Journey* (London, 1945), 131.

pointing out that the *Nation* had been 'the first British journal to commend and press the President's policy' and inquiring about the possibilities of an interview. The upshot was that Massingham met with the President on Monday evening, 10 February, at rue de Monceau. Massingham arrived on the scene in the last days of the discussion of the preliminary draft of the Covenant of the League. What response he had from the President we do not know. But the next day Massingham reported his anxiety to House:

> I fear that if the constitution of the League of Nations does not contain any representative element, the force of popular interest and enthusiasm, which has been the President's great support in all countries, will have a shock, and be seriously diminished in volume and confidence.

On the 12th he conferred with House and then with General Smuts whom he considered sympathetic and at House's suggestion submitted a Memorandum on a Parliament for the League. 'It is clear', Massingham wrote House 'that the important matter is to get the *principle* of representation embodied in the draft, and that if this is done it can safely be left to the Council to settle the constitution of the assembly . . . I gather that this is General Smuts' view.' And his letter concludes: 'We are at the cross-roads. Pray God the president's way is taken.'[1]

But nothing came of it – there is no evidence that Massingham made any serious impression. Even the tone of his own report of proceedings is uncorroborated. He wrote to Smuts that both the President and House were sympathetic, that House 'jumped' at the notion of a specific proposal and 'was anxious and much alive to the importance of the draft-plan not going out without a proposal . . . on representative lines'. But House himself jotted down in his journal (12 February): 'I had a great many callers today, but none of them particularly interesting. Massingham of *The Nation* is disturbed over the way the League is arranging for representation. He believes there should be a representation of the minority.' He noted that the President had given this matter consideration 'but we have been able to draw up nothing which seems to us practical'. Smuts, in various correspondence, merely refers to snags in preparation of the draft of the Covenant

---

[1] Massingham to House, 30 Jan. 1919 (Copy) and Tuesday [11 Feb. 1919] (Copy); 12 Feb. [1919] (Copy); telegram, House to Massingham, 8 Feb. 1919. House Papers. A copy of the Memorandum, n.d., is in House Papers.

which was completed 13 February by the Commission on the League. On that day Wilson addressed a brief note to Massingham thanking him for the volume of essays, *The Idea of Public Right*, comprising the winning essays in the *Nation* contest conducted in 1917 on the subject of equal opportunity for all states, weak and strong. Wilson did not mention representation in the League, merely remarking: 'It was a great pleasure to meet you and to be able to feel that I know you.'[1]

On his return to London, Massingham was greeted by a large *Nation* Lunch, Nevinson recording (24 February): 'HWM back again with a much reduced opinion of President Wilson.' In July 1920 Colonel House was in London on a visit. To a small group at the Reform Club, House declared that the American President was persuaded that the Versailles Treaty did in truth embody his 'points' and his 'principles'. Massingham wondered how that could be when the discrepancies were so glaring. C. P. Scott, noting the occasion in his diary, added that House gave no satisfactory answer, possibly out of loyalty to Wilson. In his comment in the *Christian Science Monitor*, 7 February 1924, after Wilson's death, Massingham said that the idea of 'giving representative parliamentary colouring to the Council of the League' fell through for lack of Wilson's support.

After his return from Paris, Massingham's remarks on the League invariably reflected disillusionment. Two signed leaders on 'The Conference at the Cross Roads' (22 February and 1 March) presented grave doubts about the published draft of the League Covenant which provided for no representation of peoples and no satisfactory arrangement for including Germany, and apparently envisaged disarmament for Germany only. In contrast he hailed the Berne International Socialist Conference, held in February, as representing free commercial intercourse, protection of national minorities and parliamentary democracy in the League. As for British policy, the Army Estimates (3 March) provided for 'a peace of armed force' and Churchill's presentation was 'the most jingo speech in support of the most indefensible Estimates ever presented to Parliament' (*Nation*, 8 March).

[1] Massingham to Smuts, n.d., Smuts Papers, Cape Town; Journal of Col. House, 12 Feb. 1919, House Papers; President Wilson to Massingham, 13 Feb. 1919, Wilson Papers, VIII-A, Library of Congress (Copy).

At just this juncture circumstance brought harmony with a long-time antagonist in the press – J. L. Garvin of the *Observer*. A *Nation* review of Garvin's *Economic Foundations of Peace*, a book which shared much of Massingham's outlook, led to correspondence, Massingham welcoming Garvin to the ranks of those who would continue to work for 'an equitable settlement'. Certain of the treaty-makers still had his confidence. General Smuts, Massingham was sure, must have signed the treaty with 'grave personal doubt'; his farewell address to Britain was 'a great political testament'. Should he ever return to England – and he may be wanted back – 'London may crown his career'.[1] There was also Lord Robert Cecil, one of the creators of the League.

From late April to late June, Massingham was on a visit to America, an experience which did nothing to revive his confidence in American leadership but which did indulge his pleasure in travel and made possible association with friends, old and new. He was accompanied by Clement Shorter; they spent an evening in Cambridge, Massachusetts, with Amy Lowell (this led to publication of some of her poems in the *Nation*) and with Padraic Colum in New York.[2] There they were guided about by Oswald Garrison Villard, editor of the American *Nation* and were entertained by John Quinn, editor and collector; Quinn and Massingham found common satisfaction in denouncing Lloyd George. Harold Laski, in Cambridge, sent Massingham on to Justice Holmes in Washington: Massingham, Laski wrote, 'represents for me all that is best and most generous in English life... He is the greatest of English editors, fearless, honest, uncompromising, with fine perception and flawless taste.'[3] In Philadelphia, in company with Christopher Morley, he visited the home and grave of a favourite poet, Walt Whitman. Somehow he found time to write a piece for the New York *Nation* (24 May 1919) lamenting the absence of Liberalism in the peace treaty.

Upon his return to England he wrote at length in the *Nation* of his

---

[1] Massingham to Garvin, 18 April 1919 and April 18 [1919], Garvin Papers. On Smuts, see 'Wayfarer', *Nation*, 26 July 1919.

[2] Massingham–Amy Lowell correspondence, Houghton; Colum to author, 22 May 1966.

[3] B. L. Reid, *The Man from New York, John Quinn and His Friends* (New York, 1968), 390; Mark DeWolfe Howe (ed.), *Holmes-Laski Letters ... 1916–1935*, I (Cambridge, Mass., 1953), 208–9.

'impressions' in America. He was at his best – perceptive, critical, appreciative. But there is also the other side – the blunt, impulsive Massingham, which produced the unguarded remarks which Nevinson recorded: 'HWM unexpected from USA. Had been unable to endure the heat and Clement Shorter. Says the people knew nothing about Europe & care nothing. Wilson universally hated.' S. K. Ratcliffe noted that 'Massingham's language about Wilson & Co. has got back to the sultriness of his *Chronicle* days'.[1]

10 Adelphi Terrace

In studying Massingham's *Nation* after the war it is instructive to examine the newcomers to his staff and their response to the editor. Leonard Woolf, who wrote for both Clifford Sharp and H. W. Massingham, found a certain 'bleakness' at the *New Statesman* office on Great Queen Street and 'a peculiar grimness' at the weekly lunch – this in contrast to the atmosphere of the *Nation* at Adelphi Terrace which was 'extremely friendly, civilized and distinguished'.[2] There he encountered the veterans (Hammond, Nevinson and Hobson) and new faces as well – most importantly, H. M. Tomlinson, the assistant editor in charge of the literary pages. Tomlinson's manner and talents lent themselves to description by those who knew him best – 'quiet, weary, sad, with his unforgettable face, carved and weather-beaten like the figure heads of the sailing-ships under whose bowsprits he walked and dreamed as a boy on the East India Dock' (J. Middleton Murry); 'his prose has a fine and not too intricate measure, and its colour lights on the ships, the sea, and the roofs and alleys of his Dockland . . . with quaint and sparkling distinctness' (Massingham).[3]

One day in February 1917, at Rollencourt in France, Tomlinson, then a war correspondent, found himself beside 'a pinched figure in a blue-serge suit' who introduced himself: 'Mr. Massingham, the editor of the *Nation*'. Seven months later Massingham wrote to Tomlinson, by that time recalled from France, 'I've pleasure in asking you to take the Assistant Editorship of the *Nation* at a salary of £10 per week.' In

---

[1] 'Some Impressions of America', reprinted in *H.W.M.*, 297–316; N.D., 25 June 1919; Ratcliffe to G. Wallas, 5 July 1919, Wallas Papers, B.L.P.E.S.

[2] Leonard Woolf, *Nation*, 12 May 1956.

[3] J. Middleton Murry, *Between Two Worlds: An Autobiography* (London, 1935), 432; *H.W.M.*, 191.

the issue of 13 October 'The World of Books' section is signed 'H.M.T.' – Tomlinson had replaced 'Penguin' Evans. The following January came another important change; the secretary, Miss Manson, was replaced by Miss Gertrude M. Cross, who became in effect another assistant editor – in Leonard Woolf's tribute, 'one of those highly-geared, super-efficient secretaries who are themselves capable of editing and often, *de facto* but not *de jure*, do edit the paper'. Oswald Garrison Villard was astonished that the *Nation* was edited by Massingham aided only by Tomlinson and Miss Cross; in the United States there would have been 'a large and expensive staff of assistant editors'.[1]

When Tomlinson joined the *Nation* he was assured by one of his friends that he might well stay no longer than six months. But Tomlinson left only with his chief, six years later. His own fame as a writer was in the making, and he had much to do with the association of the *Nation* with promising young writers – Edmund Blunden, John Middleton Murry, Frank Swinnerton, Aldous Huxley, as well as Sassoon and Sitwell, whose poems continued to appear. It was in November 1920 that Sitwell, in Italy, decided to attempt an interview with Gabriele d'Annunzio, then in power in Fiume. By telegraph Sitwell received permission to represent the *Nation*, and accordingly in the issue for 1 January 1921 appeared his account of the interview.[2]

From 1917 on J. Middleton Murry wrote occasional political articles but after 1919 he was also editor of the *Athenaeum* which was merged with the *Nation* in February 1922. While Massingham did not favour the merger he was so beholden to the Rowntrees that he had little choice. Murry continued on the staff. A young poet, Edmund Blunden, 'discovered' by Sassoon, was promptly introduced to Massingham and Tomlinson, at the Reform Club of course. 'I'll do anything for young Blunden', Tomlinson wrote to Murry; Blunden's contributions were frequent and by 1922 he was dropping in weekly at the *Nation* office.[3]

Frank Swinnerton wrote dramatic criticism regularly in the post-war years and Massingham's eldest son, Harold, was a frequent contributor

---

[1] *H.W.M.*, 121; Massingham to Tomlinson, 28 Sept. 1917, U. of Texas; Woolf, *Downhill All the Way*, 92–3; Oswald Garrison Villard, *Fighting Years: Memoirs of a Liberal Editor* (New York, 1939), 375.

[2] Osbert Sitwell, *Noble Essences* (London, 1950), 115.

[3] Massingham to Arnold S. Rowntree, 26 Jan. 1921, Rowntree Papers; Tomlinson to Murry, 1 Oct. 1921, U. of Texas.

on literature and natural history, with occasional responsibility for the 'World of Books' section; his passionate concern for the Plumage Bill (which finally became law in April 1922) received strong support in the *Nation*. One of Harold Massingham's friends was Aldous Huxley. Almost his first published poems appeared in the *Nation* in 1916; after the war he wrote signed and unsigned articles including several instalments of 'World of Books'. Though H. W. Massingham's personal associations with the literary world waned somewhat, we find him turning up from time to time at literary gatherings as a guest of Shaw, of Bennett, of Sitwell. In general, on the *Nation* staff we do not find the gulf between political and literary interests which Woolf noted in his experience with the *New Statesman*. And the sharp divergence in attitudes, so significant before and during the war, is now noticeably absent.

The political staff was changing. When Brailsford assumed the editorship of the *New Leader* in 1922 he was replaced as leader-writer on foreign affairs by Leonard Woolf who earlier, from August to October 1920, had temporarily filled that role when Brailsford went off to Russia. It became Woolf's practice to confer with his editor for a half hour or so each Monday morning and we have no better picture of Massingham, the editor, in action at this time, than that provided by Woolf, all the more instructive in that Woolf and Massingham never became close friends.

He invariably asked me to suggest the subject of my article and notes and left it to me to tell him what I proposed to say. I do not remember him ever not accepting my subject or line of policy. . . But though he said very little when we were talking as professionals on the week's job, there is no doubt that he was a first-class editor in that somehow or other he impressed his personality on those who wrote for him and what they wrote. The consequence was that the paper too had a personality, a flavour, a smell of its own.[1]

Bertrand Russell's association was revived. In the summer of 1920 he contributed five articles on his 'Impressions of Bolshevik Russia', including conversations with Lenin, Trotsky and Maxim Gorki. The following year a visit to the Far East brought three 'Sketches of Modern China'. Young Harold Laski became a disciple of Massingham.

[1] Woolf, *Downhill All the Way*, 93.

When Laski's book *Authority in the Modern State* (1919) was reviewed with praise in the *Nation* on 16 August 1919, he wrote to Bertrand Russell: 'I owe Massingham many debts, but none so great as this.' A brilliant conversationalist, Laski became a valued attendant at the Lunch and contributed occasionally to the *Nation*. The association with G. D. H. Cole – his articles had appeared frequently during the war – ended abruptly in 1919 when the *Nation* returned an article as 'too extreme', writes Mrs Cole. The *New Statesman* promptly accepted the article and published Cole steadily thereafter.[1]

In 1920 Massingham reached his sixtieth year; the younger members of his staff note qualities of mind and spirit not emphasised earlier. Murry later recalled a man in whom passion was always near the surface. Blunden never forgot his editor's constant movement of hand and body as he talked. Evidently the contradictions in his personality became more apparent – Leonard Woolf found him a very sentimental man, 'high-minded' and 'gentle', but also 'bitter and violent'.[2] Behind this was poor health; his problems, which were indigestion, colitis, gout, and nervous exhaustion, increased. His holiday trips away from London – to Monte Carlo, to Paris, to Wiesbaden, to the Hague, to Corsica – became more frequent.

But the tempo at 10 Adelphi Terrace did not moderate. To consult the *Nation* editor in the post-war years came many visitors, some of low estate and some with careers in the making. Some examples: in the summer of 1918 Maxim Litvinov, unofficial Soviet ambassador, stopped by in shabby dress to say farewell before departure to Stockholm and Russia; after the war came small groups of Cypriots, Armenians and Eastern Europeans asking, in poor French, for support; and there was Ramsay MacDonald, out of Parliament until 1922, waiting patiently in the outer office for an appointment.[3] Personal references abound, often in 'Events of the Week' which was supervised and in part written by the editor, sometimes in the first leader which was usually written by Massingham, and especially in 'A London Diary', where Massingham always spoke in the first person. There we often

[1] Russell, *Autobiography*, II, 111–12. Margaret Cole, *The Life of G. D. H. Cole* (London, 1971), 70.
[2] Murry, *Between Two Worlds*, 431–2; author's interview with Blunden, 4 Jan. 1965; Woolf, *Downhill All the Way*, 94.
[3] Conversations with Miss Gertrude Cross.

learn of the sources of his knowledge. Thus there are references to Clemenceau; they became acquainted in the days of the Dreyfus Affair and Massingham when in Paris often called at rue Franklin. After the war he came to know the German Ambassador in London. In Wiesbaden and in London he talked at length with Walther Rathenau the brilliant Minister of Reconstruction and later Foreign Minister of the Weimar Republic; in London, early in 1922, with the young Czecho-Slovakian statesman, Dr Eduard Beneš; during the Labour Government in 1924, with K. G. Rakowsky, the Russian Chargé d'Affaires.

'The catastrophe of Paris'

The Peace Conference is a failure because all the Governments alike are using the victories won by the democracies of the world for the old selfish ends, because each one of them still believes in the old ideas of national prestige and pursues the old schemes of national ambition.

These words by J. L. Hammond[1] might well have been written by Massingham, much of whose inspiration in the next few years was born of his conviction of the 'catastrophe of Paris'. He dwelt on the weaknesses of the Treaty and ignored its strengths, often in a manner which seems irrational to us. John Maynard Keynes' brilliant but partisan *The Economic Consequences of the Peace*, published in England in December 1919, was a shot in the arm. Massingham wrote in congratulation: 'You have crushed the treaty under your arguments'; the book 'has set scores of minds on fire, and will go on lighting such conflagrations until the work is done, & the movement for revision has gathered a force that the statesmen cannot (& probably won't want to) resist'. Arnold Rowntree urged Massingham to use his influence for an inexpensive edition.[2]

In examining Massingham's attitude towards British foreign policy after the war, one confronts a recurrent problem: to what extent does his position grow out of the merits of the situation and to what extent is he merely opposing Lloyd George? It is therefore all the more interesting to notice those occasions when the Prime Minister's efforts

---

[1] *Nation*, 7 June 1919.
[2] Massingham to Keynes, 11 Dec. [1919] and 29 Dec. [1919]; Arnold S. Rowntree to Keynes, 5 Jan. 1920. Keynes Papers, Marshall Library.

win Massingham's approval. The circumstances are usually those in which Lloyd George seeks to solve problems in 'open conference'. Here he was at his best, in manner and objective, and so in December 1921 Massingham hailed the early achievements of the Washington Conference. It was, he said, a shift 'from Force to Conference'. Then again in January 1922 at Cannes, when the vexed question of French security seemed on the verge of solution, Massingham said without qualification that Lloyd George 'is making a large and imaginative effort to undo the disaster which he helped to bring on Europe at Versailles'. Although both Washington and Cannes ended in frustration Massingham did not hold British policy responsible, and he was still able to find kind words for Lloyd George when the Genoa Conference of May 1922 was wrecked by the French.[1]

The fate of the German Republic was for Massingham a central concern. Before the war Eduard Bernstein often set the *Nation*'s tone on Germany. Now, in 1920, there is a series of articles by Theodor Wolff, noted liberal and editor of the *Berliner Tageblatt*, and frequent articles 'from a neutral correspondent', S. F. Van Oss, at The Hague. At times Massingham was close to the decision-making process. On the occasion of the London Conference on reparations, from 21 February to 4 March 1921, when proposals presented by Dr Simons, the German Foreign Secretary, proved unacceptable, Massingham lunched with the German Ambassador (Dr Friedrich Sthamer) and conferred with Dr Simons.[2] These conversations were behind the leader, 'The New German War' and the remarks of 'Wayfarer', both in the 12 March *Nation* and both of which ignored the unconciliatory aspects of the German proposals. Here is Massingham's tone: 'It is not so much the failure [of the Conference] to settle the indemnity question which matters. What is of far greater moment is the moral anachronism of these proceedings. The talk of "sanctions" had begun even before the Germans had spoken.' But he took heart six months later with the Rathenau–Loucheur agreement for German payment of reparations in

[1] *Nation*, 17 Dec. 1921; 14 Jan. 1922; 20 May 1922. But he opened his columns to the iconoclasm of Bernard Shaw once again – in November 1921 the *Nation* carried articles in which Shaw said he had refused to attend the Washington Conference as a professional journalist because nothing would be accomplished there.
[2] N.D., 4 March 1921.

kind. Massingham talked with Rathenau at Wiesbaden – conversations which provided the basis for the leader (15 October 1921) in the *Nation*, 'The Ruin of Reparations'. But further negotiations failed and, the summer following, a trip to the Rhineland[1] was the basis for Massingham's 'The French War on Germany' (*Nation*, 12 August 1922) – a strong castigation of French occupation. 'They do not occupy. They settle.'

In the Upper Silesian Question it was Massingham's view that the rehabilitation of Germany took precedence over Polish national interest. He was convinced that the Poles, supported by France, were determined to get Silesia by hook or by crook. A German defeat in Upper Silesia 'means more even than despair and economic ruin. It is simply an act of decivilization'. The plebiscite (March 1921) he regraded as favourable to Germany, and so the final settlement in October 1921, while assigning two-thirds of the land to Germany, for granting most of the mineral wealth to Poland was to him a disaster for Germany.[2]

British foreign policy under the Coalition was so generally suspect in Massingham's mind that in Greece, where Venizelos was staunchly supported by Lloyd George, the *Nation* looked favourably on the monarchy, which remained in exile after the war until Constantine I returned to power in November 1920. Massingham always had a special interest in Greece, often to the point of sentimentality ('I am an old friend of Greece' is his refrain); and he usually had his own sources of information, now including G. Streit, the Greek Minister of Foreign Affairs under Constantine, and Prince Nicholas, brother to the king.

It was the *Nation*'s lament that 'Liberalism' was no longer manifest in the British policy which attracted the attention of the Greek Monarchist Party. Streit, writing from Lucerne in January 1920, insisted that the Monarchist Party had always been friendly to the Entente and he welcomed the opportunity to set forth 'the present dictatorial conduct of our internal policy by Mr. Venizelos [which] is repudiated by the Greek people'. He enclosed documents of 1913–17

[1] 1 July 1922 ('Wayfarer').
[2] *Nation*, 24 Mar. 1920; 4 June 1921; 15 Oct. 1921.

from the Greek White Book for Massingham's perusal, and an article for the *Nation*. But Massingham, probably in an exercise of caution, did not publish the article. Then from January until June Massingham received a series of letters from Prince Nicholas, also from Switzerland. The intellectual of the family, Nicholas, it seems, was a regular reader of the *Nation*. Writing on 21 January he exclaimed: 'At last here [in the *Nation*] is somebody who sees things different and who has the courage to say so' and then proceeded to set forth in sixteen closely-written pages the wickedness of the Venizelos regime. Massingham, while still cautious, did refer to Venizelos's electoral manipulation in his own interests, his rigid control of public opinion and 'the aggrandizement of Greece' at the expense of Turkey. A sharp response from the Greek Embassy in London appeared in the *Nation* for 17 April and enlisted Massingham's comment: 'We hold no brief for any party in Greece and simply desire the return of a more liberal and tolerant regime than now appears to exist.'[1]

But he did take sides; he refused to recant his strictures on the Venizelos rule and continued to deplore his 'reign of terror' against the Monarchist Party. Even after the return of Constantine to power in November 1920 Massingham held Venizelos, along with Lloyd George, accountable for the reverses to Greek fortunes which followed on the revival of Turk nationalism. Two years later, after the disastrous conclusion of the Greek occupation of Smyrna and the abdication of Constantine, Massingham still held Venizelos responsible.[2]

Well before allied intervention ended in Soviet Russia, a *Nation* leader (20 September 1919) declared 'For our part we hold that the world may have to adjust itself to the permanence of the Soviet System in Russia.' From this tone the *Nation* never deviated. The Bullitt mission and report in 1919 were received with praise. In the summer of 1920 Massingham hailed the leadership of British labour in forestalling British intervention on the side of Poland against the Soviet. 'Workmen set the great peace fire alight, but it has swept all over Britain', wrote 'Wayfarer' (14 August). In May the *Nation* provided enthusiastic support to an appeal received from Russian intellectuals favouring

---

1 The correspondence with Streit and Prince Nicholas is in M.P.
2 *Nation*, 'Wayfarer', 26 June, 21 Aug. and 6 Nov. 1920; 16 and 30 Sept. 1922.

resumption of economic intercourse and normal political relations. This 'Appeal' was widely distributed by the *Nation* with a covering letter from Massingham, which read in part

I am very anxious that you should give your name to a movement of general sympathy with the document... It is suggested that if the Government are willing, a deputation of this more or less non-political type should be invited to visit this country and lay before it the case for the general resumption of relations with Russia.

Replies were received and published from A. N. Whitehead, G. Murray, G. P. Gooch, Bennett, Galsworthy, Wells, Shaw, Haldane, J. A. Spender, W. E. Orchard, L. T. Hobhouse, J. L. Garvin, C. P. Scott, W. Robertson Nicoll, Havelock Ellis, J. M. Keynes, William Archer. It was a striking example of how, on occasion, the *Nation* marshalled public opinion. Then Massingham wrote to Maxim Gorki urging him to send such a deputation with the consent of the two governments.[1]

In the *Star* and *Chronicle* years Massingham was committed to Irish Home Rule. Now after the First World War he was equally devoted to the cause of Irish independence. Irish visitors to Adelphi Terrace were frequent and in Constantine P. Curran the *Nation* had a remarkable correspondent in Dublin. Massingham himself was personally acquainted with prominent Irish figures, including Lady Gregory, Michael Collins, and T. M. Healy.

Massingham condemned as worthless the Government of Ireland Act introduced in 1919 and finally enacted in December 1920; it was, he said, an imposed settlement without negotiation, and a partition which violated the principle of nationalism and perpetuated religious separatism.[2] But well before that, 'The Troubles' – the state of undeclared guerrilla war between the Irish Republican Army and the Royal Irish Constabulary supported by the Black and Tans (special British police) – occupied his attention and stimulated his passions. The *Nation* disseminated information and stirred emotions in circles wider than its limited circulation.

In April 1920, Massingham, at the suggestion of Shaw, invited

---

[1] Massingham to G. Murray, 26 April 1920, Murray Papers; *Nation*, 1, 8, 15 May 1920.
[2] *Nation*, 24 Dec. 1920; 3 Jan. 1921.

Lady Gregory to write on the Irish situation out of her own observation and experience.[1] Soon the *Nation* referred to a letter from a distinguished Irish writer who was a landlord and not a politician and who wished to tell *her* story of *Sinn Fein*. Some months later her articles appeared in five issues; they constituted excerpts from 'the diary of an Irish writer and landlord' and illustrated 'atrocities' and 'outrages' against the Irish, cited in *Nation* leaders.

J. L. Hammond devoted much of 1921 to Ireland, writing extensively for the *Manchester Guardian* and the *Nation*. His eight-page 'Irish Supplements' in the *Nation* (in January and April 1921) entitled 'A Tragedy of Errors' and 'The Terror in Action' were widely circulated in pamphlet form. Sir John Simon, Violet Bonham-Carter and Vaughan Nash, among others, testified to their influence. An article, ardently sought from Lord Morley, did not materialise. Massingham found him, in Morley's own words, 'self indulgent', and 'saving himself up for an early voyage to Heaven'.[2]

Week in and week out, in 1920 and into 1921, the *Nation* attacked Government policy in Ireland. Thus in the autumn of 1920: the Lloyd George Cabinet is charged with 'The Proclamation of Anarchy'; the Lloyd George speech at Carnarvon draws the leader 'Killing No Murder'; an appeal is made to the British people in 'The Call for Public Action' and the Government is accused of 'The "War" on Ireland.' The *Nation* proposed a settlement with the Prince of Wales as Regent of Ireland, a declaration of amnesty and a new constitution for Ireland drafted by a body representative of all elements in the land and from Britain and the Empire as well.

But no journalist, least of all Massingham, could pen such leaders without manifesting his feelings in other ways. When the Government of Ireland Act was enacted it is no surprise to find Nevinson jotting down that his editor was 'burning with rage'. And he was thus in a mood to welcome the report at the end of 1920 of a Labour Delegation to Ireland, 'compiled with care and discrimination', which was favourable to Sinn Fein and damning for the Black and Tans. But Massingham had more constructive ideas as well. At the end of 1920 he was in

---

[1] Massingham to Lady Gregory, 30 April [1920], Berg; Lennox Robinson (ed.), *Lady Gregory's Journals, 1916–1920* ([London] 1946), 128, 139.
[2] Letters to Hammond, including Massingham, 'Friday', n.d., J.L.H.P.

communication with Irish Catholic moderates – Lord Macdonnell, Lord Monteagle and Timothy Healy. The idea of 'an interregnum of the moderates', urged by Healy, influenced some of Massingham's passages in the *Nation*. Massingham learned that the Cabinet was indeed seeking some intermediary force and he recommended this role for Lord Monteagle.[1]

In March 1921 the killing of leading citizens of Limerick brought one of the *Nation's* strongest leaders, 'The Outrage on Ireland'. The report of the inquiry by the American 'Nation' was 'distressing and humiliating reading for English people'. But by July the *Nation* welcomed a conciliatory note inaugurated by the King's speech at Belfast: 'The progress of the Irish peace negotiations gives reasonable grounds for hope... We start at a parting point in history.' Kind words are found even for Lloyd George. His proposal is a fair one and a Massingham leader (27 August) tells 'Why Ireland Can Accept' and 'Wayfarer' says 'it is too good to fail'. 'Liberals and Radicals who fought the Prime Minister when he was wrong over Ireland can be generous in their help when he is indubitably right.' In December, the *Nation* finds 'the final stages . . . as dramatic as anything in history', and 'Wayfarer' gives credit to Lloyd George, Birkenhead and the Irish leaders. A year later, when Saorstat Eireann was proclaimed, the *Nation* hailed the appointment of Timothy Healy as the first Governor-General. Soon after Massingham wrote to Lady Gregory: 'We had a good fight over Ireland, and the victory, I am sure, is not going to be to the devil and his angels.'[2]

On Ireland Massingham was pretty much on target, but on India he was wide of the mark. While he took a long view – the Empire was breaking up and India would go – and while to him the road to progress was in Home Rule, he was without sympathy for Mohandas K. Gandhi and 'civil disobedience'. Massingham was baffled without knowing it. To him Gandhi was merely 'a bewildering mystic' who did not represent ideas and therefore could not be handled politically. Gandhi revealed 'the intellectual crudity of India'. Such remarks brought considerable correspondence to the 'Letters' section but Massingham was

---

[1] Massingham to Healy, 31 December 1920 [Copy], M.P.
[2] *Nation*, 1921, *passim*, especially 19 March, 9 April, 9 July, 3 Sept., 10 Dec. *Nation and Athenaeum*, 9 Dec. 1922. Massingham to Lady Gregory, 7 June 1923, Berg.

stubborn. When Gandhi was imprisoned (April 1922) Massingham expressed admiration of his dignity but considered his policy 'endless vacillation' and 'idealism without vision'; his career 'is not a step on India's march to freedom; it is a long step backwards'.[1]

An alternative to Lloyd George

How would a Liberal Radical brought up in the tradition of peace, retrenchment and reform, confront the depression of production and trade and the crisis of unemployment which beset the land in the period of Reconstruction? Would a commitment to Free Trade and to the liberty of factory owner and factory worker alike provide answers? As always more facile in putting questions than in answering them, Massingham himself stated the issue in his final word in the *Nation* of 28 April 1923. 'The great dilemma of modern statesmanship', he wrote, 'is how to revise the industrial contract without destroying it.'

Massingham had no ideological solution. But he steadfastly believed in rational processes, especially those in the democratic-parliamentary context, and he rejected violence and force of any kind. If changes came smoothly and were salutary he was likely to accept them. If measures were ineffective he would seek for the cause. He was particularly impatient with inaction, for that verged on apathy, a deadly sin. Thus he tended to deal pragmatically with social and economic problems as they arose. He accepted the Housing and Town Planning Act of 1919, perhaps partly because it met no opposition and did not become a political issue. But failure of the Government to deal successfully with unemployment led to the judgment (2 December 1922) after the fall of the Coalition: 'one of the worst chapters in the history of the late Government is the record of its treatment of the unemployed'.

Towards coal, of all industries in the most critical condition, the *Nation* was bold: nationalisation was the answer, a relatively new note for Massingham. The Sankey Commission of 1919 was praised for its courage and optimism. The coal crisis of September-October 1920 which threatened to involve the Triple Alliance led the *Nation* to support the general policy of the miners: the conversion of coal into 'a public service under democratic control'. In the more severe crisis of April 1921 the Government was held responsible for 'Chaos in the

[1] *Lady Gregory's Journals, 1916–1920*, 210–11; *Nation*, 4, 18 Feb. and 1, 15 Apr. 1922.

Coal Trade'. In discussing the rights and the interests of owners, miners and the public, Massingham observed that 'in equity and truth though not in law, the land of a country, including the underground part, belongs to the nation as a whole, and is certainly held in trust for it'.[1] Siegfried Sassoon contributed a sympathetic account of conditions of the Glamorgan mine at Tonypandy in Wales. The prospect of a General Strike, 'Black Friday', and the demoralisation of trade unionism and the coal industry alike led to the *Nation*'s observation: 'The disastrous deadlock in the coal industry is the result of that fatal habit of disregarding realities and leaving all important decisions to the event which marks the conduct of Ministers in every crisis'.[2]

But the 'Geddes Axe' (February 1922) recommending drastic economies in Government services offered Massingham perhaps his best opportunity to combine with dissatisfaction over policy his violent hatred of the Government which produced it. Now, said the *Nation*, it is clear that

political comedy must nearly have reached bottom. Having spent several hundred millions in making the world a more dangerous place than the Peace had left it, an entirely unprincipled Government finds itself confronted with a deepening trade depression and a desperate finance.

And Massingham spoke with obvious relish and anticipation of the 'demi-Coalition' or 'ex-Coalition' and 'the coming Government'.[3]

In his weekly meetings with the editor of the *Nation* Leonard Woolf tells us that on nine out of ten occasions Massingham would launch into a tirade against Lloyd George. Massingham 'hated him with an almost crazy violence and bitterness'. Nearly always suspicious of his motives, Massingham did not join the chorus of praise from the Liberal press for Lloyd George's defence in the Commons, 16 April 1919, against the attack of the Northcliffe papers on what they called his leniency towards Germany. It was merely a 'tactical or electoral movement' said Massingham.[4] And so it went that Lloyd George seldom won Massingham's approval; the Irish settlement in December 1921,

[1] *Nation*, 4 Sept. 1920; 2 Apr. 1921, p. 9; 16 Apr. 1921, p. 52.
[2] *Nation*, 7 May 1921, p. 201.
[3] *Nation*, 18 Feb. 1922, pp. 743, 748; 4 Mar. 1922, pp. 815, 818.
[4] Woolf, *Downhill All the Way*, 94; *Nation*, 26 Apr. 1919.

the Washington Arms Conference and the policy towards France on reparations in 1922 come to mind as about the only exceptions.

As a rule the *Nation* spoke of Lloyd George and the Coalition in absolutes. 'Lloyd George races *after* opportunity instead of *with* it' (26 April 1919, in comment on Lloyd George's attack on Northcliffe); 'the final duty of the nation is to get rid of them [the Lloyd George Government] as a common nuisance and peril' (16 April 1921, in comment on the coal crisis); Lloyd George 'has tried to govern with a Coalition and *without* a House of Commons. He has failed' (28 January 1922). Nevinson unburdened himself to Oswald Garrison Villard: 'As long as this atrocious Government holds power, I fear nothing will be done to wipe out our shame. . . Hammond, Massingham and I pour out denunciations and satire in the *Nation*.' As for Lloyd George himself he had long since dismissed the *Nation* as unlikely to be of any value to him. During the Peace Conference, speaking of the *Daily News* and the *Nation*, he remarked to C. P. Scott: 'I never heed them because I know that in their eyes I never can do right. I know beforehand what they're going to say.'[1]

What was the alternative to the Coalition? Hardly the Liberal Party as constituted, though Massingham was reluctant to admit it. He still hoped 'Liberalism' would favour responsible Government in India, Ireland and Egypt, would advocate withdrawal from Russia, and would seek to accommodate the Peace Treaty with the principles of the League of Nations. After all 'Liberalism' remained 'the creed of open-minded men' and should range far and wide in attracting disciples. Asquith's task, upon his return to the Commons in February 1920, was that of restoring Liberalism to its proper place in the national consciousness in order to rescue the country from the existing Government.[2]

This would be accomplished, Massingham concluded, by bringing together in a new 'democratic' or 'people's' party the ideas and philosophy of historic Liberalism and the organisation and constituency of Labour. However, this notion, though mentioned as early as October 1917, never in his language took viable form. It was easy

---

[1] Nevinson to Villard [22 Mar. 1921?], Houghton; Wilson (ed.), *Political Diaries of G. P. Scott*, 371.
[2] *Nation*, 19 July 1919 ('Wayfarer'); 27 Sept. 1919; 31 Jan. 1920.

enough for 'Wayfarer' to speak in general terms: 'Sooner or later the Radical Left and Labor must come together and work out the salvation of progressive England.'[1] And MacDonald was provided space (3 July 1920) to trumpet the accomplishments of the Labour Party Conference at Scarborough; the programme adopted, he said, 'remains the most comprehensive and consistent view of our foreign and domestic problems which any political party in this country has yet expressed'.

But the essential of electoral cooperation was another matter. Labour's dependence on working-class support, particularly the predominating influence of trade unionism, disturbed Massingham, and the divisions within the Labour Movement disquieted him still more. At *Nation* Lunches discussing a possible Lib.-Lab. combination, the most gloomy voice was that of the editor.[2] C. F. G. Masterman and James Ramsay MacDonald in successive articles (*Nation*, 22 and 29 May 1920) on the same topic, 'The Case for the Liberal Party', failed to agree on anything. While Masterman found the Liberal Party's outlook sound and healthy and Labour hopelessly divided, MacDonald found the Liberal Party in complete disarray and declared that anyone who would return politics 'to great issues and masterful effort' must associate with Labour. Such disagreement became emotional in an exchange between Ponsonby and Masterman (*Nation*, October-November 1920), prompted by a plea from 'Wayfarer' (9 October 1920) for Lib.-Lab. cooperation in turning out Lloyd George. *Nation* leaders exhorted the N.L.F. to revive the traditional programme (Free Trade, economy, land reform), A. G. Gardiner appealed for a Radical rebirth, and Laski (a Labourite) expressed scepticism of any possible rapprochement of Liberalism with Labour.[3] Altogether there was much talk of the challenge to Liberalism, but not much prospect that the challenge would be met.

No doubt Massingham himself had more sense of accomplishment in attacking the efforts at fusion in the other camp. Churchill's call in July 1919 for the merger of 'the democratic forces in Conservatism and the patriotic forces in Liberalism' in a new 'Centre Party' was termed by 'Wayfarer' 'anti-Labourism' and promptly dismissed. Lord

[1] *Nation*, 20 Mar. 1920.
[2] N.D., 18 Oct. and 8 Nov. 1920; 10 Jan. 1921. For view on trade unions, see *H.W.M.*, 96.
[3] *Nation*, 29 Jan., 14, 21 May 1921.

Birkenhead's talk of 'A National Party' to fight Labour was based, said Massingham (17 January 1920), on 'Imperialism and Militarism'. And he made merry with Conservatism fighting 'a phantom communism' in England. 'Wayfarer' seemed to relish even more commenting (20 March 1920) on Lloyd George's difficulties with his 'Central Party' for 'it admits of no parties, only a claque and a crowd'.

Check has been administered to Mr. Lloyd George's proposals to turn the Coalition into a party for himself... At first all went well ... [but then] a frost set in. There were references to principles, to benighted beings who had been Liberals all their lives, to the chance of a revolt among those grovellers, the Liberal Associations, and even to such degraded people as constituents.

By 1921 elements opposed to the Lloyd George Coalition had found a rallying point in the Conservative Lord Robert Cecil, who had been treated with respect by the *Nation* ever since his appointment to the Cabinet in February 1916. Then, in 1919, his dedication to the League of Nations and his services at the Peace Conference appear, said the *Nation*, 'to promise the arrival of a new political force'. Massingham added, 'Failing him, I see no other.'[1]

Two years later this possibility seemed to be approaching reality. Correspondence on Cecil's prospects poured into No. 10 Adelphi Terrace. When, in February 1921, Cecil crossed the floor in the Commons, Massingham decided that an effective parliamentary Opposition was in the making. He drew up an alternative Cabinet headed by Lord Robert and spoke of his leadership of a Lib.-Lab.-neo Tory combination. Paralleling this development Massingham briefly anticipated an early collapse of the Lloyd George Government – but such optimism alternated with despair. So he writes (26 March 1921) of 'The Coming Fall of the Coalition' which will leave Lloyd George 'essentially a party-less man'. But then (14 May 1921), 'Lloyd George For Ever and Ever?' asked the *Nation*.

If Liberal policy continues to be as timid and infertile as it is today; if the Labor Party cannot rise beyond the statesmanship of wage-fixing; if Lord Robert Cecil will not lead, and Mr. Asquith neither actively leads nor retires from leadership ... then Mr. George must continue to govern England.

[1] *Nation*, 12 July and 23 Aug. 1919.

Now Massingham's attention was caught by the return of Lord Grey to politics, in October 1921, after six years of silence. Massingham shared the enthusiasm engendered by the demonstration of the Free Liberals ('in effect a revival meeting') at the N.L.F. Conference in January 1922, where Asquith and Grey were welcomed with 'something like Gladstonian hero-worship' as they 'took the field on the issue of "Down with the Coalition"'. 'Wayfarer' suggested a Grey Government with Lord Robert Cecil as Foreign Secretary.[1] All this was the more exciting in that talk of an early General Election was rampant. But, for Lord Grey Massingham's admiration was stronger than his confidence. He warmly applauded two articles (*Nation*, 11 and 18 February) by William H. Dawson on 'A Plea for Light: Our Foreign Policy and Lord Grey', underlining Grey's close association to the 'old' secret diplomacy.[2] In any case there was little prospect of Asquith making way for Grey's leadership of the Liberal Party.

Massingham's hope for the future remained with Cecil. Who else could elicit such a demonstration from all political elements as he did at a League of Nations rally late in November 1921? And when Lloyd George, checked by the Conservatives in the Coalition early in 1922 in his design for an early General Election, turned to re-establishing his leadership of the Liberal Party, Massingham went to work. A signed Massingham leader, on 25 March 1922, showing remarkable knowledge of the political situation, urged the affiliation of Cecil with the Liberal Party, for he was the one statesman who embodied 'the conscience and thought of Liberalism both in European policy and in industry'. Massingham wrote many letters – two are available. He reopened communication with Northcliffe. Writing on 27 March, Massingham expressed great concern at the prospect of Lloyd George as the *de facto* leader of the Liberal Party.

It is therefore necessary to put before the country some figure who, being as far as possible a contrast to L. G. in honesty and straightforwardness, is also a man of his times, able to transact, when necessary, with the right wing of Labour. Grey, of course, helps things with the Conservatives who would prefer him to Asquith, but not with what I may call the forces of the future. I know that the Labour men would enter a Cecil Government willingly...

[1] *Nation*, 15 Oct. 1921, pp. 99, 107; 28 Jan. 1922.
[2] Massingham to Dawson, 13 Feb. 1922, U. of Birmingham.

Cecil, though not ideal, and in my mind too cautious, is a man, who by a progressive policy can save the country from Bolshevik extremes, and equally dangerous reaction.

But Cecil must have a better press – 'there isn't a Liberal daily that's worth a damn... Now can't he [Cecil] be given a better show?' Northcliffe undertook to report Cecil more fully. Massingham also wrote to Haldane urging support for Cecil.[1] Massingham found encouragement in Cecil's manifesto (15 April), 'the best statement of the Liberal creed and its modern application I have seen'. And he brought together at dinner Cecil and some of the Liberal editors.[2]

All this indicates that Massingham's mind was still set on defeating the Lloyd George Coalition by a counter-coalition. How hopeful he was of success we cannot say. He followed with more assurance the difficulties of the Coalition, leading to desertion by the Parliamentary Conservative Party and Lloyd George's resignation on 20 October. The alternatives in the Coalition – Bonar Law and Baldwin – were treated with some favour. But 'Wayfarer' sighed 'for a Liberal-Labor *entente* as the best available organ for governing England strongly and well'. Still, 'that is for the future. The next best thing is to keep Liberalism in being – and in health'.[3]

Thus Massingham had hoped for and worked for a reformed and revived Liberal Party or, as an alternative, a Lib.-Lab.-neo Conservative alliance. He was hardly realistic. On the other hand, Northcliffe, in his letter of April 1922, had predicted the emergence of a Conservative Government with a strong Labour Opposition. Thus it was in the General Election of November 1922. Massingham then moved rapidly to the Left – for him the important development was the election of James Ramsay MacDonald as the leader of the Parliamentary Labour Party. His electoral campaign was termed 'the most dramatic' of the Labour contests and the *Nation and Athenaeum* carried his 'How I Won at Aberavon'. Arthur Ponsonby dramatised for *Nation* readers the scene in the Commons when an ex-Prime Minister retired to a corner below the gangway while a private member who had never occupied Government office was acclaimed the Leader of the Opposition.

---

[1] Massingham to Northcliffe, 27 Mar. 1922 ('Private'); Northcliffe to Massingham, 1 Apr. 1922 (Copy), Northcliffe Papers. Massingham to Haldane, 12 Apr. [1922], H.P.

[2] *Nation and Athenaeum*, 22 Apr. 1922; Howe (ed.), *Holmes-Laski Letters*, I, 432.

[3] *Nation and Athenaeum*, 28 Oct. and 4 Nov. 1922.

Oswald Mosley, as independent candidate for Harrow, was singled out as 'the most attractive personal element in the campaign'.

> If character, a brilliant and searching mind, a sympathetic temperament, and a repugnance from mean and cruel dealing, fit men for the service of the State, Mr. Mosley should rise high in it... I regard him as something of a star – and of no common brightness.

But of all the things to be thankful for, said Massingham, 'I utter my chief "Jubilate" over Dundee' – there Churchill, 'a public danger', was defeated. 'And it is fitting that Pacificism, represented by Morel, even more than Laborism should have brought down our Man of War.'[1] So far in his estimation had fallen one of H.W.M.'s heroes.

So the period closed as it began, with 'Wayfarer' warning against Lloyd George. Liberals were admonished to range themselves with Labour 'as the only party with a scrap of principle left'. 'The great Georgian film "Liberal Reunion" has suffered a little in popularity owing, perhaps, to the exposure of the author's design not so much to unite with free Liberalism as to supplant it.' We find Massingham writing to Garvin: 'I see all I've cared for in politics lapse helplessly into such hands as L.G.'s. He's not a villain, but a totally irresponsible, non-moral personality.'[2]

'Vale'

Nothing in Massingham's long tenure with the *Nation* is more revealing than the manner of his leaving it, in April 1923. The circumstances reveal his own character and personality, reflect the nature of his relation to the Rowntree Trust, put to the test his ties with his staff and emphasise the reputation the *Nation* had achieved. Fortunately, it is an episode with ample documentation. But, as always when Massingham is concerned, a matter of human relations is a matter of controversy. Was Massingham's resignation from the *Nation* the outcome of protracted quarrels with the Rowntrees over policy towards Lloyd George and the Liberal Party? That was how it was widely regarded at the time. At once recalled were Robert Donald's unceremonious departure

[1] *Nation and Athenaeum*, Nov.–Dec. 1922. Of Massingham, Sir Oswald Mosley has written the author (14 Nov. 1968): 'I have vivid recollection of him as the most brilliant journalist of his time and a singularly attractive personality.'

[2] *Nation and Athenaeum*, 9 Dec. 1922; Massingham to Garvin, 10 Dec. [1922], Garvin Papers.

from the *Daily Chronicle* in October 1918, and, about a year later, A. G. Gardiner's resignation from the *Daily News*, the latter not so much a 'riddle' to Massingham as he innocently suggested (*Nation*, 13 September 1919). Was Massingham 'driven from the Nation under circumstances beyond print'? (Laski).[1] Was it a 'scandal' resulting from the general 'wholesale marketing of recognized organs of public opinion in recent years'? (*Daily Herald*, 29 August 1924). Or, as the Rowntrees insisted, was it a simple matter of obtaining additional financial support or selling the paper, and turning to the Oxford 'Summer School' Liberals when Massingham and his friends had failed to locate sources of support? But was Massingham given sufficient opportunity to find a solution and so remain as editor? Were the Rowntrees somewhat secretive; did they in truth welcome circumstances which would remove Massingham from the editorial chair? Was Massingham himself sympathetic to problems faced by the trustees; was he consistent in his own position?

An account of what happened will come as close to answering these questions as may be. Massingham's relations with the Rowntree Trust over the years had generally been cordial, but with Massingham seeking no advice on policy, assuming no interference and looking to the Trust for financial support only. On editorial policy during the Great War some directors expressed differences with Massingham but other directors always came to his defence. Circulation increased from 8,000 in 1916 to 11,600 in 1918 when a net profit of £73 was recorded, any profit at all being quite unprecedented.[2]

In the end it was finance, not policy, which brought a crisis. From November 1920 this remained a chronic problem, with economic conditions adversely affecting circulation, advertising revenue and costs of production. Arnold Rowntree, the chairman of the directors, in reporting to the Trust in June and July of 1921, summarised the situation: a loss in the *Nation* account during the financial year 1920 of £4,679 and an anticipated loss for 1921 of £6,240. After conversations with Massingham and A. J. Bonwick, the business manager, Rowntree proposed drastic economies (a smaller paper, larger advertising section, reduction of editorial expenses). Only Seebohm Rowntree raised the

---

[1] Howe (ed.), *Holmes-Laski Letters*, I, 475.
[2] Minutes, Rowntree Trust, 19 Feb. and 21 May 1918; 14 Mar. 1919, Rowntree Papers.

question of editorial policy. He declared that if the decision were his he would terminate the *Nation* at once. But the venerable Joseph Rowntree, the founder of the Trust, in statements generally approved by the others, asserted and reasserted the view that the *Nation* had rendered great service. He was reported as saying that the *Nation* 'must be kept going at all costs'.[1]

Extended conversations and correspondence between Arnold Rowntree and Massingham led to an agreement, as Rowntree understood it, for a reduction of the reading matter of the paper by four pages, and large cuts in the weekly editorial expense. Rowntree wrote to Massingham that the Trustees would continue support of the *Nation* for another year, only on condition that these economies be effected, and advertising be increased with four pages at the front of the larger issues. Massingham, clearly in something of a huff, proposed discontinuing the 'London Diary' to find space for 'Letters to the Editor', but Rowntree responded that 'Wayfarer' by all means should continue. The trustees, with one exception (no doubt Seebohm Rowntree) went on record (17 February 1922) 'that every possible effort should be made to continue the "Nation" even if this involved using some of the Capital of the Trust'.[2]

Nevertheless irritations grew. Rowntree was disturbed when sufficient economies were not effected while Massingham declared that he was responsible only for the editorial department. He was annoyed when the directors refused to sanction a return to a 6*d.* (from a 9*d.*) paper 'as a positive policy of enterprise'. In June 1922 the Trustees declared they could underwrite losses for the current year only to £2,000, and by May the deficit had reached £1,600. Now Arnold Rowntree proposed a search for a prospective buyer, with interests similar to those of the Trust so that Massingham might remain as editor. But negotiations in August and September with his friend, S. F. Van Oss, the proprietor of a successful Dutch weekly, broke down. Soon after, in October, Massingham requested a return to a

[1] Minutes, Rowntree Trust, 8 Nov. 1920; 3 June and 28 July 1921; 'Memorandum on the Present State of the *Nation*', presented to Trustees meeting, 28 July 1921. Rowntree Papers.
[2] Arnold Rowntree to Massingham (copies): 4 and 15 Aug., 29 Nov. 1921 and 5 Jan. 1922. Massingham to Rowntree, 4 Jan. 1922. Minutes, Rowntree Trust, 17 Feb. 1922. Rowntree Papers.

36-page issue to prove 'we are giving a little more for our 9*d*. than the Spectator's 6*d*.'. He boldly proposed a new 3*d*. *Nation* with more popular appeal aiming for a circulation of 30,000 to 40,000. He anticipated that capital of £20,000 would be required and urged the Rowntree Trust to join the new venture to the extent of £2,000 or £3,000. He himself pledged the rest of his working days to such a paper. He felt assured of support elsewhere, notably from A. G. Gardiner, now a free lance. He introduced this proposal with expression of 'a most friendly and cordial feeling' towards Arnold Rowntree. 'I could not have had kinder treatment than I have always had at your hands.'[1]

Unfortunately we do not have Rowntree's response; there is now a hiatus in our record. We pick up the story on 10 December when Massingham, rather suddenly it appears, sent Arnold Rowntree a letter of resignation. It was a cheerful and friendly letter and must be quoted:

This is not in any way the signal of a permanent difference with you or your colleagues in the Trust. On the contrary I shall part with only the warmest feelings of friendship and regard. My reasons are as follows:

(1) I think the re-union of the Liberal [Party under] L. G., inevitable. Under these circumstances my position would be impossible. I could only go over to the Labour Party. This in any case I have decided to do. I should not blame you or anybody for deciding under such circumstances to keep to Liberalism. . .

(2) I am tired of Editorship – not well – and wanting fresh work and interests. . .

(3) I think the effort to put the 'Nation' on its legs again will need greater union among the Proprietors than now exists, and will not be furthered therefore, by my personality. Pray don't think this is a complaint. Everyone has a right to his opinions. Mine may be wrong; Seebohm's may be quite right.

Massingham's resignation was promptly accepted by the Directors 'with regret'.[2]

But he was then unaware that shortly before, in November, the Rowntrees had inaugurated discussions with a group of independent Liberals, known variously as the 'Manchester Group' or the 'Oxford

---

[1] Minutes, Rowntree Trust, 1922: 8 Mar, 14 June, 21 July, 5 Sept. Arnold Rowntree to Massingham, 14 Mar. 1922 (Copy); Massingham to Rowntree, 16, 17 Mar. and 11, 13 Oct. 1922. Rowntree Papers.

[2] Massingham to Arnold Rowntree, 10 Dec. 1922; Minute, Directors of *Nation*, 13 Dec. 1922. Rowntree Papers.

Summer School Group', including Maynard Keynes, Walter Layton (the new editor of *The Economist*), Ramsay Muir (historian and director of the Summer School) and others. Arnold Rowntree was confident they would accept at least a half-share in financing the *Nation*. Massingham, on hearing of these negotiations, at once inquired of Joseph Rowntree, the founder of the trust; the reply was most cordial: 'To myself it is a great disappointment that the "Nation" could not be continued on the old lines.' Massingham then complained to Arnold Rowntree that he had not been informed of these negotiations. 'I offered last week to raise the necessary sum. I think my suggestion should take precedence.' To this Arnold Rowntree answered at length, rehearsing the course of events: a reference by Massingham early in 1922 to retirement by the end of the year, the search for financial support, the failure with Van Oss and then the turn to the Oxford 'Summer School' Liberals. An offer had now been made to them and could not be withdrawn.[1]

Massingham's voice rose. Impatiently he appealed to Layton who responded courteously, outlining the plan to continue the *Nation* as a Liberal organ, and offering Massingham a place on the Editorial Committee (with Keynes and Layton) and the continuance of his 'Wayfarer' diary. 'I have declined this insulting offer in a sentence', Massingham wrote to J. L. Garvin. He declared to Keynes his opposition to the 'iniquitous proposal', and poured his complaints into the more sympathetic ears of Sir Robert Hudson, political agent with the Asquith Liberals.[2]

By now the issue was of general interest – the relation of an editor to his proprietors and the future of the *Nation* and H. W. Massingham. *The Times* (January 20) corrected a rumour that Massingham was leaving at once. But, said the *New Statesman* (13 January): 'while we recognize the *Nation* as our most formidable rival in weekly political journalism we shall most sincerely regret even the temporary disappearance from that field of so brilliant and sincere a journalist'. Such

---

[1] Minute, Rowntree Trust, 22 Dec. 1922, Rowntree Papers. Joseph Rowntree to Massingham, 21 Dec. 1922; Massingham to Arnold Rowntree, 22 Dec. 1922 [Copy]; Arnold Rowntree to Massingham, n.d. and 21 Dec. 1922. Copies in M.P.

[2] The exchange with Layton, 15 Jan. 1923 and 18 Jan. 1923 (Copy) is in M.P. Massingham to Garvin, 16 Jan. 1923, Garvin Papers. Massingham to Keynes, 5 Jan. 1923, Keynes Papers, Marshall Library. Keynes to Massingham, 7 and 16 Jan., copy in M.P. Hudson to Garvin, 10 and 11 Jan. 1923, Garvin Papers.

regret, declared the *Manchester Guardian* (10 January) 'would be found in more quarters than he would expect'. The *Spectator* (20 January) said that while Massingham was 'one whose views are not ours', his loss would reflect 'the lack of stability in the press – a tragedy for readers, writers and for editors'.

With J. L. Garvin of the prestigious *Observer* the episode completed the way to reconciliation and affection. Somehow they had been in touch. On 10 December 1922, the day of his resignation, Massingham had written to Garvin of his decision. But very soon in further correspondence he wrote of grievances against the Rowntrees to which Garvin responded sympathetically. Massingham gave way:

Your letter is incomparably sweet to me. It has caused me the only emotion I have felt through the struggle with the people who have done me in. I only regret with deep penitence that I misjudged you and did not know and prize you earlier.

The *Observer* for Sunday, 14 January carried a story, 'The Soul of "The Nation" '. One by one, Garvin wrote, Liberalism had stifled its most vital forces in the press: Cook, Gardiner, Spender, and now Massingham. The *Nation* has been nothing

but the creation of his own soul. . . He has made it without exception the most brilliant review of advanced Liberal opinion in the world. It has been indispensable, like the 'Manchester Guardian'. You might agree with it or not. You had to read it.

Massingham, with full heart, thanked Garvin. He wrote that the *Observer* had put the Rowntrees and the Oxford Liberals in wrong with the press and had broken the attempt to accomplish all 'in silence and secrecy'. Thrusting one of Garvin's letters at Tomlinson, Massingham cried: 'Read that! I've spent all my life for the Liberals, and here we are, and they don't care. But that man [Garvin], I've gone out of my way to mock.' J. L. Hammond reported developments to C. P. Scott who called the situation 'a tragedy both public and private. Nothing which the new "Group" can contribute is likely in the least to compensate for what we shall lose of a fine and courageous Liberal initiative in Massingham and the organization he had built up'.[1]

---

[1] Massingham to Garvin, 10 Dec. 1922, 18 Jan. [1923], and an undated letter, Garvin Papers. *H.W.M.*, 126. C. P. Scott to J. L. Hammond, 24 Jan. 1923, J.L.H.P.

In mid-January Massingham went off to Monte Carlo for a rest, but with only one thought – to launch a new paper of his own. Perhaps references to a possible combination of the Oxford Liberals and the *New Statesman* spurred him on. He wrote with enthusiasm to Harold Laski that they would put out the best paper in London – an independent paper. With capital of £12,000 they could proceed, but support from Haldane and Morley was indispensable.[1]

Characteristically, Massingham did not inform his staff of the crisis, but when word reached them they rallied to his support. Nevinson concluded with Tomlinson and Laski that the Rowntree action seemed to have been 'underhand and mean'. Tomlinson wrote to Murry, 'They've done in Massingham' and reported to Blunden that he did not care for 'the new colonel and his staff' and had refused the offer to continue with the new group. Hammond (speaking for Tomlinson, Laski and Nevinson) proposed to Hobson that if Massingham left the *Nation*, the chief contributors depart with him. In the end Leonard Woolf was the only regular contributor to remain, and the only one apparently who found the delay in settling the fortunes of the *Nation*, a personal annoyance. 'It is unpleasant waiting in a dependent kind of way to know what Massingham will do', Virginia Woolf noted in her diary, 7 February.[2]

In mid-February, back in London, Massingham, annoyed by newspaper reports that H. D. Henderson had been appointed the new editor of the *Nation* with no official word sent to him, renewed to Arnold Rowntree his offer to find capital for carrying on himself. After some delay Rowntree, early in March, informed Massingham that arrangements with the Oxford Liberals were complete, suggesting formal transfer of the *Nation* with the issue of 6 May and Massingham's salary to be paid through June.[3]

No significant progress was made towards Massingham's new weekly. C. P. Scott, all sympathy, doubted that Massingham's energies would be equal to such a task. Laski approached Haldane but without

---

[1] Massingham to Laski, 11 and 15 Jan. 1923, M.P.
[2] N.D., 10 and 23 Jan. 1923; Tomlinson to Murry, 19 Jan. 1923 and Tomlinson to Blunden, 12 Feb. 1923, U. of Texas. Hammond to Hobson, 28 Jan. 1923 (Copy), M.P. Quentin Bell, *Virginia Woolf: A Biography*, II (London, 1972), 92.
[3] Massingham to Arnold Rowntree, 15 and 28 Feb. 1923 (Copies), M.P. Arnold Rowntree to Massingham, 19 Mar. 1923 (Copy), M.P.

results.[1] Nonetheless Massingham, the journalistic adventurer, persisted. He outlined his ideas to H. G. Wells. It would be an independent journal, 'indispensable if the politics of the Left are to be kept going'. Much as he had advocated to the Rowntrees four months before, he said it would be a 3d. paper, more popular and more varied than the old *Nation*. He now had prospect of £5,000 of the £12,000 capital required. But then he proceeded to sketch a still bolder proposition – the formation of 'a great Reform Party (not a sect) able to replace Liberalism & present itself as an Opposition today, a Government tomorrow, with all [?] stars in it & definitely working to that end. Nothing less'. They arranged to talk it over. Shaw told Nevinson they should start 'a boldly Bolshevik paper'. In April Laski was still nourishing the prospect and Massingham was writing to Felix Frankfurter: 'I shall try to revive the old effort in a new form, as soon as I get strong again.'[2] He was referring to a heart attack he suffered in the office on 20 March. Confined to his bed Massingham brooded over his 'shameful treatment' from the Rowntrees, especially from 'turnip-headed Arnold, who never faced facts and refused to answer letters'.[3]

While convalescing, 'Wayfarer' contributed paragraphs to his declining *Nation* and for his last issue, 28 April, Massingham wrote 'Vale', a simple straightforward statement of the position taken by the *Nation* in foreign and domestic policy. The next issue, under the new staff, contained a formal tribute to him. The press, generally, took note of the change, usually in terms complimentary to Massingham. He himself was, as he said, 'deluged with letters, saying (and for this I *do* thank the gods) that the writers have been moved to some kind of activity in work and thought by what they have read in the *Nation*'.[4]

But controversy over Massingham's separation from the *Nation* lingered on. The issue was simple enough, as found in an observation, 16 April 1923, by Hobson to the new editor, H. D. Henderson. 'I do not consider that the change has been brought about with proper

[1] Scott to Hammond, 18 Feb. 1923, J.L.H.P.; Laski to Haldane, 1 Mar. 1923, H.P. 5916/7.
[2] Massingham to Wells, 19 and 26 Feb. [1923], Univ. of Illinois; N.D., 14 Mar. 1923. Laski to Garvin, 19 Apr. 1923, Garvin Papers. Massingham to Frankfurter, 23 Apr. 1923, M.P.
[3] N.D., 21 Mar., 16, 30 Apr. 1923.
[4] *H.W.M.*, 141–3.

consideration for Mr. Massingham on the part of the proprietors.' Hammond remarked to Henderson that the paper was sold over Massingham's head without consulting him. To these complaints Arnold Rowntree made the official reply. He pointed out that at the end of 1921 Massingham spoke of resigning for reasons of health a year hence. Rowntree emphasised the financial problem and the Trustees' decision by the summer of 1922, with Massingham's full knowledge, to find outside support. Massingham's health somewhat improved, but although both he and the Trustees sought that support, it was in vain. Then, Rowntree's account has it, he told Massingham that the Trustees would continue the search on their own. Accordingly, negotiations with the Oxford Liberals began in November; of this, it so happened, Massingham was not informed until after his resignation on 10 December. Rowntree concluded:

It is difficult for me to see what more the Trustees could have done. They took the view that H. W. M. was the first man to consult about the paper, and they did this and he did not succeed. . . Having decided to sell the paper, or get financial help for it, and having made the offer to H. W. M. surely the Trustees were justified in then looking out themselves.[1]

From Massingham's point of view C. P. Scott, back in January, had seen the central issue; even after negotiations were under way with the Oxford Liberals Massingham should have had the opportunity to find the necessary capital. J. L. Hammond's judgment was well balanced. In May 1923 he wrote to Gilbert Murray: 'I have been hearing the other side of the N[ation] affair. I still think that Massingham was badly treated but there is more to be said of the Rowntrees than I thought. M[assingham] certainly behaved very foolishly.'[2]

One cannot disregard Leonard Woolf's remark that Massingham's 'queer, secretive, complex character' had much to do with the rift with the Rowntrees.[3] Massingham had registered little sympathy with the financial problem. After his own abortive proposal in October 1922 for a new, more popular *Nation*, he held himself aloof for some weeks. In his resignation he said quite frankly that his support of Labour

[1] Hammond to Henderson, 29 Mar. 1923 (Copy), J.L.H.P.; Arnold Rowntree to Hobson (Private), 16 Apr. 1923, J.L.H.P.
[2] Hammond to Murray, 17 May 1923, Gilbert Murray Papers; C. P. Scott to Hammond, 18 Jan. 1923, J.L.H.P.
[3] Woolf, *Downhill All the Way*, 96.

would make an impossible situation for the Rowntrees. So, no doubt, they thought as well but there is no evidence that they deliberately forced him out. But Massingham's unfortunate and impulsive resignation eased negotiations with the Oxford Group and was taken as justification for proceeding without further consideration of his interests.

In 1936, in a Rowntree re-examination of Massingham's departure, Ernest E. Taylor, a financial officer of the Trust, wrote to B. Seebohm Rowntree:

Massingham had a *habit* of resigning and 'the Nation' Board had a habit of asking him to withdraw his resignation. When at last his resignation was accepted I feel sure, from memory, that an opportunity was given to H. W. M. to interest his own friends in the purchase of the property but I feel equally sure that there was some misunderstanding about the period of the option.

'The period of the option' – this seems to be the question. Taylor refers to this as the 'one weak link in the chain of evidence'. And from Arnold Rowntree's own account in 1923, the option was not open when Massingham resigned.[1]

[1] Ernest E. Taylor to B. S. Rowntree, 12 Aug. 1936, Rowntree Papers.

CHAPTER II

The Final Chapter (1923–1924)

'On the spur of the moment', Massingham 'would turn out a dramatic notice, or a review, or a political leader of first rate quality.' The instant performance and the versatility, to which S. K. Ratcliffe pays tribute, continue to characterise Massingham's writing from the time of his departure from the *Nation* in April 1923 until his death in August 1924. For a time he still nursed the notion of a new paper, a 3*d.* paper, in format like that of a *Times* supplement, 'advanced Liberal, tending to Labour but free to criticize' (Nevinson's words), and he even dreamed of acquiring one of the monthly reviews.[1] But he settled down as free-lance writer, ranging more widely in subject matter than ever and promptly finding space in a broad range of periodicals and papers. And all the while ill health plagued him.

Very soon after the transfer of editorship of the *Nation*, *The Times* announced (19 May) that 'Wayfarer's' diary would continue in the *New Statesman* and then (26 June) that Massingham would contribute a series, entitled 'The Other Side' to the *Spectator*. From 26 May 1923 until 2 August 1924, with but six omissions, 'A London Diary' by 'Wayfarer' appeared in the *New Statesman*. Leafing through these weekly notes one knows at once that none but Massingham could have written them; however, one soon senses that it is hardly the 'Wayfarer' of *Nation* days, with his sting, his intensity of conviction, his outrage, his enthusiasm. After his death the editor of the *New Statesman* readily acknowledged some such distinction: 'We could not give him, and he never sought to take, that complete independence which was a necessary condition of his very best work.'[2] Behind that remark is the fact that Massingham and Sharp (the editor of the *New Statesman*) were incompatible.

Massingham confided to his daughter, Dorothy, that the friendly

---

[1] Ratcliffe in *New Statesman*, 30 Aug. 1924, p. 586 (unsigned article); N.D., 11 June 1923.
[2] *New Statesman*, 30 Aug. 1924, p. 585.

atmosphere and spirit of the *Spectator* was more to his liking. With this influential Unionist weekly, Massingham exercised complete independence in his writing and enjoyed the full confidence of an editor, John St Loe Strachey, with whom he differed on many points of public policy. Their informal correspondence warmed their hearts as it does that of the reader today.[1] After Massingham's death Strachey wrote to J. Ramsay MacDonald that *Spectator* readers considered Massingham's articles one of the best features of the paper.[2]

The *Spectator* connection began in March 1923 when Strachey, aware of Massingham's imminent severance from the *Nation*, invited him to contribute a weekly letter. Massingham responded: 'It would, indeed, be a most pleasant and interesting job to talk to your powerful and important public'. In introducing Massingham Strachey told his readers

The general title of Mr. Massingham's articles will be 'The Other Side', which implies that we want him to feel as free as possible to express opinions which normally will be opposed to our own. We do not pretend that this is virtuous on our part. In the first place it is a pleasure to give a hearing to so distinguished a writer and commentator on public events as Mr. Massingham, and in the second place it is good business, as our readers probably prefer to reach their conclusions on any given subject after considering both sides and not only one.[3]

In this spirit Massingham's articles, which continued until shortly before his death, were written and received. His initial contributions on Liberalism, and on Labour, published in June and July 1923 were welcomed by Strachey as 'very remarkable . . . all decent and sensible people liked them and profited by them'. When Massingham had doubts about the appropriateness of the article, 'The Necessity of a Labour Party', Strachey wrote (7 July) that it was 'not a bit too extreme. I want you to feel absolutely free, and then I shall feel absolutely free also to controvert you'.

That month Massingham went off on holiday to Bavaria and the Black Forest, his letters to Strachey and Laski from Bad Kissingen

---

1 Dorothy Massingham to Strachey, n.d. The Massingham–Strachey correspondence is in Strachey Papers.
2 Strachey to MacDonald (Copy), 11 Nov. 1924, Strachey Papers.
3 Massingham to Strachey, 27 Mar. [1923] Strachey Papers; *Spectator*, 23 June 1923, p. 1,031.

reflecting improved health and strength. The trip led to his article 'Why Should Germany Perish?' in the *Spectator* of 1 September. Then Strachey sent Massingham a 'really remarkable' article, by Lord Leverhulme, on Henry Ford as a kind of hero of capitalism. Massingham answered in 'The Other Side': 'All praise to him [Ford]. But the unreformed rest of the capitalist system remains.'

In December came 'Journalism as a Dangerous Trade'. The Rothermere Press, Massingham declared, was 'a *masked* power ... a *monopoly* power ... a *non-moral* power'. The article was 'very much liked by our readers', commented Strachey. When his little book, *The Referendum*, appeared, Strachey invited Massingham's criticism: 'Please hit me as hard as you like.' Massingham's comment appeared on 26 January 1924; Strachey had written (19 January) that it was nice to have a controversy with him because he discussed 'the real points and not the sham ones'.

No article which Massingham wrote in the final year of his life attracted more attention or stands up better than his essay on 'The Book of Common Prayer' (*Spectator*, 19 April 1924). Revision of the Prayer Book was under consideration and Strachey invited from Massingham a layman's position. At first Massingham wished the article to be published unsigned: 'Religion is a terrible subject, and I approach it with fear and trembling', he wrote, and warned 'I am an abject literalist. Not a syllable, not a comma of change.' The article was greeted by Strachey as 'one of the most moving as well as one of the most brilliant things written even on a subject so august as that of the Book of Common Prayer'. One does not hesitate to underline that comment today. Massingham wrote, as one accepting the Christ of the Gospels but not of St Paul, as one outside the Church in a formal sense. But 'I live in a Christian world and ... I cannot escape from it.' The Church is 'a national Society' and the Prayer Book 'a national possession'. We should keep this treasure handed down to us, he said, a spiritual document for men of all or no theological professions.

The English Church of today still offers an open door to all those who regard religion as a thing of spirit and life, not a metaphysic; a means of common profession and aspiration, not merely of intensive spiritual culture ... Its liturgy is a noble invocation of the finest in man; of his charity; his power to forgive the injuries of others as he hopes to be forgiven his own ...

of his aspiration after truth; of his active benevolence; of the freedom of his will, and its final surrender to the Will of God.[1]

There were occasional book reviews and (28 June 1924) a review of Fernald's play *The Mask and the Face*. Strachey wrote to Massingham that it was the kind of commentary which attracted him: 'I am very proud to have it in my paper', and invited him to be the regular dramatic critic for the *Spectator*. 'I know what wonderfully poignant stuff you used to give your readers ... in pre-war times and I do not see why you should not relight the flame upon that altar.' Massingham hesitated – the previous December he had turned down a similar proposal from Garvin of the *Observer* – and finally suggested undertaking the assignment on an experimental basis. But this was soon postponed until autumn.

All this time, at home, at the Reform Club, on holiday, Massingham was turning out other articles. For the *Observer* there were notable reviews – among them, J. L. and Barbara Hammond's *Lord Shaftesbury*, A. G. Gardiner's *Life of Sir William Harcourt* and J. A. Spender's *Life of the Rt. Hon. Sir Henry Campbell-Bannerman*. Massingham and Garvin were mutually appreciative of common viewpoints which developed after the war. And 'Wayfarer' stood aside from his usual partisan position to admire Garvin's critical insight into Labour politics as well as his proficiency in his support for Liberal and Tory attitudes. In Garvin's rough notes for an obituary tribute to Massingham we find the phrase, 'our long enmity and charm of final friendship'.[2]

Upon Morley's death Massingham's widely-read article 'Morley the Humanist' appeared in the *Fortnightly* (November 1923). For Brailsford's *New Leader* there were book reviews. From 11 October 1923 to 31 July 1924 he cabled each week his 'A British Onlooker's Diary' to the *Christian Science Monitor* in Boston. It was much the same piece, with some adaptation 'for Americans and world readers', which he wrote for the *Haagsche Post* for which he had been London correspondent since 1922.[3] From September to December 1923 he wrote occasional articles for the *Daily Herald*, the Labour paper, including a severe critique of Asquith ('The Tragic Comedy of Liberal

---

[1] *H.W.M.*, 281.
[2] Massingham to Garvin, 11 Dec. 1923, and Garvin's notes on 'Massingham', Garvin Papers; 'Wayfarer' in *New Statesman*, 15 Dec. 1923.
[3] Massingham to Braithwaite, 8 Oct. 1923, M.P.

Imperialist Blunders and Intrigues', 13 September); a series attacking Grey's pre-war foreign policy; 'Appeal to the Young Liberals' (22 November); and 'Twenty Reasons for Voting Labour' (4 December). These led to an invitation in February 1924 from Hamilton Fyfe, the *Daily Herald* editor, that he contribute regularly, perhaps twice a week, on political questions and Labour positions.[1] But he chose rather to write on political questions for a variety of journals – the New York *Nation*, *Century* (New York), *Fortnightly*, *New Leader*, as well as for the *New Statesman* and the *Spectator*. A paper on 'The Press and the People' was prepared for Co-operative Congress at Nottingham, at Whitsun 1924. But Massingham was unable to attend and his paper appeared in the *Co-Operative News* of 28 June, 5 July and 12 July.

One project of considerable moment to him was his 'reminiscences' to which he first put his mind while recovering from his heart attack in March and April 1923. He had many offers from publishers, he tells us, and he made a good start in 1923 with an essay on his religious attitudes; this was posthumously published as 'The Religion of a Journalist' in the *Spectator* for 27 September and 4 October 1924. Also he had written from time to time some autobiographical pieces on his early years in Norwich which no doubt would have been included. But the 'dreadful book I am trying to compile about my unspeakable past' was put aside indefinitely with the Election of December 1923 and the advent of the Labour Government.[2]

Defection from Liberalism

When Massingham died in August 1924, the Prime Minister, J. Ramsay MacDonald, was in Scotland. He immediately telegraphed Mrs Massingham:

Have just learned with most profound sorrow of the death of your husband. How hard fate is. He has been taken away just when he saw new hope and felt a new energy for work and reason for living. In the name of all my colleagues I offer you my deepest sympathy.[3]

During the last nine months of his life Massingham enjoyed an

---

[1] Parmoor to Massingham, 2 Feb. 1924, Copy, M.P.
[2] Massingham to Ratcliffe, 4 Dec. [1923], M.P. Jonathan Cape to J. L. Hammond, 18 Sept. 1924, J.L.H.P.; *H.W.M.*, 276. Dean Inge contributed to the *Spectator*, 25 October 1924 a comment on 'The Religion of a Journalist'.
[3] 29 Aug., Copy, M.P.

informal and confidential relationship with MacDonald which we may trace through correspondence often marked by MacDonald as 'private', 'confidential', 'very confidential', and hitherto unused in accounts of the first Labour Government.[1] This relation gives special meaning to Massingham's political articles which reflect the attitude and tone not of the critic but of an adviser in the formation of policy.

Though Massingham did not formally announce his affiliation with the Labour Party until the Election of December 1923, his defection from Liberalism had been evident since the poll the year previous. He had so informed the Rowntrees in December 1922. He wrote to Beatrice Webb in January 1923: 'I feel a load off my mind now that I'm definitely done with Liberalism.'[2]

In March 1923 in accepting Strachey's invitation to write for the *Spectator*, Massingham said that he wished 'to talk over the great Socialist Problem'. This he did, after his own manner, in his first group of 'Other Side' articles in June and July 1923. First he took note, without sorrow, of 'The Passing of Liberalism'. 'The Liberal Party has shrunk to a group and the Labour Group has expanded to a Party'. In post-war Liberalism 'there is no life . . . no humour, no play, no quick responsive intelligence'. Then he turned to Labour. 'A new dynamic force' has arisen in the Labour Party, a repository for a new conception of the role of the State in society. At once there was controversy in the *Spectator*'s 'Letters to the Editor'. One reader called Massingham's ideas 'a dose of deadly poison to the reading public'. Strachey (14 July) defended his desire 'to hear the other side, both out of fairness to our opponents, and . . . still more as a method of opposing and defeating the aims of Labour wherever they are injurious to the State'. But Massingham's conversion to Labour was not without reservations. It was not easy to give his confidence to the Labour Party as constituted. In its approach to power, he said, there were perils – inexperience, the dominance of trade unionism, 'a class party', the dangers of 'ca 'canny' in an easy-going Socialistic society. *Spectator*'s readers followed an argument within Massingham's mind. Even during the Election campaign in November-December 1923 he had, privately, grave misgivings. In a personal letter he dwelt upon the narrow out-

[1] Copies of the MacDonald–Massingham correspondence cited in this chapter are in M.P.
[2] P.P., Massingham to Beatrice Webb, 27 Jan. [1923].

look of a Labour Party, a class organisation concerned primarily with hours and wages, with an irreconcilable Communist wing. To survive, it must attract a large middle-class element.[1]

But Massingham, the opportunist, had committed himself. The Labour *Daily Herald* carried a piece from this 'formerly most famous of Liberal editors'. Massingham admonished young Liberals:

Join the Labour Party, as I have joined it. It is your proper place. You will gain with it a repository for the faith that many of you have lost as members of an almost exclusively middle-class Party, in detachment from the mass of your countrymen and countrywomen.[2]

And in the *New Leader* (30 November 1923); 'As a party of definite principles, Liberalism has ceased to exist, and no longer supplies the vital needs of the nation... One party alone [Labor] can find room for the best and freshest thought that stirs in Britain today.'

Massingham's insistence that Sidney Webb's estimate of Labour strength in the new Parliament (170 to 180) was too low was borne out in the poll which returned 191 Labourites and reduced the Conservatives to 259. At the overflowing victory meeting in the Albert Hall, on 8 January, Massingham sat on the platform, with others, 'to show where we belong'. In the *New Statesman* he interpreted MacDonald's remarks as 'an appeal for a great moral transformation of politics'. When A. G. Gardiner asked him what he thought of the Labour meeting, Massingham answered: 'I have not been to a Labour Meeting. I've been to a religious meeting.' Or in another version, Massingham responded: 'I was born again.'[3]

This language was characteristic; the Labour Government became Massingham's last crusade. He put aside his autobiographical reminiscences and turned down other writing opportunities to devote his time and energy to Labour whose cause now replaced that of the Lib.-Lab. alliance which he had sought so insistently since the war. Beatrice Webb with some glee noted the shift. Shortly after the poll Massingham dropped in at 41 Grosvenor Road

to implore us not to allow the Labour Party to enter into any relations with the Liberal Party – even with regard to conventional support of a Labour

[1] Massingham to S. K. Ratcliffe, 4 Dec. [1923], M.P.
[2] 22 Nov. 1923, as quoted in *H.W.M.*, 101n.
[3] *Beatrice Webb's Diaries, 1912–1924*, ed. Cole, 250; *New Statesman*, 12 Jan. 1924; *British Weekly*, 14 Sept. 1924.

Government by the Liberals or *vice versa* (we did not remind him that it is barely a year ago that he was denouncing Sidney for being the main obstacle to such an understanding).[1]

The Labour Government

In his new role as counsellor to the Prime Minister it does not appear that Massingham's advice directly influenced Cabinet decisions, but it is evident that MacDonald prized it highly. He says as much. Overwhelmed with the duties of the Foreign Office as well as those of the Prime Minister, he answered Massingham's letters promptly, sometimes in his own hand and often by return of post, and not only solicited Massingham's views but often provided, in confidence, advance information as to his own intentions. To MacDonald, beset on all sides – from Labour as well as from Liberal and Conservative – with criticism and abuse, this association provided outlet for his feelings, disinterested advice separated from power, and a relation based on confidence and respect.

On 11 December 1923, the *Daily News* reported on 'the highest authority' that if Labour were invited to form a Government MacDonald would accept. At the same time, the *Daily News* added, since he would have no majority he would not seek to legislate major partisan programmes. That same day MacDonald wrote to Massingham:

I can whisper in your ear that the information [in the *Daily News*] is quite sound. I shall play for confidence and shall hope that before I go out the country will be accustomed to the hand of a Labour Government and will lose, in consequence, some of its nervousness and restlessness.

At MacDonald's request Massingham had made inquiries, probably through McKenna, concerning the attitude of financial leaders in the City towards a Labour Government. Massingham was able to report favourably. He also made suggestions about Cabinet appointments.

MacDonald left London on 13 December for Lossiemouth, where he remained until 3 January. In the interim, consultation with Massingham continued, with Liberal tactics the chief concern. On 18 December, as all the accounts emphasise, Asquith, addressing the Liberals of the newly-elected Commons, said he had no intention of supporting

[1] *Beatrice Webb's Diaries, 1912–1924*, ed. Cole, 255.

the Conservative Government; he assumed it would be replaced by a Labour Government which 'could hardly be tried under safer conditions'. But he added, and this is often omitted, that the power to dissolve Parliament did not rest in a Prime Minister who controlled but 31 per cent of the Commons, and should MacDonald fail in his efforts to govern, the Crown might well turn to other ministers. Both Massingham and MacDonald took a dim view of Asquith's statement. Massingham (writing on 21 December) thought that Asquith had every intention of turning out Labour at the first opportunity. 'I am convinced,' he wrote, that Asquith 'has utterly mis-stated the constitutional position in regard to Dissolution'. MacDonald responded at once (24 December):

I quite agree with your constitutional view. I think Asquith's speech one of the most wicked that has been made. . . I must get the absolute confidence of my own people before anything happens in Parliament; and nothing will help me more in this than taking a very stiff line regarding the Liberals. . . My hope is that, as soon as we begin to do things, we shall appeal to the best elements amongst the Liberals.

MacDonald proposed to Massingham that they talk the situation over when he returned to London. On 29 December MacDonald wrote of the effects of his Elgin speech (22 December) in which he expressed concern that 'the democracy of this country might not have fair play given to them'.

By 2 January, MacDonald seemed more confident:

I shall assuredly do everything I can to protect Liberals feeling any loss of self-respect in the House of Commons. . .
If we could once get going in the House itself, I am sure things will go smoothly enough unless the Liberals try to be tricky. Then they will get it.

He continued that while he had no intention of asking for a pledge in support of his right to call for a dissolution ('to ask for a pledge on taking office would be improper'),

there are ways and ways. . . But I shall not let down the constitutional practice whatever happens. . . However, I am satisfied (you must not breathe this to anyone) with my soundings. So far as I have any desire to go the signals are 'all clear'.

This correspondence led to 'Wayfarer's' remarks in the *New Statesman* concerning the constitutional right of a Prime Minister, even one without majority control of the Commons, to call for a dissolution. The Labour Government took office on 22 January. Ten days later diplomatic recognition was extended to Soviet Russia. In negotiations before recognition and in the discussions thereafter which produced two treaties in August, the key figure for Russia was Khristian G. Rakovsky, a Bolshevik who had lived long in exile in Switzerland and had accompanied Lenin in the sealed car to the Finland Station in 1917. Now, in September 1923, he came to England as the Russian trade representative. He met Brailsford, E. D. Morel and others, including Massingham – that introduction was made by a mutual friend, Harold Grenfell, a naval attaché at the British Embassy in Petrograd under Czarist Russia who had turned pro-Bolshevik.[1]

When Massingham mentioned his acquaintance with Rakovsky, MacDonald responded that even before the Election poll he had commenced conversations with Rakovsky. He wrote, on 19 December: 'I have no doubt at all of being able to fix the whole matter up. If you could do anything in the meantime to clear the way I should be very much obliged.' Then he outlined the questions on which agreement must be reached. By return post (21 December) Massingham reported at length on 'a long conversation' with Rakovsky who, he said, favoured a general understanding at once, with a joint commission to work out details as to trade, credits, pre-war debts, and guarantees against Communist propaganda. In expressing agreement with Rakovsky's statements, Massingham observed: 'The great thing, is it not, is for Labour (a), to establish the new relationship, and (b), to get going its big scheme for the relief of unemployment through a drastic extension of our foreign trade.' MacDonald replied (22 December) that he would keep Massingham's letter at hand as a guide, but added: 'Of course I did not expect that I could get all that I had laid down, but I must have a general understanding. It would smash up everything if, after recognition and, perhaps, even, because of it, they began giving trouble.'

Knowledge of MacDonald's intentions is apparent in Massingham's

[1] Louis Fischer, *The Soviets in World Affairs*, II (London, 1930), 472–3. Information from Miss G. M. Cross. After British recognition of Soviet Russia Grenfell sought Massingham's support in opposing consular appointments which he (Grenfell) considered anti-Bolshevik. Grenfell to Massingham, 3 Mar. 1924, Copy, M.P.

censure of Neil MacLean, a Labour M.P., for writing to the *Herald* a few days after MacDonald took office, expressing scepticism of the Government's intention to recognise Russia. Massingham commented:

The task of readmitting Russia to European society . . . is being pursued by a perfectly harmonious Government with vigour and in a broad spirit, and, in principle at least, has been already accomplished. . . there is no reason whatever to suppose that the issue will be long delayed.[1]

With formal recognition (1 February) Massingham and Rakovsky exchanged notes, Rakovsky thanking Massingham for his 'friendly letter' and expressing the hope that all difficulties would be surmounted and Anglo–Russian friendship established. 'Wayfarer' gave Rakovsky much credit and hoped he would be Soviet Russia's first diplomatic representative. Rakovsky did remain as Soviet Chargé d'Affaires. In June Massingham attended Madame Rakovsky's party at Claridges, and pronounced it 'lively, and at the same time serious, for it was attended by a great many important people, and there were some serious things to talk about'. The Anglo–Russian Conference to settle political and economic questions was by then in the midst of pro-tracted discussions. Massingham's comments which reflected consider-able knowledge expressed confidence in the judgment and good will of the Russian deputation, called for patience and were optimistic about the outcome.[2]

By the time MacDonald took office Massingham's journalistic commitments were almost running away with him. Immediately after the poll in December he wrote 'The Case for a Labour Government' which appeared in the *Fortnightly* in January. 'It would', he said, 'be a denial of the uses of Parliament to refuse to a constitutional Labour Party under moderate leadership, the chance of working, as statesmen' for a solution of Britain's problems. Somewhat more popular articles appeared in the New York *Nation* (6 February 1924) and in the *Century* (New York) in April. Week after week his regular commitments continued. He had recognised the need for a paper which 'would

---

[1] *New Statesman*, 2 Feb. 1924: George Lansbury wrote Massingham in MacLean's defence, saying that he, like Lansbury himself and Duncan Carmichael, secretary of the London Trades Council, had been under pressure to use their influence to hasten recognition. Lansbury to Massingham, Sunday [3 Feb. 1924], Copy, M.P.

[2] Rakovsky to Massingham, 14 Feb. [1924], Copy, M.P. 'Wayfarer' in *New Statesman*: 16 Feb., 12 Apr., 17 May, 21 June.

steady and inform Labor opinion', and Beatrice Webb mentioned the possibility of 'a really competent press department' for Labour with perhaps Massingham, Hammond and Laski in charge. But nothing came of these suggestions.[1] Massingham found it impossible to accept an invitation from E. D. Morel (probably for *Foreign Affairs*) for an article on MacDonald. Nor did he respond to a suggestion that he write for the Agence International de la Presse Socialiste in Brussels.[2]

Engagements included a dinner of the old *Nation* Group, with Garvin as guest, on 16 February, and a dinner tendered by the *Nation and Athenaeum* to Edmund Blunden, on 11 March, in recognition of his appointment to the chair of English Literature at Tokyo University. 'Wayfarer' (*New Statesman*, 11 March) provided his own send off: 'I know of no figure among our younger writers deriving so evidently from the soil from which our great ones have sprung.' Massingham himself arranged a luncheon, on 21 March, at his home at 21 Bedford Square, bringing together MacDonald, Strachey, Garvin, C. P. Scott and Dean Inge (whom Massingham hoped to win over to Labour), an occasion pronounced very useful by the Prime Minister. Dean Inge was impressed and recorded the discussion in some detail in his diary.[3]

Late in January Strachey suggested an 'Other Side' article on MacDonald. But the result was a piece, informed by Massingham's correspondence with MacDonald, which dealt as much with Liberals as with Labourites. Massingham wrote to Strachey on 16 February:

> I've only been fierce over Asquith's tactics, which are contemptible, and threaten, of course, a speedy defeat of the MacDonald Ministry, before it has time to make good (or the reverse). The Liberals have all the small-mindedness of Little Bethel, with some of its fervor.

'Is Labour to Have Fair Play?' appeared in the *Spectator* on 1 March. Somehow he found time to review, in a moving piece of writing, a biography of Olive Schreiner for Brailsford's *New Leader* (21 March).

Massingham's connections in Germany, Austria and Belgium gave weight to his opinions on foreign policy. Towards the end of January

---

[1] Massingham to S. K. Ratcliffe, 4 Dec. [1923], M.P.; B. Webb to J. L. Hammond, 30 Jan. 1924, J.L.H.P.
[2] Massingham to Morel, 7 Feb. [1924], Morel Papers, B.L.P.E.S.; L. de Brouckère to Massingham, 13 fevrier 1924, Copy, M.P.
[3] N.D., 14 Feb. 1924; Memo of C. P. Scott, 21 Mar. 1924, B.M., Add. MS. 50907/93. W. R. Inge, *Diary of a Dean, St. Paul's 1911–1935* (New York, 1950), 93.

it was briefly rumoured that he was to be Ambassador to Germany, but the *Daily News* said, on 25 January, that Massingham had denied the report. According to *The Times* (28 and 30 January) Massingham was then spending a few days in Belgium and consulted with the Prime Ministers and Socialist leaders concerning German reparation payments. Massingham had great confidence in his friend, Monsieur Horn, a Councillor at the Belgian Embassy in London. In March, Massingham sent MacDonald Horn's views on the political situation in Belgium and on the deliberations of the Experts' Committee on reparations. When German Social Democrats, worried over the possible separation of the Rhine province from Prussia, carried their concerns to Massingham, he passed his visitors on to Arthur Ponsonby, the Under Secretary in the Foreign Office.[1]

On the sensitive question of Singapore, where the Labour Government decided to abandon the construction of naval defences, Massingham asked for information and direction. MacDonald responded (4 March, 'VERY PRIVATE AND CONFIDENTIAL') that the protest was 'just one of those little stunts which our Liberal friends promote in order to keep their importance alive'. He discounted any possibility of a Cabinet Crisis. Beatty, the First Sea Lord, objected as a matter of course but was not causing any serious trouble, and if Chelmsford (a Conservative) at the Admiralty produced a showdown, 'I would accept his resignation. I tell you this so you may feel confident in waiting for results.' MacDonald's letter inspired Massingham (*New Statesman*, 8 March) to declare that there was no cause for anxiety, that the Government would not be frightened, and that, while there would be no excessive expenditures, the services would be maintained on their existing level 'pending the development of the Prime Minister's pacific policy'.

Strained relations with the Liberals in March and April threatened to hamstring MacDonald's efforts to negotiate successfully with France and Belgium the forthcoming proposals of the Experts' Committee on German reparations. In a letter to Massingham on 24 March, MacDonald poured out his troubles. Unless he had 'some sort of security at the Foreign Office until, say, Christmas, the work that has to be done there cannot possibly be done'. Negotiations would

[1] Massingham to Ponsonby, 'Private and Confidential', 14 Feb. 1924 (Copy), M.P.

soon take him frequently to the Continent and his position there would be impossible, if parliamentary crises constantly threatened at home. If there were to be a change in the Government, possibly a Coalition, it should come at once. Otherwise he thought he was entitled to some demonstration of support. As to ominous reports from the Experts' Committee, he wrote 'I can tell you – but you must not use me as your authority – that the rumours about the disagreements are altogether exaggerated. Our representatives have adopted a very wise policy.' Massingham, Strachey and Garvin discussed the possibility of broadening the Government, perhaps by bringing in Lord Milner, a Conservative, a proposal originating with Strachey. The suggestion was passed on to MacDonald who found it 'well worth considering' though another official appointment from the outside at just that time would, he said, increase his difficulties with Labour.[1]

It was without doubt MacDonald's communications with Massingham and the discussions at Massingham's lunch (21 March) which led Strachey to write the article 'France and Mr. MacDonald' (*Spectator*, 29 March):

> If Mr. MacDonald has to leave the Commons for a time, let there be a truce openly proclaimed by the leaders... [Mr. MacDonald should] be able to make it quite clear to Foreign Powers that... abroad he speaks with the full authority of the nation. Mr. Baldwin is the very man to invest Mr. Mac-Donald temporarily with that power by a speech in the Commons.

This came from the leading Unionist weekly. Massingham must have seen an advance copy of the article. He wrote to Strachey on 27 March: 'The article seems to me perfect – most wise and useful. The Prime Minister is, I know, very grateful for your helpful attitude.' Strachey's statements in the *Spectator* were echoed by 'Wayfarer' in the *New Statesman* for 29 March. It was about this time, a Saturday in early April, that the Massinghams went down to Chequers on MacDonald's invitation. And MacDonald took time (14 April) to write Massingham a *bon voyage* note for a holiday to Corsica. This produced one of his best travel pieces, 'Corsica in Spring', which appeared in the *Spectator* on 19 July. After returning from Corsica Massingham was laid up with one of his ever-recurring ailments and henceforth was less active.

[1] Massingham to Strachey, 27 Mar. 1924, 'Private', Strachey Papers; MacDonald to Massingham, 24 and 26 Mar. 1924, Copy, M.P.

MacDonald's schedule had grown beyond all control and the Massing-ham correspondence almost ceased. In July we do find Massingham reporting to MacDonald conversations with Horn at the Belgian Embassy that the Theunis Government which disapproved of the Dawes plan would probably soon fall. MacDonald (about to leave for Paris for a conference with the new Herriot Government) responded the next day in a brief note in his own hand that while he did not expect much from the Dawes Plan as to actual payments, it would give a fresh start – 'if France will take it'.[1]

At the end of May, Strachey, pushing Massingham for more 'Other Side' articles, suggested a series on Liberal leaders: Asquith, Simon, Masterman and Pringle. 'I am sure nobody could give us better charac-ter studies of those people than you could.' Eventually Massingham prepared a composite article. 'It may amuse some readers and slightly scandalize others' he wrote (28 June). Strachey responded that the article, 'The Liberal Caravan', was 'one of the most brilliant pieces of political anatomy you have done'. Massingham readily deleted some opening remarks making sport of the Liberals. In the 2 August issue appeared Strachey's signed article 'The Tragic Predicament of the Unionist Party' ('I am going to castigate the Unionist Party for all I am worth', he had written to Massingham) with 'The Liberal Caravan' the week following. Strachey wrote to Massingham (5 August) 'I shall be able to say [that] if the *Spectator* goes for the Conservatives, it does not spare the Liberals.'

Despite his uncertain health July 1924 proved an active month for Massingham, the journalist. He was thinking of *Spectator* articles to follow 'The Liberal Caravan'. Strachey sent along a set of proofs of his book, *The River of Life*; Massingham was enthusiastic and offered to write a piece about it. The three instalments of his 'The Press and the People' appeared in the *Co-Operative News*. What proved to be his final article in the *Christian Science Monitor* was in the issue for 21 July, and his last 'Wayfarer' contribution was in the 2 August *New States-man*. The *New Leader* for 15 August carried his 'The Workers' Party Can Govern: Labour's First Session' and for 22 August, his review of James Marchant's *Dr. John Clifford*.

---

[1] Massingham to MacDonald, 7 July, 'Private and Confidential' (Copy); MacDonald to Massingham, Tuesday [8 July], 'Very private'. Copy, M.P.

Nevertheless for some time Massingham's family had been aware of his depleted spirit and ebbing energy. He sometimes remarked that his work was done. From time to time he aroused himself and a complete rest in early August seemed to revive him. He wrote to his son with his accustomed 'vigour, praise, passionate denunciation' and to his secretary that now 'ideas were coming more freely'. But a life dedicated solely to journalism was close to its end. Late in August he went with his wife and his son Richard for a brief holiday to Tintagel in Cornwall. His daughter, Dorothy, was also briefly with them. He seemed to be feeling much better. But on 27 August, the evening of the third or fourth day in Tintagel, when playing cards with his family in the Castle Hotel, he was stricken with a heart attack and died soon after. The verdict at the inquest was 'death from angina pectoris'.[1]

'That Boanerges of an Editor'

Massingham's autobiography if written would no doubt have filled in certain details of family life, would certainly have informed us more fully about holidays and travels, might have told us something of 'Mayertorne Manor' in Buckinghamshire. It might also have explained Massingham's great knowledge of human affairs and the manner of its steady replenishment despite a hectic schedule as journalist and editor. But no work of reminiscence is likely to have added much to an understanding of his character and personality, his talents and his achievements. Of his contemporaries Shaw knew him better than most and he said that Massingham 'lived ... eagerly in the present ... his mind was far too active and comprehensive to be occupied with himself or the past'.[2]

So we turn to Tomlinson for a sympathetic yet perceptive delineation of his personality, to Hammond for an extraordinary analysis of his gifts as a writer and to Shaw for a generous but discriminating interpretation of his editorial career. Their essays together with Brailsford's comment on Massingham's 'Political Development', Nash's 'Massingham at the Chronicle' and Nevinson's essay on 'His Sense of Literatere' adorn the impressive memorial volume published

---

[1] Harold Massingham to Hammond, 5 Sept. 1924, J.L.H.P.; information from Miss Cross; *Daily Herald*, 30 Aug. 1924.
[2] *H.W.M.*, 214, 216

in 1925. Prepared as tributes they stand up astonishingly well a half-century later and testify to Massingham's genius for attracting some of the finest talent of his day.

While the enigma of Massingham still eludes analysis, at the end of his story it loses force. It now seems quite natural that though he knew nearly everyone he was friend but to few. It seems to us no contradiction that though proud to a degree he was without vanity or personal ambition. Though he associated with the leading political and literary leaders of his day he kept no appointment book, jotted down no diary and preserved little correspondence. His dignified but almost fragile figure attracted little attention at first meeting but association with him was not soon forgotten. Some found his voice high-pitched and toneless, yet he made his mark in any discussion of which he was a part. Leonard Woolf discovered that his 'gentle high mindedness' might give way to 'absurd verbal violence'. Middleton Murry noted that when Massingham employed the word 'bloody' it 'has the effect of an oath on the lips of a saint', and Vaughan Nash spoke of 'his brooding brow and mocking eyes'.[1] And so on. We accept him for what he was without understanding him any more fully than did his contemporaries. Some extracts have survived from his personal correspondence in later years but tell us little we do not already know. 'I doubt if he ever sought or needed human intimacies', wrote Harold Massingham of his father; especially, after the death of his first wife, he remained aloof. 'He was a very shy and secretive man and revealed his essential self neither to man nor woman.'[2]

But what do we make of Massingham the journalist and editor? – a nervous, impatient man who, all testify, was a superb moderator at the frequently acrimonious *Nation* Lunches; a mercurial individual who gave an unmistakable tone to each of the papers he edited; a social critic whose judgment of men was erratic but who was read as much without his own camp as within. And what do we say of his politics?; a Liberal usually at odds with his own party and to whom a Liberal Imperialist was worse than a Tory; a reformer who found in politics the road to social progress and yet for the most part eschewed all political activity himself.

[1] Woolf, *Downhill All the Way*, 95; Murry, *Between Two Worlds*, 431–2; Nash in *H.W.M.*, 296.　　[2] *H.W.M.*, 234, 140, and *passim* for extracts from Massingham's letters.

When Gladstone introduced the First Home Rule Bill in the Commons on 8 April 1886, young Massingham was in the Press Gallery. Nearly forty years later, he was there on 12 February 1924, aged sixty-three, when James Ramsay MacDonald outlined the policy of the first Labour Government. Beyond his main concern of politics and society was a wide range of other interests – the theatre, literature and history, travel, sports and classical music. He was moved to action not only by prison conditions in England but by 'modern slavery' in Portuguese Angola. In 1923 he signed the 'Animal Charter' listing measures to reduce suffering of animals and birds; he sponsored the Plumage Bill in Britain and agitated against pigeon shooting at Monte Carlo.

Each concern became a cause on behalf of which Massingham became a crusader. 'Each paper he edited he turned into a pulpit', remarked an obituary writer, and to Robertson Scott he was 'that Boanerges of an Editor'.[1] 'The Mind of An Age' (*Daily News*, 24 November 1913) reads like a sermon and who else would have penned these lines (*Observer*, 26 August 1923) on Lord Shaftesbury:

We only draw closer to a notion of what Shaftesbury really was, and of where he drew the sustenance of his wonderful career, when we acknowledge that he was one of the men, like Paul or Augustine, on whom religion confers a vastly magnified power of action and influence on the world. These men live, as Tolstoy says, 'for God.' But when they turn their eyes on life, it is with a range of vision, and a concentration of purpose, which will yield them an unusual mastery of its secrets.

When A. G. Gardiner in March 1921 ceased writing for the *Daily News* Massingham's regret (*Nation*, 21 March) is summarised in the words that Gardiner was the *News'* 'only preacher'. Massingham's own mind often dwelt on religious and spiritual thought, extending from a concern for institutionalised religion to a fascination with the possibility of psychic perception. But he had no interest in dogma as such and after his early years seldom attended a conventional service. Early in the Great War he did find a clergyman to his liking: Dr W. E. Orchard of the King's Weigh House Church in London. It was probably in April 1923 or 1924 that Massingham wrote to Orchard: 'I'm a shy person but I should like to thank you for what you've done

[1] *Co-Operative News*, 8 Aug. 1925; Robertson Scott, '*We*' and Me, 136.

for me, in drawing me back to the love for Him who has always been in my heart, though not, alas, in my life.' Yet – and once more the biographer is startled – Massingham, his eldest son tells us, was quite indifferent to any religious instruction for his children, not one of whom he had baptised.[1]

By definition dated and ephemeral, journalism has other dimensions – the drama of writing under pressure of circumstances, the insight which can only come from being on the scene, the adventure of giving meaning to events in progress. In these terms Massingham's writing stands up well against the best work of his contemporaries. Once again we turn to Shaw to say what we have in mind. Massingham

proved himself to be one of the best feuilletonists in London. . . The feuilletonist is the man who can write a couple of thousand words once a week in such a manner that everyone will read it for its own sake, whether specially interested or not in its subject, which may be politics, literature, music, painting, fashion, sport or gossip at large.[2]

Some would say that it was as 'Wayfarer' that he exerted his greatest influence. But he excelled also by sheer output. Day after day, week after week, he wrote in a constantly changing context, turning quickly from a leader on current news to a political portrait, and then to the theatre or a book review (this 'Paddington of diverging lines of mental interests'), all written at incredible speed and in the midst of a multiplicity of editorial detail and distraction. He was seldom banal, never stupid. The unexpected phrases which stopped people short in his day arrest our attention today. Douglas Jerrold, though hostile to the *Nation*'s spirit and purpose, wrote later that there was 'not a line of the old *Nation* that was not well written'.[3] Not many journalists have been asked to write for rival papers as Massingham was for the *New Statesman* and the *Spectator*.

E. T. Raymond, in an unsympathetic comment on Massingham's career after his death, remarked that Massingham was more of a

[1] Massingham to Orchard, 1 Apr., possession of Mrs Betty Massingham. On psychic perception, *Nation*, 31 May and 14 June 1913; 15 Mar. 1919. Massingham, *Remembrance*, 5.
[2] *H.W.M.*, 210.
[3] Douglas Jerrold, *Georgian Adventure* (New York, 1938), 272–3.

character than a force, that he lacked geniality and refinement. His judgment fluctuated and his charity began abroad and ended at home. He was 'widely narrow, Quakerishly belligerent, sometimes piously un-Christian'.[1]

A good case could be made for each of these strictures with their emphasis on the uneven temper of Massingham's ways. But such censure loses relevance when assessing his stature as an editor. Brailsford put it briefly but to the point. 'Journalism, as Massingham practised it, was leadership' – leadership in performance and industry, and above all in conviction and dedication. The remark that the *Nation* bore the imprint of a single mind is more than rhetoric, though it may be more appropriate after 1918 than before. Individuals as wide apart in mentality and temperament as Nevinson and Woolf felt constrained to employ this language.[2] Massingham's example brought out the best in his staff and it could be successfully argued that members of his staff wrote much better for him then they did for other editors. He was able to gather first-rate men, usually for unsigned articles and modest remuneration, and he held them for five, ten, fifteen years and more – Nevinson, Hammond, Hobson, Brailsford, Tomlinson. Some – Norman, Brailsford, Masterman – stayed on despite sharp differences of opinion. When Massingham as editor of the *Daily Chronicle*, broke with his proprietor, the important members of his staff went with him – a story repeated when he left the *Nation*.

Massingham's leadership had another quality. Harold Laski tells us that Massingham was a great editor 'as long as the reins were in his own hands'. He never took well to a position of subordination in authority; he was never given to compromise. He not only differed with his superiors but clashed and broke with them – O'Connor of the *Star* and Fletcher of the *Daily Chronicle*. Yet he succeeded them both. As parliamentary reporter, as leader-writer, as dramatic critic, as editor, he required complete independence to do his best work. When writing for the *Manchester Guardian* in 1900 he enjoyed no such freedom and this was the briefest, the least successful and the least satisfying phase of his career. His uncompromising stance in turn

---

[1] E. T. Raymond, *Portraits of the New Century* (New York), 1928, 263–6.
[2] Brailsford in *H.W.M.*, 93; Nevinson in *Labour Magazine*, 3 Oct. 1924; Woolf, *Downhill All the Way*, 92–4.

towards the proprietors of the *Star*, the *Daily Chronicle* and the *Nation*, each revealed, in pragmatic terms, weaknesses in his personality and character. A man of another mind and spirit might well have reconciled the differences and retained his position. But, as Shaw said, 'his defeats ... were the evidences of his integrity'.[1] Only a man of his quality could profit by such setbacks and move from one journalistic genre to another with enhanced reputation and widening public.

What happened to the papers he left behind? After January 1891 the *Star* remained a successful paper without much distinction – historians of journalism find little occasion to refer to it. In November 1899 he left the *Daily Chronicle* which continued as a respected paper, but now with a client (the Liberal Party) without a clearly-defined cause. We pause longer to compare Massingham's *Nation* with that of the Manchester Liberals when the *Nation and Athenaeum* was ably edited by H. D. Henderson from 1923 to 1930, and not so ably by Harold Wright, 1930–1. We'll let the Manchester Liberals speak for themselves. In 1925, two years after he assumed editorship, we find Henderson writing to Keynes:

I've been reading old volumes of *The Nation* with the effect of being disconcerted at how much better the political part of it used [to] be. . . The old *Nation* gives much more the impression of really covering the field of events, and fulfilling the function of a political review than we do.

In October 1926, Keynes himself writing to H. G. Wells remarked that 'The *Nation*, which has been an up-hill affair looks as though it was beginning to budge.' Circulation of the *Nation* dropped to 6,000 or less. In the words of the historian of the *New Statesman* with which the *Nation* was merged in 1931, the latter had become 'rather a flabby sort of paper'.[2]

We have employed the term 'Radical Journalist' to bring together Massingham's career as parliamentary reporter, leader-writer and editor. As we have seen, 'Radical' is an elusive term, particularly when applied to journalism. One looks in vain in certain standard treatments

[1] *New Republic*, 20 Jan. 1926; *H.W.M.*, 212.
[2] H. D. Henderson to Keynes, 25 Apr. 1925, Keynes Papers, Marshall Library; Keynes to Wells, 11 Oct. 1926, H. G. Wells Papers, University of Illinois. Hyams, *The New Statesman*, 119.

of Radical thought for reference to Massingham or his journals. On the other hand A. J. P. Taylor finds journalism at the heart of 'New Radicalism' before the First World War and Simon Maccoby by 1922 sees Massingham 'rightly regarded almost as the Radical oracle'.[1]

But the fact is that Massingham himself merely toyed with terminology and his 'Radicalism' was an attitude, not a doctrine. At the end of his editorship he declared that 'during the entire period of its existence the *Nation* has remained an independent paper, a journal "of the Opposition".' Use of the term 'Radical' put him in proper relationship both with those with whom he generally agreed and those with whom he usually disagreed. He might well dissent from both. Massingham in his final issue of the *Nation* quite simply summarised his own role:

The problems of the Great War, and of the years of its preparation, no less than the state of arts and letters, and the reflections of these activities on the faith and practice of our times, have seemed to us to call less for the acceptance of existing standards than for a candid examination of them.

It was this independence of mind that caused him to be read regularly by political leaders extending from William E. Gladstone to J. Ramsay MacDonald. Massingham's shrewd, often acid, and merciless but informed comment could not be ignored by such as Rosebery, Joseph Chamberlain, Balfour, and Churchill. Why else did Lloyd George, in his attack on the Radical press from 1916 on, almost invariably single out the *Nation* as the most notorious example? And why else was it that what the *Nation* said on Saturday so often became the text of the leading article in a provincial daily the following Monday?

Massingham and his journals find little place in studies of the organised Liberal Party. Thus there has been extensive study of 'The Entry of Liberals into the Labour Party, 1910–1920'[2] with no reference whatsoever to Massingham or the *Nation*. When Massingham died his career received more complete and more sympathetic attention from the Conservative press (e.g., *The Times*, the *Morning Post*) and from Labour journals (*Daily Herald*, *New Leader*, *Co-Operative News*) than

---

[1] Taylor, *The Trouble Makers*, chs. IV, V; Maccoby, *English Radicalism: The End?*, 364. But Maccoby in *English Radicalism, 1886–1914* (London, 1953) makes only incidental reference to Massingham's journals.

[2] Robert E. Dowse, in *Yorkshire Bull. of Eco. and Soc. Research* (Autumn 1961).

from the orthodox Liberal. His old paper, the *Daily Chronicle*, carried a routine notice of his death and editorial comment more critical than appreciative. The *Liberal Magazine* for 1924 made no reference to his death.

I feel pretty certain that the magnetic field surrounding journalism induces the editor and staff of every newspaper to believe that their paper is much more important and influential upon public opinion than it really is.

This caveat by Leonard Woolf[1] would probably have little impressed H. W. Massingham. Journalism was his entire life. Along with Woolf's remark, equally beside the point is the occasional comment that Massingham 'just failed to realise himself' and that his temperament and personal idiosyncrasies interfered with the most effective use of his great talent. All this is merely to say the obvious, that a different Massingham would have had a different career. The Massingham we know lived in the era of 'New Journalism' when the newspaper (the daily and the weekly) was the chief source of news and an important moulder of public opinion. Also, he was fortunate to live in the heyday of the editor when the proprietor usually remained in the background (Northcliffe was the great exception), when great editors like Stead, Garvin, Gardiner, Scott and Massingham themselves pronounced on policy, and when the most influential journals did mirror the personality and outlook of their editors.

After the First World War this era moved to an end, though perhaps not as rapidly as envisaged by Massingham who was affected by his own unceremonious departure from the *Nation*. While he had only vague forebodings about radio and could not foresee television, he was singularly sensitive to the shift from journals of policy or opinion to 'organs of business'. The syndicated press was becoming a capitalistic press and 'a purely commercial Press is, and must be, an anti-social thing'. It was with the consequences of this development that Massingham became preoccupied in the final years of his life. So he wrote in the *Spectator* (30 June 1923):

Syndicated journalism may have come to stay, but its sameness, snobbery, triviality, timidity, colourless clothes, unimpressive character, inveterate

[1] *The Journey not the Arrival Matters* (London, 1969), 146.

commercialism, and unscrupulous addiction to sport, will never make or sustain a great political movement.

Some months later (*Spectator*, 1 December 1923): syndicated journalism is 'a non-moral power, amenable only to "business" considerations, and rejecting any intellectual or fixed political basis'. Yet his last published words on the subject, in the *Co-operative News* for 12 July 1924, were aggressive and opportunistic, as well as moralistic.

I think still that the Press which created these dangers will also open a door of escape from them. . . It is not in the nature of things that the power of writing – the intercommunication of mind with mind – should perish, or that it should always be abused as it is today. Human values fall, but they also rise, and it is on this power of moral recovery that the hopes of such a society as yours are fixed.

Here is Massingham, the evangelical, the critic, the crusader and the Radical – in character to the end.

Bibliography

UNPUBLISHED MATERIAL

Manuscript collections

Norman Angell Papers, Ball State University, Muncie, Indiana.
Viscount Bryce Papers, Bodleian Library, Oxford.
William H. Buckler Papers, Yale University, New Haven, Conn.
John Burns Papers, British Museum, London.
Sir Henry Campbell-Bannerman Papers, British Museum, London.
Sir Charles Dilke Papers, British Museum, London.
Fabian Society Papers, Nuffield College, Oxford.
Baron Fisher Papers, Lennoxlove, Haddington, East Lothian.
A. G. Gardiner Papers, in possession of Mr Patrick Gardiner, Wytham, Oxfordshire.
J. L. Garvin Papers, University of Texas, Austin, Texas.
David Lloyd George Papers, Beaverbrook Library, London.
Viscount Gladstone Papers, British Museum, London.
William E. Gladstone Papers, British Museum, London.
Viscount Haldane Papers, National Library of Scotland, Edinburgh.
J. L. Hammond Papers, Bodleian Library, Oxford.
Edward M. House Papers, Yale University, New Haven, Conn.
Henry Demarest Lloyd Papers, State Historical Society, Madison, Wisconsin.
Reginald McKenna Papers, Churchill College, Cambridge.
H. W. Massingham Papers, possession of the author.
Gilbert Murray Papers, Bodleian Library, Oxford.
Henry W. Nevinson Papers, Bodleian Library, Oxford.
Diary of Henry W. Nevinson, Bodleian Library, Oxford.
Viscount Northcliffe Papers, British Museum, London.
Passfield Papers, British Library of Political and Economic Science, London School of Economics.
Arthur Ponsonby Papers, Bodleian Library, Oxford.
Earl of Rosebery Papers, National Library of Scotland, Edinburgh.
Joseph Rowntree Social Service Trust Papers, York.
Viscount Runciman Papers, University of Newcastle-upon-Tyne.
C. P. Scott Papers, British Museum, London.
C. P. Scott Papers, the *Guardian*, Manchester.
Diary of George Bernard Shaw (transcription by Miss Blanche Patch), British Library of Political and Economic Science, London School of Economics. For 1892, the transcription by Stanley Rypins was used.
George Bernard Shaw Papers, British Museum, London.
John St Loe Strachey Papers, Beaverbrook Library, London.

Dissertations

Dorey, A. J. 'Radical Liberal Criticism of British Foreign Policy, 1906–1914'. Ph.D. Thesis, Pembroke College, Oxford, 1964 (MS. copy in Bodleian, Oxford).

Weiler, Peter. 'Liberal Social Theory in Great Britain, 1896–1914'. Ph.D. Thesis, Harvard University, 1968 (MS. copy in Harvard University Library).

PUBLISHED MATERIAL: BOOKS

Only the more important items for this study, including recent publications, are listed. Other works, as used, are cited in the footnotes. Biographies and monographs consulted primarily for correspondence and other contemporary material are listed under 'Primary sources'.

Primary sources

Asquith, Margot. *An Autobiography.* Vol. II, New York, 1920.

Bennett, Arnold. *Journal of Arnold Bennett.* 3 vols., New York, 1932–3. *The Letters of Arnold Bennett.* Ed. James Hepburn. Vols. II, III, London, 1968, 1970.

Bernstein, Eduard. *My Years of Exile: Reminiscences of a Socialist.* Trans. Bernard Miall. London, 1921.

Bonham-Carter, Violet. *Winston Churchill as I Knew Him.* London, 1965.

Bullock, J. M. (ed.). *C.K.S., An Autobiography: A Fragment of Himself.* London, 1927.

[Burrows, Herbert and Hobson, John A. (eds.)]. *William Clarke: A Collection of his Writings, with a Biographical Sketch.* London, 1908.

Churchill, Randolph S. *Winston S. Churchill*: vol. 1, *Youth, 1874–1900.* Boston, 1966. Companion volume 1, 2 parts, Boston, 1967. *Winston S. Churchill*: vol. 2, *Young Statesman, 1901–1914.* Boston, 1967. Companion volume 2, 3 parts, Boston, 1969. and Gilbert, Martin. *Winston S. Churchill*: vol. 3, *The Challenge of War, 1914–1916.* Boston, 1971.

Churchill, Winston Spencer. *Liberalism and the Social Problem.* London, 1909.

Cline, C. L. (ed.) *Letters of George Meredith.* 3 vols., Oxford, 1970.

Engels, Friedrich, and Lafargue, Paul and Laura. *Correspondence.* Trans. Yvonne Kapp. Vol. II, Moscow, 1960.

Fabian Tracts Nos. 40, 41, 47, 49.

Garnett, Edward (ed.), *Letters from W. H. Hudson, 1901–1922.* New York, 1923. (ed.), *Letters from John Galsworthy, 1900–1932.* London, 1934.

Gathorne-Hardy, Robert (ed.). *Ottoline: Memoirs of Lady Ottoline Morrell.* New York, 1964.

Haldane, R. B. *An Autobiography.* New York, 1929.

Hamilton, Mary Agnes. *Remembering My Good Friends.* London, 1944.

Hancock, W. K., and Van der Poel, Jean (eds.), *Selections from the Smuts Papers.* Vols. II-III, Cambridge, 1966.

Hart-Davis, Rupert (ed.), *The Letters of Oscar Wilde.* London, 1962.

Hirst, Francis W. *In the Golden Days.* London, 1957.

Hobson, J. A. *Confessions of an Economic Heretic.* New York, 1938.

Holroyd, Michael, *Lytton Strachey.* 2 vols., London, 1967-8.

Howe, Mark DeWolfe (ed.), *Holmes-Laski Letters . . . 1916-1935.* Vol. I, Cambridge, Mass., 1953.

Hutchinson, Horace G. (ed.). *Private Diaries of the Right Hon. Sir Algernon West, G.C.B.* London, 1922.

Hyde, H. Montgomery, *Oscar Wilde: The Aftermath.* New York, 1963.

The Idea of Public Right. London, 1918.

Jerrold, Douglas. *Georgian Adventure.* New York, 1938.

Jones, Thomas, *Whitehall Diary*, ed. Keith Middlemas. Vol. I (1916-1925), London, 1969.

Laurence, Dan H. (ed.). *Bernard Shaw: Collected Letters*, vol. 1, *1874-1897.* New York, 1965.

London Reform Union Proceedings. 1892-3.

MacCarthy, Desmond. *Humanities.* London, 1953.

Marder, Arthur J. (ed.). *Fear God and Dread Nought. The Correspondence of Admiral of the Fleet Lord Fisher of Kilverstone*, Vols. II and III, London, 1956, 1959.

Marrot, H. V. *The Life and Letters of John Galsworthy.* New York, 1936.

Massingham, H. J. (ed.). *H. W. M.: A Selection from the Writings of H. W. Massingham.* London, 1925.

Remembrance: An Autobiography. London [1941].

Massingham, H. W. *The London Daily Press.* London, 1892.

The Life and Political Career of the Right Hon. W. E. Gladstone. London [1898].

The Gweedore Hunt: A Story of English Justice in Ireland. London, 1889.

(ed.). *Labour and Protection.* London, 1903.

Why We Came to Help Belgium. London, 1914.

Masterman, Lucy, *C. F. G. Masterman.* London, 1939.

Mottram, R. H. *For Some We Loved: An Intimate Portrait of Ada and John Galsworthy.* London, 1956.

Murry, J. Middleton. *Between Two Worlds: An Autobiography.* London, 1935.

Nevinson, Henry W. *Changes and Chances.* New York, 1923.

More Changes, More Chances. London, 1925.

Last Changes, Last Chances. London, 1928.

O'Connor, T. P. *Memoirs of an Old Parliamentarian*. Vol. II, New York, 1929.

Pease, Edward R. *History of the Fabian Society*. London, 1916.

Pennell, Joseph, *The Adventures of an Illustrator*. Boston, 1925.

Phillips, Harlan B. (ed.). *Felix Frankfurter Reminisces*. New York, 1960.

[Pope, Wilson, and others], *The Story of 'The Star'*, *1888–1938*. London [1938].

Riddell, Lord. *Lord Riddell's War Diary, 1914–1918*. London [1933].

More Pages from My Diary, 1908–1914. London, 1934.

Robertson-Scott, J. W. *'We' and Me*. London, 1956.

Robinson, Lennox (ed.). *Lady Gregory's Journals, 1916–1920*. [London] 1946.

Rosebery. *Lord Rosebery's Speeches (1874–1896)*. London, 1896.

Roskill, Stephen (ed.). *Hankey, Man of Secrets*. Vol. I, London, 1970.

Rothenstein, William. *Men and Memories, 1900–1922*. 2 vols., New York, 1931–2.

Russell, Bertrand, *Autobiography of Bertrand Russell*. Vol. II, London, 1968.

Russell, George W. E. (ed.), *Malcolm MacColl: Memoirs and Correspondence*. London, 1914.

Sassoon, Siegfried. *Memoirs of an Infantry Officer*. New York, 1930.

Shapcott, Reuben (ed.). *The Autobiography of Mark Rutherford, Dissenting Minister*. London, 1936. ('Memorial Introduction' by H. W. Massingham.)

Shaw, Bernard. *What I Really Wrote About the War*. New York, 1931.

How to Become a Musical Critic. Ed. Dan H. Laurence, London, 1961.

Sitwell, Osbert. *Laughter in the Next Room*. Boston, 1948.

Noble Essences. London, 1950.

Spender, Harold. *Fire of Life*. London, 1926.

Spender, J. A. *Life, Journalism and Politics*. 2 vols., New York, n.d.

Swinnerton, Frank. *Swinnerton: An Autobiography*. London, 1937.

Villard, Oswald Garrison. *Fighting Years: Memoirs of a Liberal Editor*. New York, 1939.

Webb, Beatrice. *Our Partnership*, Ed. Barbara Drake and Margaret I. Cole. London, 1948.

Beatrice Webb's Diaries, 1912–1924. Ed. Margaret I. Cole. London, 1952.

Whelen, Frederick (ed.). *Politics in 1896: An Annual*. London, 1897.

Wilson, Trevor (ed.), *The Political Diaries of C. P. Scott, 1911–1928*. London, 1970.

Woolf, Leonard, *Downhill all the Way*. London, 1967.

The Journey not the Arrival Matters. London, 1969.

Secondary Sources

Annual Register, 1896. London, 1897.

Archer, C. *William Archer: Life, Work and Friendship*. New Haven, 1931.
Bealey, Frank, and Pelling, Henry, *Labour and Politics, 1900–1906*. London, 1958.
Bettany, F. G. *Stewart Headlam: A Biography*. London, 1926.
Butler, Jeffrey. *The Liberal Party and the Jameson Raid*. Oxford, 1968.
Clegg, H. A., and others. *A History of British Trade Unions Since 1889*. Vol. I, Oxford. 1964.
Destler, Chester McArthur. *Henry Demarest Lloyd and the Empire of Reform*. Philadelphia, 1963.
Dunbar, Janet. *Mrs. G. B. S.* New York, 1963.
Ervine, St John. *Bernard Shaw: His Life, Work and Friends*. London, 1956.
Fyfe, [Henry] Hamilton. *T. P. O'Connor*. London, 1934.
Gardiner, A. G. *The Life of Sir William Harcourt*. 2 vols., London, 1923.
Sir John Benn and the Progressive Movement. London, 1925.
Gilbert, Bentley B. *The Evolution of National Insurance in Great Britain*. London, 1966.
Gollin, Alfred M. *The Observer and J. L. Garvin, 1908–1914*. London, 1960.
Balfour's Burden: Arthur Balfour and Imperial Preference. London, 1965.
Gooch, G. P. *Life of Lord Courtney*. London, 1920.
Grenville, J. A. S. *Lord Salisbury and Foreign Policy: The Close of the Nineteenth Century*. London, 1964.
Gross, John J. *The Rise and Fall of the Man of Letters*. London, 1969.
Guinn, Paul, *British Strategy and Politics, 1914–1918*. New York, 1965.
Gwynn, S., and Tuckwell, G. M. *Life of Sir Charles Dilke*. London, 1917.
Hale, Oron James. *Publicity and Diplomacy ... 1890–1914*. New York, 1940.
Hamer, D. A. *John Morley*. Oxford, 1968.
Liberal Politics in the Age of Gladstone and Rosebery. Oxford, 1972.
Hammond, J. L. *C. P. Scott of the Manchester Guardian*. London, 1934.
Hanes, David P. *The First British Workmen's Compensation Act, 1897*. New Haven, 1968.
Hearnshaw, F. J. C. (ed.). *Edwardian England, A.D. 1901–1910*. London, 1933.
Henderson, Archibald. *Bernard Shaw, Playboy and Prophet*. London, 1932.
George Bernard Shaw: Man of the Century. London, 1956.
Herd, Harold. *The March of Journalism*. London, 1952.
History of The Times. Vols. III–IV, London, 1947, 1952.
Hobson, J. A., and Ginsberg, Morris. *L. T. Hobhouse: His Life and Work*. London, 1931.
Hope, James F. *A History of the 1900 Parliament*. Vol. I, London, 1908.
Hyams, Edward. *The New Statesman*. London, 1963.
James, Robert Rhodes. *Rosebery: A Biography of Archibald Philip Primrose, Fifth Earl of Rosebery*. London, 1963.

Jones, Kennedy. *Fleet Street & Downing Street.* London [1920].

Kent, William. *John Burns.* London, 1950.

Koss, Stephen. *Lord Haldane, Scapegoat for Liberalism.* New York, 1969.

Sir John Brunner: Radical Plutocrat, 1842–1919. Cambridge, 1970.

Lea, F. A. *Life of John Middleton Murry.* London, 1959.

Lowe, C. J. *Salisbury and the Mediterranean, 1886–1896.* London, 1965.

McBriar, A. M. *Fabian Socialism and English Politics, 1884–1918.* Cambridge, 1962.

Maclean, Catherine Macdonald. *Mark Rutherford: A Biography of William Hale White.* London, 1955.

Mallet, Sir Charles. *Herbert Gladstone: A Memoir.* London, 1932.

Martin, Kingsley. *Harold Laski, 1893–1950.* New York, 1953.

Martin, Lawrence W. *Peace without Victory. Woodrow Wilson and the British Liberals.* New Haven, Conn., 1958.

Martin, Wallace. *'The New Age' under Orage.* Manchester, 1967.

Meynell, Everard. *The Life of Francis Thompson.* New York, 1913.

Mills, J. Saxon. *Sir Edward Cook, K.B.E. A Biography.* London, 1921.

Moody, T. W. 'Michael Davitt and the British Labour Movement, 1882–1906', in *Transactions of the Royal Historical Society*, 3 (1953), 53–76.

Morison, Stanley, *The English Newspaper, 1622–1932.* Cambridge, 1932.

Poirier, Philip P. *The Advent of the British Labour Party.* New York, 1958.

Pound, Reginald. *Arnold Bennett: A Biography.* London, 1952.

Rae, John. *Conscience and Politics.* London, 1970.

Rappaport, Armin. *The British Press and Wilsonian Neutrality.* London, 1951.

Robertson Scott, J. W. *The Life and Death of a Newspaper* [*Pall Mall Gazette*]. London, 1950.

Rowland, Peter. *The Last Liberal Governments: The Promised Land, 1905–1910.* London, 1968.

Sassoon, Siegfried L. *Meredith.* London, 1948.

Speaight, Robert. *William Rothenstein.* London, 1962.

Spender, J. A. *The Life of the Right Hon. Sir Henry Campbell-Bannerman.* 2 vols., Boston, 1924.

Stansky, Peter. *Ambitions and Strategies.* Oxford, 1964.

Stone, Wilfred. *Religion and Art of William Hale White.* New York, 1967.

Taylor, A. J. P. *The Trouble Makers.* London, 1957.

Politics in War Time. London, 1964.

Taylor, H. A. *Robert Donald.* [1934].

Thompson, E. P. *William Morris, Romantic to Revolutionary.* London, 1955.

Thompson, Paul. *Socialists, Liberals and Labour: The Struggle for London, 1885–1914.* London, 1967.

Tschiffely, A. F. *Don Roberto, Being the Account of the Life and Works of R. B. Cunninghame Graham, 1852–1936.* London, 1937.

Tsuzuki, Chüshichi. *H. M. Hyndman and British Socialism.* Oxford, 1961.

Watson, R. Spence. *The National Liberal Federation 1877–1906.* London, 1907.

Weintraub, Stanley. *Journey to Heartbreak: The Crucible Years of Bernard Shaw, 1914–1918.* New York, 1971.

Whyte, Frederic. *The Life of W. T. Stead.* 2 vols., London, n.d.

Wilson, Trevor. *The Downfall of the Liberal Party, 1914–1935.* Ithaca, New York, 1966.

Winkler, Henry R. *The League of Nations Movement in Great Britain, 1914–1919.* New Brunswick, 1952.

PUBLISHED MATERIAL: JOURNALS AND NEWSPAPERS

Journals and newspapers consulted include: *British Weekly, Contemporary Review, Cosmopolis, Daily Chronicle, Daily News, Daily News and Leader, Eastern Daily Press, Fabian News, Fortnightly, Justice, Liberal Magazine, Manchester Guardian, Morning Leader, Nation, New Statesman, Norfolk News, Pearson's Monthly, Review of Reviews, Speaker, Spectator, Star, The Times, Westminster Gazette.*

Index

Haldane, R. B. *(cont.)*
    ground with H.W.M. on secondary
    education, 209–10; defended by
    Nation against charges of pro-
    Germanism, 237–8; mentioned, 19,
    61–2, 184, 191, 199, 219, 283, 299
Hale White, William ('Mark Rutherford'):
    writes 'London Letter' for *Norfolk
    News*, 11, 13; H.W.M. identifies
    'Mark Rutherford', 63; shares many
    qualities with H.W.M., 168; wins
    H.W.M.'s admiration and apprecia-
    tion, 168–9; published in *Nation*, 3,
    169, 174
Hamer, D. A., 91
Hamilton, Sir Ian, 260
Hamilton, Mary Agnes, 265
Hammersmith Socialist Society, 47
Hammond, J. L.: as pro-Boer, 115; edits
    Speaker, 119, 143; as member of
    Nation staff, 145; supports British
    intervention (1914), 228–9, 235;
    writes for *Nation* and *Manchester
    Guardian* on Irish question (1921),
    284; on H.W.M.'s departure from
    Nation, 299, 301; mentioned, x, 108,
    117, 120, 141, 198, 314, 322
Hankey, Sir Maurice, 253
Harcourt, Sir William: position on
    Armenian question, 89–90; and
    Rosebery's resignation as Liberal
    leader, 90–1; resigns Liberal leader-
    ship (1898), 102; mentioned, 73–4,
    109, 208
Harcourt, Loulou, 73, 89
Hardie, Keir: on H.W.M.'s resignation
    from *D.C.*, 108; mentioned, 45, 130–1
Hardy, Thomas; contributes to first issue
    of *Nation*, 157; association with
    H.W.M., 157; mentioned, 171
Harmsworth, Alfred: *see* Northcliffe, 1st
    Viscount
Harmsworth, Cecil, 129
Harris, Frank: correspondence with
    H.W.M. concerning Shaw's review
    of Harris' *Shakespeare and his Love*,
    159–60
Harrison, Frederic, 15, 105
Harvey, George, 153
Headlam, Stewart, 16, 19, 23, 67
Healy, T. M., 283, 285
Henderson, Archibald, 157
Henderson, Arthur, 265

Henderson, H. D., 1, 299, 323
Herbert, Jessie, 130
Herriot, Edouard, 317
Hirst, F. W.: on H.W.M.'s political
    judgment, 6; as pro-Boer, 115; on
    Nation staff, 146; supports the
    Anglo-Russian Entente (1907), 182–
    3; mentioned, 1, 119, 141, 195–6, 199,
    217–19, 228, 246
Hobhouse, L. T.: on H.W.M.'s political
    judgment, 6; comments on H.W.M.'s
    resignation from *D.C.*, 103–4; and
    H.W.M.'s attachment to *Manchester
    Guardian* staff, 112; member of
    Nation staff, 146; opposes Asquith's
    succession to premiership, 184;
    breaks with *Nation* Group, 235;
    mentioned, 197–8, 199, 205, 228,
    233, 283
Hobhouse, Emily, 228
Hobson, J. A.: comments on H.W.M.'s
    resignation from *D.C.*, 108; aids
    H.W.M. in drafting a Prospectus for
    new paper, 111; as member of
    Nation staff, 146, 217; protests at
    H.W.M.'s forced resignation from
    Nation, 299–300; mentioned, 1, 58,
    104, 136, 197, 199, 205, 228–9, 243,
    250, 267, 322
Hofmeyr, J. H., 135
Holmes, Justice Oliver Wendell, 274
Holyoake, George Jacob, 127
Horn, Monsieur, 317
House, Col. Edward M.: as President
    Wilson's personal representative,
    244; receives reports on English
    press, 245, 247–9, 256; appreciates
    H.W.M.'s support, 249; supports
    H.W.M. during overseas ban on
    Nation, 255; finds H.W.M. more
    helpful than Scott and more useful
    than Donald, 258; interviewed by
    H.W.M. at Paris Peace Conference,
    271–2; meets with H.W.M. and other
    journalists in July 1920, 273
Hudson, Robert, 122, 297
Hudson, W. H., 148
Hughes, Hugh Price, 33
Huxley, Aldous, 4, 277
Hyndman, H. M., 15, 25, 34–5, 62, 107

Ibsen, Henrik, 61, 64–5
Illustrated London News, 99

North American Review, 61

Northcliffe, 1st Viscount: H.W.M.'s attack on the 'Harmsworth Brand' (1908), 176; discusses Coalition with H.W.M., 239–41; and H.W.M.'s appeal for support of Lord Robert Cecil, 291–2; mentioned, x, 23, 55, 215, 255, 264

North East Lanark, 129, 132

Norwich: in H.W.M.'s youth, 7–8, 11–12; bye-election (Jan. 1904), 130–1; mentioned, 13, 141, 168, 170

Norwich Grammar School, 8–10

Noyes, Alfred, 171

Observer, the, 2, 23–4, 176–7, 214, 306

O'Connor, T. P.: as editor of the *Star*, 18, 20–3, 25–6, 28–32; employs H.W.M. and Shaw, 21; breach with Shaw, 25, 29–30; breach with H.W.M., 25, 28–32; mentioned, 322

O'Connor, Mrs T. P., 30

Old Age Pensions, 139

Olivier, Sir Sydney, 161, 246

Olney, Richard, 81

Omar Khayyam Club, 63–4

Orage, A. R., 2, 145, 155–6

Orchard, Dr W. E., 283, 320

O'Shea, W. H., 33

'The Other Club', 224

Outlook, 5, 85, 108, 114

Owen, Wilfred, 263

Oxford Liberals: *see* Manchester Liberals

Page, Walter Hines, 235

Pall Mall Gazette, 17, 18, 22, 33, 71, 116, 213–14

Pankhurst, Mrs Emmeline, 213

Paris Peace Conference (1919), 271, 273, 279

Parke, Ernest, 21–2, 61

Parker, Joseph, 16, 86

Parliament Act of 1911, 201, 209

Parnell, C. S., 19, 33

Parsons, Alfred, 76

Partridge, Bernard, 60

Pater, Walter, 63

Paul, Herbert, 117

Pauncefote, Lord, 84

Pearson's Monthly, 28, 37, 42

Pease, Edward R., 41, 47–8

Pennell, Joseph: and the *Star*, 21; on D.C. staff, 57, 59, 75–6; mentioned, 3, 40, 62

Penrhyn, Lord, 97

Persia, 202, 217, 222

Plural Voting Bill, 139

Ponsonby, Arthur: contributes to *Nation*, 147; consults with H.W.M. on political matters, 185–7, 191–2, 198; mentioned, 199, 201, 217–28, 231, 243–4, 255, 289, 292

Possibilists, 35–6

Power, O'Connor, 47, 56

press censorship in war time, 234

prison reform, 26, 65–9, 162–3

Progressive Review, 77

Progressives, 26–8, 31, 49, 72, 76, 78, 98

Pulitzer, Joseph, 85

Putnam's Magazine, 198

Quinn, John, 274

Radical journalism, 54, 179, 226, 323; *see also Star*

Radicals: and the *D.C.*, 50, 54; their philosophy and views as presented by H.W.M., 78–9, 175, 177–9, 323–4; hopeful of leadership in Liberal Party, 124, 184–5; position on House of Lords issue, 190, 198; attack Liberal Government foreign policy, 179, 182, 187, 202, 205–6, 216–25; welcome Lloyd George back to social reform, 208–9, 212; divided on issues of First World War, 226–33; *Nation* as forum for their views during First World War, 226–7, 267; their views presented to Col. House, 245; extol Wilson's 'Peace without Victory' speech, 249; seek Anglo-American unity on war aims, 263; *see also Star* and *Nation*

Rainbow Circle, 96

Rakowsky, K. G., 279, 312–13

Ratcliffe, S. K. 1, 109, 303

Rathenau, Walter, 279–80

Raven-Hill, Leonard, 76

Raymond, E. T. (pseud. for Edward Raymond Thompson), 321

Redmond, John E., 177

Reform Club, 166, 245

Review of Reviews: praises H.W.M. and the *D.C.*, 55–6, 60, 79; reports H.W.M.'s break with T. P. O'Connor and Professor Stuart, 30, 33, 37, 55;